A HISTORY OF
TEXTILE ART

A HISTORY OF
TEXTILE ART

A Selective Account

AGNES GEIJER

Pasold Research Fund
in association with
SOTHEBY PARKE BERNET

First published 1979 by
the Pasold Research Fund Ltd in association with Sotheby Parke Bernet Publications
Philip Wilson Publishers Ltd
Russell Chambers
Covent Garden, London WC2

Edition for the USA available from
Sotheby Parke Bernet Publications
c/o Biblio Distribution Center
81 Adams Drive
Totowa, New Jersey 07512

Reprinted with corrections 1982

ISBN 0 85667 055 3

Printed and bound in Great Britain by the Pitman Press, Bath
Illustrations printed by BAS Printers Ltd, Over Wallop, Hampshire

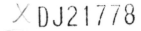

CONTENTS

Preface

This volume is a revised translation of my handbook *Ur Textilkonstens Historia* and surveys the world history of textiles from ancient times to the twentieth century. Much of my work has been done in the Scandinavian countries where textiles from all parts of the world have been particularly well preserved. In this same area there is also a living tradition of crafts and implements which has continued until recent times — a situation resulting from the fact that the Industrial Revolution, which obliterated most of the domestic crafts elsewhere in Western Europe, came very late to the less urbanized northern countries. In addition, most parts of Scandinavia have suffered less from the effects of war and revolution than the rest of Europe.

Many European and Oriental textiles date from the medieval period and were once ecclesiastical property, while others, of earlier date, have come to light as a result of archaeological excavations. In Sweden, material of this kind comes under the supervision of the Central Council and Museum of National Antiquities (Riksantikvarieämbetet and Historiska Museet) in Stockholm. The present handbook, first published in 1972, is based on a life's work in textiles within the latter institution.

The book begins with basic technical data concerning materials, looms and weaves before going on to discuss problems relating to technical developments. This discussion in turn is an introduction to historical accounts of special topics such as silk manufacturing, knotted pile fabrics, dyeing and textile printing, and the textile trade. A chapter on textiles and textile crafts in Scandinavia places this important material in its European context for the first time ever. Parts of this material, and some of the ideas put forward here, have previously been limited to a narrow circle of readership, if indeed they have been published at all.

After I had been called upon from various quarters to publish this book in an internationally viable language, I received grants from the Magnus Bergvall Foundation and the Berit Wallenberg Foundation towards the English translation, which has been most creditably done by Mr Roger Tanner, M.A. (Cantab.). The terminological aspect of the translation process was a joint effort, in accordance with the international vocabularies of CIETA and NTT.

My thanks are due to the above mentioned authorities and helpers as well as to colleagues and friends at home and abroad. I am profoundly grateful for all the assistance and encouragement I have received over all the years.

Finally, I wish to take this opportunity of thanking Mr K. G. Ponting of the Pasold Research Fund for the interest he has shown in this project and for all the work he has incurred in connexion with it.

Stockholm

April 1979

Agnes Geijer

I. *Sumptuous gold-velvet fabric of Italian manufacture, finest Flemish 'broadcloth' and a 'Turkish' rug. Madonna and Child, painted by Hans Memling in the 1490s. Staatliche Museen, Berlin.*

Introduction

Sigurd the Crusader, King of Norway, after spending some time in the Holy Land, decided to travel to Miklagaard, which was the Norsemen's name for Constantinople, Byzantium or Istanbul. He sailed with his fleet first to Cyprus and then to a Greek island called the Point of the Angels, where he ordered his ships to cast anchor and get ready for their entry into the Byzantine capital. There was a following wind and he could have sailed straight on, but Sigurd wanted to have the wind on his beam so that he could set his sails fore and aft. For two weeks or more they lay off the island waiting for their cross wind, and when it came Sigurd gave orders for both sides of the sails to be hung with *pell*, costly silk 'fabrics which he had had given to him, or perhaps seized by force of arms, during his previous voyage round the coast of Spain and through the Mediterranean. When they had entered the Sea of Marmora, Sigurd drew his ships close in to land, past many strongholds and towns, from which the people could follow his progress. The ships with their golden prows sailed stem to stern, their billowing sails forming an unbroken screen. Along the shore great crowds stood gazing in wonder. When the Emperor Alexius heard tell of King Sigurd's splendid retinue, he ordered the Golden Gate to be opened, an honour otherwise reserved for the Emperor himself when he returned from some great victory, and the road which the Norse King and his followers were to tread was lined with rich hangings . . . Their subsequent stay in the Byzantine capital was no less impressive. When King Sigurd eventually returned home it was claimed that 'no Norseman had ever made a more glorious journey'. This event took place in about 1110, when Sigurd was only twenty years old![1]

It was Snorri Sturluson, the famous thirteenth-century Icelandic poet and historian, who described this spectacle in which costly and sumptuous textiles played a predominant role and endowed the young King with the status he so ardently coveted. The account is unusually graphic, but in spirit it is typical of its time. Knowing what we know today of the textile art of that period, we can easily imagine what the silks adorning the sails of Sigurd's fleet must have looked like: great eagles, lions, elephants and propitious beasts of fable; princes engaged in the chase; Cufic inscriptions and even more recondite symbols, all resplendent in gold and various colours.

The textiles that have come down to us bear witness to a spectacular range of colours. This predilection for brilliant hues, which can only be achieved with silks and jewellery, is typical of the Middle Ages. The luxurious textiles of the period were depicted by artists in the Low Countries during the fifteenth century, when new techniques of painting made it possible to create realistic pictures embodying the aesthetic ideals of that time. Hans Memling's *Madonna and Child* (colour plate 1) is a superb example of this, but it also reflects the international character of textile art, showing how fabrics of completely different origin and character can be used together. The Madonna's robe and gown are of Flemish woollen cloth in brilliant blue and red, the canopy is of Italian gold cloth with a magnificent design in green velvet, while on the floor lies a 'Turkish' rug of rural manufacture. A further series of historical pictures of this kind would give us an exact portrayal of leading textile arts and of the values put on them by different periods. But this is only *one* side of textile art — the supreme achievements. What we must also ask is, how did it all begin?

Textile work (*opus textile* in Latin, from the verb *texere*, meaning to weave or plait) has gradually come to include far more than the term originally implied. Of all textile techniques, the art of weaving is the fundamental one and this book will therefore be primarily concerned with the development of weaving. In very early times, hardly any other product of human workmanship meant so much to mankind as woven fabric. First of all men learned weaving in order to protect themselves from the elements. The utilitarian fabrics were followed by ornamental textiles. Developments were conditioned by local circumstances, above all by the exigencies of climate and the availability of raw materials. Gradually, in highly civilized countries, the art of weaving developed into a medium of craftsmanship and creative artistry. Where conditions were favourable production was established on a large scale and the choicest works became the most sought-after commodity in world trade. As a result of these wide-ranging contacts, patterned silks in particular provided designs for other textiles and served as vehicles of stylistic impulses and decorative themes. This brings us back to the story with which we began. We would very much like to know what Sigurd the Crusader brought back with him to Norway. No doubt his acquisitions included silk fabrics with exotic patterns which would tempt the womenfolk of the royal demesne to experiment on their looms with new designs.

The scholars who first began to study ancient textiles were chiefly concerned with patterns and motifs and less interested in techniques. Since then, however, the fundamental importance of various technical factors has been generally realized. The nature of the raw materials, the construction of the weaving implements and, above all, the multitude of weaving techniques determining the details of the woven pattern must all be carefully considered and analysed in order to ascertain the age and origin of surviving fabrics and trace the course of development.

Since the material on which this study is based is now scattered all over the world, and is also worldwide in origin, the evolution of textile art has to be considered in international terms. At the same time, however, certain products must be viewed from a national vantage point. There is no contradiction here. It is an advantage to be able to illustrate this account with specimens from a wide repertoire of textile art, ranging from more or less primitive folk art to sophisticated works of great craftsmanship, and also including textiles of native, European or Oriental origin from a variety of periods down to the present day. The large stock of ancient textiles still extant in Scandinavia together with the remains of traditional handicraft, which flourished in these countries until recent times, may therefore be of wider relevance.

The history of textile art constitutes an extensive and many-sided subject field which, to various degrees, impinges on archaeology, ethnography and ethnology, art history (including iconography, ornamentation and costume), social and economic history and so on. But it is also worth pointing out that insight into textile techniques might add to the possibility of bringing out all the information embedded in the object regarding, say, the classification of a single object or a more or less probable influence from alien areas. It is considerations of this kind which have dictated the outlines of this book.

I   *Materials*

Until quite recently, when artificial fibres of various kinds began to be used, the majority of spinning materials were taken directly from nature, from the animal or the vegetable kingdoms. Some exceptions to this rule will be considered at the end of the present chapter. Since natural conditions and climate vary a great deal from one part of the world to another, the incidence of the natural spinning materials also varied a great deal, and this had far-reaching effects on the development of textile art in different civilizations.

Animal fibres are either hair formations from certain mammalian species, or cocoon filaments from caterpillars, that is silk. Quite a large number of vegetable fibres can be used for textile work, but only flax and hemp and to a certain extent the nettle fibre — all of them relatively similar in structure — together with cotton, have achieved international historical significance. Of these textile materials, four can fairly be termed paramount: wool and silk, linen and cotton. Each of these materials has its particular aesthetic and technical properties, which have shaped the course of textile development. Highly sophisticated technical processing has made it possible for each of them to be transformed into a medium of artistic creativity well worthy of the epithet 'textile art'.

Wool and other animal fibres

Most of the animal fibres used as textile materials come from various species of the sheep, goat and camel, but other quadrupeds have also supplied the raw materials for textile work.

Wool varies enormously with regard to coarseness, length, lustre, colour, etc. Variations also occur within one and the same animal species depending on pasturage and climatic conditions, which can influence fibre formation in one way or another. A chilly climate and high altitudes have a favourable influence on the quality of wool. Accordingly the animal species with the finest hair are to be found in the highest mountain regions of the world: the Kashmir and Angora goats of Tibet and the Pamirs and the timid vicuña, whose home is in the Andes. The character of the hair also varies between different parts of the same fleece and between young and old beasts of the same species.

I, fig. I.   Greek vase painting from *c.*550 B.C. showing various stages of wool processing. The uncarded wool is being shaped to porous weft yarn, the warp yarn is being spun on a spindle and the material is being weighed. Two women are working at the warp-weighted loom. Finished pieces are being folded

Basically, it is possible to distinguish the following types: the soft wool, which may be curly to a greater or lesser degree, the longer, straight and shiny hair, and the rather inferior kemp, with a pronounced medulla which is coarse and stiff and therefore breaks easily. The proportions of wool, hair and intermediate variants differ considerably from one breed of sheep to another, as do the length, coarseness, colour, curliness and lustre of the fibres. Throughout the ages, selective sheep-breeding has aimed at isolating certain properties and developing them to suit the changing requirements of various forms of textile production. Thus in certain breeds the hair as well as the kemp has been eliminated to such an extent that the fleece consists almost exclusively of fine wool.

There are two very different ways of collecting wool. The most primitive method is to pluck the wool off the animal by hand. This is done during the spring, when in the natural course of events the animal would shed its winter wool anyway. In the case of wild animals (such as the Angora goat), the wool comes off by itself and clings to bushes and rocks, where it can be collected by people who venture up into the mountain regions inhabited by these animals. A more rational method is to shear the entire fleece off the sheep's body. This method is newer though still very old. It

is not thought to have been practised in the Scandinavian countries until the twelfth century.[2]

There are also two distinct methods (and implements) whereby the wool is prepared for spinning; these are combing and carding. The latter method is the newer. Combing is also used to separate the curly wool fibres from the straighter and longer hair in the plucked or sheared fleeces. The latter are spun into worsted while the finer wool is used for fabrics which are to be fulled or felted.

Wool is undoubtedly the oldest spinning material in human history, and it is easily converted into a simple fabric. Apart from animal hides, wool was originally the material that enabled man to withstand a cold and rigorous climate. And it is in these climates, especially in upland regions, that wool is naturally available. It is also possible to make wool into a thread without any elaborate preparations.

The oldest civilizations of the ancient world may be termed 'woollen' cultures. We have evidence of this in the detailed narratives of the Old Testament as well as in the works of Homer, Herodotus and other classical authors, and also in vase-paintings (I, fig. I). The details that have come down to us concerning the sheep-breeding and wool trade of the Roman

Empire indicate that manufacture was organized on an international basis. This tendency survived into the Middle Ages. Wool and woollen products then became one of the most widespread commodities of world trade and were of the utmost political and economic importance. The Iberian peninsula and the British Isles became prominent exporters of wool, and new towns based principally on the woollen industry sprang up along the Channel coast.

Plain woollen fabrics can vary enormously in appearance and weight. If the yarn is spun from a really fine and soft light wool the woven fabric will be particularly soft; worn as a garment, this gives a 'drape' which no other material can achieve. On the other hand, if the wool is coarse the fabric will be heavy, especially if it is dense, and after shrinking and fulling it can become so stiff as to be reminiscent of leather. Variants in this respect may be studied through the medium of classical and medieval sculptures, showing variously draped garments. Some of these garments seem to be as soft and thin as muslin while others appear thick and bulky.

Silk

The silk filament consists of a very long fibre produced by the fibroin secretion of the silkworm, *Bombyx mori*, when it pupates, that is, spins itself into a cocoon. From this cocoon there will eventually emerge a silkmoth, provided nothing unforeseen happens. Every worm or chrysalid secretes two parallel strands together with a gum, sericin, which rapidly solidifies, glueing the two strands together to form a single thread.

When the silkworm larva is ready to leave the cocoon, usually after eight to ten days, a special secretion is discharged which dissolves the gum sericin but which also has the effect of damaging the silk thread. This has to be artificially prevented so that the silk thread can be unwound in its full length. The chrysalid is therefore killed with boiling water, which also dissolves the layer of sericin surrounding the cocoon. The end of the thread is then found so that it can be wound off or reeled. The 'hard' silk thus obtained is still saturated with sericin, which makes the thread relatively dull. The sericin is removed (the silk is 'degummed') by washing it in warm water, either while it is still yarn, or after it has been woven into a silk fabric. The latter method is easier and is probably older. Washing makes the silk softer and shinier, but the same procedure is also required if the silk is to be dyed, otherwise the dye will not 'take' evenly.

If the silkworm is not killed, it will eat its way out of the cocoon, in which case the fibres will be 'short'. The only method of making a thread out of a naturally abandoned cocoon is to card and spin the fibres in the same way as wool. This thread is called 'spun silk'. It is therefore usual to speak of 'spun' or 'wild' silk in contradiction to 'cultivated' silk. There are, however, many varieties of silk cultivation, the caterpillar being domesticated to a greater or lesser degree. Basically sericulture (silk cultivation) involves supervising and directing the speed at which the chrysalid develops, so that reeling can proceed regularly, giving a uniform product. But this uniformity is also very much dependent on the species to which the caterpillar belongs and the type of tree or plant on which it feeds. Thus the caterpillar is also dependent on climatic and other natural conditions.

Silkworms are divided into two separate families, *Bombycidae* and *Saturnidae*. There are no less than sixty species of the former. The most important of them, *Bombyx mori*, lives on the leaves of the cultivated 'white' mulberry tree. In India there are six different *Bombycidae* in Bengal alone. One species is known from China, *Bombyx mandarinae Moore*, which lives on the wild mulberry tree and may conceivably be a remote ancestor of the domesticated caterpillar or *Bombyx mori*. The saturnids include one species living on different kinds of oak trees in Northern China and another which lives on *Ailanthus glandulosa*, 'the tree of Heaven', which is found in both India and China. The product derived from these and other 'wild' species related to them, which is sometimes termed 'tussah', exhibits a great deal of variety.[3]

Under the microscope the fibre from the wild silkworms is quite different from that of *Bombyx mori*, which has a more even surface and therefore gives a better shine than the others. The latter often have a somewhat undulating surface and an angular or flattened cross section. The *Bombyx mori* fibre is also finer: its diameter, measured in microns (= 0.001 millimetres) varies between 20 and 30 microns. The Chinese *Bombyx mori* is finer than the western species, while various species of *Saturniidae* are said to be up to 90 microns in diameter.

The reeled silk of *Bombyx mori*, improperly termed 'pure' silk, is also superior in terms of the length, strength and elasticity of its fibre. It is normally several hundred metres long, sometimes as much as 800–900 metres. After the sericin has been washed away, the two strands (or Fr. *brins*) are exposed; in the processing that follows they are combined with another two or more pairs of strands, and all these strands are 'thrown' or twisted together to form a thread. This so-called 'grenadine' thread is much stronger in relation to its fineness than any short-fibred material. Moreover, it is elastic and its tensile strength may be further increased by doubling and plying.

BAST FIBRES[4]

Flax

Among bast fibres, flax is an agricultural product, which, given very careful processing, can be made into a luxury commodity. The Latin name of the plant, *Linum usitatissimum* (very useful) indicates that it can be used for many purposes. While the stalk yields a beautiful and strong spinning fibre, the fruit is nourishing, and beneficial to the health and also supplies linseed oil, which has a multitude of technical applications. These various practical properties have led people in many parts of the world to credit linseed with miraculous powers.

In order to develop into good spinning material, flax needs fertile soil, a relatively mild climate and laborious processing: retting, breaking, scutching, hackling, bleaching and, by no means the least exacting, spinning. Retting is very much dependent on access to suitable water. If the flax is to give a really fine thread, it must be harvested while it is still green. If it is left standing until the fruit has ripened, the fibre will be coarse.

Whether it is cultivated for spinning fibre, for its fruit, or for both, flax is a pre-eminently civilized product, dependent on sophisticated agriculture. For this reason the cultivation of flax and the skilled work entailed by its processing and spinning has established it since the dawn of history in one of the richest agricultural areas of the world, Egypt. True, various opinions have been propounded concerning the origins of flax growing. Egypt's claim in this respect is supported by finds of processed flax from as long ago as Neolithic and Pre-Dynastic times and also by the comprehensive organization developed under the Pharaohs for the grading of woven linen products. Detailed particulars concerning this have come down to us from Roman authorities. The pre-eminent position of Egyptian linen on the world market during the Middle Ages points in the same direction.

Spun and woven linen has a property which is unsurpassed in a warm climate, namely a capacity for moisture absorption which causes it to feel cool against the skin. To this must be added the aesthetic quality of the properly bleached fabric. Small wonder that linen garments were the only ones permitted to visitors to the temples of Egypt: wool was considered unclean. Egyptian linen was always woven in plain tabby, which for thousands of years has remained the classical technique for this material. It is significant that this very type of linen weave (tabby) has a special name in many languages, for instance Fr. *toile*, Da. *lærred*, No. *lerret*, Sw. *lärft*, Old Norse *lerept*.

Compared with most other textile materials, a linen thread is somewhat stiff and has a shiny and slippery surface. These properties are enhanced by suitable treatment, above all by heavy pressure in a damp state, without any heat. Over the centuries several methods have been employed to utilize the ability of woven linen to retain the shape given to it while wet. One such method, a form of pleating produced by gathering narrow pleats together by sewing, is well exemplified among the Birka graves of the Viking period (Pl. 91b). Ancient Egypt provides other instances of skilful pleating of costume material, both in pictorial art and in archaeological finds.[5] During the Renaissance, heavy linen presses were used to bring out the shine of the patterned linen damask. The same purpose is served by the 'mangle' (*calendre*) with rollers.

From the early Middle Ages there are records of Byzantine imports of Russian linen cloth, which was specially used for linings;[6] it was probably quite coarse. These fabrics were presumably made from flax grown on the fertile steppes of southern Russia and along the Black Sea coast from where the area of cultivation gradually spread northwards towards the Baltic. 'Russian linen' was imported to Scandinavia during the Middle Ages and later as well. The question of the origin of flax cultivation in southern Russia brings us to Herodotus's statement that the Egyptians and the Colchi (living in the plains north of the Caucasus) wove their flax using a technique unknown to other peoples.

During the late medieval period the countries south of the English Channel — the Low Countries and northern France — were an important flax-producing area. The so-called *toile de Reims*, linen tabby from the French city of that name, is said to have equalled the finest linen tabbies in the world, namely the Egyptian ones. At the close of the Middle Ages this same region also began to use linen thread for weaving patterns, above all in damask for table linen, which also became a highly esteemed commodity.

There are various factors to suggest that flax was grown early in the history of Scandinavia (excluding Iceland). For instance, there are numerous place-names associated with the plant. But to what extent this cultivation was combined with the complex chain of processes needed to convert the flax into spinning material, or whether it was solely concerned with linseed, a nourishing food in its own right which was also treasured as a remedy with magical powers, has yet to be established.

Isolated finds indicate quite definitely that flax was already being produced in Scandinavia for spinning during the Iron Age. Numerous medieval statutes from Sweden and Finland show that processed or unprocessed flax was used as a unit of value and this use as currency seems to reflect a long standing production on a large scale. The earliest written evidence dates from the twelfth century and concerns a tithe paid to the Archbishop of Uppsala in the form of linen tabby from the province of Hälsingland. Although flax has been grown in many Swedish provinces, Hälsingland, which during the Middle Ages also included the northernmost seaboard provinces of Medelpad and Ångermanland, was paramount in every respect, a position which it has retained down to our own century. Great hopes were entertained of this part of the country during the eighteenth century and special bounties were disbursed as part of the efforts made by the state to encourage crafts. It was above all in Ångermanland that the fine 'bounty linen' was manufactured, while it was in Hälsingland that the famous Flor damask factory was established in 1729.

Hemp

Hemp, *Canabis sativa* (Sw. *hampa*, Ger. *Hanf*, Fr. *chanvre*), grows wild in large areas of inner Asia, where it flourishes in poor soil and withstands a rigorous climate. Botanists distinguish between two or three main types. One species, whose female flowers contain the drug hashish, came originally from southern India. In southern Europe another species is cultivated which grows to a considerable height. A third, Siberian-Russian, type ripens during a brief summer. This northern species is probably that most commonly grown in Scandinavia and northern Europe and is thought to have found its way there via Russia and Finland. Hemp was cultivated at an early stage for the sake of its fibre and its oil-yielding fruit. It may even have been known to western Europe in pre-Roman times.

The oldest known example is a textile find from Gordion in Asia Minor which has been dated to about 800 B.C. A Russian find shows that hemp was used over 2,000 years ago for the production of narcotics: one of the great Pazyryk tombs contained apparatus for this purpose.[7] Concerning the use of hemp fibre in China, we know that under the Han dynasty it played an important part in the manufacture of costly lacquer vessels, hempen fabric being used as a kind of reinforcement for the originally viscous sap forming the main ingredient in this complex manufacturing process.

Hemp would seem by all accounts to have been grown practically everywhere in northern Europe throughout the Middle Ages, to some extent because it was needed for marine cordage. On the other hand we do not know how widely it was used as a weaving yarn. Concerning the relationship between linen and hemp weaving in France, it is interesting to note that there was a guild of hemp weavers (cannevasiers) in Paris in 1258. Linen tabby, which by all accounts was a luxury article, would seem, on the other hand, to have been imported from Normandy. In Finland hemp was more widespread than flax during the Middle Ages, and hemp fabric was generally produced in the eastern parts of the country.

Nettle plants

The nettle family includes several species providing excellent spinning materials notably the *Boehmeria nivea* species, originally cultivated in India and China, of which the bast fibres are termed *ramie*, while the finished thin fabric has long been known as 'nettle cloth'. Gradually, however, this name has come to be applied to thin fashion fabrics of other materials, and during the nineteenth century it was above all applied to cottons.

Our common stinging-nettle, *Urtica dioica*, which grows wild in many parts of the world, is related to these plants. The stinging-nettle has a variety of uses both as spinning fibre and as a food and medical herb; it has also been credited with magical properties. This plant has been used both in Scandinavia and by primitive peoples in other parts of the world.[8]

It is uncertain, however, to what extent the stinging-nettle was used for spinning and weaving in prehistoric times. There is one archaeological find which sheds considerable light on this problem, and contributes evidence to the interesting wider question of which kind of bast fibre was first used for spinning in Scandinavia. About 100 years ago an early Bronze Age grave in Denmark (Voldtofte) yielded some fragments of a tabby weave which were at first considered to be linen and were therefore taken as evidence of the occurrence of linen and flax cultivation in Scandinavia during the early Bronze Age. Renewed scientific analysis of this find has since revealed that the fibre comes from our common stinging-nettle.[9]

COTTON[10]

The cotton plant, *Gossypium*, occurs in the form of a tree, a bush or a plant. Its fruit is a brown capsule the size of a walnut which opens when ripe, causing the long seed hairs to swell out, so that the fruit seems to resemble a snowball. When people from the Mediterranean countries first set eyes on a tree of this kind the seed hairs reminded them of wool, which explains such names as the German *Baum-Wolle* (tree wool) from which comes the Swedish equivalent, *bomull*. As a spinning fibre, cotton is softer and generally even finer than the bast fibres, and it is also easier to dye. On the other hand cotton yarn lacks the shine which, to a greater or lesser degree, is present in all bast fibres.

Cotton cultivation originated in India, where cotton has been the main spinning material for thousands of years. The material reached the Mediterranean countries with the Arabs, who exported both cotton fabrics and the raw material from India to China as well as to the western world. The raw material soon became very important for ecclesiastical purposes as well; it was the best material for candle wicks. During the late Middle Ages cotton yarn was often also used as weft in conjunction with a linen warp. However, painted and printed cottons were the main commodities exported to the West.

Eventually the cultivation of cotton plants spread from India to the Mediterranean countries, but it was not until the eighteenth century that cotton growing acquired the tremendous industrial significance that made North America the world's greatest producer; only a fraction of world production now comes from India.

Cotton as a raw material probably did not enter Sweden until the 1730s, via the East India Company. The spinning of cotton yarn was introduced at the Alingsås factory in 1733 and by 1739 it had also been established in the more remote province of Darlecarlia (Dalarna), as witness an ordinance published in 1757 by the Board of Trade, dividing the country into spinning districts and allotting cotton spinning to Dalarna. This decision was justified on the grounds that for the past eighteen years cotton had been spun there on an outwork basis under the auspices of a number of merchants who forwarded the finished yarn to factories in Stockholm.

METAL THREAD[11]

In writings from the Homeric age down to late Roman times, we often read of garments interwoven with gold. Understandably enough, few specimens have been preserved, and of these only very fragmentary remains have come down to us in the form of archaeological finds. The main reason for this is that when such clothes were no longer used they were burned so that the precious metal could be re-used.

There are two completely different methods of making metal thread. One of them, doubtless the older of the two, involves cutting out narrow tinsel strips from beaten gold or silver. This tinsel or 'lamella' (Fr. *lame*, Ger. *Lahn*) can be used flat or spun round a textile core. 'Beaten gold', *aurum battutum*, of this kind is very bright and shiny and was therefore still being used for embroidery as late as the thirteenth century. The other method consists of pulling thin rods of gold or silver through progressively smaller holes in a disc. The drawn metal thread, or wire, originally had a round cross section and was solid. This technique occurs at a very early stage in the art of the goldsmith, but where textiles are concerned it would not seem to have been used prior to the ninth century A.D. In northern Europe this type appears as a distinctly oriental phenomenon, in contrast to the beaten 'lamella' which completely dominates all contemporary and earlier textile finds from western Scandinavia and from central and western Europe generally.

The next stage of development, which may have come during the thirteenth century, is for the drawn silver wire to be gilded and mangled flat, that is, into a 'lamella', which is then spun round a silk core. This type of 'spun gold thread', which in French inventories is termed *or fin*, was used as a weft for silk weaving. The same type, gilded drawn silver, flattened and spun, has been in general use in Europe ever since the fifteenth century for weaving and for embroidery, as well as other techniques of precious textile production.

But this kind of gold thread had certain inconveniences. For one thing it was expensive, but above all it was heavy, and this put a strain on the textile materials forming the constructive element of the fabrics. This state of affairs prompted several kinds of imitations. The imitations were cheaper and in turn made it possible to use more of this kind of gold and silver thread. There ensued an accelerating course of development which may be said to have culminated in the Italian silk weaving of the fourteenth and fifteenth centuries.

The most important imitations are now generally referred to as membrane gold and membrane silver. They consist of an animal membrane or gut of one kind or another (especially the intestines of cattle, according to Italian documents) which has been gilded or silvered. There has been a considerable amount of conjecture as to the technique used for this gilding, which in the majority of cases has gradually worn off, with the result that the gold threads are now a dull brownish or greyish colour, often with a shade of violet.[12]

The earliest known evidence of this type dates from the twelfth century: in this case the membrane strip is twisted round a silk core and is sparingly brocaded into silk textiles of Spanish-Islamic origin. A probably later type, known from Italy, is coarser and spun round a core of linen or hemp. This was manufactured in various places but is also known to have been made in Cologne from whence it was exported to Lucca.

I, fig. 2. Lapp woman pulling pewter wire with her teeth. From Shefferus's *Lapponia* 1673

Gilt and silvered membrane also occurs in certain Chinese (or possibly central Asian) silks which probably date from the thirteenth century (Pl. 29). Here the membrane is not twisted round a thread but woven flat into the silk fabric. This type of substitute for metallic gold may have been devised in China, where there was a greater shortage of gold than in countries further west. The membrane was later replaced in China by rice paper. Rice paper gold occurs both flat and spun round a silk core, the latter kind often being used in embroideries.

On the subject of metal wire, mention should also be made of the pewter wire which has been made for centuries by the Lapps of northern Sweden, who used it for their costume embroideries. As a rule this pewter wire was very closely twisted round a reindeer sinew, the utility thread which was used by the Lapps for all their needlework. Its manufacture is illustrated in I, fig. 2, which comes from Johannes Schefferus's *Lapponia* (1673). The structure of this otherwise rare 'spiral wire' is identical with some of the gold and silver wire in the finds from Birka.

OTHER KINDS OF TEXTILE MATERIALS

Mention is sometimes made in historical texts of textile fibres which have proved hard to identify, and which are certainly not related to the common principal species. Three such phenomena are described below:

Pinna marina, or *squamosa*, is the name for certain mussel species living in temperate sea water, especially in the Mediterranean and off the coast of India. The mussel clings to underwater rocks by means of long tufts of hair growing out of its shell. After they have been cleaned, these tufts make a lustrous spinning material which was used even in prehistoric times for weaving fine fabrics. Arab merchants called this material 'sea-wool'.

Asbestos (from the Greek for 'unquenchable') is a mineral substance occurring in several rock formations and used in modern times mainly for thermal insulation. During prehistoric times and in the Middle Ages, it seems to have been put to some textile use, and western European medieval texts refer to asbestos fabrics (under a variety of names) as something more or less miraculous.[13]

Byssos (Lat. *Byssus*) is one of the most controversial of all textile terms and often appears in medieval texts. It is universally agreed that it was a thin, costly fabric but it has not been established what it was made of. Convincing evidence has recently been provided on this point by the Polish historian Wipszycka in a work dealing with the Egyptian textile industry under the Romans. Papyrus texts often refer to byssos and to the professional term *byssourgi*, which designated a special branch of linen weaving. The manufacture of byssos, of which there were various degrees of fineness, was a monopoly of the Egyptian priests, but the Romans abolished this monopoly. We can thus take it as proved that byssos was a top quality linen, the Egyptian luxury product through the ages.[14]

THE PRODUCTION OF THREAD

Spinning methods[15]

With the exception of certain materials — reeled silk and a number of synthetic fibres which can be described as imitations of silk — all spinning materials consist of short fibres, of variable length, which have to be twisted together in order to make a thread. But it is fairly easy to make a kind of thread with one's bare hands, as three of the women are doing in the Greek vase painting shown (1, fig. 1). A weft yarn can also be formed by pressing a tuft of wool against the thigh with one hand, a method which has been practised in various primitive civilizations. Both methods yield a full, porous yarn with little or no twist. It is not strong enough to be used as a warp, but in certain cases it makes an excellent weft yarn and it is for this special purpose that the method has survived until later times.[16]

In order to strengthen the woollen yarn it has to be twisted, that is, spun, and the harder the twist, the stronger the thread. The simplest spinning method requires a weight. In 1, figs 3 and 4 are shown different implements used for this purpose. The spindle is an excellent tool which

1, fig. 3.   Improvised spinning tool used by a Mongol caravaneer

1, fig. 4.   Distaff and spindle used by the Tebbu Tibetans

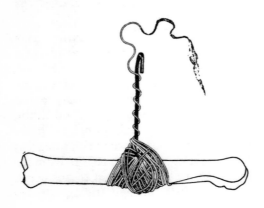

was known during the European Stone Age and has been used all over the world in many guises for various materials.

The spindle consists of a straight rod, usually of wood, hooked at one end, and a spindle-whorl which is threaded on to the rod. The whorl can be made of stone, ceramic or other material heavier than the rod and serves as a fly-wheel to keep the rod rotating so as to twist the thread material already shaped by the hands of the spinner. The thread is wound on to the rod, either above or below the spindle-whorl. With this implement one can spin an even and, indeed, an extremely fine thread. The spindle can also be used to ply threads together.

1, fig. 5.   Simple spinning-wheel for wool spinning. From an English manuscript of 1338

As time went on, however, more efficient methods were devised: the spindle-whorl was replaced by a spinning-wheel and later a treadle arrangement. The oldest of these implements was rotated by hand and was used in India, especially for spinning cotton, but also for spinning wool. It must have reached the western world in the early Middle Ages, possibly in conjunction with new types of looms and other implements for more efficient wool processing. This type is shown in an English manuscript from about 1338 (1, fig. 5).

The form of spinning-wheel in use today, represents a later development, and is provided with a spindle with flyer attachment and a treadle. Opinions vary as to the origin of this invention, which was more efficient for flax than the earlier type, since it automatically gives a harder twist. It was presumably developed in Europe and the earliest known illustration is in a German manuscript from 1480 (1, fig. 6).

In western Europe the older type with the big wheel long remained in use for spinning wool; even in the eighteenth century British woollen manufacturers were said to produce better results with this type than on the treadled spinning-wheel with flyer. From England or Scotland the big wheel spread to Denmark and Norway, where it was commonly referred to as the *skottrock* ('Scotch wheel'). It is known that in both Denmark and Norway spinning with it was taught to female inmates of penitentiaries, which were in fact called 'spinning houses'. One of the Swedish names for this implement, which was introduced for cotton spinning in the eighteenth century, was therefore known as the cotton wheel.[17]

1, fig. 6.   Spinning wheel with spindle and flyer attachment

1, fig. 7.   Diagram showing notations of the twist by spun and plyed yarn

The spinning-wheel with flyer attachment and treadles, on the other hand, is ideal for flax, with its long fibre, which requires a particularly strong twist. In the Swedish provinces of Dalarna and Hälsingland, if not elsewhere, it was called the German wheel which tells us something of its origin and in England, the Saxony wheel. Judging by Olof Broman's *Glysisvallur* (the classical description of life in the province of Häsingland) the German wheel was ranked as an innovation at the beginning of the eighteenth century. It is hard to say whether this only holds good for

Hälsingland, but it seems reasonable to suppose that both the German and the cotton wheel were centrally sponsored in line with the official efforts being made at that time for the promotion of manufacturing industry. Domestically, the ancient method of a simple spindle survived in many areas until quite recently.

Terms for the direction of the twist in spinning and plying

Whatever the implement used, thread can be spun in two different directions, 'with the sun' or 'against the sun'. Earlier these characteristics of the yarn were termed in various languages by the words for 'right' and 'left' respectively. It was found, however, that the application of this principle of nomenclature had gone astray, with the result that both terms had become ambiguous. A completely different designation therefore had to be introduced (see 1, fig. 7), and this was achieved by an international agreement concluded at the beginning of the 1930s, which introduced the terms S and Z.

The spinning of different fibres

Wool can be spun in various ways: with a hard twist into a dense and strong thread, perhaps for use as warp, or with a loose twist to give a light and porous yarn to be used as weft. Wool can be spun either with an S or with a Z twist, as can cotton and wild silk. But it is not uncommon to find that warp and weft have been deliberately spun in opposite directions in the same weave, for the sake of the final effect. The direction chosen affects the 'texture' of the weave.

This is not the case with bast fibres, which have a natural spiral movement which can be said to dictate the direction of spininng, in other words, to make it easier to spin in one direction than the other. Consequently a single linen thread will usually be S spun, while hempen thread is supposed always to have a Z twist.

On the strength of this casual connexion — not observed until quite recently in the study of textile history — the spinning direction has been taken as a means of determining the species of a fibre. Judgement should perhaps be reserved on this point for the time being. It is not entirely clear as yet whether the rule for the species of flax and hemp now common also applies to all the other species of these plants, including those which have long since fallen into disuse. Nor is it entirely certain how this rule applies to the nettle.

Spinning method and origin

It is in the light of these physiological properties and the habits probably induced by them that certain scholars have ventured to make geographical attributions to textiles whose origin has previously been disputed. This has applied especially to certain woollen textiles from late antiquity which have been found in Egypt, some of which species consistently display an S twist while others display a Z twist. Since flax in Egypt was the genuine and, from time immemorial, the overwhelmingly predominant spinning material — unlike the native sheep's wool, which never acquired any great importance in that country — it has been concluded that flax inculcated a habit or a technical tradition of spinning with an S twist. This argument is confirmed by the fact that the woollen textiles which even for other reasons can be assumed to be of Egyptian origin, consist of coarse and inferior wool. The latter opinion is seconded by Pliny, who refers to the poor quality of Egyptian wool. In contrast to the inferior Egyptian woollen products, there is a series of consistently high-class woollen fabrics with Z spinning for which there is other reasons to disprove an Egyptian origin. Pfister, judging by completely different indications, considered these textiles to be of Syrian or Persian origin.

Reeled silk does not have to be twisted (or thrown) even to make a warp. It was not usually twisted in China, but it was normally in the west. Patterned silk textiles which, for various reasons, can be assumed to have been made in the Near East or the Mediterranean region, as a rule have twisted warp threads. This rule may no doubt be attributed to tradition, deriving from the use of short-fibre spinning materials: flax, hemp and different kinds of wool, which were widespread and native throughout this extensive region. An observation of this kind must imply that the manufacture of the object concerned is native to this wide-ranging geographical region. On the other hand, contrary to what has sometimes been alleged, any detailed conclusions regarding the place of manufacture should not be based on the tightness of the twist ('the harder the twist, the further to the West').

Weaving Implements[1]

Faced with the task of elucidating at least some of the outlines of the long evolution of weaving, difficulty can very often be experienced in distinguishing between the concepts of method and implement. Implements may be so rudimentary that they are only understandable with a particular procedure or method. Because so very few specimens of authentic weaving tools, or even parts of them, have come down to us, our only possible recourse is to grope our way forwards on the strength of isolated facts, which, to make matters worse, are not always completely reliable.

The following are our main sources of information for present purposes: 1. Ancient implements and methods which have survived in the traditions of modern civilizations; 2. Implements and methods still used by primitive peoples, that is, ethnographic material; 3. Archaeological remains of weaving implements; 4. Depictions in contemporary art; 5. Various historical details, originally supplied by contemporary observers, as well as literary sources of other kinds; 6. Observations resulting from the examination of existing weaves from periods and geographical areas which may be relevant in particular cases.

By dint of systematic collection, ethnologists and ethnographers have rescued material of fundamental importance to this subject. Categories 4 and 5 present great problems of interpretation, not least linguistically, which have quite naturally given rise to conflicting opinions. Finds coming under category 3 are extremely rare, except for loom weights (made of stone or burnt clay); the looms themselves being made of wood have usually long since rotted away or been burnt.

Finally we come to category 6, a vast mine of information. In many cases, it is possible to proceed, by means of analogy, detailed analysis and observations of later weaves and surviving methods, to draw reliable (or at least highly probable) conclusions regarding the nature of the ancient weaving implement used in a particular case. But there are risks attached to this method. Quite often weaving specialists in our own time have arrived at assumptions which are historically absurd. Starting with a contemporary type of loom in which the specimen under consideration is made or could be made, today, they have drawn categorical conclusions regarding the construction of the original loom, even though the specimen itself was made hundreds or thousands of years ago.[2] The reconstructor has failed to understand that the same result can be achieved in more than one way, with greater or lesser human effort and with a greater or lesser degree of mechanization of the loom. It is all the more important for the person compiling a description to be on the look-out for this kind of pitfall, since methodically conducted investigations of textile techniques may have far-reaching effects on the subsequent course of research.

THE BASIC PRINCIPLES OF WEAVING

Before going on to describe the chief kinds of weaving implements in existence, and there are any number of variants, we will begin by considering the general principles that characterize a weaving process. The first step in producing a weave is the setting up of the yarn for the warp. The warp must be secured at both ends so that it can be stretched. It should also be provided with a mechanical arrangement of some kind whereby the shed (Sw. *skäl*, Ger. *Fach*) can be opened and closed by a movement of the hand or foot, or by the weaver's body. The warp ends must then be divided in such a way that they come alternately above and below the shed. Normally this is arranged automatically in the warping process.

Weaving requires at least two sheds, resulting in tabby, the simplest of basic bindings. A distinction is drawn between the natural shed and the countershed. The simplest form of shedding involved the following two operations:

1.   During warping the warp threads are divided in such a way that, after they have been stretched, they lie alternately above and below a shed rod, which thus represents the natural shed. Normally the shed rod is retained throughout the weaving procedure, in which case the natural shed can be activated by inserting a thin stick or lath, which is turned up on one edge as required. In this way every other thread, say the threads with 'even' numbers, can be lifted simultaneously to form an opening above all the 'odd' threads.

2.   In order to obtain the other shed (the countershed), the even warp threads have to be lowered, or the odd ones lifted, so as to form the shed opening above the even threads. This can be arranged by fastening all the odd threads to a shaft via a thread crossing the warp to form loops (heddles or half-heddles). This entire arrangement is called a heddle rod. At a more advanced stage (our loom type 6), this device has developed

into a full heddle rod with complete heddles. A complete heddle has a loop in the middle through which the warp thread passes, and larger loops above and beneath. By these loops the heddles are linked to transverse bars, the uppermost of which is the true 'shaft'. Certain suspension devices or supports are needed in order for these two operations to work. These supports can take such very different forms as a tree, poles driven into the ground or the roof and walls inside or outside a house.

In discussing different weaving arrangements it has been usual to employ the designations 'horizontal' and 'vertical', referring to the position of the warp. Likewise it is customary to distinguish four main types, two of which are termed horizontal and two vertical. For various reasons I shall not follow this classification. In my opinion one is compelled to distinguish between more than four main types. Besides, the position of the warp is not really significant, for in principle the same weaving arrangement can exist even if the warp goes horizontally in one case and vertically or diagonally in another. Seven types must therefore be regarded as the minimum number. Finally, it is necessary to emphasize that there are variants and even intermediate forms of the seven main types which will be described below. These intermediate types may be the result of influence from several main types as well as from practical necessities or new requirements. In some of the seven cases I venture to use more specific names instead of the hitherto current terms.

Type 1. The most primitive loom: the four-edged weave of the Indians

This loom, which in principle may be taken as representing the origin of all weaving devices, consists of two sticks with the warp stretched between them. It also includes a shed stick left in the warp to give the natural shed and a simple heddle rod for the countershed. The latter is obtained by each lower thread in the natural shed being picked up and bound by a loop (half heddle) which is gradually secured to a stick, the heddle rod. When this stick is lifted, the warp threads attached to it are also lifted, to allow a pick to be inserted in the shed (= the countershed). After the rod has been lowered again, the weaver can insert a flat stick next to the shed stick and raise the latter on to one edge, thus bringing the natural shed into operation.

This type of weaving device is illustrated by means of a drawing in the remarkable petition to the Pope — a very moving human document — written in about 1600 by Don Felipe de Ayala, a high-ranking prince of the Incas and probably the only member of his class to have survived the cruelties perpetrated by the Spaniards during their conquest of Peru.[3]

The woman in Ayala's picture (II, fig. 1) has hung the upper warp 'beam' from a tree, while both ends of the lower beam are secured to a belt, known as the back strap, passing behind her hips. In this way she can stretch and relax the warp as needed by means of 'body tension'. In practice, however, it is difficult to carry on weaving right up to the upper stick. Not only is it difficult for the weaver to reach up far enough, but it is impossible to obtain a clear enough shed with a very short warp.

II, fig. 1.   The 'primeval loom' — rectangular fabric woven by a Peruvian woman using a back strap. Manuscript of the Inca Prince Ayala c.1600

II, fig. 2.   Peruvian tapestry loom from the same manuscript c.1600

To get over the latter difficulty she must 'cheat', using a pointed stick of some kind or a needle, to insert the weft thread by thread. One solution to both problems is to invert the whole weave after reaching about half-way, in which case the 'cheat threading' can be made decorative. The whole procedure results in a rectangular piece of cloth with a selvedge on all four sides. Even today the same type of loom can be found in use both among the Indians of Latin America and in other parts of the world.

Ayala's voluminous account also depicts another, somewhat similar loom which gives an impression of greater stability. Here the upper stick or beam rests in forks on a pair of stout uprights, and the lower beam is also firmly anchored. But otherwise this construction resembles the weaving device already described. It was probably on looms of this kind that the ancient Peruvians made the admirable tapestries that have been discovered in graves. Thus this picture can serve to illustrate the type of loom which we shall now turn to consider.

Type 2. The tapestry loom

This weaving device is often referred to as 'the vertical loom with two beams'. There is no doubt that the precursor of this loom must have been a primitive weaving device resembling that shown in II, fig. 2, irrespective of the direction of the warp. But in order to weave a tapestry, with its densely-beaten wefts, the warp must be even and tightly stretched, which also requires a stable frame, especially as the technique used is a slow one and the work must therefore be left from time to time without fear of disturbance. Moreover the construction has to be firm in order to stand the beating of the weft. All these considerations made it natural for the uprights to be anchored vertically, preferably by driving them into the ground. In this case they could also be made to support a beam on which to roll up the woven product, as well as another beam for the warp. The Egyptian loom in II, fig. 3 probably had a transversal beam which could be lowered as required. The European tapestry loom, in use since the Middle Ages, is unlikely to have differed very much. At the bottom it had a rotating beam and at the top another beam for the warp, or else a transversal stock with stout pins on which the warp could be wound up in groups. The latter device is that commonly used in small looms.

Shed-changing proceeds in much the same way as in the primitive loom. The countershed may be formed by loose half-heddles collected in bundles pulled forward by hand as required, which provides greater opportunity of working freely. The weaver sits in front of the loom. Work invariably starts at the bottom and continues upwards. The weft, which has to cover the warp completely for the sake of effect, is packed or beaten from the front, first with a few blows from the spools on which the weft yarn is wound, and then perhaps with a hafted comb beater. Both these implements are beaten downwards, with their pins inserted between the sparse warp threads.

This type of loom is without doubt indigenous to the ancient civilized countries of western Asia, where it is of very great antiquity. The two looms depicted in about 1500 B.C. in a burial chamber (II, fig. 3) represented an innovation in Egypt at that time. They are roughly contemporary with the earliest tapestries, found in the very rich tombs of Tuthmosis IV and Tutankhamen.

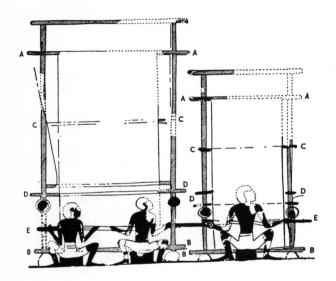

II, fig. 3.   Tapestry looms from an Egyptian grave painting. Thebes *c.*1500 B.C.

Even if it is correct to assume that multicoloured tapestries were of minor importance under the Pharaohs, this kind of weaving, and with it the loom, must have been in use ever since that period. For this we have the testimony of Herodotus, who visited Egypt in the middle of the fifth century B.C. and was surprised to note that people there 'worked the weft downwards, whereas in other places the practice is to beat it upwards' — as in the warp-weighted loom (Type 5) which he was accustomed to see at home in Greece and Asia Minor.

Evidence from the Middle Ages suggests that most of the work (i.e. the patterning) was done free hand, only the main contours often being marked out in advance by drawing directly on the warp. Since the Renaissance, the weaving has followed a model, usually in the form of a painted cartoon, placed behind the warp and thus visible between the threads. In simpler workshops, however, the cartoon would be replaced by a woven piece. In both cases, since weaving is done from the reverse side, the new woven picture is in reverse, with right in the model becoming left in the woven product and vice versa.

Another device was used at the Gobelins and other French tapestry manufactories, though we do not know exactly when it was introduced. The contours from the model are drawn on the warp, but the cartoon is placed behind the weaver, who thus has to turn round to compare colours, etc. This arrangement makes it possible to install an adjustable mirror behind the warp, thus enabling the weaver to see the result of his work from the face of the weave.

The tapestry loom with vertical warp, the *métier de haute lisse* or high-warp loom is first mentioned in Paris in 1303 but which had existed earlier. At the same time mention is made of a *métier de basse lisse* or low-warp loom, evidently a new type, with a horizontal warp, and presumably fitted with treadles. The treadles may have made the work easier but at the same time it made the front of the tapestry inaccessible, and was probably used for tapestry of lower quality. The high-warp tapestry loom was long considered the superior type.

A loom which to some extent combined the advantages of both the original types is said to have been invented in the mid-eighteenth century. It could be described as a pivoting high-warp loom and was used in the Beauvais factory, where it was mainly used for weaving upholstery and small works.

It should be added that a vertical loom of a very stout construction is still used in the Orient for knotted pile carpet weaving.[4]

Type 3. The linen loom of ancient Egypt

This weaving device consists of a horizontal warp stretched in its entire length between two beams supported by low posts driven into the ground. One shed of the tabby weave is the natural shed. The countershed is obtained by lifting a simple heddle rod. The weaving could be done by two persons sitting on either side of the weave and lifting and lowering the shed together, but it could also be done by a single person so long as it was confined to small widths. The weft is beaten in the shed with a sword beater.

This procedure is quite clearly illustrated by the burial chamber painting reproduced in II, fig. 4, showing a horizontal loom which is seen in a modified bird's eye view. At the very top of the picture we see the transversal beam and the posts, which in fact are a fair distance away, at the far end of the stretched warp. In the foreground can be seen the shedding device and the two weavers. The woman on the right is beating the weft with her sword beater while her partner is lifting the heddle rod to change

II, fig. 4.   Bird's-eye view of horizontal linen loom with two weavers. Beni Hasan, Egypt, *c.*1900 B.C.

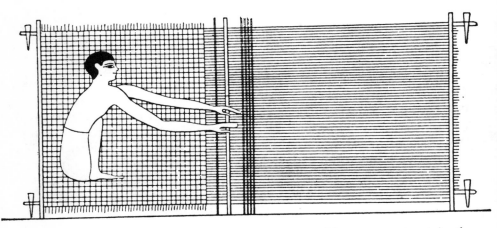

II, fig. 5.   A single weaver working on a horizontal loom pegged out in the ground. Beni Hasan, *c.*1900 B.C.

the shed. As the weave grows, the weavers have to change both their own position and that of the heddle rods. The other picture from the same period and place shows a man weaving a mat with a weft of rushes. He works sitting on top of the woven fabric, so as to be able to reach over the entire loom width. Wall paintings in burial chambers from Pharaonic times quite often depict scenes of working life, especially textile work, the looms shown being of the type we have described. But the best demonstration of how a loom worked is given by the charming doll-sized model of a weaver's shop, found in the tomb of Meket-re (c.2000 B.C.). Mummy bindings of extremely fine linen dating from about the same period must have been woven in the same way. The dimensions of the complete pieces of linen that have been found, widths of 1½ metres and lengths of 20 metres, bear witness to the capacity of this equipment. The appreciation of this kind of production is attested by the huge bundles of linen found in the tomb of the architect Kha, living during the fourteenth century B.C.

In more recent times, variants of this type of loom persisted among Bedouins and other nomad peoples both to the east and to the west of Egypt. They are usually narrow eaves with the warp collected in a long, thick cord. The warp behind the heddles is then made to pass through a coarse comb which spreads out the threads to the width of the finished weave.

Type 4. Weaving with tubular or circular warp[5]

The expression 'tubular' weaving covers a large group of different weaving methods exemplifying varying solutions to the external problem of getting a warp of the right length for the purpose in mind and also

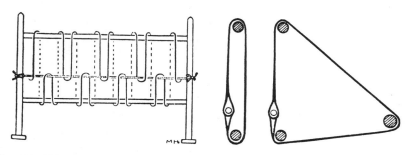

II, fig. 6. Diagram of tubular (circular) warp. Front view and cross sections with two and three beams respectively

evenly stretched. This method also makes full use of the valuable warp material. One warping method, much used for band weaving, involves winding the warp yarn in the same direction, that is, spirally, round two sticks or 'beams', the distance between which determined half the length of the warp. By the *other* procedure, the 'loop method', an extra stick is inserted round which the warp thread always returns in the opposite direction. An additional third beam may serve to increase the length of the warp (II, fig. 6). In both cases weaving proceeds in the normal manner: alternation between the natural shed and the countershed is obtained by lifting simple heddle rods, as with the types we have already described. The heddle rod may be flexible, for example consisting of a thick string, as used by Indians in Latin America.

II, fig. 7.   Loom with tubular warp and back strap. Used by the Tebbu Tibetans, twentieth century

In the former case (spiral warping) the result is inevitably a cylinder whose circumference equals the length of the warp. Alternatively, a warp set up using the loop method can be concluded in two different ways after the entire warp has been woven up (filled with weft). Either the stick is replaced by a thread which 'locks' the loops formed by the warp — in which case the result will also be a cylinder, for example a skirt without seams — or the stick can be pulled out of its position in the opposing loops, giving a rectangular weave with selvedges on all four sides. Since, after some amount of use, the original warp loops are soon filled out by the weft, they are generally hard to distinguish, especially if the fabric has been in the ground for a long time.

Two-beamed looms of this kind can be placed both horizontally, as with the Tebbu Tibetans (II, fig. 7), and vertically, as with the Indians and the carpet-weavers of Syria, but there are also other variants with three beams (II, figs. 6 (*right*) and 8). The purpose of these constructions is to elongate the warp without it having to be rolled up on to a revolving warp beam, which is always liable to result in uneven stretching of the warp, especially when working with very large warps and heavy material.

The great black tents used by the Bedouin of the desert are woven on tubular warps stretched by three thick beams. Here the yarn is spun from coarse goat hair. The tent cloth is woven in one piece, with no aperture, like an enormous ring about 20 metres in circumference. The height of the tent wall, that is to say, the loom width, is almost 2 metres. Large dimensions such as these also require very stout loom constructions, with thick poles driven into the ground and wedged with heavy stones, which in turn requires all work to be done more or less out of doors (II, fig. 8).

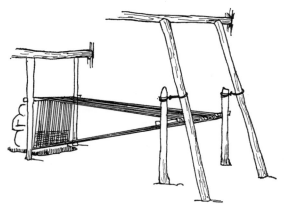

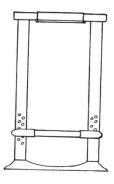

II, fig. 8.   Big loom with tubular warp. Syria 1950s

II, fig. 9.   Weaving frame from the Oseberg ship burial, probably used for tubular warp

The tubular method of stretching the warp has been used by primitive peoples all over the world and may be used for weaving large fabrics or narrow bands, the supporting arrangements sometimes being of such a temporary nature that one is hardly entitled to speak in terms of weaving equipment at all. All the more remarkable, then, is the well-preserved and perfectly made tool which was found in the Oseberg ship (II, fig. 9), consisting of two uprights rising vertically from a footpiece and joined at the top by a transversal beam. There is a deep groove in the bottom of the upper beam, and a detachable pin, which fits the groove perfectly, has been inserted there and tied to the beam with a string. Lower down there is a sliding beam which can be raised and lowered. The uprights have holes in which plugs can be inserted to fix the position of the sliding beam for streching the warp.[6]

Type 5. *The warp-weighted loom*

The west Norwegian term *oppstadgogn* is a general Scandinavian, and to some extent internationally accepted, name for the warp-weighted loom, the construction of which is illustrated in the schematic drawings, II, figs 10, 11.[7] This loom has a warp beam from which the warp is suspended. The warp is stretched by loom weights made of burned clay or stone, fastened in pairs at the bottom. The warp beam is supported by two up-rights propped against the wall, which are also fitted with supports for the heddle rod. The sheds are changed in the following ways:

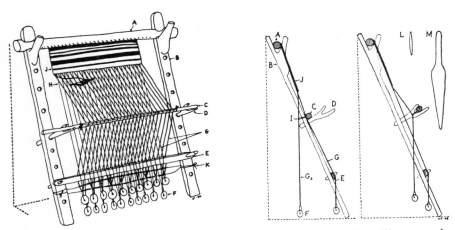

II, figs 10–11.   Diagram of warp-weighted loom. Cross sections illustrate the shedding procedures. M = sword beater

One series of threads remains stationary parallel with the uprights while the other series is fastened with half heddles to a shaft (C), which is movable. The natural shed is formed when the movable warp threads hang vertically. The countershed is obtained by lifting the heddle rod (with its warp threads) upwards and forwards and placing it in its cradle (D). This is for tabby.

Four-end twill can also be woven on this loom, in which case the warp must be divided during warping into four series (instead of two), one series of threads being vertically suspended (so as to form part of the natural shed). The other three series are looped on to three separate rods. By lifting the three heddle rods alternately and then utilizing the natural shed four successive sheds are obtained, producing an ordinary four-end twill. (In Iceland, when a weave was made in this way it was therefore termed 'three-shaft' (*þriskept*).)

The weaver or weavers always work standing in front of the loom (I, fig. 1). The weft is beaten upwards, inside the shed, with blows from a sword beater. In Norway this implement is still known as *sked*, a word related to the verb 'skilja' meaning 'to separate'. A fabric produced on a warp-weighted loom can be recognized by the 'starting border', generally formed as a band (sometimes a cord), resulting from the special warping method, which is essential for weaving on this kind of loom. Band warping proceeds in the manner shown by the schematic drawing (II, fig. 12). The

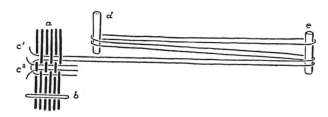

II, fig. 12.   Warping on band, schematically shown: *a* woven band, *b* place for tablets or a rigid heddle, *c* the weft of the band to be used as warp in the weave of fig. 10

band can be woven either with tablets or with a rigid heddle. The weft of the band, which is to be the warp of the final weave, is drawn out on the one side of the band, being regularly laid round two or three pins (d, e) projecting from a frame, so as to give sufficient length for the height of the loom piece to be produced. The work thus produced resembles an enormous fringe. This must be carefully tied on to the warp beam before the latter is placed in position on the uprights and the weights hung on to it. Thus the starting border plays an important functional part: it should be solid and firm so as to keep the warp threads from sliding.

Traces of the warp-weighted loom have been found from the eastern Mediterranean through central Europe and up to the far north of Scandinavia and Iceland and its history covers a period of more than nine thousand years. It is depicted on several Greek vases from the sixth century B.C. (I, fig. I) and in the north of Norway the tradition survives to this day.[8]

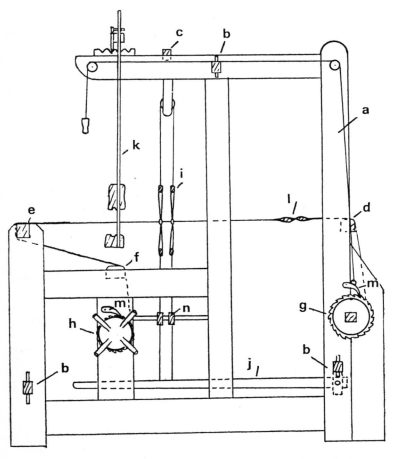

II, fig. 13.   Construction of the ordinary treadle or shaft loom

Type 6. The treadle or shaft loom

The essential construction of the ordinary hand loom, with its generally horizontal warp, is shown in II, fig. 13. Two uprights are joined by transverse beams and support two rolling beams: the warp beam (g) and the cloth beam (h), together with a fixed breast beam (e), in front of which a seat is generally provided for the weaver. Heddle horses or pulleys are suspended from an upper cross beam (c). These in turn support the shafts (i) and heddles. Each heddle rod consists of several heddles stretched between two bars. A complete heddle consists of three loops, with the smallest in the middle, through which the warp thread is pulled. The treadles (i) are secured to the frame at the bottom and are tied to the shafts via *lams* (n). The weft is beaten with the beater (k). A reed inserted in the beater serves to spread the warp threads evenly. As a rule the beater is suspended from the front of the uprights, but it can also be attached to the bottom of the loom.

II, fig. 14. Broad loom with two weavers. Ypres MS of 1363

Several variants of this basic type are known, which contains the essential components of the weaving equipment that entered Europe during the Middle Ages. One manuscript from the fourteenth century shows a loom for two weavers (II, fig. 14),[9] and another depicts a simple construction with poles driven into the ground and with heddle rods hung from the roof (IV, fig. 9). From Eastern Europe and more recent times we know of similar constructions supported by the walls or roofs of the room where the loom is placed.

The treadle loom is thought to have come to western Europe in connexion with the organized woollen industry which led to the foundation of the cities of the Low Countries in the eleventh and twelfth centuries. This technical innovation may have come from the Near East, probably by way of Italy. Its distribution is attested by other pictures but also by archaeological finds of loom components. There is one pulley from Sigtuna (IV, fig. 1) and another from Lund, found in strata ascribed to the twelfth and thirteenth centuries respectively. Comprehensive excavations of settlement sites in Danzig (Gdansk), Opole and other Polish towns have unearthed loom components and innumerable fragments of cloth, some of which display properties showing that they may have been made on treadle looms (cf. Chap. IV).[10]

II, fig. 15.   Silk loom similar to fig. 16. From a Chinese stone relief, Han period

II, fig. 16.   Chinese loom with one treadle and back strap

One of the advantages of this type of loom was that it could produce far longer woven pieces than the weaving tools mentioned previously. A very long warp could be wound up on the beam, which gave rise to a new method of winding the warp. After the warp has been wound on to the beam, the threads are drawn, one after the other, through the heddle loops and then through the reed. In this way the warp threads are not restricted to a particular binding number (two or four) as in the case of the warp-weighted loom. The new type of loom and the warping method used with it made it possible to have odd numbers of shafts, hence the many woollen fabrics of three-end twill that appear not only in the Polish but in medieval Scandinavian finds as well.

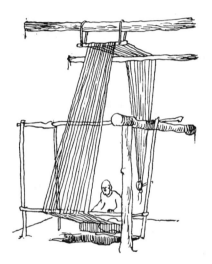

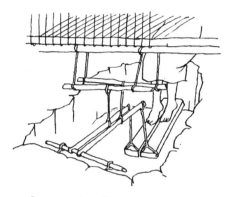

II, figs 17–18. Treadle loom with a long warp stretched to the ceiling, and a pit for the treadles. Syria 1950s

The origins of the treadle loom doubtless go back to Chinese silk weaving, which may have been at an advanced stage of development 2000 years before the Christian era. A loom of this kind is depicted in stone reliefs from the Han period (II, fig. 15). It seems delicately constructed and generally appears to have a gently sloping warp. These pictures seem to resemble popular looms occurring more recently in China and Japan (II, fig. 16). which are typical tabby looms with a single treadle and a body tension device, the back strap. The novelty of this type of loom, compared to the types described earlier, is that a heddle is connected to a treadle. The treadle device, which was probably invented by the Chinese, eventually spread westwards, in the first instance presumably to Iran and India. It has also been combined with tubular warps.

Until relatively late (the seventeenth century), Chinese silk fabrics were usually long and very narrow — a practical result of warping procedures. The precious polychrome silks from the Han period, made solely in imperial workshops, were bound by law to be at least 50 centimetres wide, but that may have signified the limit of what was possible. The plain weaves from the same period and later are generally much narrower. Here too the warp predominates, but the density is generally uneven, which shows quite clearly that the beater and reed of the ordinary European hand loom were not in use. The weft must have been beaten into the open shed, as indeed was the practice with many other weaving devices (types 1, 3, 4, 5, and 7). Further consideration will be given to the development of the treadle loom in Chapter IV.

Type 7. The Indian cotton loom and similar weaving devices with a pit for the treadles

Various weaving devices based on roughly the same principle, often combined with a pit dug in the ground for the treadles, occur within an area ranging from India in the east to North Africa in the west, and were apparently used for various materials. Archaeological excavations in the Hungarian village of Razom revealed two small houses, each containing traces of a loom of this kind, probably dating from the seventh or eighth century.[11] Basically, this weaving device could be described as a combination of the Egyptian linen weave and the heddle- and treadle-device of the old Chinese silk loom. Here the heddle rods are suspended on a transverse beam resting on a pair of uprights. Exactly underneath this there is usually a pit for the treadles and the weaver's feet. The weaver thus sits on the level ground with his legs down in the pit. Across his thighs is the cloth beam, which rests on low supports driven into the ground. Behind the heddles the long warp passes through a thread spacer (a kind of trellis) to a stout pole a distance away, after which it can be anchored in different ways, even in the roof if the weaving is being done indoors.

If the weave is narrow and the work is done outdoors, as is commonly the case in India, the entire arrangement can easily be moved according to the prevailing climatic conditions. The treadle pit method also has advantages in connexion with tasks that are best done indoors and require stout timber constructions. If the poles can be driven into the ground, as shown in II, fig. 18, they will stand quite firm.

TOOLS AND APPLIANCES FOR WEAVING BANDS

Theoretically speaking, it should be possible to weave bands on any of the types of weaving implements described above. Apart from professional work, however, this has been more the exception than the rule. In many cases band weaving devices, some of them so primitive that they can hardly be termed implements at all, perpetuate ancient implements which appear to be primitive forerunners of more mechanized and rational weaving methods. There are also band methods which do not in any way correspond to what we have defined as weaving.

The complete bandloom, until recently in use by Nordic handicraft workers, partly resembles the ordinary treadle loom (type 6). It consists of a stand made of two solid uprights directly supporting two rollers, corresponding to the warp beam and the cloth beam of a big loom. Between the uprights is a transversal beam supporting a holder for the heddles, which can be connected with two treadles at the bottom. Another type of bandloom, resembling the above device, has no treadles. Instead the shedding is activated by the weaver's hand, lifting or lowering the heddles. Neither of these bandlooms having a regular beater, the weft is packed within the shed with a knife (bandknife), thus acting as the counterpart to the sword-beater of the warp-weighted loom.

Here may also be mentioned a technically related construction without any wooden parts, namely the Icelandic 'footweaving', for which the weaving implement consists of a string. It works as follows: the warp is held in the left hand and stretched between this and the right foot, which is placed within the shed (the natural shed). The countershed is opened with the right hand by pulling a number of simple heddles tied to a long string. The natural shed is opened by inserting the right hand into the shed near the foot and moving the shed upwards.[12]

The rigid heddle

The rigid heddle (Sw. *bandgrind*, Ger. *Webegitter*) consists of a frame enclosing a number of laths (II, fig. 19). There is a hole in each lath and together these holes form a horizontal line. The warp threads are threaded alternately in one hole and in the chink between two laths. Usually the warp is stretched between a fixed support and the weaver's belt. Shed changing is obtained by pressing the implement alternately upwards and downwards, causing it to work in the same way as two heddle rods.

The age and origin of the rigid heddle have yet to be determined. The ingenious simplicity of the implement might seem to suggest great antiquity. But the earliest known specimen, from Pompeii, is no older than the Christian era.[13] The rigid heddle is not thought to have reached Scandinavia before the Middle Ages, since there is no trace of it in the

II, fig. 19.   Rigid heddle

archaeological finds — a remarkable gap in the Norwegian Viking finds, which have yielded specimens of many other textile implements. Another reason for this view is that the rigid heddle is unknown in Iceland, a country which has preserved very many antiquated working methods introduced by the Norwegian colonists during the first settlement period, in the ninth century.

Tools for Tablet Weaving

The construction of a tablet weave and the implements used differ from every other kind of weaving. The weaving implement consists of a number of identical tablets, usually square plates with a hole in each corner through which a warp thread is drawn. The tablets are kept parallel and close together so that they can be rotated simultaneously with a single movement of the hand. Six-holed and hexagonal tablets are also known. However, a previous assumption concerning triangular tablets has proved incorrect. Thus the triangular object shown in II, fig. 21 was no doubt used as a pulley.[14]

The tablets, which have to be equal in size and fairly thin and smooth, are generally made of wood, horn, or stiff leather. More recently they have also been made from playing cards or hard cardboard. Like rigid heddle weaving, the tablet warp with its parallel tablets can be fastened to a fixed support and stretched by body tension. But very wide tablet bands or those which have a complex pattern require a kind of stand or frame to keep the warp under constant tension and to provide support for the individual tablets.

Traces of tablet weave technique have been discovered in archaeological finds from very ancient periods, while geographically it extends throughout Europe and Asia all the way to China.[15]

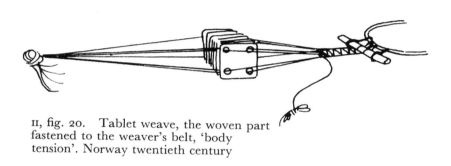

II, fig. 20.   Tablet weave, the woven part fastened to the weaver's belt, 'body tension'. Norway twentieth century

II, fig. 21.   Weaving tablets with 4 and 6 holes. The triangular tablet was used as a loom pulley, not for band weaving. Sweden

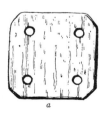

a

d

c

Band weaving frames

Band weaving implements and methods which are presumably of great antiquity still survive in isolated parts of Norway. One such implement (II, fig. 22) consists of a high, vertical frame with notches to support the heddle rod, some cross-sticks and a rotating beam or roller on which the finished band can be wound up. The band produced resembles those made elsewhere, executed on various bandlooms or on a rigid heddle. In some of the Norwegian band frames the warp is stretched by a suspended weight, which is reminiscent of the warp-weighted loom.[16]

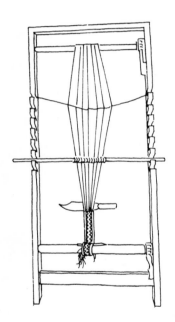

II, fig. 22. Upright frame for weaving bands with an extra warp producing pattern. Norway nineteenth century

Band weaving box

Another very primitive implement is still commonly used in Hallingdal (Norway), where it is used to make the ancient type of band which is known as *kelim-band*. Normally this implement consists of a small, rectangular box (II, fig. 23) supporting holders for two rollers, one for the warp and one for the finished braid. There is no shedding mechanism at all. The weft is darned into the warp using a flat, pointed wooden needle (resembling the 'net needle' used for net-making). One such needle is needed for each colour. There are medieval pictures showing similar boxes, which probably were used tor making braids of this kind.

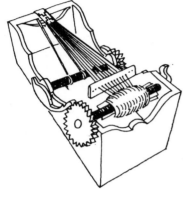

II, fig. 23.   Box loom for weaving Kilim bands. Norway nineteenth century

III *Woven Fabrics and Weaving Techniques*

What is a weave? The first requirement is that there must be a warp and a weft, that is, two systems of threads interlacing with one another at right angles and in such a way as to be bound together in a uniform system. Such a system is called a 'binding'. But this is not the complete definition, for the same effect could be obtained by a needle-and-thread darning across the warp ends. A weave also requires a regular shed, that is, a mechanical arrangement whereby a movement of the hand or foot will open one shed to allow the 'pick' to enter and then change over to the other shed.

ELEMENTARY TERMS[1]

The 'binding repeat' is the smallest unit in the system, which is graphically depicted by means of a 'binding pattern' on squared paper, each square denoting a crossing of the warp and weft. According to the number of 'binding points' occurring in the binding pattern, a weave is said, for

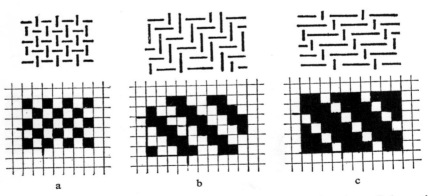

III, fig. 1. Basic weaves. In the upper row, schematic drawings. Below, the corresponding 'binding patterns' on graph paper; each filled-in square denotes a depressed warp end

example, to have a three-end or four-end construction. The term 'extended binding' denotes that the threads have been regularly doubled. It should be noted that the word repeat is also used in the sense of 'pattern repeat', referring to the pattern unit of a mechanically repeated design. 'Interruption' is a term indicating the number of warp threads by which a binding point is moved, from one weft thread to the next. The number for twill is one, while for satin it is at least two (cf. III, fig. 1).

The repeat of a twill may also be expressed as a numerical ratio, the first figure indicating the number of picks over which an end passes and the second the number of picks under which it passes. Thus 3/1 is a four-end warp twill; 1/3 is a four-end weft twill; 2/2 is a four-end twill binding which is equal on both sides of the weave. Unfortunately, in every language this code is applied in a different way. The proportion between warp and weft very much affects the appearance of the weave. If the warp predominates over the weft, it is a warp-faced weave. If the weft predominates, the weave is weft-faced. Alternatively, such terms as 'weft twill', 'warp twill', etc. can be used.

The notes to the subsequent descriptions of weaves start with the 'basic binding' systems: tabby, twill, and satin. This will be followed by various combinations of techniques and types, most of them for producing patterns. The technical types have been arranged in groups and sub-groups in order to indicate their degrees of proximity: A1, A2, etc. In the absence

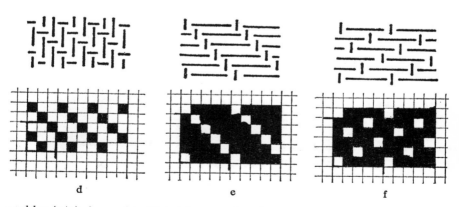

a tabby (1/1), *b* 4-end twill (2/2), *c* 4-end weft-faced twill (1/3), *d* 3-end warp-faced twill (2/1), *e* 5-end weft-faced twill (1/4), *f* 5-end weft-faced satin, interruption (stepping) 2

of exact English terms (and in some other cases as well), Swedish names will be used or added as explanation, because they have already to some extent been internationally adopted for textile terminology. In many cases also non-English equivalents are added, between brackets, in order to facilitate understanding for readers of different nationalities. In most cases the definitions are followed by described examples and notes on the occurrence of the techniques in question.

THE BASIC WEAVES

1. Tabby (Sw. *tuskaft*, Fr. *taffetas*, Ger. *Leinwandbindung*). The binding repeat includes only two binding points. Variants: ribbed fabric and panama which is an extended tabby binding with two or three threads accompanying each other in both warp and weft.

2. Twill (Sw. *kypert*, Fr. *sergé*, Ger. *Köper*) is characterized by the diagonal lines formed by the binding points. The binding repeat usually contains three or four binding points (three-end and four-end twill respectively) but can include more. Variants: chevron twill, herring bone or lozenge twill which are produced by reversing the sequence of threading, the turn-over being made in the direction of both warp and weft. The turn-over may be symmetrical or asymmetrical (cf. IV, figs 4–5, 7).

3. Satin is distinguished by the interruption, that is, the spacing of the binding points. Together with widely divergent porportions of warp and weft, this binding helps to make certain surfaces of the weave smooth and shiny.
   A plain weave consisting of one warp and one weft can generally be ascribed to one of the three basic types of weave. When producing a pattern, two or more basic weaves can be combined (types C2 and C3).

CLASSIFICATION OF TEXTILE TERMS/WEAVES

A   Weaves with uniform binding, patterned by colour changes.

A1 Weaves with one warp and one continuous weft: striped, banded, checkered, rosepath.

A2 Tapestry weaves, i.e. weaves with discontinuous wefts: all-over and 'inserted' tapestry, Flamskväv, Rölakan, Rutevev, Kashmir shawls, K'o-ssu.

B   Basic weaves with additional yarn worked in various techniques.

B1   Pile weaves: knotted pile, rya-rug, half pile, looped weave or bouclé.

B2   Weaves with floating pattern wefts on a plain tabby ground: 'Weft-patterned tabbies': Munkabälte (monks belt), Opphämta, Skälblad 'Brocaded tabbies': Krabbasnår, 'tabby brocaded on the counted threads' (Dukagång), Soumak, overshot weaves (Daldräll).

C   Monochrome weaves, the patterns produced by changing the binding systems (i.e. self-patterned in a wide sense).

C1   Twills: plain, chevron, lozenge or extended twills.

C2   Self-patterned weaves in restricted sense ('Han damask' and similar).

C3   Damask (true damask).

C4   Gauze.

D   Weaves in which either the warp or the weft system — or both systems — are doubled:

D1   Warp-faced compound weaves, either tabby or twill.

D2   Weft-faced compound weaves, either tabby or twill (Samitum).

D3   Double-faced weft weaves, one warp system.

D4   Double weaves and 'pick-up doublecloth' (Dubbelväv, Finnväv).

D5   Lampas/tissue weaves.

E   Ground weaves supplemented with a pile warp (velvet): solid, voided, cut, uncut, pile-on-pile respectively.

A.   PATTERNING USING COLOUR CONTRASTS IN PLAIN WEAVES WITH UNIFORM BINDING

A1.   *Weaves with one warp and one continuous weft*

In a simple weave stripes are obtained either in the length, by warping yarn of a different colour, or else by changing the colour of the weft, in other words, the fabric is banded. A chequered effect is obtained by a combination of both methods. In an evenly balanced twill, the diagonally emphasized binding pattern will stand out if warp and weft are differently coloured.

In a chevron weft twill with a warp so thin and spaced as to be covered by the weft, quite a variety of patterns can be obtained by changing colour. Rosepath (Sw. *rosengång*) is a kind of chevron twill with multi-coloured wefts which cover the warp. There are variations: either 'bound', that is, one-sided with a clearly patterned face — the reverse being filled by long floats — or 'reversible', with short floats on both sides. This technique is very common in Scandinavia (III, fig. 4) but also occurs in many other parts of the world.[2]

A2.   *Tapestry weaves: weaves with discontinuous wefts*

All tapestry weave is characterized by the fact that the weft is inserted by hand using yarn of different colours, and also by the fact that the weft covers the warp. The binding system is mostly tabby, but twills also occur, as well as free, irregular bindings. Open slits occur where the boundary between two areas of colour is parallel with the warp (III, fig. 2a). The slits can be avoided by interlocking the weft threads before reversing direction.

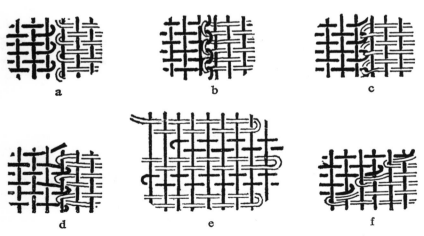

III, fig. 2.   Colour change methods in tapestry techniques. *a* slit tapestry, *b–c* interlocked tapestry, *d* dovetail or toothed tapestry, *e* 'hachures', *f* slanting join

If this is done every time, a chain will be formed on the reverse; if it is only done every other time, both sides will be roughly similar, but the change will be less distinct. Other types of colour change are called 'dovetailed' and 'toothed'. A shaded change is sometimes known by the French term 'hachures' (hatchings).

Apart from the all-over tapestry there is a type called inserted tapestry in which limited patches of various shapes are worked in as ornamentation in a plain fabric (as a rule in tabby, from which they differ both in colour and in texture). The weft ends in the inserted tapestry ornaments pass over and under groups of the ground warp, as shown in the diagram in III, fig. 3b. Sometimes small details are added free-hand on top of the tapestry surface, using the technique called *Fliegende Nadel*, or flying needle (III, fig. 3). This term is applied to details in white linen thread worked on to the regular tapestry surface with fairly long, irregular stitches while weaving is in progress. Inserted tapestry weaves frequently occur in Egyptian and Near Eastern texiles from late antiquity.

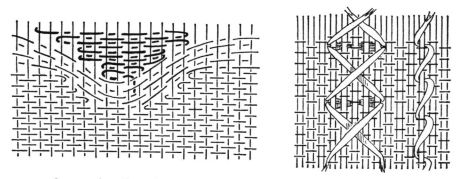

III, fig. 3 a–b.   Details from an Egyptian textile with tapestry motifs inserted into the tabby ground: *a* several warp ends from the ground weave are joined to groups when used in the tapestry weave; *b* Sometimes irregular stitches are added with the 'fliegende Nadel'

As a rule tapestry weaving is done on a vertical loom. True tapestry is distinguished by its rounded outlines. The multicoloured wefts generally follow the contours, so that the weft yarn is not exactly at right angles to the warp. This free working procedure is the reason why the technique has been preferred to other weaves for representing figurative scenes. Since elongated forms are best produced with the longest possible weft, human figures and other vertical shapes are usually woven horizontally and depicted recumbent across the warp, so to speak. The free mode of work requires a great deal of skill and artistic talent on the part of the weavers. In this technique particularly, it is the eye and the hand of the weaver that determine the quality of the finished product. Even coarse and primitive tapestry is a decorative technique. The higher its quality, the more refined and costly a work of art it becomes.

III, fig. 4.   Motif from 'bound' Rose-path weave, N. Sweden
III, figs. 5–6.   Motifs from Rölakan, S. Sweden

Whatever the stage of development, tapestry weaving always requires yarn of various colours, above all fine woollen yarn. Wool was almost the only material that could be dyed with a good result, a fact which makes it likely that this technique was created in territories with a good supply of dye stuffs and plenty of good wool suitable for dyeing. This in turn points to the ancient civilizations of the Near East and Central Asia. All-over tapestry weaves were probably produced there at a very early stage.

The art of tapestry which flourished in France and in central Europe, was introduced in Scandinavia in the sixteenth century by professional tapestry weavers emigrating from Flanders. For this reason the folk art variety, which was coarser and worked in smaller sizes, went by the name of *flamskväv* (Flemish weave). It was woven on a simplified tapestry loom. Both Swedish *rölakan* (III, figs. 5–6) and the Norwegian *rutevev* have predominantly geometrical patterns. The main difference between them lies in the manner in which the vertical colour change is effected. The name *rölakan* has nothing to do with red (röd = red) but comes from a word resembling *rygg laken*, meaning a woven material hanging on the wall behind one's back. The Latin term was *dorsale*.

Kelim is an oriental type of tapestry, used for large covers with geometrical patterns of coarse wool, which are recognizable by vertical slits at the colour changes. Production areas were mainly Anatolia and Central Asia.

The true Kashmir shawl was made of the precious and extremely fine Kashmir wool, which was obtained from the goats found in the mountains of Tibet. These shawls, bearing witness to an extremely high standard of craftsmanship, were highly prized in European fashion from the eighteenth century. They were mostly woven in four-end twill and executed on an ordinary treadle loom.

Chinese *k'o-ssu* much resembles the ordinary tapestry weave but is always executed in silk, sometimes with the addition of gold thread. This technique presumably came to China from Iran during the Sassanian period.

B. GROUND WEAVES WITH ADDITIONAL YARN INSERTED IN VARIOUS TECHNIQUES

B1. *Pile weaves*

KNOTTED PILE. This term denotes a weave with short tassels, called 'knots', tied in by hand, raised above the ground weave and made of a different yarn from the latter. This yarn is knotted around the warp threads in rows between the ground weft. The knots, which are principally of two types — normally termed Ghiordes (Turkish) and Sehna (Persian) — can be made in two different ways. Either they consist of short, ready-cut ends of different coloured yarns, or the yarn is worked in continuously, in which case, between each knot, it is taken across a narrow rod so as to form loops, which are cut afterwards.

Using pile of a single colour only, this technique originally served a purely practical purpose, supplying a warm cover with the same function as a sheepskin fleece. Unlike fleeces, which harden when exposed to the wet, these thick woollen covers had the advantage of always staying soft. Eventually this technique came to be applied to decorative purposes: the knots were made of differently coloured yarn and arranged in patterns — in much the same way as the stones in a mosaic.

Both the oriental knotted pile rug and the Nordic *rya* (Ger. *Knüpfteppich*) have played such an important part in the history of civilization that they require exhaustive treatment. We shall therefore be returning to the subject (Chap. xi).

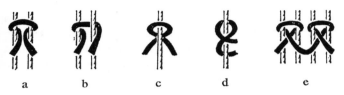

a   b   c   d   e

iii, fig. 7.   Pile knots of ordinary types (*a*, *b* and *e*) and the 'Spanish' or one-warp knot (*c*, *d*)

HALF PILE WEAVE.   This term denotes a weave in which only the design motifs are executed in pile, thus standing out in relief against the plain ground. The half pile weave occurs among Egyptian finds from late antiquity, in large pieces of eminently decorative character which were presumably used as curtains between the columns that were a common feature of general classical architecture. These textiles often included large figurative compositions standing out in multicoloured wool against a white linen background. As a rule the older specimens are of good classical style, in contrast to the later ones, presumably dating from the late Coptic period, which are characterized by grotesquely deformed figures.

Another type of half pile is known from the Spanish Renaissance, namely woollen bed coverlets — rather than carpets, as they are sometimes called — with patterns which are obviously enlarged designs from silk velvets of the voided ciselé variety. These Spanish coverlets seem definitely to be professional products, but folk art imitations are also to be found in Spain.

A related kind of folk-art occurs in northern Europe. The Norwegian half pile forms a fairly closed group, mainly confined to Gudbrandsdalen, where it seems to have been executed by specialist women weavers. It takes the form of pillow covers, generally, like the Spanish coverlets mentioned above, reminiscent of velvet patterns. Compared with these, their counterparts from Skåne (south Sweden), Denmark and Schleswig-Holstein have a more provincial character.

A very peculiar half pile weave in miniature is known from Iceland, where it was used as trimming for women's coats. These products seem to be imitations of certain trimming borders executed in patterned silk velvet of the kind once very much in vogue in southern Europe.

BOUCLÉ, or looped weave. This effect is obtained by means of additional wefts drawn up into long or short loops (III, fig. 8). The technique was practised in Egypt under the Pharaohs; for instance a unique and very beautiful specimen of pattern bouclé from the eleventh Dynasty (*c.*2000 B.C.) is now in a museum in Cairo. Made with very long loops of the same linen material as the ground weave, but without any pattern, the 'looped weave' often occurs in the later Egyptian finds.

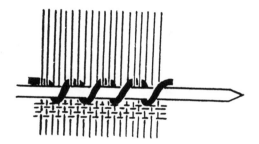

III, fig. 8. Bouclé weave

In the most sumptuous Italian velvets from the fifteenth and sixteenth centuries, prominent pattern effects were executed in bouclé of gold and silver thread. A less precious kind of bouclé, sometimes called boutonné, executed with coarse yarn in contrasting colours, was practised as popular textile art in many countries, usually for bed-covers and similar items. A related type, reminiscent of the 4,000 years old Egyptian weave just mentioned, was almost always made entirely of white cotton. The first specimens of this type date from late eighteenth-century England and were used as bedspreads. In Lancashire during the nineteenth century large numbers of these were manufactured as a 'cottage industry' centred on Bolton, north of Manchester. So-called 'Bolton quilts' were produced in large quantities, both for the domestic market, and for export to the Continent and to North America. This novelty gained great popularity and even inspired imitations, particularly in Canada, and from about 1860 to a considerable degree also in Sweden, where the technique was often adapted for native patterns.

III, figs. 9–10.   Brocaded tabby, type Krabbasnår.
Technique and pattern

B2.   *Weaves with floating pattern wefts on plain tabby ground*

The additional pattern weft may be either brocaded, or shuttled from selvage to selvage (Fr. *lancé*), the latter technique in English termed 'weft-patterned tabby', which name corresponds to a number of Swedish terms referring to the different types described below.

KRABBASNÅR is a brocaded tabby generally worked with multicoloured yarns forming diagonally shaped motifs (cf. III, figs. 9, 10). Several examples of this kind of weave are known from the Viking era and the Middle Ages.

The 'weft-patterned tabbies' are characterized by long floats of weft passing over and under the ground weave. As a rule the pattern yarn is shuttled but it may also be brocaded. Originally these weaves must have been done by the *skälblad* method (see below under *opphämta*). In order to facilitate weaving patterns of a similar kind other methods were eventually invented.

III, fig. 11. Weft-patterned tabby, type Opphämta, picked-up on a rod by hand

III, fig. 12. Weft-patterned tabby, Opphämta, threaded on shafts

MUNKABÄLTE (Monk's belt) (III, fig. 14) is the name of the simplest type of weft-patterned tabby, in which the pattern consists of alternating small blocks or squares. Here the sheds are opened by two pattern rods. The pattern is generally shuttled.

DUKAGÅNG (III, fig. 13; Pls 85a, 88a) is 'tabby brocaded on the counted threads' (Fr. *toile brochée à liage vertical*) and is characterized by all pattern wefts being tied down by one or two regularly spaced warp threads which give the design a striped surface. *Dukagång* is always brocaded.

There are a number of late medieval wall-hangings in this technique, once belonging to Nådendal Convent in Finland, now in Helsinki Nationalmuseum (Pl. 85a). They are especially interesting in relation to numerous hangings from southern Sweden, which, however, are later (Pl. 88). All have a rich ornamentation more or less influenced by the Romanesque style. The *dukagång* weave frequently occurs in ancient Icelandic textiles and it has also been woven in Finland, Norway and the British Isles as well as in Egypt, the latter variety occurring in Coptic burials.

III, fig. 13.   Tabby brocaded on the counted thread, Dukagång

OPPHÄMTA (meaning 'to raise' the shafts) is the most variable among the 'weft pattern tabby' techniques (III, fig. 11; v, fig. 6; Pl. 88b). Before a pattern weft can be entered a special shed must be prepared. Originally this was done by selecting the groups of warp ends needed for the pattern, collecting them on a narrow rod, and transferring them to a flat and broad stick (Sw. *skälblad*). When this is raised on to its edge a shed is formed for entering the pattern weft. By alternately inserting rods and the stick a shed can be transferred to behind the shaft where it is kept attached to a rod, in order to allow new sheds to be opened. More details of this method are given in Chapter v.

Many years ago the painstaking *skälblad* method was probably replaced by a heddle-and-treadle method engaging a few additional pattern shafts and treadles with which one could make small and uncomplicated patterns. This was the case with monk's belt (see above) and especially the type called in Swedish *solvad opphämta*, or '*Opphämta* threaded on shafts', generally not more than six shafts. This less time-consuming method has been very commonly used in all the Scandinavian countries. The resulting small-patterned weaves (III, fig. 12) were originally made of coloured woollen wefts on linen ground, mostly for use as bed-covers, table-cloths, etc. The production of such weavings seems partly to have been organized as a home industry for sale. This was especially the case in the surroundings of Borås in western Sweden from where the textiles were distributed by pedlars all over Sweden and also in Norway.

The true old *opphämta* in English overshot weaves, however, continued to be woven when rich and large patterns were desired, mainly forrectangular coverlets with coloured wools on linen ground. The richest and most varying patterns occur in a special form of textiles: the very long, horizontally placed wall-hangings, called *drättar*, that were woven for festival occasions in the great farm houses in Skåne in southern Sweden. They consist of alternating white areas of plain tabby and large borders in *opphämta*, usually of blue linen yarn. As with the *dukagång* hangings (see Pls 88–89), two loom widths were carefully joined. The entire pieces, often measuring a length of ten metres, were hung around the room, covering a great portion of the walls. In the beginning of this century this kind of weave was still being woven domestically, but using the laborious *skälblad* method. We

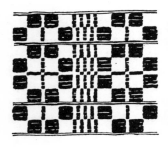

III, fig. 14. Weft-patterned tabby, Monk's belt

III. fig. 15. Brocaded tabby, Halvkrabba

will be returning to this interesting phenomenon in Chapter v. Nowadays this method is generally replaced by some kind of drawloom.

Overshot weave may be the same as a certain type of monk's belt, but it is generally synonymous with what is known in Swedish as *daldräll*. It is characterized by the pattern weft, passing the ground weft as well as on both sides of the ground weave. It is threaded on four shafts. This technique has existed in many countries, from Greece to Norway, where it was sometimes called 'Swedish weave'. In North America the *daldräll-overshot* type was very common and several eighteenth-century specimens are still preserved.[3]

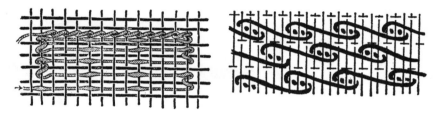

III, figs 16–17.   Swedish Soumak brocading techniques: from the Viking age, and the Middle Ages

SOUMAK is the name of an oriental type of weave sometimes related to tapestry. Discontinuous wefts in various colours are carried manually over a group of warp ends, each stitch being passed back under and around parts of the group, thus continuously filling the surface of the textile. Some early medieval weaves of northern Swedish origin with figure subjects (Pl. 87a) exhibit a similar technique used as brocading, alternating a tabby ground weave. A related but more varying technique was practised during the Viking era, as witness the finds from the Oseberg ship and from Birka (III, fig. 16; xv, fig. 1).

C.   MONOCHROME WOVEN PATTERNS

Various types of patterning can be produced by modifying or partially changing the binding system of a basic weave.

C1.   *Twills*

A large group is based on the twill system, in which the diagonal lines formed by the binding points are reversed in the direction of the warp or the weft (chevron twill, herring bone) or again in both directions (lozenge twill, diamond twill).

C2.   *Self-patterned weaves*

Various types of patterning can be achieved by modifying the regular binding system. For instance, in a regular tabby certain series of ends may be permitted to float, thus giving a kind of damask effect — shiny surfaces contrasting with a lustreless tabby weave (Fr. *damassé*). The earliest known type appears in the Chinese silk weave known as 'Han damask' (III, figs. 18–19). In western European linen manufacture, especially in Holland, related types were being produced from the sixteenth and following centuries, above all for use as table linen (cf. Pls 9c–d, 82b–g).

III, figs 18–19.   Chinese silks in self-patterned tabby. Diagram of the technique face and reverse, Palmyre. Diagram of pattern, Birka

C3.   *Damask*

A true damask (the same word in most languages) is a monochrome figured textile with one warp and one weft forming satin. The pattern is produced by reversing the binding so as to contrast the warp and weft faces of the same weave, thus showing different degrees of gloss. In its classical form, a damask is reversible (Pls 54–55, 60–63, 74–75, 80). Satin may be replaced by twill, and two different binding systems may also be employed. The name derives from the Syrian capital Damascus, an important centre of the silk trade and silk production.

C4. *Gauze* (Fr. *gaze*, Ger. *Dreherbindung*)

In principle every second warp end is fixed, the others — known as doup ends — being carried either to the right or to the left, around the fixed ends, after which the position is locked by a pick. Open patterns are achieved by varying the doup end twists. The doup ends may be selected by hand or by a special kind of heddle known as a doup. The gauze

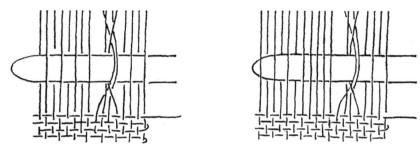

III, fig. 20.   Pick-up gauze weave, linen. Finland, Karelia

technique developed in Chinese silk weaving under the Han dynasty and was employed for fine open-work patterns. Executed in linen the technique is known from medieval Europe (Pl. 8) and from the folk-art of Karelia, eastern Finland, where it is called *spetsopphämta* ('pick-up lace weave'). Here perhaps it may be a relic of Far Eastern influence across Russia.

D.   WEAVES IN WHICH EITHER THE WARP OR THE WEFT, OR BOTH SYSTEMS, ARE DOUBLED

D1.   *Warp-faced compound weaves*

Each weave employs two or more series of warp ends and one weft. Alternate picks serve to separate the series of warp ends so that only one of them appears on the face, while the other or others are kept to the reverse. The remaining picks bind the warp ends. The ground and pattern

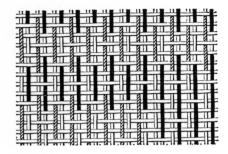

III, fig. 21. Two-coloured Chinese silk in warp-faced compound tabby. Han period

are formed simultaneously and the entire surface is covered by regular warp floats which hide the weft.

The binding of the warp ends may be in tabby or twill, hence the terms 'warp-faced compound tabby' and 'warp-faced compound twill'. Produced in polychrome silks, they are typically Chinese, the tabby being developed prior to the Han period and the twill occurring later on, during the T'ang period (see Pls 9a and 10–11).

D2. *Weft-faced compound weaves*

This type has two warps with different functions — a main warp (Fr. *chaîne pièce*) and a binding warp (Fr. *chaîne de liage*) — and a weft composed of two or more series of threads, usually of different colours. By the action of the main warp ends, only one weft thread appears on the face, while the other or others are kept to the reverse. The ends of the binding warp bind both series of wefts and the ground and the pattern are formed simultaneously. The entire surface is covered by weft floats which hide the main warp ends.

If the wefts are bound in tabby, the construction is called 'weft-faced compound tabby' (Fr. *taqueté*, Ger. *Leinwand-Schuss-Komposit-Bindung*). If the passes are bound in twill, the construction is called 'weft-faced compound twill' (Fr. *samit*, Ger. *Köper-Schuss-Komposit-Bindung*), also designated in Swedish and several other languages by the medieval term *samitum*.[4] This technique may have been developed in Iran in the second or third century A.D. No doubt it was influenced by the Chinese warp-faced compound weaves, in which the warp plays a similar role to that of the weft in the western weaves (cf. III, fig. 22).

Both techniques occur in various materials, that is to say, entirely in silk, in silk and extremely fine woollen yarn, or even in cotton and coarse wool. In patterned silks (mostly polychrome), it is the dominant technique during the first millennium A.D. (cf. Pls 12–22, 83c).

Some rare variations of the *samitum* technique without colour-effects, that is, monochrome, appeared in about A.D. 1000: on one hand the exquisite type with 'incised' linear designs, termed in German *Ritz-Muster*, on the other the 'pseudo-damask' which is characterized by areas showing the effect of coarse tabby contrasting with the regular glossy surface of a *samitum*. Both types may have come from Syrian looms, possibly to be localized to Antioch and mostly dated to the eleventh century (see Pls 23 and 30 respectively).

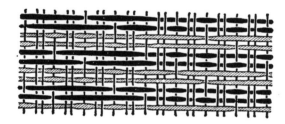

III, fig. 22. Weft-faced compound twill ('samitum'), two-coloured

There is also a later type of *samitum*, in which the main warp is of coarse linen or hemp yarn, enlarging the design, which is often distinguished by features more or less debased. Such 'half-silks' have long been called 'Regensburg' fabrics, a consequence of a totally erroneous attribution by O. von Falke of a remarkable altar frontal (in fact not a half-silk) belonging to the cathedral of that German town. Subsequently specimens of half-silk of good quality were identified at Las Huelgas and the type was generally attributed to Spain. In a paper published in 1969, however, D. King showed not only that the Regensburg altar hanging was made in Venice, but also that figured half-silks were produced in this prominent silk weaving centre. The economical use of silk made them less costly than whole-silk fabrics, but this fact did not necessarily affect the quality of the design. Among the numerous half-silks which have been preserved in various places in Europe there are, in fact, examples exhibiting a perfect execution — which indicates that they are probable Venetian — as well as poor, probably later, specimens characterized by debased features, of different origin. The place of production of the latter specimens seems difficult to decide.

D3. *Double-faced weft weaves*

These are weaves with one widely spaced warp system and a weft composed of two series, of which one appears on one side of the textile, while the other appears on the other side. This is done by arranging the binding points of each series in such a way that, from the opposite side, they are concealed by the floats of the other series. In patterned double-faced weaves wefts from the two series, which are of different colours, change places as required by the pattern.

This technique is known from some silks dating from the twelfth or thirteenth century and considered to be of Spanish origin. The technique also occurs in half-woollen cloths — the warp of linen or hemp — of which about ten have been preserved in Finland, Norway and Sweden (Pl. 83b). The patterns are in Romanesque style, with paired birds etc. and related to some of the silks just mentioned. All these woollens are certainly imported but the area of manufacture is difficult to decide.

D4. *Double weave and double cloth*

According to current international practice (CIETA, see Chap. XVII) the term 'double weave' denotes various types of fabrics consisting of two separately woven layers which can be of different binding systems and may be linked together by stitching ties. In Scandinavian tradition the term *dubbelväv* has a more specialized meaning, exactly equivalent to the English term 'pick-up double cloth', Fr. *taffetas double-étoffe faconnée*. The Scandinavian *dubbelväv* always consists of two separate layers in tabby binding simultaneously woven in contrasting colours, one layer above the other. Patterns are executed when the layers change position, always appearing in reversed colours. The pattern is picked up by hand on pattern rods or sticks (*skälblad*). (See Pls 84b–c, 86, 87b and also Pl. 56.)

The oldest extant examples of *dubbelväv* in Scandinavia date from the thirteenth century and are executed in wool and linen (Pl. 86). The technique was at its height between about 1400 and 1600. Since then it has been perpetuated as folk-art, especially in those parts of Sweden which border on Norway: the technique also occurs in both Norway and Finland. Terms such as *finnväv* and *ryssväv* (Russian weave) occurring in old Swedish and Finnish records would seem to suggest an oriental origin. This technique appears in ancient Peruvian textile art, skilfully executed with the primitive equipment; it also occurred in the finest Persian silk weaving from about 1600 (Pl. 56).

D5. *Lampas*

According to the CIETA vocabulary (the English version of 1964):

Figured textiles in which a pattern, composed of weft floats bound by a binding warp, is added to a ground fabric formed by a main warp and a main weft. The ground may be tabby, twill, satin, damask etc. The weft threads forming the pattern are normally pattern or brocading wefts; they float on the face as required by the pattern, and are bound by the ends of the binding warp in a binding ordinarily tabby or twill and which is supplementary to the ground weave.

It was only at a late date, probably after 1900, that the word 'lampas' was adopted as a technical term in French silk weaving.[5] This term, however, has not been generally accepted. Since the eighteenth century English silk manufacture has used the word *tissue* in roughly the same sense, and it is still employed by some scholars.[6] The Scandinavian vocabulary (NTT 1974) has a descriptive term (*sammansatt vävnad*) as a general equivalent to lampas but maintains the old term *diasper* introduced by von Falke as a designation for the special type of weave occuring in the Italian thirteenth and fourteenth century silks. In the latter sense *diasper* may be classified as a variety of lampas, but also (and more exactly) as a kind of 'double weave' — but not 'double cloth', cf. D4) — consisting of two separate layers in weft-faced and warp-faced binding respectively, forming pattern by alternating on the surface. See Pl. 35a and colour plate 2).[7]

E. VELVET

Velvet (Fr. *velours*, Ger. *Samt*) is a pile weave. The pile is produced by a 'pile warp' (Fr. *chaîne poil*) which is raised in loops above the ground weave by the introduction of thin rods during weaving. When the ground is entirely covered with pile, the velvet is said to be 'solid'. When areas are left free, it is termed 'voided velvet'. In 'uncut velvet' the loops formed by the pile warp are left uncut. Another variant is 'pile-on-pile' velvet, i.e. velvet in which the same type of pile is woven in two or more heights in order to achieve a pattern. Other types are *broderie* or *ciselé* velvet, in which the pattern is formed by composing cut and uncut pile and voided areas.

Velvet may be enriched with various forms of brocading, often with loops of metal threads, forming bouclé (cf. Pls 44, 46).

Note that the German and Swedish synonyms (*Samt,* and *sammet*) are not to be confused with *samitum,* a common Latin term for weft-faced compound twill. Instead they may derive from the Italian term *scamito velluto.* A further step forward in the artistic and technical refinement of velvet production was practised in the Imperial workshops of Persia, of the sixteenth and seventeenth centuries.

IV *Development of Plain Weaving*

In this and the following two chapters, an attempt will be made to put the technical aspects into an evolutionary context and to relate them to probable historical periods. Most accounts of the history of textile art have been confined to design and ornament. Plain weave, on the other hand, although the foundation of pattern weaving, has been neglected by textile historians. It was first and foremost an unpretentious everyday commodity and a vitally important one too, especially in a chilly climate. But plain weaves — brilliant white Egyptian linen fabrics and softly draped Flemish broadcloth, gossamer thin cotton from India and lustrous silk taffetas from China — could also rank as luxury articles. Eventually they became much sought-after trading commodities of great economic significance.

Delight in unpatterned fabrics was governed by a number of factors, primarily the quality of the basic material and the craftsmanship of the weaver, but also, particularly where woollens were concerned, by the complex procedures of after treatment and by the dyeing of the material. Both the preparation and the dyeing of woollens were highly specialised crafts. During the Middle Ages the dyers were a very exclusive group and their recipes and methods jealously guarded secrets.

Woollen fabrics from sheep and other animals tended to come from cold and temperate climates, above all because the people living in such regions needed warm clothing, but also because the animals living in cooler climates generally produced better wool than those living in warmer ones.

MATERIAL, WEAVES AND LOOMS

Various tendencies appear in the development of weaving methods which are obviously connected with the raw materials concerned, and with their specific character. Certain implements and types of loom must therefore be presumed to have been devised and developed in connexion with work using a particular textile material. But a specific relationship of this kind does not preclude the subsequent application of a particular type of loom to a different material from that for which it was originally used. This has undoubtedly been the case with the treadle loom, constructed in China for weaving reeled silk, where the warp predominated. As it moved further west, this loom was adapted for weaving woollens where the weft predominated and acquired a stouter and somewhat different construction in the process.

There is an obvious connexion between the two-beam loom (type 2) with its vertically stretched, well spaced warp well covered by the woollen weft which was easy to dye — one of the prerequisites of tapestry weaving. But used as weft it had to be beaten up very hard in order to give distinct colour effects. A similar development applied to the Egyptian linen loom with its horizontal warp (type 3) and the admirable linen fabrics preserved from Pharaonic times. This loom was ideally suitable for weaving the glossy and smooth linen yarn.

There is a great deal to suggest that the warp-weighted loom was originally devised specifically for woollen yarn. It was easy to weave in woollen yarn, which is relatively light, from the top downward and as it is fairly rough the woollen weft does not slip on the stretched warp. Although the shed is open downwards, the weft stays in place as long as is necessary before the shed changes. Using linen yarn, which is rather slippery, it would have been very difficult to make the weft stay in place in a shed which opens downwards.[1] This hypothesis concerning the properties of the yarn and its effect on loom construction raises problems concerning the earliest linen weaving in Sweden, which may also be of general interest. Excavations in the old trading town of Sigtuna revealed, in twelfth-century layers, a loom pulley, which is a typical component of the treadle loom. The pulley was extremely skilfully wrought in elk bone, the same excellent material as was used for combs and other tools found in the area, all of which bears witness to the existence of a centre specializing in this kind of craftsmanship.[2] The Sigtuna pulley (IV, fig. 1) constitutes the earliest Scandinavian evidence of the treadle loom. At first it was assumed to have been used for weaving woollen fabrics. But considering that the warp-weighted loom or perhaps the tubular loom (types 5 and 4) had been used for weaving woollen fabrics ever since the Bronze Age and, no doubt, continued to be used for the same purpose long afterwards, the newer type of loom with horizontal warp seems more likely to have been introduced for weaving linen, for which purpose it was seriously needed.

It is not known for sure when and where flax first began to be used for textiles in Scandinavia. A great deal of the evidence points to Hälsingland and other provinces along the eastern coast of Sweden, which for centuries were famous for their flourishing flax cultivation and their linen industry. Written documents from the twelfth century onwards show that the people of Hälsingland paid their taxes in flax or woven linen, which suggests that the linen industry there developed at an early date. It is also known that the Sigtuna merchants extended their trading route via the Baltic ports to include Hälsingland. The whole of this Baltic trade route presents a cultural highway that may have helped propagate knowledge concerning the complex technology of flax processing. It is not unlikely that the Sigtuna pulley came adrift from a larger consignment with which some enterprising merchant set out to rationalize the linen industry in Hälsingland, where the soil and water had proved so amenable to the cultivation of flax.

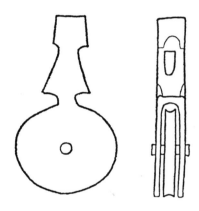

IV, fig. 1.   Loom pulley of elk horn excavated in Sigtuna, probably twelfth century

CLIMATE AND WEAVING IMPLEMENTS

The development of weaving implements has also been influenced by climate. In places where the weather for the greater part of the year enabled work to be done out of doors, considerations of space cannot have played a very important part. In such cases it would have been possible for the warp to be stretched out on the ground to its full length. This is still done today and has been the established practice for thousands of years with linen weaving in Egypt and cotton weaving in India. On the other hand, in countries with a variable climate, once the weaving implement has been set up it may need, to a greater or lesser extent, to be protected from the elements. Even the simplest form of shelter, a roof plus two or three walls, requires space, and accordingly favours looms that take up less room. For instance, the warp behind the beam furthest away from the weaver may be laid up over bars in the roof or a rack above the loom — and yet still leaves the weaver half outdoors (II, figs 8, 18). But in latitudes with prolonged periods of cold weather and rain or snow, working indoors is a necessity and the question of space is thereby rendered more acute. To a Scandinavian this comes as a truism. What types of looms, then, would have appeared in this part of the world?

Viewed solely in terms of economies of space, all of the three types of looms with vertical warps would be eligible. But in areas where utility weaves for warm clothing are an imperative physical necessity, only two of these types can really have been conceivable at an early stage of civilization, namely the loom with tubular or circular warp and the warp-weighted loom. The vertical tapestry loom, on the other hand, can never have been a practical implement for weaving plain everyday fabrics; it seems more likely to have been developed for ornamental weaves. In the ancient world therefore this loom might have been used at the same time as other weaving implements. There is a great deal to suggest that the two loom types which are suitable for plain weaving (types 4 and 5) occurred in those areas of the Mediterranean which primarily formed part of the Greco-Roman world.

TUBULAR LOOM AND WARP-WEIGHTED LOOM: CHARACTERISTICS AND INCIDENCE

First, the tubular loom, the occurrence of which in prehistoric Scandinavia was first extablished by Margrethe Hald, who found several reliable specimens including the virtually complete woman's costume from the bog of Huldre as well as the relatively well-preserved bog finds from Jutland and Schleswig-Holstein. The bog finds in question are attributed to Celtic and Roman times, between 400 B.C. and A.D. 400. To these must be added, it would appear, other possible examples which lack, however, the technical characteristic, the 'lock', which would definitely link a weave to this method. But Hald has also studied other variants of tubular weaving still in use in the Near East and in South America, where evidence has even been found from the Stone Age. Comparisons with this material have led her to conclude that tubular weaving is more primitive and, in principle, older than warp-weighted weaving. She has compared Iron Age costume with depictions in Greek and Roman art. The Huldre costume can be arranged in such a way as to resemble a Dorian *peplos* as depicted on vase paintings etc. This Danish *peplos* takes the form of a large cylinder, about 170 centimetres high (i.e. the width of the fabric) the top of which was folded outwards like a cape or pelerine, and fastened over the shoulders by some kind of pins. The great, soft folds of the fabric measuring a width of no less than 264 centimetres, were presumably gathered in by a belt round the waist.

Unlike the tubular loom, the warp-weighted loom has long been familiar to students of the history of Scandinavian and classical civilization, but the first complete account of the dispersion of this type of loom in time and area, and of its technical potentialities, came with the well-known publication by Marta Hoffmann. There are two kinds of archaeological evidence left by warp-weighted looms. (1) the loom weights, which, being made of clay or stone, have been spared the destruction that has overtaken the rest of the loom, and, (2) still to be found in surviving textile fragments, the more or less prominent 'starting borders' which provide direct evidence of the warping method on which warp-weighted weaving is technically dependent.

Archaeological excavations in Anatolia and Syria have yielded finds attesting to the occurrence of warp-weighted weaving as long ago as the sixth or seventh millennium before the Christian era.[3] Great numbers of ceramic loom weights have also been found in Greece, clearly testifying that this loom was commonly used there; it is moreover depicted on many vase paintings from the sixth and fifth centuries B.C. (1, fig. 1).[4] According to Vogt the fragmentary textile remains from the Swiss settlements of the Neolithic period (roughly corresponding to the second millenium B.C.) have also been found to include starting borders, suggesting that they may have been woven on a warp-weighted loom.

A series of virtually complete costumes have been preserved in the famous Bronze Age tombs of Denmark. Particularly interesting in this connexion are the sizeable pieces of woollen cloth — undoubtedly woven in a warp-weighted loom — whose dimensions show that the beam must have been revolving so that the finished cloth could gradually be rolled up at the same time as the weighted warp was lengthened from below. All these fabrics are woven in tabby.

In the salt-mines of Hallstatt in Austria, in the vicinity of the famous graves of the mine masters (*Bergherren*) from the period 800–400 B.C., some textiles were found which should be mentioned because, according to J. H. Hundt, they would have been contemporary with the *Bergherren* period. They are worn rags of very coarse wool found in the mining galleries, some of which, being twill weaves with starting borders are evidence of a warp-weighted loom. The fact that the mines were in use until comparatively late (eighteenth century), together with the social difference between the textiles and the splendid metal objects from the world-famous Hallstatt graves obviously speaks for different dates of origin. The textiles themselves seem to show no basis for dating other than the connexion with the warp-weighted loom, which would indicate the first millenium A.D.

The bog finds and other textile remains from northern Europe include specimens of twill and also furnish evidence of both warp-weighted weaving and tubular weaving, the latter, according to Hald, being probably the older method of the two. Presumably both methods were used simultaneously but for different purposes. The starting border of the warp-weighted weave, usually tablet woven, was often repeated on the sides and bottom forming an edging which was both durable and decorative. The supreme example of this is the famous cloak from Torsberg in Schleswig-Holstein first described by Stettiner and later by Schlabow. A related type is evident in Swedish and especially Norwegian finds from the Roman Iron Age and it is also found in Finland and the east Baltic areas, though in much later burials and of coarser quality.

In vase paintings and other specimens of archaic Greek art one can sometimes recognize rectangular cloaks and other garments which seem to have been embellished with decorative borders of a similar kind. The most beautiful specimens in this connexion and apparently overlooked, are the lovely maidens from Erechtheion, now in the Acropolis Museum in Athens (Pl. 91a). The borders show obvious traces of gold and painted colours, while the fall of the folds, which are reproduced in the white marble with consummate skill, gives the impression of the thinnest woollen muslin, a testimony to the capacity of a warp-weighted loom.

Since the textiles which have long been buried in the ground or in bogs are often incomplete, it is generally not possible to determine the implement used to make them. The oval cut cloak found in the bog of Gerum, Västergötland (Sweden) and first described by von Walterstorff, is one of the weaves which might be thought to have been produced by means of the tubular method. Its original dating to the later Bronze Age, which was queried for some time because of the twill weaving technique, has been substantiated by a dated Danish find (from Haastrup in the island of Fyen) also woven in twill.

As regards the further diffusion of the two types of loom, we may add that the warp-weighted loom was still in general use in central and western Europe during the first millenium A.D. It was generally used for the rural handicraft production of coarse woollen covers, made by women living on farms or in the workshops of convents. This product was woven in rectangular pieces, usually of standard size with dimensions regulated by law in order to be used as regular currency. A piece of this kind was termed *Wede*, the same word as the Swedish *våd* occurring in *vadmal*, a word which in the Scandinavian languages remains the common term for domestically produced woollen fabrics.

 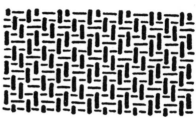

IV, figs 2–3. Diagrams of 4-end twills, plain and broken, warp Z-spun, weft S-spun, the fabric slightly fulled. Thread counts: 11 × 8, 14 × 10, 18 × 11 per cm. Birka

EVIDENCE OF A WORLDWIDE PRODUCTION OF FINE WOOLLENS

The trading town of Birka, on the now rural island of Björkö in Lake Mälar, was the most important trading centre in northern Europe during the ninth and tenth centuries. It was the point of intersection between the trading routes from western Europe and the Orient (via Russia), and here the monk Ansgar was sent by the Church of Rome to preach the Gospel. The world famous burial finds from Birka, excavated between 1871–81, constitute our main source of knowledge concerning the textiles and costumes of the Viking era.[5] Among the number of graves which have been excavated (about 1275), more than 180 contained textile remains of different kinds: silk fabrics, bands inwoven with metal, costume trimmings of gold and silver wire made in various techniques and shapes, numerous pieces of plain woollen and a few linen fragments and even some patterned weaves of linen and woollen material. It is the woollen fabrics, almost one hundred in number with which we are concerned here. Only one tenth of them, of coarse and poor quality, are likely to have been of native origin, the rest must be considered as imports. But from where?

A group of twelve (IV, figs 2, 3) may be classified as tweeds: plain four-end twills of Z-spun warp and S-spun weft, the cloth finally napped and fulled — in other words, a fairly ordinary product which, although of foreign make did not necessarily come from very far afield, perhaps from the British Isles.

In contrast to this is a group of about seventy-five specimens with the following characteristics, indicating that they share the same country of origin, and a remote one at that. Micro-analysis has shown that the material consists of fine, originally white wool manufactured into 'worsted' (i.e. yarn). The yarn is uniformly fine and evenly spun, always with a Z-twist, and of exactly the same kind, in both warp and weft. Another characteristic feature is that the warp is far denser than the weft, as a rule twice to three times as dense. About ten items in the group are woven in warp-faced tabby with a warp density of up to thirty threads per centimetre against eight to nine in the weft. A small group contain three-end twills, to which we shall be returning presently. The majority — more than fifty very similar variants — may be described as self-patterned four-end twills. The patterning is achieved by reversing the diagonal lines of the binding, generally in the direction of both warp and weft, resulting in a lozenge or diamond twill (IV, figs 5, 6). It is characteristic of these bindings that the 'turn-over' is asymmetric ('broken'), which is a natural result of the warping method connected with this loom. Fortunately several pieces with woven edges have survived, partly selvages, partly starting borders (IV, fig. 6), indicating that the warp was set up by bandweaving, basically following the system illustrated by the diagram in II, fig. 12. The correctness of this conclusion was shown beyond any doubt by the practical results obtained by following an old Icelandic description found by Hoffmann.

IV, figs 4–5.   Worsted woollens in 4-end twill, forming broken chevron or lozenge patterns. Usual thread counts: 35 × 12, 36 × 16 per cm. All yarn Z-spun. Birka

The binding patterns vary somewhat but as a whole they agree with the standard type (IV, figs 5–6), of which some forty pieces were observed in Birka. The slight variations of the thread count can be seen from the following examples: 32 × 12, 38 × 16, 40 × 18 and up to 55 × 21 threads per centimetre in warp and weft respectively. It should be noted that the warp is invariably more than twice as dense as the weft. Similar examples have emerged in several finds from Sweden and Norway (Kaupang, Oseberg etc.), from Bornholm, the British Isles and Iceland and from Germany (a seventh-century Merovingian grave).

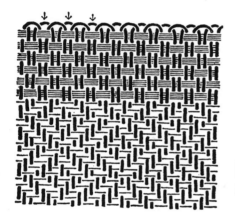

IV, fig. 6.   Broken lozenge or 'diamond' twill, with starting border. Birka

Turning now to a type which is rare in Birka and hitherto unknown from other contemporary finds from northern Europe — the three-end twill (IV, fig. 7) — we find that the yarn is even finer and the difference between warp and weft densities greater, e.g. 50 × 17, 52 × 14, 55–60 × 17 threads per centimetre. All nine specimens (except for one which seems to be completely plain) display a pattern formation with regular turn-overs. Unfortunately these pieces do not possess any woven edges to prove which is warp or weft. We observed earlier that three-end weaving might be technically incompatible with the 'band warping' method associated with the warp-weighted loom, and this would seem to suggest that these fabrics were made on a loom with treadles and horizontal warp. The question now arises as to where all these fabrics were made.

The so-called pallium frisonicum of the Vikings: was it made in Syria?

The fine woollens described above cannot possibly have been made in any of the Scandinavian countries. In view of the high and uniform standard of the material as well as the execution, all these fabrics must originate from an extensive and professional system of production developed by successive generations of craftsmen.

In *Birka III* 1938 I ventured to identify this industry with the trade commodity *pallium frisonicum* (Frisian cloth) known to us from historical documents and vigorously discussed by several historians, especially the Belgian scholar Pirenne. These historians surmised that the woollen fabrics sold by the Frisian merchants — but of which none of them had ever seen specimens — were manufactured in the areas bordering the Channel coast which later became the centre of a large-scale woollen industry. However, the Norwegian scholar Marta Hoffmann in her doctoral thesis of 1964, proved that this hypothesis was untenable, because, among other reasons, the historical documents quoted in support of it are not reliable. Coupled with the various other arguments propounded, this would seem to establish once and for all that the areas in question lacked, during Viking times, both the practical knowledge and the political-social background for a textile production of the sophisticated standard illustrated by this material.

IV, fig. 7. Three-end lozenge twill of very fine worsted yarn. Thread counts: 50 × 17 to 52 × 14 per cm. Birka

Instead Hoffmann suggested that the entire production came from Syria, a hypothesis which I have no hesitation in seconding. Her opinion was founded on specific examples which are undoubtedly of Syrian manufacture, viz, three specimens exactly resembling our four-end twills. Two of these were found in Palmyra, so that they can hardly have been woven later than A.D. 200, while the third forms part of a find from

Antinoë and should thus be a century or so later. The Antinoë specimen seems identical to our standard type, while the Palmyra specimens, also four-end twills, appear even finer and denser than our three-end twills. As no selvages have been preserved in any of these instances, one cannot distinguish with complete certainty between warp and weft. We must therefore allow for the possibility of the Palmyra fabrics having been weft-faced weaves, in which case they may have been made in a treadle loom. Syria, renowned for its textiles, had for centuries been a great meeting point where novelties of textile technology from east and west came face to face with inherited craftsmanship. Anything can happen in such an area. We also have reliable evidence of three-end weft-faced weaving from here, both in tapestry and in silk (type D2). Furthermore, this area also had access to first-class wool of all kinds, including the greatly prized Kashmir wool of which, according to Pfister, the two Palmyra specimens were made.

In spite of slight differences in the quality of the material and the weave, the overall similarities are so well marked that we are obviously confronted here with evidence of continuous large-scale production. Considering the great length of time involved — from about A.D. 200 to the eleventh century (finds from Iceland) — the uniformity is striking. On the other hand this production must obviously have been preceded by a prolonged development of weaving implements and of methods of preparing raw material and spinning the yarn. The historical perspective grows ever wider.[6]

REELED SILK VERSUS SHORT-FIBRED SPINNING MATERIAL

It often seems that textile researchers generally are not sufficiently conscious of the fundamental importance of the textile material itself — its varying character and quality — in weaving practice and production. The practical problems connected with large-scale production tend to be overlooked, especially when this is built upon short-fibre material, for example, wools of different qualities. Above all the difficulties in the necessary co-ordination of spinning with the preceding and subsequent treatment of the material — while all this work remained dependent on the manual skill of the individual are generally ignored. With regard to quality as well as quantity, these questions always posed major problems in the management of large-scale textile manufacture, especially before the

Industrial Revolution. Even small differences in the fineness of the yarn, its density or porousness, its evenness and, not least, the twist, will soon become evident in the course of weaving. In a limited working unit, on a domestic basis, these variations need not present any disadvantage: all sorts are needed and there is a use for everything. But the sorting and standardization of the yarn is of vital importance in the large-scale production of cloth which must be sold in uniform qualities. This requires a very high output of yarn, facilities for sorting and long-term storage, and thus a high standard of economic organization in general.

If we try to imagine the practical requirements that had to be met in order to produce, say, the fine Egyptian linens from Pharaonic times or the Syrian woollens at present under consideration, we can understand that all this would have been impossible without many generations of professional training coupled with a suitable economic and social background, in short, a developed capitalist system. The development of high quality textile production is a multifarious enterprise that is bound to take a very long time to accomplish.

In primitive circumstances, both in early and in later periods, weaving methods had to be adapted to the capacity of the spun material, instead of vice versa. Since the warp is subjected to the greatest strain, the yarn for it has to be spun harder and more evenly than would be necessary for the weft yarn. If necessary the strain could be reduced by shortening the warp. The precious yarn could be made to last longer by spacing the warp threads in comparison to the weft. At the same time the woven fabric could be made as wide as the occasion demanded.

Reeled silk led to a complete transformation and simplification of the weaving procedure and also to the inception of a completely new trend of development. This textile material must have amazed the Chinese when they first discovered it, perhaps more than five thousand years ago — the thread was practically ready for weaving. This was a different matter from the ancient short fibre materials, wild silk, wool, and hemp, which always had to be spun first in order to produce a thread. One can readily understand how the wonderful product yielded by the silk worm could only be explained in terms of the supernatural. Thus arose the myth of the good Empress Hsin Ling Shih, who according to the oldest Chinese chronicles found the silk worm while walking in the woods. She was henceforth worshipped as the goddess of silk. This much revered legend is not necessarily contradicted by the fact that the new thread must have been the result of many years' persevering and deliberate labour on the part of the Imperial silk growers. The dramatic début of the long shiny thread, whose fineness belied its uncanny strength, generated something of a technical revolution. The exigencies of the situation brought forth radically improved weaving implements. The silk loom was made as small as possible so as to facilitate indoor weaving, thus helping to protect the precious material, and this may have been the situation that prompted the epoch-making invention of the treadle loom.

THE FIRST TREADLE LOOM

The first treadle loom probably resembled that portrayed on a funeral monument from the Han dynasty (II, fig. 15). The graceful little lady sitting at the loom has her foot on the single treadle, which is lifting the heddle rod for the countershed, while the other shed of the binding, the natural shed, is activated by means of body tension. The slender frame supports two beams, so that the long warp can be rolled off and the finished fabric rolled on as work progresses. The principle of the early loom illustrated hardly differs from that of the later ones. It is probable that this apparatus was devised more than 4,000 years ago. Large quantities of Chinese silk fabrics from the same period as the stone relief depicting the loom have been saved by archaeological excavations: the finds preserved in Leningrad alone include more than two hundred pieces of different sizes, all from the Han period. Some of these are pattern woven (about which more in the following chapter) but the majority (approximately 90 per cent) are plain taffetas, that is, the simple domestic product in which the Chinese peasant paid his taxes. But everything seems to indicate that essentially the same type of loom was employed for the costly patterned fabrics as for the simple ones: the difference between them was purely a matter of individual manual execution, but it was nevertheless a great difference. In no case did the width of the fabric exceed 50 centimetres. This corresponds exactly to the 2 *ch'ih* 2 *ts'un* of the officially dictated dimension of the multicoloured silk fabrics, the manufacture of which was subject to state supervision. No doubt these fabrics were made exclusively in closed workshops, where the statutory width was a professional maximum. The domestic production of plain silk mentioned above also existed long afterwards and could vary in width down to 20 or 30 centimetres. In seventeenth-century Europe variously-coloured thin silks of this kind were joined together to make large flags.

Chinese silk weaving consistently exploits the functional properties of reeled silk. The great length of the cocoon thread, running into hundreds of metres, made it possible to set up a very long warp and thus derive the greatest possible benefit from the work entailed by entering the warp ends into the heddles. It was the same practical approach that caused the textile to be made narrow and the warp relatively dense.

THE TREADLE LOOM SPREADS TO THE WEST

Experience has shown that implements — and not only textile implements — usually spread in combination with a new material. This alone makes it probable that the Sassanian empire, the easternmost region of the 'western world', at that time learned of the treadle loom at about the same time as it started weaving with silk. In the next chapter we shall see how this innovation in Iran gave rise to a revolutionary technical invention connected with the patterning mechanism.

One consequence of this innovation was that the silk loom underwent a transformation. It was made wider, an alteration which must have been founded in native tradition. Not only the tapestry loom and the warp-weighted loom but also the linen loom, which were the weaving devices native to this area, could easily be made very wide. This influence is clearly illustrated by single pieces of silk, up to 130 centimetres wide, which are known to have been made in the eastern Sassanian territory during the eighth or ninth centuries.

As one might suppose, although until recently there was no evidence to prove it, the same area of civilization also produced plain, monochrome woollen fabrics which, like the patterned silks of the Sassanian empire, were evidently famous, not least as export articles. The evidence for this kind of manufacture is to be found in the 'riding-coats' of oriental cut, embellished with patterned silk fabrics of Sassanian manufacture, which were discovered by the excavations at Antinoë in 1898. These elegant caftans with their characteristic extra long sleeves, had apparently been adopted as a token of eminence by high-ranking Byzantine officials, who wore them over their ordinary Roman garment, the tunic. Doubtless the coats had been imported ready-made from the Sassanian empire, some time between A.D. 300 and 500.[7] The main material of these coats consists of a thin warp (about eight threads per centimetre) and a thick weft of soft, loosely-spun Kashmir wool. The woven material has been dyed and then napped and pressed to give a soft nap of long, shiny hair completely covering the surface of the fabric. Judging by the great loom-width (130 centimetres approx.) and the tightly beaten weft, the loom must have been stoutly built and fitted with a heavy beater. In other words, the Chinese silk loom had been adapted to another kind of material, wool, and also to another mode of weaving — weft-faced weaving.

DEVELOPMENTS IN MEDIEVAL WESTERN EUROPE

There is a great deal to suggest that during the eleventh century the treadle loom reached the countries north-west of the Alps, where the innovation, with all that it implied in the way of new implements and craftsmanship in the processing of woollen materials, led to a radical trans-formation of economic and social life. This is particularly true of the area we now call Holland and Belgium; the production of textiles had formerly been a domestic craft in the farms and monasteries sparsely scattered all over the country. During that period of the medieval history of northern Europe known as the Dark Ages, most weaving was done by women producing short rectangular loom pieces, the typical product of the warp-weighted loom.

The new type of weaving implement and the new order made it possible to organize production on a more efficient basis. The various tasks were differentiated and centred in a number of places which eventually developed into towns and cities. The new loom was worked by men; weaving became an organized occupation. The main advantage of the new loom was that it could produce long pieces of fabric, since both the warp and the finished cloth could be rolled up. There must also have been a certain social significance in the fact that the male weaver sat while he worked, whereas the women, still using the ancient warp-weighted loom, had to stand and walk all the time.

This situation is neatly though rather journalistically summed up in a statement from the eleventh century, the period of transition between the two kinds of weaving apparatus: 'Men weave with their feet while the women have a stick which moves up and down.'[8] Clearly the writer, a man by the name of Rashi who was born in Troyes (France) in 1040, was well informed. The procedures and tools he is comparing are connected with the identical function in the two looms, namely the shedding. The move-able stick — the loose heddle rod of the warp-weighted loom — cor-responds to the treadles in the new loom (cf. II, figs 10c, 13j).

A thirteenth-century English manuscript includes a picture of a treadle loom (IV, fig. 8), showing the weaver sitting on a separate chair in front of a slender loom with a narrow, horizontal warp. The loom is fitted with two treadles and their associated heddle rods, connected by a pulley (he is weaving tabby) but there seems to be no beater, which may indicate that

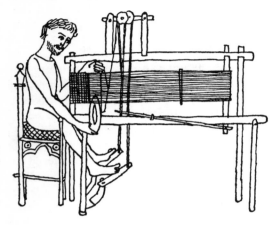

IV, fig. 8.   Loom with two treadles, English MS thirteenth century

the weft was being packed within the shed. A hundred years later four-end twill could be woven on a treadle loom of stout construction made for two weavers weaving 'broadcloth' (II, fig. 14). Such a loom was depicted in 1363 in the regulations of the cloth-makers guild in the town of Ypres. A similar construction, though of simple execution, with the uprights pegged in the floor and the working devices hung from the ceiling, is shown in the *Mendelsche Hausbuch* (IV, fig. 9; drawing from *c.*1425). Although some nine hundred years older than the loom pictured here, the Iranian coats of Kashmir wool mentioned above may serve as examples of the luxurious Oriental woollens which may have given some Florentine merchant the brilliant idea of organizing a similar manufacture. *Calimala*, the powerful Florentine guild of woollen manufacturers, operated as an enormous trading enterprise from the Iberian peninsula to the British Isles, importing fine wool in its own ships, both in the form of raw material and as un-processed woollen fabrics. Most of these half-finished goods were processed in Florence. It was this far-ranging and well-organized business that opened the way for the fabulous prosperity of the Florentine republic and at the same time a different but similar organization gave rise to the flourishing Flemish woollen industry, *la draperie flamande*.

The processing of raw cloth was a skilled craft, but the result was to a great extent dependent on the softness and fineness of the wool itself. Apart from dyeing, the main processing operations were: fulling, napping, shearing, and pressing. The best cloth, already termed 'broadcloth' in medieval English, was a costly, fashionable product the soft drape and brilliant colours of which can still be admired in the paintings of the late fourteenth and fifteenth centuries. Its leather-like solidity was a prerequisite of the dress trimmings skilfully cut out into leaf-shapes, for instance shown in Jan van Eyck's famous portrait of the Arnolfinis, and in many of Pisanello's imaginative fashion sketches. The genuine fine 'broadcloth' (Fr. *drap*, Ger. *Tuch*, Sw. *kläde*) of which small quantities are still produced is clearly distinguishable from the coarser and relatively more summarily processed woollens in which the texture of the weave remained more or less apparent. In broadcloth, as in the Kashmir cloth of the Iranian riding-coats, the binding is completely hidden by the lustrous nap.

IV, fig. 9.   Loom with four treadles, Nuremberg, *c.*1425

A very precious kind of broadcloth was termed *scarlatum* in medieval Latin (*skarlakan* in Old Norse). This fabric could be of various colours and it was not until later that the term came to be applied to a particular colour, scarlet (cf. It. *scarlatto*, Fr. *écarlat*). The origin of the word itself has occupied the attentions of many scholars, but it remained a mystery until a few years ago. The word has now been traced, through a number of widely varying linguistic forms (*siklaton, sakirlat, saqalat* etc.) current in the Near East ever since the early Middle Ages, to a Latin word, *sigillatum,* meaning 'stamped' or 'sealed'. The term probably originated from a particular kind of cloth which was imported into the Roman Empire and marked with an official seal, presumably of lead. When this 'sealed' cloth began to be imitated — at first in Italy — it was natural for the imitation to be given a name alluding to the original commodity.[9]

NORTH-EASTERN EUROPE

Our knowledge of medieval textile production in this part of Europe is based solely on archaeological evidence, and this evidence falls into two very different technical and social categories. A series of similar burial finds containing quite well-preserved costumes from the time of the Crusades (1000–1200) have long been known in Finland and the countries on the eastern shore of the Baltic (published by Appelglen-Kivalo). These costumes are characterized by a rectangular cloak with tablet-woven borders such as was commonly worn in the west a few centuries earlier — resembling the Torsberg cloak — and which can itself be traced back to a far more ancient, and classical tradition, probably based on the warp-weighted loom.

The other category of finds has emerged comparatively recently as a result of systematic excavations in Danzig, Opole, Wolin and other towns and cities in northern Poland, but also in the Russian city of Novgorod. The textile material has been analysed by Polish scholars such as Kaminska, Nahlik and others. Stratigraphical notation of the finds has made possible a relative dating of the various strata from the mid-fifteenth century back to the mid-tenth century A.D. These finds are invariably made up of unrelated fragments, being refuse of all kinds. Very coarse weft-faced woollens are particularly common in the Danzig finds and display a sparse warp and a thick weft, sometimes differently coloured. These rather uniform, coarse and unpretentious fabrics are remarkable in one respect: they are usually in the three-end twill, the kind of weave which is considered not to have been produced on a warp-weighted loom, since odd bindings require a loom with independent shedding, which in practice means a treadle loom where shedding and threading are done *after* warping. Fortunately the wooden remains of an implement which probably formed the side piece of a treadle loom (IV, fig. 10) were found in related strata. This find may be considered as conclusive evidence that the fabrics were made on the spot: presumably this was the craftsmen's quarter of the medieval city.

How are we to account for this sudden appearance of the treadle loom in north-east Europe? It has no connexion with the introduction of the treadle loom into the Low Countries. Of one thing there can hardly be any doubt: the production indicated by the finds from Danzig is a crude and simplified off-shoot of a more refined kind of manufacture which probably existed not too far away. This (hypothetical) quality production, concerning the existence of which, unfortunately, nothing appears to be known, may have arisen one way or another as a result of southward connexions, via the Byzantine Empire. This would explain the three-shed system, early traces of which are known from that particular area of the eastern Mediterranean.

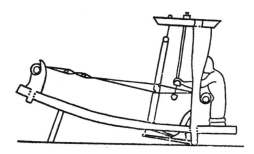

IV, fig. 10. Treadle loom as reconstructed from fragmentary wooden pieces excavated in Danzig (Gdansk). Middle Ages

Research is still needed to elucidate the course of development alluded to here, which would seem to have started earlier than its western counterpart. Perhaps it was by this route that the three-shed system spread further north. The medieval textile remains discovered in recent years by excavations of medieval Swedish towns — Lund, Gamla Lödöse, Nyköping, Söderköping and Uppsala — show that the three-shed system was becoming more and more common for weaving woollens.

V *Individually Patterned Weaves*

This chapter will deal with the category of patterned weaves which are executed directly by hand, as weaving progresses, that is, weaves worked in the warp already stretched in the loom. The resulting ornamentation will necessarily be a unique product as distinct from patterns produced by a pre-arranged control of the warp by means of the heddles and other mechanical devices. The latter methods will be treated in the following chapter. Even among initiated writers the view is often encountered that a regular repetition of similar motifs is typical of textile art, in fact a technical pre-condition of weaving itself. This is true only in the cases just mentioned, where mechanical appliances produce real 'pattern repeats', but it is far from being a rule applicable to weaving in general, or even to weaving alone. There are, indeed, instances of individually patterned weaves showing designs of repeated motifs, but in such cases this is for aesthetical reasons. On the other hand there are many decorative techniques involving uniform repetitions which are used in connexion with woven fabrics or applied on completely different materials: as in block printing, stencil painting, and the application of metal ornaments, either stamped or cast.

In this and the following chapter we shall try to put some of the most important techniques of textile patterning in their correct historical context. The course of development proceeds naturally from 'primary' methods, with exclusively manual operations, to techniques executed with the aid of certain mechanical devices which gradually facilitate increased standardization and, at the same time, a relative reduction of the manual labour involved. These primary patterning techniques inevitably result in unique products. This category includes, in the first instance, all types of tapestry weaves and also knotted pile weaves, plain weaves with variously worked pattern wefts, either shuttled or brocaded, as well as some types of doublecloth.

TAPESTRY TECHNIQUES

A distinction is drawn here between the three main types which can be designated as follows: (a) all-over tapestry with a uniform binding system, (b) the same but with varying types of binding ('free tapestry'), and (c) 'inserted tapestry', or sections of multicoloured tapestry worked into a plain ground weave, usually tabby. The two latter types predominate in the earliest material. While all-over figurative tapestries seem not to become common until the Middle Ages.

Originally tapestry would be woven with no other equipment than a frame or some other device for keeping the warp evenly stretched so that the weft yarn could be inserted with a form of needle. In the absence of a shedding mechanism the weaver was not forced, technically speaking, to adhere to the tabby binding and could equally well make the weft yarn pass over two or more warp ends. He could consistently follow the same binding system or alternate freely between different systems. In this case the ordinary tabby (or 'rep') would be replaced for purely aesthetic reasons: e.g. by areas of weft floats (over two or more warps) emphasizing the lustre and the colour effect of the weft yarn.

The earliest tapestry weaving

American excavations at Chatal Hüyük in Anatolia revealed traces of a remarkably sophisticated Neolithic civilization, including dwellings with multicoloured wall paintings in the form of rectangular panels with geometrical designs (v, fig. 1). Those panels have been interpreted as

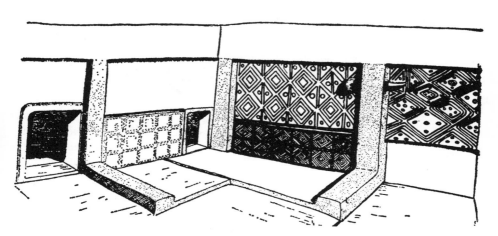

v, fig. 1.   Painted wall decoration imitating some kind of tapestry. Chatal Hüyük, Anatolia, c.6,000 B.C.

imitations of woven pieces of the Kelim type, and are thus probably the earliest evidence of primitive tapestry weaving. The oldest *extant* tapestries were found in the tombs of the Pharaohs Tuthmosis IV and Tutankhamen, dating from between 1400 and 1330 B.C. The richly decorated tunics in the latter tomb are thought to be of eastern, probably Syrian, origin. But specimens have also survived which seem, as far as we can judge, to have come from Iran. One interesting example, a border depicting a row of walking lions (v, fig. 2), was found in Siberia, in one of the Pazyryk tombs of the fourth or fifth century B.C. This tapestry-woven border bears such a close resemblance to sculptured details on the canopy of the throne of Xerxes in Persepolis that it may well have been intended to imitate the latter. A contemporary example, no doubt Iranian, comes from a princely grave at Kertch in the Crimea and was described by Stephani. Certain fragments found in Egypt are also of Iranian origin, dating from the Sassanian period. Some of those specimens were found in Antinoë, the town established by the Romans, whose links with the Orient are amply documented. Other specimens of a somewhat later date were found in Fustat, in the richly-productive refuse strata which have been related to the location there of the headquarters of the Persian army during the occupation of Egypt between 619 and 629.

v, fig. 2.   Tapestry border from the Pazirik finds, *c.*400 B.C.

All of these textiles are characterized by a stylization and iconography very typical of Iranian art. Several of them are made of extremely fine wool stated by Pfister to be of the precious Kashmir type. One of the textiles exemplifies the rare 'free' technique; at some places the weft passes through the warp on the principle of 'over two threads, under one', in other words, according to a weft-faced three-end twill binding; in these cases the sheds must have been picked up separately for each pick. In a second series of fragments, probably from a large hanging, this type of binding has been regularly executed. When pieced together the surviving fragments shows a stylized cock standing on a plinth encrusted with jewels, all done in bright colours against a brilliant red background (v, fig. 3).

One more item can be added to this interesting catalogue of examples. The finds from Kertch just mentioned included the remains of an extremely fine tapestry, showing ducks and deer heads, subjects which immediately remind us of Iranian art. The publication by Stephani offered a description which, although incorrectly phrased, tells us that it was woven according to the same twill binding as the last mentioned example from Fustat, dating from Sassanian times.

v, fig. 3.   Cock motif from a Sassanian tapestry of very high quality, *c.* A.D. 600. Fostat

Pictorial tapestries

Large pictorial pieces executed throughout in tapestry weave constitute a form of art which eventually gained widespread currency and importance. Most of the development of this costly art took place north of the Alps and is closely connected with the climate and the architecture of those countries, both of which gave rise to a natural need for decorating and warming chilly rooms. The beginning of this art must have occurred in the Orient. The sparse remains of early tapestries from the Near East described above, bear clear witness to a highly developed art of this kind. Before proceeding to the numerous groups of tapestry hangings made in Europe, we must consider an outstanding piece which might be classified as a transitional version of Oriental origin and which may have been made before this art was adapted by the West.

I refer to the so-called shroud of Bishop Gunther in Bamberg Cathedral (Pl. 4), known to scholars through a drawing from about 1850, but only recently examined in the careful investigation by Dr Sigrid Müller, Munich (*Bayerisches Nationalmuseum*).[1] The entire tapestry is made of silk, both the warp and the multicoloured wefts. The original dimensions were considerable, about 2.60 by 2.10 metres, and the piece was presumably made to serve as a hanging between two coloumns. It shows a monumental composition of an emperor on horseback, flanked by two symbolic female figures, against a background pattern of small lotus buds. Above and below is a large border of ornamental lotus flowers. On account of the all-silk weave and its bright colours, the tapestry must have looked splendid, especially with the light passing through it, when the effect may have been similar to that of a stained glass window. It is recorded that the powerful Bishop Gunther, on his return from a pilgrimage to the Holy Land, spent some time at the Imperial court and that he died on the way back in *c.*1065. Nobody has called in question that the costly textile which was buried with the Bishop had been a gift from a Byzantine Emperor and that it had been manufactured in an Imperial workshop. But the question is: when was it made, and in honour of which emperor? The problem has been exhaustively studied by A. Grabar, the great specialist in Byzantine art, who, after much hesitation, finally concluded that this pictorial textile may have represented Basil II Bulgaroctonos and his triumphal entry into Constantinople in A.D. 1017. However, while agreeing with Grabar's earlier comparison of it with the Mozac silk in Lyons (Pl. 20) dated to about A.D. 750, I would suggest the possibility of an earlier date for the tapestry. That and some other questions will be discussed in a forthcoming article in the *Münchener Jahrbuch für bildende Kunst*.

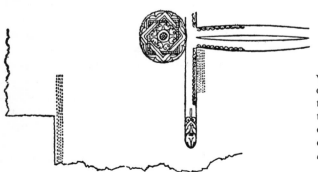

v, fig. 4. Fragment of a Syrian linen tunic with inserted tapestry. Shoulder ornament beside neck opening. Palmyre, *c.* A.D. 200

European tapestries[2]

The Cathedral of Halberstadt owns three remarkable wall hangings which stand out as an introduction to tapestry art in central Europe. Typical in format, low and very long, as well as in the figure style but reflecting the influence of contemporary Byzantine art, all three pieces were manufactured in a monastery in Saxony between the middle of the twelfth century and about 1220. The Apocalypse tapestries of Angers represent a step towards a new style which was developed in France. This giant series of scenes, together measuring 144 metres in length, was commissioned from the Parisian tapestry weaver Nicolas Bataille in 1375. The cartoons were created by Jean Bandol of Bruges, court painter to Charles V. The surviving portions are impressive works of art in their own right, though we can only surmise what the work must have looked like in its entirety.

The first craftsmen in Paris recorded as weaving tapestries were referred to as *sarrasinois*. They were probably Syrians of the Mohammedan religion. The south of France by this time had trading connexions with Syrian and other Mohammedans. The First Crusade (1096) and all that followed in its train led to increasing contacts from which the city of Paris was not slow to benefit. The collection of guild statutes from 1258, known as *The Book of Etienne Boileau*, shows that the craft was by then firmly established. The *faiseurs de tapis sarazinois* are mentioned there among other guilds of high repute. The extensive regulations applying to these exclusive craftsmen are informative. A master was not allowed to have more than one apprentice at a time and the apprentice must remain with him for at least four years. The best woollen yarn had to be used. Work should only be done during the day — while it was easy to see — and orders should only be accepted from churches and the nobility.

In an ordinance of 1303 appears for the first time the professional designation *tapissiers en haute lice* which, no doubt, referred to the 'Saracen' craftsmen who employed vertical looms, as distinct from the *tapissiers nostrez*, who may have been the native weavers. It is evident from the context that the 'Saracen' weavers were at first an identifiable group, but these foreign workers soon vanish from the documents: presumably they were assimilated, and native craftsmen gained the upper hand taking over the 'Saracen' workshops. The workshop traditions, looms and other implements survived.

Paris soon acquired a serious rival in the city of Arras, and from there the art of tapestry weaving spread to Flanders, the heart of the Burgundian Empire, whose art-loving rulers created the necessary conditions for the prosperity of the costly tapestry craft which existed there in the fourteenth and fifteenth centuries. A typical feature of the period was the close collaboration maintained with the great artists of the period, just as was the case with the Angers series mentioned above.

During the mid-seventeenth century, Colbert, Louis XIV's indefatigable Minister of Finance, extended his organizing zeal to include the Parisian tapestry manufacture. A large building, which had belonged to a family of dyers by the name of Gobelin, was bought for the purpose, and the name of the erstwhile proprietor was immortalized after the workshops were established there. In 1667 'les Gobelins' were designated a royal manufactory. Gradually the name was applied to the products of the royal workshops and in the course of time it became a technical term for tapestry, which, although illogical, is used in many languages.

Works of tapestry became an important status symbol at the courts and great palaces of northern Europe. At a time when courts were often on the move from one castle to another, tapestry wall hangings satisfied the practical need for easily transportable and decorative trappings. The walls of rooms and apartments could be covered with sets of tapestries depicting coherent themes. Sets of this kind were ordered from distinguished workshops in Brussels and Paris and they were acceptable gifts for princes. Alternatively tapestry weavers were summoned from abroad, usually from Flanders and Holland. This was the practice adopted by Gustav Vasa, the King of Sweden (1523–1560), and still more so by his ostentatious son, Erik XIV. The same example was followed by the Danish kings, Fredrik II and Christian IV (1542–1645).

Following the immigration of foreign craftsmen into Scandinavia, some local manufacturing centres developed towards the close of the seventeenth century in such towns as Malmö (Sweden) and Bergen (Norway), many of them directed by skilled business women who also trained apprentices. These workshops generally produced small size furnishing pieces and from there the knowledge of tapestry weaving passed on to country parsonages and the homes of the wealthier farmers. These peasant weavers, usually women working for domestic requirements, but occasionally tramping professionals, seldom had any cartoons to follow. Instead they would copy older tapestries to the best of their ability — often at several removes. As a result the details were misunderstood and the designs became more and more debased. Coarser yarn, and consequently a coarser technique and a more limited repertoire of colours accentuated the transformation of the original models. But in fortunate instances, where the country weaver was gifted with imagination and a sense of colour, these 'degenerate' phenomena could incorporate artistic qualities of a completely different kind from those which may have characterized the original.

Inserted tapestry

In default of an adequate technical term for this special adaptation of the tapestry technique the writer ventures to introduce the expression 'inserted tapestry' which type of textile forms a category of its own. The principal part of the textile is always a plain tabby, mainly linen, into which coloured woollen ornaments contrasting with the ground weave have been inserted during the weaving process. Originally these were transverse borders in the weft direction to which rounded ornaments were added (v, fig. 4). This type is well known to us from the large quantity of Egyptian finds originating from late antiquity and from the Coptic and Islamic periods. Egyptologists attribute the flourishing of the later and predominantly multicoloured weaves to a fashion imported from the Orient. Previously the Egyptians had for the most part worn clothes made of plain white linen.[3]

However, rare specimens found in Syria (Dura-Europos and Palmyra) are older than most of the existing Egyptian ones. The same applies to a few costume decorations in gold and purple silk, the very finest of which (Pl. 2a, now in the Hungarian National Museum in Budapest), was discovered in a provincial Roman sarcophagus together with various items of gold jewellery which date it to the beginning of the third century A.D. The Syrian fragments, from richly decorated garments, are interesting for a number of reasons. They provide surviving specimens of the gold-inwoven clothing often mentioned by classical writers from Homer onwards. They obviously represent the costly precursors of the well-known Egyptian burial textiles of white linen decorated with dull 'purple' wool, in which the expensive true purple has been replaced with a mixture of indigo and madder. The gold thread on the other hand has been replaced by white linen yarn mostly lying over the 'purple' areas and worked in the 'flying needle' technique (III, fig. 4). The surviving fabrics, originally rectangular covers or tunics, were woven as single pieces of a size suitable to the purpose in hand. When fashion dictated that the tunic should have sleeves, this problem was solved by adding two extra sections of warp during weaving, as shown in the schematic drawing (v, fig. 5).[4] The great loom width characteristic of this tunic and many other similar pieces indicates that the cloth beam must have been extremely wide, but this is as much as can be deduced about the construction of the loom. It is generally supposed to have resembled the looms shown in ancient Pharaonic paintings (II, fig. 3), representing what might be called a real tapestry loom. However, it seems to me to have more in common with the ancient

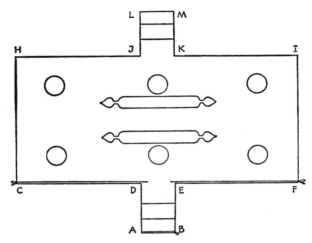

v, fig. 5.   Diagram showing the sequence of procedures when weaving a Coptic tunic. The narrow warp (A–B) is set up first and one sleeve woven. When this is finished two other warps (C–D and E–F) are attached to the beam, and the entire body is woven and finished off. Next comes the other sleeve (J–K) which is duly finished off. The entire cross-shaped piece is finally folded double in the direction of the warp and sewn together at the sides

Egyptian 'linen loom' with its horizontal warp (type 3). The latter seems probable since the plain areas comprised most of the textiles which were originally linen. It would presumably have been more difficult to do plain weaving in a tapestry loom than to weave limited tapestry areas in a plain weave provided with a proper shedding mechanism.

The tapestry-decorated textiles from the Egyptian finds may be roughly divided into the following five groups: (1) Linen fabrics decorated with inserted tapestry areas of a dark colour, in imitation of purple, often in geometric or purely ornamental patterns, related to the finds from Palmyra. (2) The same fabrics mostly with polychrome decoration consisting of human figures and plant motifs depicted in naturalistic style, sometimes executed with a virtuosity suggesting highly skilled specialist workshops. Both these groups betray a close relationship to surviving Roman floor mosaics and, in common with the latter, seem to be directly modelled on paintings. (3) A variety of products, some of them from Antinoë and others from Fustat, display typically Persian motifs, and at least some of them, no doubt, were made within the Sassanian Empire while others may probably be Egyptian imitations. (4) The group which can rightly be termed 'Coptic' comprises products of folk art which, using a coarse technique, reinterprets and debases themes from the preceding groups, the principal change being that the pagan figures take on a Christian significance. (5) The art of the Arab conquerors does not penetrate this sphere until towards the end of the millenium. Then once again we encounter professional work of a high standard, though the best of it, thin veils of silk and cotton with tapestry woven bands containing cufic letters and various ornaments, is later and seldom seems to be included in burial finds.

OTHER WEAVES WITH INDIVIDUAL DESIGNS: SINGLE OR PAIRED

Beside the tapestries there are also some other types of weave which are individually produced, with either single or reversing designs. But while the patterning methods are essentially the same the structures of the weaves may be of various types. Primarily to be mentioned here are the types belonging to the multifarious group of weaves which in the schematic list (Chap. III) are summarized as 'ground weaves with additional floating wefts' — either 'weft-patterned tabbies' or 'weaves with additional floating wefts'. But a similar patterning method may also have been employed for double-cloth (*finnväv*) as well as for some kinds of self-patterned weaves. Note, however, that this patterning method might certainly have been practised in several places all over the world — before some mechanical devices were invented and added to the simple loom. The technical principle of this method consists in the individual, and extremely time-consuming preparation of each pattern shed, made before(!) the pattern weft is entered. This is done by 'picking up' certain warp ends on a stick from which the entire pattern shed successively is transferred on to the pattern rod. The following details from the carrying out of a special kind of weaving method — which until lately has been preserved in Sweden — might also give an idea of some further development of this method.

The old Swedish opphämta ('weft-patterned tabby') with large and rich patterns was executed by means of a method, now out of use, which is of fundamental interest in connexion with other weaving techniques of considerable antiquity. Formerly opphämta could be woven on an ordinary treadle loom for weaving tabby, which was temporarily supplemented with a number of narrow shed rods and one especially flat and broad rod or stick, the *skälblad*. All these rods or sticks are usually removed from the loom as soon as they have been used. Note that this is a method for executing patterns and not a special kind of loom, as is sometimes stated. It is characteristic of the 'rod' method that it can be developed further in such a way that the pattern is repeated inversely, that is, to form a symmetrical design with a transverse axis. The clearest way of explaining this technical principle is to describe the operating procedures, of weaving opphämta of the old Swedish type shown in Pls 88–89.[5]

(1)   After weaving one section in plain tabby, the groups of warp ends needed for each 'step' of the coloured pattern are picked up and collected on a thin rod, and thence transferred to the broad shed rod. This is raised on its edge and the pattern weft is entered. The first step, including four to five picks of each pattern weft (and in between ground wefts) is then finished.

(2)   As the shed thus formed would obstruct the following picks it is transferred through the reed and the heddles to behind the main shafts, which procedure is done by alternately inserting rods and the skälblad, the latter raised onto its edge. Behind the shafts each thread group is finally collected with loops onto a rod.

(3)   For each new 'step' of the pattern a completely new shed has to be picked up, collected on the rod, used for all the picks and finally transferred through the reed and the heddles to behind the shafts. Here successively all the pattern rods are 'stored', lying on the stretched warp, one rod above the other. There will be quite a number of them before the middle of the pattern border is reached (cf. v, fig. 6, the arrow).

(4)   After finishing the arrowed pick the weaver will have to bring forward all the pattern shed rods one by one in the order in which they are lying, and successively remove them from the loom. All this involves, for each pick, a series of manipulations in which the weaver needs the assistance of at least one other person.

v, fig. 6.   Opphämta weave of the Skälblad type: the pattern sheds are successively picked up on rods, of which the sheds are moved behind all shafts to be kept there until returned

The old Scandinavian 'pick-up doublecloth' (sometimes called *finnväv*) incorporates the technical principles of points 1 and 2, resulting in a unique piece. Several examples of such work have come down to us from the Middle Ages. If we are studying the oldest known specimens (Pl. 86) it is easy to see how the weaver has picked up the white threads from the underlying warp to form a pattern, of which the free-hand details are obviously copied from a more regular original, probably silk fabric. The blue and white doublecloth hanging with its regular design of beasts (Pl. 87) may be about two hundred years later. This design of 'animal inhabited' squares, is so regular that at first sight one is tempted to classify it as consisting of true pattern repeats and therefore produced in a draw loom. But on closer examination one finds that the whole design extends across the entire loom width and includes, besides the six animals, a large border with dragons. It is clear that a unit of this size is far too large to have been produced in an ordinary drawloom. This conclusion was subsequently proved by a meticulous analysis of the entire fabric, showing small irregularities which could only be attributed to each shed having been picked up by hand. That means that as soon as one section of the design was finished the weaver had to start all over again, all the time working free-hand (Pl. 10f).

The 'skälblad' method practised in other weaves

The weaves described above are all characterized by the absence of regular pattern repeats, in other words, there is no exact repetition within the loom width. On the other hand, one certain kind of self-patterned weave does present a similar 'transversal symmetry', that is a pattern repetition round an axis which is parallel to the weft. This form of patterning is typical in Chinese monochrome silks, especially those of the Han dynasty, but it sometimes also occurs in the polychrome 'warp-faced compound weaves' of both types (see VI, figs 1–3). It appears that this kind of resemblance between the finished products must be due to a similarity of procedure, which may have been executed more or less in accordance to the Swedish method described above. However, this view concerning Chinese silk weaving does not agree with a certain idea sometimes expressed in print. Impressed by the general complexity of the polychrome Han silks, various writers have argued that such patterns were produced by means of a drawloom, thus implying that this intricate mechanism already existed in China under the Han dynasty (Pl. 6).[6]

I would not be so bold as to claim that the resemblance here to the old Scandinavian methods is conclusive evidence to the contrary. But it does tend to support and illustrate the view previously put forward by the late Harold B. Burnham of Toronto in 1965 and 1967. By close analysis of a series of Chinese polychrome silks, in warp-faced compound tabby, and by comparison with other material, this eminent textile scholar convincingly showed that the drawloom theory is completely unrealistic. He established the important point that there was no repetition of pattern units within the entire loom width in any single instance. The warp-faced compound tabbies consisted of two or three differently coloured warp systems forming patterns as a result of the threads being lifted up to the face of the weave. It is known that the statutory width of cloth produced in the imperial workshops corresponded to 50 centimetres. The difficulty of the work is evident from the number of warp ends per centimetre: 100 to 160, which means 4,000 to 7,800 raised warp ends throughout the entire width of the loom. The absence of true pattern repeats shows that every thread change must have been manipulated by hand, probably with the aid of pattern rods, and presumably also with at least one assistant.

Note that Burnham, as well as other writers in English and French, preferred to call the whole ensemble of implements a 'pattern-rod loom' (Fr. *métier aux baguettes*). Although this method is in itself a supreme weaving achievement, it precludes the mechanical aids belonging to the drawloom.

Burnham only briefly deals with the patterning of the monochrome Chinese silks (the so-called Han damasks). But in the same article he writes that the pattern-rod loom would also have been suitable for this kind of weave. Although the technique here is simpler, as is generally the case, too, with the ornamentation, the pattern disposition is roughly the same in both types. The monochrome silks have only one system of warp and weft, forming a tabby ground, while the pattern consists of warp floats. This effect is generally obtained by raising some warp ends before every other pick. The pattern shed then may have been produced by selecting a series of warp ends over the entire loom width and collecting them on a rod. By co-ordinating a number of such sheds one obtains a very low pattern unit which is reversed around a transverse axis (v, fig. 7; vII, figs 1–2; Pl. 9d). The 'transversal symmetry' is apparent in a large number of Chinese silks from various early archaeological sites (above all Palmyra) but also fabrics of later date.[7]

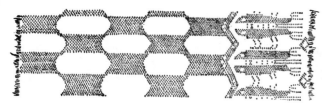

v, fig. 7. Self-patterned Chinese silk. The turn-over axis is transversal as in the Skälblad weave, fig. v:6

The blue and white hangings from southern Sweden (Pls 88 and 89) exemplify the same system of repetition. We know in detail how the latter textiles were woven: on an ordinary treadle loom supplemented by a number of narrow shed rods and a broad and flat pattern stick, the *skälblad*. The simple loom of the Han period seems to have had only one treadle and a back-strap for body tension (II, fig. 15). However, I venture to conclude that the patterns of the Chinese 'Han damasks' as a matter of principle were produced similarly to the Scandinavian *skälblad* method.

VI *Mechanical Patterning*

TECHNICAL DEVELOPMENTS

Unlike the individual methods dealt with in the preceding chapter, mechanical patterning denotes the repetition of patterns by means of a mechanical appliance built in while the warp is being arranged in the loom. The unit of pattern thus created is termed a 'pattern repeat'. The mechanical appliance generally termed the 'drawloom figure harness' makes it possible to control certain warp ends or groups of ends according to a predetermined arrangement. In other words, all the mutually corresponding warp ends in the entire loom width are simultaneously raised or lowered in order to open the shed for a pick. In this way the same motif or pattern unit can be exactly repeated several times both across the width and in sequence.

This, roughly defined, is the principle of the mechanical patterning, which was developed in the Near Eastern silk manufactories. Superficially, there may not seem to be much difference between the first designs executed by mechanical patterning and various types of pick-up patterns, especially as the latter have in many cases been inspired by mechanically produced patterns. Seen in a longer-term perspective, however, the difference is very great indeed, and the effect of the new invention was revolutionary. The various constructions known to us today have taken a long time to evolve. For instance a variety of patterning mechanisms must have been evolved to suit the different weaving techniques that continually succeeded one another. Unfortunately we do not know what these mechanical appliances looked like. The long period in the textile history of the western world (down to the end of the fifteenth century), when technical activity would seem to have been at its height, has bequeathed us no evidence whatsoever apart from the products themselves, and they cannot tell us everything we would like to know.

One patterning method involves extending the binding, for example, twill, by fitting the ordinary loom with several shafts connected to treadles; in practice this means making the loom bigger. Another method, often used for patterned tabbies with floated wefts, involves placing a few pattern shafts behind the main shafts. Groups of a certain number of warp ends are then entered in the pattern shafts, which are connected to special treadles, so that whole warp groups can be raised and lowered for the

pattern weft. However, both these methods are confined to small, geometrical patterns.

The drawloom

A wider range of patterning facilities is afforded by the various devices
collectively termed drawlooms (Fr. *métier à la tire*, Ger. *Zugwebstuhl*, Sw.
dragvävstol).[1] The construction of the parts known as the binding harness
and the drawloom figure harness and other details must have changed
in the course of time, but this is not to say that the older apparatus
vanished as new inventions made their appearance. On the contrary
experience has shown that old-fashioned implements were often retained
for special purposes. It must be assumed that several types of loom were in
use simultaneously throughout the entire development period. An
essential feature of the drawloom figure harness system is the special
'leashes' (vi, fig. 1) fitted with 'lingoes' (weights), which make it possible

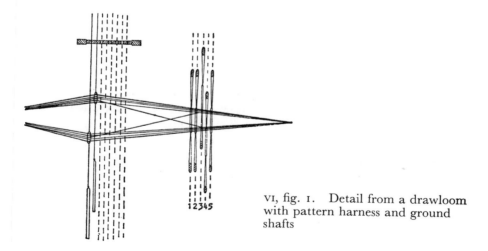

vi, fig. 1.   Detail from a drawloom
with pattern harness and ground
shafts

for them to be raised and lowered independently of the main shafts. The
leashes to be raised and lowered simultaneously are joined at the top to
necking cords and pulley cords, one for each pattern shed to be opened
(vi, figs 2a and c). The 'comber board', which can take the form of a
wooden frame with a number of slats, was originally a board pierced with
holes through which the pulley cords were drawn (to prevent them from

becoming entangled). One comber board and its necking cords generally corresponds to a comber repeat, or rather, the comber board controls the warp ends belonging to the repeat, giving the same number of single or grouped warp threads in every repeat. The repeat may be a 'point repeat', that is, the pattern unit 'turns over' regularly around a vertical axis, thus forming a symmetrical design. Or it may be 'straight' giving an asymmetrical effect.

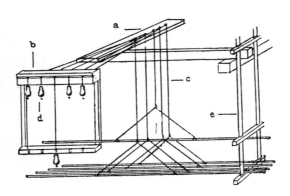

VI, fig. 2.   Diagram showing the harness system

Pulling the leashes on a drawloom could be a laborious and time-consuming business, especially with large designs. This task was therefore given to one or more assistants, known as 'drawboys' (Fr. *tireurs*), who were usually positioned somewhere aloft in the great loom (VI, fig. 4). There could be anything up to four of these drawboys to a single loom.

The origin and development of the drawloom figure harness

The basic concept of mechanical patterning has now been defined, and a schematic description of the drawloom figure harness with leash and cords given. In the previous chapter the Chinese patterning techniques of the Han period were considered, and it was noted that there is no longer any reason to suppose that a loom construction essentially similar to what is generally meant by the term 'drawloom' was already known to the Chinese during the first two centuries of the Christian era. But when and where did the drawloom first appear?

It should now be time for a general acknowledgement that the patterned silk fabrics known to have been produced by the famous silk manufactories of Sassanian Iran, the earliest high quality production of this kind in the western world, possess the very properties which testify to the use of some kind of drawloom. The textile specimens that have come down to us display regularly repeated pattern units, invariably with the same number of warp ends in each pattern repeat — a relatively small number in the oldest specimens, gradually increasing in the later ones and thus implying progressively larger patterns and pattern units.

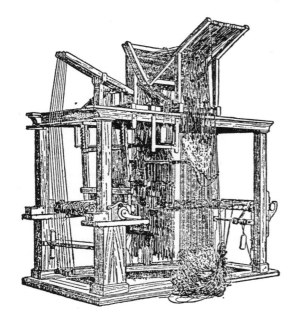

VI, fig. 3. Drawloom or 'metier à grande tire' according to a model from 1855, Musée des Arts et Metiers, Paris

Most of the fabrics in question were discovered at Antinoë in Egypt. Following the first finds there, from 1896–97, leading oriental scholars of that period (Strzygowski and later Herzfeld) declared on the strength of the designs that this artistically and technically superb silk production must be attributed to Iran under the Sassanian dynasty (224–651). Nevertheless the German art historian Otto von Falke, in his magnum opus *Kunstgeschichte der Seidenweberei* (1913) put forward arguments in favour of the manufacture of these silks in Antinoë itself; his categorical hypothesis was adopted with a surprising acquiescence by many authors dealing with the history of silk weaving. The French scholar Rudolf Pfister did more than anybody else to place the study of this very complex problem on the right track again, his final efforts to this end appearing in an important article on the role of Iran in connexion with the finds from Antinoë. This is not the place for a full account of Pfister's analyses and multifarious arguments, but present purposes require us to mention some of his discoveries, particularly the specimens of mechanical patterning which must have come from Sassanian territory.[2]

The earliest specimens are three unique and very fine woollen fabrics in the form of cushion covers which, in view of the associated grave finds, can be dated to the third century. The Antinoë finds include a great number of silks (see VII, figs 9–11), generally to be ascribed to the period between A.D. 300 and 500. Mention should also be made of some silk fabrics from the post-Sassanian period, discovered in Central Asia, and of a number of specimens preserved in the treasuries of European churches. The technique used in all these fabrics is that termed 'weft-faced compound weave' (type D2), the two chief variants of which, tabby and twill, are represented, the latter mainly in silk. It is of great importance to the problem under consideration that the specimens found in Antinoë can be dated fairly precisely, viz, to the period 200–500, for these fabrics are the most refined specimens of this technique that are known to us. Both the Central Asian finds and most of the specimens which have been found in European churches are coarser, as too are all the later products produced in the same technique, which continued to dominate the silk manufacturing of the Mediterranean countries, including the Byzantine court workshops, until the eleventh century.

The facts quoted above provide very convincing evidence for the case that the 'new' type of weave and the technical apparatus connected with it were invented and developed in Iran. To this must be added the fact that the Silk Road, along which great quantities of silk products from China were transported westwards, passed through territories which were under Iranian suzerainty. Iran was in all respects the nearest recipient of the much sought-after Chinese raw material, far nearer than the Mediterranean countries.

II. *Italian silk fabric in the 'diasprum' or 'lampas' technique with animals brocaded in membrane gold thread. Early fourteenth century. Stockholm, Historiska Museet.*

COMPARISON OF EASTERN AND
WESTERN WEAVING TECHNIQUES

A direct comparison between the Chinese and the Iranian types of weave, which were chronologically consecutive (types D1 and D2), would seem to be appropriate at this point. The difference can be stated with drastic simplicity, though technically speaking not quite correctly, in the following terms: 'if the Chinese binding were turned through an angle of 90 degrees, it would resemble the Iranian binding'. The weft in the latter plays the same part as the warp in the Chinese weave, in that it is visible and covers the surface of the weave. But whereas the Chinese type of technique has only one weft, serving different functions every other pick, in the Iranian technique the warp is divided into two separate systems of warp threads serving distinctive functions. One warp is a 'binding warp' which is guided by the ground harness, the other is the 'main warp' and it is the movements of this warp that form the pattern. It is the ends of the main warp which are controlled by the leashes of the figure harness. The idea of operating two warps simultaneously doubtless originated in China, but the use of one of the warps for a completely different function (patterning) must rank as an invention in its own right. Moreover the method of using a special patterning warp controlled by the figure harness continued to be practised even when other techniques were adopted.

Some technical observations

Sometimes the surviving textile material enables us to make detailed observations which can supplement our imperfect knowledge of the construction of different looms. In both earlier and later specimens of the Iranian type of weave (D2), including those of a very high standard, one often observes an irregularity in the pattern which proves to be caused by an uneven warp density (for instance, Pl. 18c). On the other hand the number of warp ends per pattern unit is constant. The unevenness in the warp must have arisen because the beater lacked the reed which in more recent looms helps to keep the thread density even throughout the loom width. The same condition seems also to be the rule in Chinese silk weaving; especially in simple plain tabbies the warp density always increases towards the edges. All this tends to show that the Asian loom had no reed. Perhaps instead there was an open comb with widely-spaced dents, not unlike the raddle used much later for mounting the loom. A device of this kind also helps to account for another detail occurring in Mediterranean silk weaving, namely the selvedges, which remain much the same until about 1400, at least where broad silk fabrics are concerned. When they have not been cut away, which, unfortunately, is quite often the case, the edges consist of several very thick cords (Pl. 34b), the purpose of which was to hold out the weft so as to give the fabric an even width. Of course, such selvedges are not compatible with the close fitted dents of a proper reed.

Another important factor is the great width of the fabric and the loom. As we saw earlier, the old Chinese silks were always narrow, never more than 50 centimetres wide. In the west, on the other hand, great widths were very common, especially where costly silk fabrics were concerned. These differences are tellingly illustrated by a report which has come down to us from a fifth-century Chinese traveller, Hwan P'san, visiting the territories bordering on Persia, who was amazed by the broad silk fabrics woven in the Sassanian Empire. Several specimens of such fabrics have survived in the treasuries of European churches in the form of complete loom-pieces about 130 centimetres wide; and from the period commencing in about 1000 we know from Müller-Christensen of several *pallia* of Byzantine and Islamic origin measuring up to about 250 centimetres width. Naturally such very wide looms called for stout construction. As a result they became heavy and also expensive: a specialized loom came to represent a capital investment far beyond the capacity of a simple craftsman. On the other hand it could be a sound investment for a capitalist with an eye to the main chance. It is recorded that the Italian painter Giotto, who was a wealthy man, owned several looms and leased them at a high rate of interest.

Development in Italy

The richly designed silks produced in Italy between the mid-thirteenth century and the early-fifteenth century are invariably 115–120 centimetres wide, no doubt a mandatory standard dimension. Later on during the fifteenth century a general revision of the loom constructions obviously occurred: the thick selvedge cords still occurring about 1450 were replaced by neat selvedges of plain weave usually striped in different colours, and the loom width was reduced generally to 60–70 centimetres. This change of standards was undoubtedly connected with the many new types of weave that were introduced in the course of the fifteenth century: pomegranate-patterned damasks, ornate velvets of rich and elaborate quality, cloth of gold of various kinds, some of which were all-silk fabrics, others half-silks of heavy quality. Each and every one of these different techniques and qualities must have demanded new, specially equipped looms. This situation is plainly reflected by the Italian guild organizations, which in the case of silk weaving distinguished between a number of different specialities.

We know very little about the actual appearance of the pattern looms used. Some simple treadle looms were depicted by Italian artists of the fifteenth century, but nobody took the trouble to portray the more complex models. We therefore have to content ourselves with a Chinese drawing, probably from the seventeenth century, showing a female 'drawboy' at work high up in the loom (vi, fig. 4).

vi, fig. 4. Drawloom with 'drawboy'. China, c.1600

Developments in France

Unlike Italy, several loom models have been preserved in France together with historical particulars concerning the development of the different inventions. This in spite of the fact that the main development of silk weaving must have taken place in Italy, which would seem by all accounts to have been the leading country in the whole of Europe in this respect.[3]

The technical collections in the *Conservatoire des Arts et Métiers* in Paris include a number of miniature model looms which, over and above their prime purpose of illustrating the development of French craftsmanship, are of general European interest. The collection as such owes its existence to the fact that the French silk manufactories in Tours and Lyons were state-subsidized enterprises, which made the Parisian training institute *Arts et Métiers* and all its collections a national concern. This is quite different from the state of affairs in Italy, where the silk industry was maintained from the very beginning by a number of rival trading cities and business houses, to whom inventions and other technical novelties were business secrets not lightly to be noised abroad. Here are some references from the French sources on which the manuals have often put an exaggeratedly nationalistic interpretation. A new loom, ascribed to a certain Jean le Calabrais, an Italian from Calabria, was installed in Tours in 1470 on the orders of the King. This loom is supposed to have been a 'button drawloom', with details more or less resembling those shown in vi, fig. 2, in other words a relatively simple drawloom of the kind usually termed *métier à la petite tire*.[4] Tradition has it that another Italian, Claude Dangon of Milan, greatly improved the drawloom system by replacing the button device with a figure harness with 'simple cords' (Fr. *cordes de semple*). A frequently portrayed miniature model (vi, fig. 3) in the custody of the *Arts et Métiers* is catalogued as 'Dangon's loom', but as this model was executed for the Paris World Exhibition of 1855, its historical accuracy is open to question. The model is a specimen of the type known as *métier à la grand tire*. Dangon was unquestionably a highly skilled weaver of *grands dessins*, for which he is said to have employed four drawboys simultaneously. But his 'invention' seems to be rather a myth, for it is hard to believe that the Italians, who were still by far the most advanced silk weavers in Europe in the seventeenth century, were not the original creators of this invention, especially as it soon spread to all the European countries where advanced silk weaving was practised. One is inclined to think that the type of loom introduced in Lyon by Dangon and known by his name had long been in use in his native country.

The circumstances of silk weaving in France were completely transformed in the latter half of the seventeenth century. The activities directed and vigorously supported from the highest level gave rise to improvements of every conceivable kind. Among other things, efforts were made to find substitutes for the extra labour demanded by the various complicated draw systems.

By the time the Lyon master weaver Jacquard succeeded, at the beginning of the nineteenth century, in establishing the ingenious invention of the automatic punched card-mechanism, parts of the problem had already been solved in principle by others. The first card system had been invented by Bouchon in 1725 and improved three years later by Falcon.

Other problems had been solved in 1745 by Vaucanson, though his loom is said to have been unusable in practice. However, Vaucanson's model came to rest at the *Arts et Métiers*, where it was found by Jacquard, who had been summoned to Paris in 1801 after working on loom problems in Lyon. It was in Paris that Jacquard contrived to combine his earlier experiments into an efficient working apparatus. The first Jacquard loom is said to have been completed in 1804 (VI, fig. 5). The thorough-going novelty of this loom is that all the heddles are joined together in a single system. The heddle rods with their treadles were eliminated and weaving was emancipated from the ancient hand loom. In Jacquard's loom the 'simple cords', the lashes and drawboy are replaced by a mechanism which is driven by a single treadle which can be controlled by the weaver unaided. The automatic punch-card mechanism consists of a series of cards of equal size, linked together and pierced with a number of small holes. These are mechanically matched with the heddles. The number of holes in a card corresponds to the number of warp ends in the pattern unit

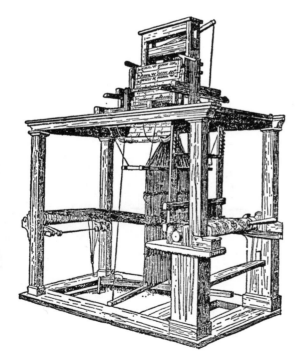

VI, fig. 5. Jacquard's loom from 1804 according to a model from 1853, Musée des Arts et Metiers, Paris

which have to be lifted in order to form a shed. When the card mechanism has completed a revolution the different sheds have been passed and the pattern unit is complete.

Jacquard's invention was an efficient means of economizing on labour. One can therefore readily understand how the many poor silk weavers of Lyon (*les canuts*), feared for their livelihoods. Serious rioting broke out on Jacquard's return to Lyons, the new loom was publicly burned and Jacquard himself had to leave the city. But the course of development was not to be restrained. By 1813 the Jacquard loom was being used in English cotton mills, though it was not introduced in the French silk weaving industry until the 1820s. During the 1830s it was adapted for completely mechanical operation.

VII   *Silk Weaving in Asia*

It was in China, the birthplace of sericulture, that silk weaving first developed into a fine art, together with bronze casting and lacquer decoration, ceramics and calligraphy, all arts that were greatly appreciated in this highly artistic civilization. As the knowledge of reeled silk and its woven products spread from east to west, silk weaving as such became steadily more appreciated. Iran was the first of the western (or west Asian) civilizations to succeed in developing an independent art of silk weaving which provided a medium for its own sense of style and its own world of symbols and beliefs.[1] The whole of this development was founded on the superior properties of the silk thread: its strength and elasticity, its flexibility and lustre. Throughout the three millennia we can now look back on, silk weaving was characterized by the close interaction of artistic creativity and technical ingenuity. Because of its favoured social and economic status, silk weaving was able to draw on the talents of the best artists of its time, ranging from the anonymous Chinese masters of the first centuries B.C. to the celebrated names of the great Italian and French epochs. As a result practically the entire evolution of textile design took place in silk weaving: silk patterns became models for embroidery and textile printing as well as for fabrics woven of other materials.

CHINA

The Chinese chronicle praising Hsi Ling Shih, consort to the Emperor Huang Ti, for discovering the miracle of the silkworm is thought by contemporary scholars to reflect a historical event. Since the Emperor Huang Ti is assumed to have lived in about 2640 B.C., the art of reeling silk would appear to be at least 4,600 years old. But there is still more tangible evidence of silk history: great quantities of well preserved silk fabrics showing what the artists of past ages have been capable of; in fact there is much more left of Chinese silk production up to and including the Han dynasty than of silks manufactured anywhere in the Near East (that is, western Asia) before approximately A.D. 1000. Due above all to fortunate archaeological circumstances, the Chinese material can be dated almost exactly, which is seldom the case with the silk specimens that have survived in European church treasuries which various scholars, with varying degrees of uncertainty and mutual dissent, have attributed to Byzantine, Iranian or Islamic workshops.

Historical data

During the first centuries of its existence, exactly how long we do not know, sericulture was an exclusive craft practised within a very limited area. Production was reserved for the court and the most privileged members of society. The secrets of silk manufacture were girded about with stringent regulations with the threat of torture and death to anybody breaking the law. But in the long run no amount of threats and sanctions could prevent this excellent material from spreading further afield. Eggs from the precious silkworms were smuggled out and the circle of initiates gradually widened, though still at first within the boundaries of China. The spread of sericulture is illustrated by the story of a Chinese princess who was married to a prince as far away in the west as present day Sinkiang, and who contrived to smuggle out some silkworm eggs concealed in her voluminous hair style. This is supposed to have happened in about 140 B.C., by which time Chinese silk production had grown in scale and had also developed technically. The lustrous silk fabrics had become commercial commodities which eventually found their way into the Roman Empire, probably at first by way of India. In the western world of those times, which included western Asia as well as the great Roman Empire, these fabrics were known as *serica*, a name derived from a Mongolian word for thread and thus directly referring to the reeled cocoon thread. This in turn caused the Chinese, the inventors of these fabrics, to be known as the *Ser* — this according to H. S. Nyberg, the famous philologist, and contrary to previous suppositions that the products were named after the people they came from.

The first Seric fabrics to enter the western world were no doubt thin, plain tabby silk, and their shine, their brilliant colours and their remarkable softness would have caused a sensation. They must have been the materials used to make the banners which Crassus's troops, with fear in their hearts, saw fluttering over the heads of the Parthian host in the disastrous battle of Carrhae in 53 B.C. — *signa auro seris sericisque vexillis vibrante.* This reference to the Parthian banners is illustrated by the enormous flags, each one composed of many narrow lengths of thin Chinese silks, carried some 1,700 years later by the Imperial armies in the Thirty Years' War, many of which now belong to the Swedish Army's trophy collection.

The first serious links with the western world were forged under the expansive Han dynasty (205 B.C. to A.D. 220), more particularly during the energetic reign of the Emperor Wu (140 to 85 B.C.). This was accomplished through the establishment of the Silk Road, consisting in fact of several trading routes leading through the deserts and mountains of Asia for the precise purpose of conveying silk and other sought-after Chinese products to the Syrian markets (cf. xv, map 2). Fortified strongholds were built to protect the precious caravans along the most hazardous stretches of the route. The Chinese would usually take their goods to the frontier of the Parthian kingdom, from whence Parthian merchants would then deliver them to such western trading towns as Dura-Europos and Palmyra. The Parthians played a very important part at this time not only as intermediaries between east and west but also as custodians of the Iranian cultural heritage prior to its resuscitation, with the foundation of the Sassanian Empire in A.D. 224. As can be seen from the map, the Silk Road was really a congeries of caravan routes which, for various reasons, had to be redirected from time to time. In Bactria some of them turned southwards, continuing by sea through the Persian Gulf and then westward and northward by way of the Red Sea.

Before the Han dynasty came to power, the Great Wall had been built to keep out the warlike Huns, a collective term for the various mounted nomads living in the interior of Asia who time and again made bloody descents upon China. But the Wall was only a partial solution to the problem. To preserve the safety of their country, the Emperors had to pay tributes, which according to the Han chronicles often contained large quantities of silk. This has proved fortunate for modern scholars, since a proportion of these treasures were buried together with the chieftains of the Huns, and, after a lapse of some two thousand years, have been recovered and saved for researchers into the history of textile art. The silk production of the Han dynasty is known to us through an astonishing number of finds. Among the most important archaeological complexes are the burial mounds, *kurgans*, in the Noin-Ula mountains of Northern Mongolia which were excavated by Russian archaeologists in 1924–25. They were found to contain among other things more than two hundred pieces of silk of various kinds and a Chinese lacquer bowl which was signed, thus dating the burial in question to a short time after the beginning of the Christian era.[2]

Earlier still the British archaeologist Sir Aurel Stein and the Swedish explorer Dr Sven Hedin had prospected for relics of civilizations along the

Silk Road. Hedin's later expeditions during the 1930s included a series of excavations carried out by Folke Bergman in Edsen-gol in Inner Mongolia and in the area surrounding the Wandering Lake of Lop-nor visited by Hedin in 1900. The textile material which was brought to light included refuse from the military garrisons and from graves, etc., belonging to a native, non-Mongolian population in Lou-Lan that had used wool. All these textiles from the Hedin expeditions were analysed and published by Vivi Sylwan before they were delivered to Peking. Most of Aurel Stein's vast material is now in New Delhi; the rest is in the British Museum.

One of the most important trading stations along the Silk Road was the once tremendously wealthy and splendid town of Palmyra, completely devastated in 273 and now a ruin in the Syrian desert. This remarkable site was excavated by French archaeologists. In a funeral tower were discovered quantities of textile fragments, including Chinese silks, an exemplary account of which was published by R. Pfister (1934, 1937, 1940).[3]

The art of silk weaving before and during the Han period

The oldest evidence of Chinese silks is known through pioneering studies by the Swedish textile expert Vivi Sylwan. In the corrosion patina of two burial bronzes from the Shang-Yin period (1500–1000 B.C.) were found some hardened remains of silk fabrics that had been wrapped around them. Microscopic analysis showed silk fibres from *Bombyx mori*. One silk was a plain tabby with a warp density of up to 72 threads/centimetre. The other had a woven pattern of lozenges very much resembling our Pl. 9c, in other words, a self-patterned tabby produced by picking up certain warp ends on rods (C2). A similar fabric (III, fig. 20) was found in a Viking period

VII, fig. 1.   Self-patterned silk with transversal pattern, so-called Han damask. Lou-Lan

grave from Birka, Sweden, thus being some 2,000 years younger. Note that none of these weaves is a genuine twill, as assumed by some scholars.

The so-called 'Han damask' (C2) is characterized by the transversal patterning discussed in detail in Chapter v. The patterns may consist of fairly simple geometrical shapes, but they can also be composed of animal shapes and other richly varied motifs (vii, figs 1–2). It was probably under the Han dynasty that the gauze weave (C4) technique was developed to give rhomboid patterns on a small scale. It is characteristic of all these monochrome fabrics that the pattern is very small and hardly discernible except at close quarters. Their main effect is that of a modulation of shades of a single colour.

vii, fig. 2.   'Han damask' with a rich pattern, also with transversal turn-over.
Lou-Lan

Not even the 'polychrome warp-faced weaves' (D2), the élite products of Han silk weaving (Pls 10–11; vii, figs 3, 4), are noted for their decorative effect from a distance. Their polychromy never aspires to grandiose effects, and the designs and the colour transitions are soft and fluid. The proportions of the figures are also quite small, even in the most sophisticated designs. Starting with the simple geometrical patterns of the pre-Han period, the trend is towards increasingly varied compositions consisting of flowers, birds, fishes and all kinds of animals in vigorous movement, as well as clouds and legible calligraphic signs.[4] It is characteristic of this art that the best specimens have been compared with wash drawings and calligraphy, the subtle arts which the Chinese themselves appreciated

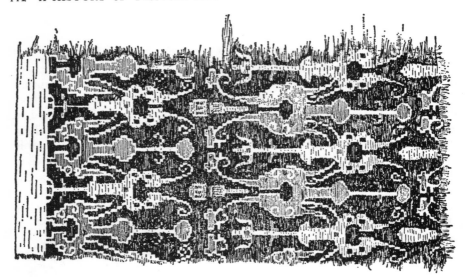

VII, fig. 3.   Polychrome silk, warp-faced compound tabby, transversal
turn-over. Han period. Lou-Lan

VII, fig. 4.   Polychrome warp-faced silk, transversal pattern unit filling the
loom width. China, Han period

most. The 'direct' method of successively manipulating the multicoloured warp threads gives the same impression of spontaneity as if the figures had been drawn with the finest of brushes.

Many of these products are superb, but of all known pieces none can rival the rocky landscape from Noin-Ula which has been called the oldest landscape in Chinese art (Pl. 11b). This is not the occasion to delve into the myth on which this evocative composition must have been based, but a summary of the principal motifs will at least convey some idea of this remarkable work of art: steep cliffs of jade sheltering a peach tree — the tree of life; on the cliffs, cranes eating an enormous mushroom — the life-giving *ling chih* which the birds of paradise can occasionally permit a mortal to taste. The colours: red, orange and yellow. No repeats and no symmetry whatever. Nothing could be more characteristic of the textile art of the Han period, in which one invariably encounters gently flowing lines and a delicate feeling for shades of colour. To appreciate this silken art properly, one should also be familiar with its parallel, the art of lacquer, another highly complex craft requiring a great deal of artistry and imagination as well as technical skill. Lacquer vessels were in fact produced in much the same area and were another major export article under the Han dynasty.

Silk weaving under the T'ang

Practically no silk has come down to us from the centuries immediately following the Han period, but with the advent of the T'ang dynasty (618–906) the material becomes abundant. A great deal of silk fabric from this period was discovered by Stein, especially in Tun-Huang, not far west of the Chinese frontier. In recent years several finds have also been made in the People's Republic of China and in Mongolia. For very special reasons, however, the great majority of T'ang silks have been preserved in Japan. The greatest Japanese collection of this kind, from the early T'ang, is known by the name of the *Shosoin* in Nara, the Imperial treasure houses containing exhibits of various kinds, which have been preserved still in excellent condition, in memory of the good and wise Emperor Shomu (724–749). Other Chinese fabrics from the early T'ang, that is, the seventh and eighth centuries, belong to ancient Buddhist temples. With a few isolated exceptions, these highly interesting textile treasures were unknown to the western world until a few decades ago, when *Gomotsu*, a major Japanese publication containing admirable colour plates, appeared.[5]

It is impossible to give any detailed account here of the innumerable *Shosoin* silks and those in other Japanese collections. Instead we may confine ourselves to the Chinese silk fabrics with Sassanian-Persian motifs which are of such international historical importance. These include, among other things, the earliest known specimen of *k'ossu*, a tapestry technique probably originating from Iran but gradually developing a purely Chinese style. Perhaps the most remarkable among the *Shosoin* textiles are a number of silks with unusually large loom-widths, executed in the typically Iranian weft-faced compound twill (D2) and showing the powerful, highly-coloured animal motifs set in circular frames, which are the most typical creations of the Sassanian textile art. A detailed investigation of these designs reveals an unmistakably Chinese sense of form, the hallmark of the Chinese master weaver, which indicates where these fabrics were actually made. There could be no more eloquent testimony to the paramount importance of Sassanian textile art than these masterly imitations.

As long as we lack a comprehensive view of the material preserved in the *Shosoin* and in other Japanese temple treasuries, it is difficult to make categorical statements concerning Chinese silk production under the T'ang and immediately afterwards. It is uncertain whether any of this production reached the west. The only reliable indication that this occurred is the fragment from Birka (III, fig. 19), which presumably came to Sweden by caravan routes to the Khazar empire, which was also reached by Scandinavian merchants before this trade route was cut.

Chinese silk production after the T'ang

The Mongol conquests in the thirteenth century reopened the routes from east to west. Thus the papal inventory of 1295 tells us that large quantities of 'Tartar' fabrics, meaning Iranian as well as Chinese products, were accumulated in the papal stores by that time. As we shall see in due course, similar luxury fabrics were also received in other parts of Europe. Probably the oldest extant specimen of this kind, a red twill damask, was adapted at the end of the thirteenth century for the remarkable head-shaped reliquary in Åbo (Turku) Cathedral in Finland. The asymmetric composition with a phoenix and a tortoise (VII, fig. 5) is typically Chinese and is of the kind that revolutionized the art of silk weaving in Italy during the fourteenth century.

One consequence of the Mongol Empire, which still included southern Russia in the early fifteenth century, was the transfer of Chinese craftsmen to its western territories. Silk manufacturing enterprises were developed

VII, fig. 5.   Chinese twill damask, thirteenth century. From a reliquary in
Åbo, Finland

in which Chinese motifs and techniques mingled with alien themes,
especially Mohammedan character, such as fabrics with colourful stripes
embellished with Cufic letters. These are pre-eminently Chinese in their
linear style as well as in the use of flat gilt membrane, but the place of
manufacture is nonetheless considered to have been somewhere in Persia
or even further west (Kühnel). Barbarically ostentatious specimens of such
gold-woven brocades — often called 'heathen pieces' in Scandinavian
records — have been preserved in the ecclesiastical treasuries of Danzig
and Regensburg. Other specimens from the same period, with patterns
more or less resembling (VIII, figs 2, 3), have survived in Verona in the
form of grave clothes for the powerful Cangrande della Scala, who died in
1329.[6]
   The importation of Chinese silk into Europe seems to have been virtually
discontinued after the mid-fourteenth century. There is a very long hiatus,
suggesting that China under the Ming dynasty was not interested in
exporting silk. The purchases which the merchants of European trading

companies managed to make in Canton do not appear to have assumed any great importance until about the seventeenth and eighteenth centuries.

Russian imports of Chinese silk

Much the same kind of silk as reached the western countries by sea had previously been imported to Russia and in this way even reached northern Europe. These silk fabrics had travelled along the caravan route across Asia to Tobolsk, where Chinese merchants exchanged them for furs. In a written report from 1674, which is one of our most important sources of knowledge concerning this textile trade (cf. Chap. xv), a member of a Swedish trade delegation to Russia described the establishment of this commercial exchange: in 1654 the Tsar dispatched an embassy to the Great Khan in Peking, who was in fact the first of the Manchu Emperors. We do not know whether the Chinese silks thus imported were resold to other countries. On the other hand Sweden possesses a large collection of these fabrics as a result of certain historical events which I have treated in detail in my work of 1951 and 1953.

After making himself absolute ruler of the Muscovite Empire, Peter the Great began to reorganize his army on western lines. Among other things this involved the production of banners and standards. Despite this reorganization, Peter was defeated at the battle of Narva and in a series of other encounters, in the course of which the victorious Swedish army captured numerous trophies — the term for weapons and standards captured in battle. These were conscientiously listed and taken to Stockholm, where a large number of them still exist today, some of them on show in the Army Museum. Nearly all these flags are made of Chinese silk damask, a material at once solid and supple and therefore ideal for the *intarsia* technique, mainly employed in Russian banners after 1696. Both the patterns and the loom-widths (approximately 50, 60, sometimes 70 centimetres, suggest that they came from different weaving centres, and they are probably also of varying ages. The oldest patterns are symmetrical or asymmetrical variants of the lotus flower on a winding stem, repeated in the same way as in the thirteenth and fourteenth centuries — in other words in the early Ming style (Pls 54–55). This was made in a characteristic style, drawing leaf shapes and other details to resemble flickering flames — a typical Chinese trait that is particularly common in early Chinese art but also in late Ming porcelain (cf. Pl. 29). A later type of pattern, which a European unacquainted with these circumstances would be inclined to call rococo or eighteenth century, consists of irregularly scattered, naturalistically depicted flower sprigs: chrysanthemums, peonies, apple blossom, cherry branches in blossom, and ripe, bursting pomegranates together with clouds and Taoist or Buddhist symbols of good fortune, etc. These two groups are overwhelmingly predominant in terms of sheer quantity. But the silks which have obviously travelled by the same route also include specimens of quite different categories: on the one hand old-fashioned types of weave, resembling some Han silks, and on the other hand individual hybrid patterns in which one suspects European influences.

In an attempt to gauge the volume of Russian imports of Chinese silk, a rough estimate was made of the amount of silk damask, in metres, used to make only the Russian flags brought to Sweden, which of course represents a mere fraction of what formerly existed. The figure thus obtained was almost 14,000 metres, not including at least some thousand metres of thin, plain silk taffeta used mostly for painted banners, etc.

Turning from this extensive and reliably documented material to the occasional specimens of Chinese silk which came to Europe during the eighteenth century — some of them with a known *terminus ante quem*, others of uncertain age and pedigree — the range of patterns does not really present any novelties, apart from a few with debased patterns of European origin. Chinese manufactured silks are recognisable not only by the motifs and the lively, nervous style of drawing but also by the characteristic quality resulting from the use of *grège* silk for the weft, which is not degummed and is therefore a trifle rigid.

PERSIA

Historical data

Greek and Roman authors praise Persian textile art on account of its great richness and splendour. This reputation had already been established under the Achaemenians, or the Medes, who were conquered in 333 B.C. by Alexander the Great, who in turn (to quote the immortal words of Tertullian) was 'conquered by the costume of the Medes', that is by the sartorial luxury of the Persians.

The rulers of the Sassanian dynasty (226–651) were not to be outdone by their predecessors in the matter of costly textiles, but unfortunately we have no exact information concerning this manufacture. Of all the Arab writers who have so vividly described the flourishing silk manufactories of Susa and the province of Fars, only one, Mashoudi, supplies any indication of the date when these industries might have been founded. But this indication seems to have been misinterpreted, due to a preconceived opinion on the part of the translator. All that Mashoudi really says is that, after winning a victory over the Romans, a King Shapur transferred captive Aramaic or Syrian weavers to his capital of Susa and the province of Fars. Unfortunately Mashoudi does not specify to which victory or which King Shapur he is referring. There were in fact two Sassanian rulers of this name, Shapur I (241–272) and Shapur II (309–379), both of them powerful monarchs, who waged successful wars against the Roman Empire. An Austrian historian of the late nineteenth century, secure in the contemporary assurance of the superiority of Greco-Roman civilization over the Orient, would only consider the latter alternative, because, in his view, the transfer of the Syrian weavers would mark the very inception and foundation of silk weaving in Persia — the implication being that no such art had existed there before. It would seem that, in addition to mis-interpreting Mashoudi's testimony, this man elaborated it to fit in with the contemporary view of history, according to which a cultural infusion of this kind must have come from Greece and Rome, the opposite would be unthinkable!

This, to modern scholars, unnecessary distortion of the Arab evidence continued for a long time to have a perverse influence on the consideration of related problems, above all those concerning the origin of the important material excavated at Antinoë. The historical concepts generally held at the turn of the century were too constricted to allow any general accept-ance of the view first propounded at that time by a small number of scholars headed by the Austrian art historian Joseph Strzygowski and occasioned by the first discoveries made at Antinoë. The conflict of opinions is best illustrated by Strzygowski's polemical essay written in 1901, *Orient oder Rom?*, and von Falke's rejoinder on behalf of the old school: 'It is simply impossible for Sassanian Persia to have surpassed the Greco-Roman sphere of civilization in the matter of creative art'. It is with this fatal misconception of history in mind that one should view and assess von Falke's fundamental error in using the silk finds from Antinoë to conjure up a picture of local production in this town, which for various reasons quite certainly could never have had a silk industry of its own. Moreover von Falke also tried to explain the style of the patterns as the product of an Archaic Greek tradition, resurrected after a lapse of six or seven centuries and transferred from Greece to Egypt. Nowadays it seems hard to understand how this idea could have been accepted and reiterated to the extent that it was. It took a long time for Pfister's methodical analyses and amply-documented arguments to set this attitude aside.[7]

The problem is complicated by the fact that not a single specimen of Sassanian textile art has been preserved within the confines of Iran itself. On the other hand there is in Iran some extremely informative evidence in the grandiose rock monuments extolling the merits of various Sassanian rulers. The most famous of these are the detailed hunting scenes at Taq-i-Bustan, formerly ascribed to the last of the great rulers, Chosroes II (590–628) but possibly a hundred years older. All these figure scenes must originally have been painted in gold and bright colours visible from a great distance. The polychromy has now vanished, but the bas-reliefs to which it was applied have preserved a host of details and patterns. These characteristically stylized animals and ornaments can be recognized as the standard repertoire of Sassanian art when they recur in textile versions, even though some motifs, such as VII, figs 6–7, originally must have depicted metal ornaments sewn onto textile materials and garments, a method of decoration characteristic of ancient Persia and its sphere of influence.

VII, figs 6–7.   Details of the great relief at Taq-i-Bustan, from the costume of the Sassanian king. Iran, sixth century

Sassanian silks

The commencement and the heyday of Sassanian silk manufacture is represented by strips and small pieces of silk, roughly estimated to represent fifty different patterns, mainly used as trimming of the so-called riding-coats from Antinoë, all found in graves approximately datable between A.D. 250 and 500. There are also isolated specimens whose themes and style are evidently Persian, dating either from Sassanian or from post-Sassanian times. These silk fabrics either belong to the oldest European ecclesiastical treasuries (e.g. Sens) or have been discovered by archaeological expeditions in Central Asia. Regarding the latter discoveries mention should be made of a fairly coarse silk with a superbly stylized head of a boar, dating from the seventh century (Pl. 18b).

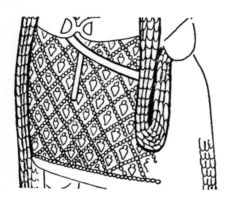

VII, fig. 8.   Detail of the costume of a Parthian King. Statue from the ruined town of Hatra, second century A.D.

It is in the Antinoë material that we encounter, for the first time in the history of textile art, mechanically repeated patterns, that is, evidence of the technical invention called the drawloom, which was dealt with in the preceding chapter. As was stressed there, the new invention occurs in a previously unknown technique, the weft-faced compound weave, the aesthetic aim of which is that of decorative polychromy. The weft entirely dominates the surface of the weave in a uniform texture which is either tabby or twill. To a certain degree this binding resembles tapestry, either of the usual type, or of the three-shed kind. The creation of the new silk technique seems to have been directly inspired, both technically and artistically, by the native tapestry weave.

The reason why twill was sometimes preferred for tapestry weaving was that the weft floats gave a more vivid effect; the lustre of the yarn came out better than in tabby. This was all the more important with silk, the lustrous surface of which needs to be brought out properly. No doubt this was the reason why the silk weavers soon exclusively adopted the twill variant (often termed *samitum*) which then became almost the only silk technique in use until the eleventh century, when other techniques began to emerge. On the other hand, as is shown by the archaeological evidence, the tabby variant was highly suitable for coarser weaves employing wool and other short-fibre yarns (VII, fig. 10).

VII, figs 9–11. Centre motifs from various Sassanian silks. Two Sassanian silk patterns. All from Antinoë, fourth to sixth century

With the weft-faced weaves the patterns are formed by the weft, divided into two or more colours appearing alternately on the face of the weave. As we know, this is aided by the inner warp, which is controlled by means of the drawloom figure harness. In the Sassanian fabrics the pattern motif is reversed as a rule, thus forming a symmetrical figure in which the axis is parallel to the warp. In fact this draw mechanism gave rise to a new type of design, which differs considerably from the fluent shapes of the Chinese designs reminiscent of brush painting. The Persian textile motifs consist of areas of contrasting colours with clearly defined boundaries. As the drawloom, even when fully developed, imposes a certain limitation on the number of main warp ends per pattern repeat, the latter became quite small, especially in the earliest specimens; but later, as the capacity of the comber board increased, the pattern repeats grew wider.

One fairly consistent feature of the Sassanian silks is that the pattern consists of isolated motifs standing out against a plain background. This trait seems to have been rooted in part in the decorative method that long distinguished Persian decorative art, that is the application of felt or gilded leather, or of spangles or other metal ornaments of gold, that were sewn onto a plain woven material. The statue of the Parthian king from Hatra (vii, fig. 8) gives an excellent example of metal decoration. No doubt this splendid but, in the long run, excessively uncomfortable luxury fashion gave rise to textile imitations, first perhaps executed in tapestry.[8] Once the new silk weaving technique had been mastered it was natural for the designs to conform to the traditionally aesthetic preferences that are typical of Persian art from Archaemenid to Sassanian times. Thus certain of the silk patterns from Antinoë are obviously related to the rhomboidal arrangement of the metal ornaments on the costume of the

vii, fig. 12. Fabric of cotton and red wool. Sassanian Iran, seventh century. Fostat

Hatra king. The individual motifs are often of an emblematic kind: swastikas, clubs, spades, hearts (the suits of playing cards), stylized leaves and palmettes. These and other motifs, arranged diagonally (vii, fig. 9), occur frequently in the two-coloured silks which form the majority of the Antinoë finds. Another group, possibly representing a later type and known to us only from Antinoë, consists of elaborate polychrome patterns including human masks, animal protomes, architectural forms, diadem ornaments and various nondescript artefacts which often give the impression of goldsmith's work (vii, figs 10, 11). But complete animals are the commonest of all: ibex, lions, cockerel and other birds, as well as fabulous beasts, and the senmurv (a dog with the tail of a peacock, vii, fig. 6), the griffin (part eagle, part lion) and the Pegasus (a winged horse). As a rule these animals are adorned with fluttering ribbons, jewelled borders and are moreover stylized in the manner of jewellery, on which many of the woven designs were probably based (cf. v, fig. 3).

vii, fig. 13. Lotus palmetto from a Sassanian stone capital

It was probably this final phase of Sassanian design that produced the motif which, directly or in a modified form, was perpetuated over the widest area: a laurel wreath or a circular band adorned with large pearls, originally a diadem with a jewel-encrusted clasp, which was often employed as a frame surrounding a central motif of symbolic significance. Originally the motif might have been a single animal or an animal's head in profile. Later on the frame was enlarged and the animals were arranged in pairs to form a symmetrical group (vii, fig. 12). Eventually they also form part of a complex symmetrical composition depicting the ruler out hunting. But there are also specimens which lack the surrounding frame, the animal figures standing out freely against the background. Less frequently, plant motifs appear, such as the sacred lotus.[9]

Persian silks from post-Sassanian times

The silk workshops in those parts of the Sassanian Empire that were conquered by the Mohammedans probably remained unaffected by political events, and it is evident that they continued for a considerable period to make silk in a purely Sassanian style. This is indicated by the two senmurv silks preserved in Rheims Cathedral which are known, from texts, to have been offerings to the relics of St Remigius.[10] The donor was Archbishop Hincmar, who consecrated the gift in A.D. 852, more than two hundred years after the fall of the Sassanian Empire. The close resemblance of this silk pattern (Pl. 24b) to the same motifs in Taq-i-Bustan (VII, fig. 6) is remarkable. But in recent years Soviet excavations in the Kuban and northern Caucasus have brought large numbers of interesting silks to light, including a complete fur coat which is covered with a silk fabric which is almost identical to that at Rheims.[11] Another design with an octagonal 'medallion' framing a pair of birds (XI, fig. 5) is a rarer but obviously related product of this high quality Persian silk weaving.

Dorothy Shepherd has convincingly associated a group of eleven silk fabrics, some of which have come to light in eastern Turkestan while others are preserved in the treasuries of northern European churches. Among these is a piece with a contemporary inscription in ink revealing the origin and the age of the entire group, namely the country of Sogdiana, with its now better-known capital of Bokhara, in about the eighth century or possibly a hundred years later. The motifs as such are typically Sassanian: either framed pairs of animals or, in two cases, a large rosette, that is, a lotus flower viewed from above. On the other hand the execution is coarse, revealing that the entire group was a provincial product, which was evidently a popular commercial commodity. The representation of this group in the finds from Turkestan mentioned above, indicates a northward branch of the Silk Road, leading to Byzantium.[12]

A more advanced stage in the deformation of similar themes is represented by the Eastern Islamic piece whose highly geometricized animal figures and Cufic inscriptions suggest that it was made in northern Persia about 950 (Pl. 19b). During the Middle Ages it found its way into the church of St Josse, in the north of France, and is now in the Louvre.[13, 14]

Persia after the Mongol conquest

As described earlier, the Asian empire of the Mongols resulted in the westward dissemination of Chinese designs and techniques. Consequently it is hard to determine in particular cases whether a fabric was made in China or considerably further west. On the other hand the traditions of craftsmanship of the Sassanian period and the practice of sericulture

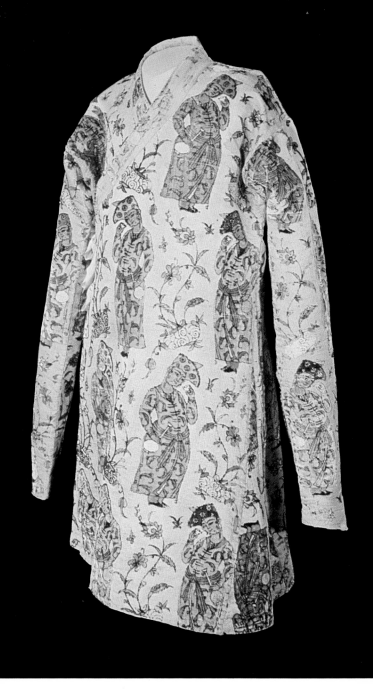

III. *Multicoloured Persian velvet on gold ground. Gift from the Russian Tsar to Queen Christina of Sweden, mid 17th C. (Stockholm, Royal Armoury).*

obviously survived and flourished in Persia. Most of the rulers of the Mongol-Timurid dynasty (1370–1500) and also of the Mohammedan Safavids (1503–1735) who succeeded them were highly cultivated art-lovers who encouraged poetry and the fine arts at their courts, which became scenes of close interaction between all kinds of art. A prominent part was played by textiles, with specialities in silk and velvet weaving as well as in carpet manufacture. Book illumination, which had already attained a high level of sophistication by the fifteenth century, had a profound influence on styles. At the same time many accurately dated specimens still extant represent an important source of knowledge concerning the various decorative arts that distinguished this civilization. It may be added that what is true of Persia under the Safavids also applies to those parts of India then ruled by the Great Mogul.

The predilection for colour and for abstract surface ornament is one of the fundamental characteristics of all Islamic art. This colourful ornamentation appears in an endless variety of materials and techniques — glazed tiles or ceramic panels, mosaics of various materials for floors and walls, roofs and façades — as well as all kinds of textiles. Almost all these techniques employ the same repertoire of motifs, often in uniformly repeated pattern units corresponding to the mechanically produced 'pattern repeat' of a woven fabric, although this repetition was not dictated by specifically technical considerations. This tradition of style endowed the art of silk weaving with pattern themes which have long proved adaptable to varying technical execution. These patterns, based primarily on diagonal frames or networks of vines, etc., were originally descended from Chinese art but eventually took on a universal and fairly timeless character (cf. VIII, figs 1–2).

At the same time as this mode of composition remained current, a completely different trend, peculiar to Persian art, developed within Safavid silk weaving. This new style is a direct application of the book painters' illustrations of epic and legendary themes: hunting scenes depicting horsemen and wild beasts or people set in romantically flowering gardens. Figure patterns were often executed in velvet, using a special technique whereby the figures stand out in differently coloured pile areas against a plain ground, often woven with gold. The famous Persian coat in the Swedish Royal Armoury (colour plate 3) is one of the few well-preserved examples of this unique Safavid method. Here the colours also alternate vertically giving a quite astonishing effect which was achieved by means of alternative pile warps of different colours between which the weaver could alternate. Unfortunately the Persian silk dyers of this period were less skilful than the weavers, with the unfortunate result that most of the surviving specimens of this technique have now faded to a dull brownish tonality that is far from the original beauty of these masterpieces.

Another equally impressive speciality is doublecloth, the same binding type as in the Scandinavian woollens from the Middle Ages (Pls 86–87b) the silks being meticulously executed with additional gold brocading. Triple cloth is a related product consisting of three differently coloured layers. In addition to these two techniques there were variants of the large group called 'lampas', either weft-faced throughout or various types with contrasting textures of warp satin and weft-structured weaves. Additional brocading or floating wefts may also occur.

VII, fig. 14.   Flower motif from a Persian silk, seventeenth century

The profound influence of book painting on the pictorial patterns of textile art is obvious. But also the floral patterns comprising the greater part of the Safavid silk manufacture were evidently influenced by the style of drawing of the miniature painters with their feeling for nature. Unlike most Chinese floral patterns, with their cut twigs scattered in various directions, the Persian garden flowers, iris, tulip, lily, hyacinth, carnation, etc., are nearly always shown as growing plants or groups of plants (VII, fig. 14). The vertical direction of growth is also stressed in a botanic-ally accurate manner. The detached single motifs often have a clearly defined shape that is repeated regularly and spaciously. Such designs were in general use but are particulary characteristic of silk patterns. Greatly simplified and with small motifs of the kind also encountered in Indian miniatures, they are sometimes reminiscent of stamped patterns, that is, cotton prints (see further in Chapter XII). This is particularly true of silk fabrics with freely arranged patterns, but the naturalistic style of painting, featuring figures and above all flowers, also took its place within the enclosing frames that had been handed down by earlier generations. One specimen reliably documented to the 1680s shows a flowering rose bush attracting flying bees, in a pointed oval area bounded by long narrow leaves (Pl. 57b).

BYZANTIUM AND ISLAM

Historical data

The luxury and splendour of an oriental court has been described in superlatives, but these cannot possibly convey the reality of it — the ruler himself, the accoutrements of his horse, the decoration of his palace apartments or the costumes worn by his courtiers. Courtiers were in fact issued with costumes as part of their wages, and the costliness or otherwise of the garments would be proportional to the status and prerogatives of the wearer. To the ruler all this ostentation was a means of asserting his own power. Consequently silk for artistic products, in common with gold and precious stones, became indispensable. In the power politics of the times, an ample supply of these articles therefore played much the same role as, say, oil and steel today. Then as now, a blockade could provoke a war. All this applies above all to the Great King and the Sassanian Empire, but similar rules also came to apply at the Mohammedan courts and at the court of the Emperor of Byzantium.

In Byzantium the acquisition of silk was an extremely difficult problem which caused enormous amounts of money to leave the country. To solve this problem, the Emperor Justinian (527–565) took an important initiative. His historian Procopius tells us that the Emperor engaged two monks (evidently of Indo-Persian extraction), who in 522 were sent to China to obtain the eggs of the silkworm and learn as much as possible concerning sericulture. The two monks did in fact contrive to smuggle some eggs out of the country, hiding them in their hollow staves, which were doubtless made of bamboo, and they brought them safely back to Byzantium, where they became the foundation of occidental sericulture.

It must have taken a long time for the Byzantine production to attain significant proportions. The silk weavers of Constantinople long remained dependent on the Chinese raw material, which came to them by one of the northern ramifications of the Silk Road, so far-off that Persia could not block it. The Islamic princes were better situated in this respect. When the Arabs conquered the Sassanian Empire they inherited a flourishing textile industry, and probably also an advanced sericulture, as well as the direct trade routes with China. Syria, which had long had an extensive production of textiles, was also part of the Islamic world. The westward advance of Islam carried with it both sericulture and craftsmanship, with the result that the Mohammedan court workshops became important centres of production and formed the basis of widespread trading activities.

In his instructive study on textile industry and trade in the Byzantine Empire R. S. Lopez refers to the detailed regulations of the degrees of sartorial luxury appropriate to each office of state as a counterpart of the salary grades of our own times. He terms the system a 'hierarchy of costume'. It was a pyramid-shaped organization which in the hands of an energetic Emperor could be made an important power factor. To secure this instrument of power, the Emperor was anxious at all costs to develop a system of production that was free from competition. The supply of raw materials was one side of the matter, and Procopius's narrative shows the importance attached to it. Unfortunately no chronicler has recorded where the Imperial workshops recruited their first craftsmen, but there can hardly be any doubt that they came from Syria or Persia. Despite strict control, the first Imperial silk weavers occupied a privileged position which, moreover, was hereditary. Lopez refers in this connexion to an 'Aristocracy of Labour'. Later, working conditions became more rigorous, with the result that many skilled craftsmen fled back to their native countries. Justinian concentrated both manufacture and trade within the capital so as to ensure effective control. A guild organization gradually evolved which was codified in *The Book of the Prefect*. Some years later (in 912) this was followed by the *Book of Ceremonies*, which gives a detailed description of the clothing appropriate to different ranks. The principal garment was a coat, the *scaramangion*, which was descended from the Persian horseman's caftan. Originally this was a purely practical garment, especially created for a cold climate, but of the same cut as the luxury garment of the Roman-Byzantine officials, sometimes called a riding-coat, of which several examples have been found in the necropolis of Antinoë.

The Imperial workshops were divided into different specialized trades, dyers of purple, weavers of different kinds, tailors, etc. There must have been a great deal of stockpiling, first and foremost to provide for regular distributions to the ministers of state, but also for the less predictable occasions when presents had to be given to visiting envoys or foreign potentates. Whereas the gentlemen had to take care to dress in keeping with their rank, the ladies were free to dress themselves as lavishly as they pleased, so long as they bought the material from the Imperial manufactories. At first the latter had a permanent exhibition building, 'The House of Lamps', that was illuminated at night, but after this building had been set alight during a rebellion the exhibition was transferred to a safer place within the Imperial Palace precincts.

Constantinople was very much the private city of the Byzantines. It was strictly segregated from the rest of the country and difficult of access for foreigners, whose movements were closely circumscribed. Infringements were severely punished. Strangers were only allowed to buy cheap fabrics, which meant fabrics of narrow loom-width, and their costume had to be plain enough to distinguish them from the Byzantines. The appearance of the latter is described by Benjamin of Tudela, a Jewish merchant from Spain who visited Constantinople in the twelfth century. 'All the people look like princes. The Second Rome is a glittering city of miracles. Everybody is dressed in silk, purple and gold.'

To be able to enter this city at all, foreign merchants had to put up in *mitata* outside the city boundary, where they were not allowed to stay for more than three months without special permission. Some of them were not even allowed to set foot in the capital. This was the case with the bearded Bulgars, called *barbati*, in their furred clothes. Since, however, their linen fabrics were needed for the lining of the silk coats, a special *mitata* was provided for them in Salonika. But there was one important exception to the general and rigorous rule. The Syrian merchants were allowed to stay almost as long as they pleased and they were allowed to sell all kinds of merchandise: spices, perfumes, Syrian silks and even ready-made clothing. Furthermore, the sale of their goods was guaranteed in advance by the Emperor. These privileges can only have meant that the clothing of the Byzantine court was to a great extent made from Syrian textiles; the court was incapable of meeting the great demand for materials without the Syrian products which were probably superior to most of the local silk fabrics. At all events, they were certainly far better than those produced by the private workshops out in the country.

All these circumstances provide an indication of the diversity that could be seen in the Byzantine capital and also among the coats and *pallia* (very precious silks of large width) that were sometimes presented to important visitors. All this emphasizes the difficulty of determining, in particular cases, where a special kind of textile was manufactured, whether in the capital or somewhere in Syria. Silk manufacture in Byzantium was not concerned with exportation. On the contrary, the export of products from the Imperial workshops was strictly prohibited. But there were loopholes. The following story about Bishop Luitpold of Cremona illustrates conditions in this period, and also the disdain shown by the Byzantines towards the 'barbarous' westerners. When Bishop Luitpold

VII, fig. 15.   Emperor Nicephoros Botaniates
between courtiers. Contemporary MS, *c.*1080

visited Constantinople in 968 as the envoy of Otto the Great, King of Germany and Holy Roman Emperor, he was allowed to purchase some precious silks from the Court manufactory. But when he reached the frontier on his way home, the silks were confiscated by the Byzantine customs officers, who scolded him: 'You Italians, Saxons, Franks, Bavarians . . . are unworthy to wear such fabrics. Should not the most exalted of all peoples also have the finest clothes?' The bishop assured them that the Byzantine Emperor himself had asked him to select the costliest fabrics for the church of Cremona, but when even this did not help he lost his temper and boasted: 'In Germany such fabrics are worn by beggars and shepherds.' When his astonished Greek questioner asked where they were able to get such fabrics, the bishop replied: 'From the merchants of Venice and Amalfi.'

But the power of Constantinople was already weakening. The Venetian fleet controlled the Mediterranean and had forced the Emperor to recognize Venice as an independent 'Byzantine city' entitled to negotiate on behalf of the capital with Italian princes and with Charlemagne. By the same token the Venetians were enabled to purchase Byzantine silks. From the end of the eleventh century, merchants from Venice and Amalfi were able to establish their own *fondachi* in Constantinople, as they had already done in other major ports of the Mediterranean. A *fondaco* corresponded to the national trading depots, containing housing accommodation as well as warehouses and sales premises, of the type used both at this time and later on by German and other northern European merchants and commonly termed by them *Hof*. One such former establishment was the famous *Bryggen* which still exists in Bergen in Norway. Another is referred to in Kihlburger's report from Russia (Chap. XIV). Significantly enough, the word *fondaco*, which is the term most generally used in the Mediterranean, is of Arabic origin.

Silks from Byzantium and Islam

Historical data from the Byzantine and Islamic worlds show quite clearly that the Islamic silk production was extraordinarily extensive. There is also the abundant written evidence published by R. B. Serjeant of a lively internal trade in all directions within the enormous Mohammedan domain, from Samarkand in the east to Spain in the west. The instances referred to above of the importation of Syrian textiles to Constantinople are described by Monneret de Villard and underline the importance of the Islamic output.

All that now remains of these innumerable products are a small number of silk fabrics, concerning the detailed origin of which we are as a rule ignorant. Most of them are badly-damaged fragments in some cases finds in church treasuries in Europe which have survived in the form of relic covers, and very seldom as nearly complete pieces. Only in exceptional cases are there inscriptions, woven into the fabric or sewn onto them, or historical data of some other kind furnishing reliable indications of their age. Indications in the place of origin are still less common. We are never likely to gain a definite idea of how certain famous manufactories worked or what they produced, for there were innumerable centres involved during a period of four or five centuries. An account such as this can only include a very brief mention of a few crucial examples, together with some general observations. It should also be emphasized that many of the attributions made here differ from those proposed in certain manuals or general studies that have been published previously.

The first thing to notice is that the gradually divergent branches of silk manufacturing, from the technical as well as from the artistic viewpoint, are mostly descended from the Sassanian court production, the last phase of which (roundels with animal motifs) must have achieved tremendous popularity. Mention has already been made of the Chinese T'ang imitations. An attempt to distinguish between what was made in Iran after the Sassanian dynasty and Byzantine imitations can also give rise to controversial problems. In the peripheral regions of the western world, for instance in old Scandinavian folk art, the influence of this style was longlasting. When a direct change of style began to appear in the Islamic silk manufacture it was primarily concerned with the manner of drawing and with the introduction of Cufic script as a decorative element: a detailed but abstract calligraphic style becomes more and more noticeable side by side with older basic themes (Pls 25–27). It is not until later that completely new motifs appear. In other fields of Mohammedan art (ceramics, crafts, metalwork, decorative sculpture in various sizes, etc.), one can often discern geographically defined schools which have been located in either the eastern or the western half of the Islamic world. But where silk weaving is concerned it is more difficult to effect any corresponding division in the present state of research.

In the case of silks manufactured in Byzantium itself there is a great deal of reliable evidence, either in the form of woven monograms incorporated in the pattern or woven inscriptions quoting names, making it possible not only to attribute the item to the Imperial workshops but also in many cases to determine the date of manufacture. The oldest specimen which has come down to us (VII, fig. 16) with a geometrical lattice pattern displays a monogram referring to the Emperor Heraclius (610–641). Similar small-patterned fabrics were reproduced in mosaics, for example in San Vitale at Ravenna (*c.* A.D. 540). The main group of identifiable Imperial products comes from the period between *c.* 900 and 1050, many of the items being securely dated. It is characteristic of these products that they closely resemble Sassanian models in terms of themes and general style (Pls 22–24), although the stylization is more extreme and unrealistic. They are also made on a larger scale than the known Sassanian fabrics, which to some extent results from the coarser quality. The Oriental, or rather Iranian influence that becomes particularly apparent under the Macedonian dynasty (867–1059) is to be seen as a manifestation of the autocratic ideology fostered by the Sassanian rulers and by their Mohammedan successors. This was a style of great decorative force, pre-eminently suited to depicting the eagle, the Imperial symbol above all others. Plates 22 and 23a show a genuine Byzantine 'Imperial fabric' and a provincial imitation. The latter, in Odense Cathedral, is supposed to have been donated to the shrine of Knut the Pious in 1101 by his widow, Queen Ethele, then married to the Prince of Apulia. This style was in fact a foreign element, quite different from the art which had formerly reigned supreme in the capital of East Rome, namely classical Greek art with its

vii, fig. 16. Byzantine samitum silk with the monogram of the Emperor Heraclius, A.D. 610–641

strong feeling for realistic features. A few mosaic pavements in the Imperial Palace are virtually all that remains of this art in Byzantium at the present time. But outside the city of Byzantium, within the far-flung boundaries of the former East Roman Empire, a number of mosaics, illuminated manuscripts and paintings on a grander scale have been preserved which provide living evidence of the stylistic development that took place before art had begun to set in the rigid Byzantine style that became established under the Macedonian dynasty (867–1028). These extra-Byzantine testimonies of the Grecian era of East Rome permit us to draw on Egypt for comparative material, above all in the form of tapestry woven textiles from late antiquity (cf. Chap. v), which employ impressionistic methods to blend colours and model forms with a sculptural effect, in a manner which is diametrically opposed to the unshaded ('flat') and mutually contrasting colours of the Sassanian style.

There are some well-known silk fabrics which, probably correctly, have been referred to in the literature of the subject as having been manufactured in Constantinople. One of the most important of these, now belonging to the *Musée des Tissus* in Lyons, is shown in Plate 20. It is recorded to be a gift of the French King Pepin the Short, who visited the monastery of Mozac in the Auvergne in 761. The composition featuring a crowned horseman hunting a lion, symmetrically repeated and with the entire figure scene enclosed in a large medallion, originally some 90 centimetres high, doubtless represents a Byzantine Emperor (a *basileus*).[15]

Another specimen in the spirit of classical Greece, though artistically inferior to the silk fabric from Mozac, is the frequently illustrated piece from *Sancta Sanctorum* (the ancient papal collection in the Vatican) depicting the Annunciation and the Nativity. Each group of figures is surrounded by a richly ornamented frame. The whole work is executed in several colours standing out against a bright red background. This piece was formerly attributed to fifth- or sixth-century Alexandria, but many recent scholars have maintained that it was made in Byzantium probably towards the ninth century. Both these silk fabrics are technical masterpieces executed with the utmost precision after models which one imagines were painted with the finest of brushes. In the case of the *Sancta Sanctorum* piece one is inclined to add that it is unfortunately done without realizing the need for stylization in order to transpose with artistic effect the naturalistic scene into a textile composition. The figural scene is too detailed for this technique and would have needed a larger scale and a freer technique, for example tapestry.

The *Sancta Sanctorum* collection contains, among other things, two more silks which are useful for purposes of comparison but which also serve to show how difficult it is to speak with any certainty concerning the place of manufacture. In both cases the motif as such is typically Iranian: birds in profile, a duck and a cock, the latter with a halo, both adorned with jewel-encrusted necklaces and standing on a pedestal, which suggests models executed in goldsmith's work. In one instance (the duck) the outline is deformed, but the silhouette effect and the division of the body into contrasted colour areas bears unmistakable witness to the Iranian sense of style. The fabric may have been woven in Persia but in a second-class workshop or in the post-Sassanian period.

The 'cock silk' (Pl. 17), so often reproduced in the literature on the subject, betrays the unmistakable influence of the impressionistic tapestry technique of late antiquity. The highly irregular execution bears witness to constant improvisations. With its freshness of colour, this specimen provides a charming and instructive example of an attempt to reconcile contradictory artistic styles. It is not impossible that the loom concerned was located in Constantinople, but if so the workshop was a fairly modest one and existed before the time (c. 900) when the court workshops, in emulation of Sassanian prototypes, began to produce the famous *pallia* with the large heraldic animals, which were mentioned above.

To sum up the Sassanian textile style was strikingly longlived. Even at the end of the eleventh century, a high-ranking Byzantine courtier would still have a full-length coat made of this kind of fabric, the pattern being so large that the length would only accommodate three medallions (VII, fig. 15). And as late as the fourteenth century the Emperor Alexius V was portrayed wearing a coat with even larger animal medallions. Understandably enough, the multicoloured silk fabrics with their exciting animal themes achieved a tremendously widespread currency and long retained their popularity, but this led to repetitions and local imitations of progressively inferior or coarsened quality, which in turn resulted in deformation of the original design. One striking result of this process is the transformation of the round medallion into a square or an octagon; the latter form, being more amenable to weaving, was unanimously adopted by Oriental as well as Scandinavian folk art (Pls 85a, 87b, 88 and 95b).

Towards the end of the tenth century there appeared, side by side with the polychrome style, which was still very much in favour, a different and, for some time, quite distinct type with patterns in one colour only. These monochrome silks occur in three different technical variants of type D2. Besides completely plain weft twills, there are two patterned types. One of them has been termed 'pseudo-damask' on account of a certain resemblance to genuine damask: apart from the ordinary glossy, weft-faced effect, it also has lustreless areas reminiscent of tabby (Pl. 23b). The second type has been called 'incised silks' (synonymous with the German term *Ritz-Stoff*) on account of the deep grooves in the warp direction, giving a fine pattern of lines (Pl. 30). The incised silks which are known to us from a number of liturgical vestments are historically associated with certain prominent personages in Germany from the period between the mid-tenth and the mid-eleventh century. These patterns have nothing in common with the Persian-Byzantine repertoire of motifs which we have hitherto been dealing with, but are almost invariably composed of abstract plant forms. A particularly characteristic feature is the division of the surface into ogival compartments. In her exhaustive publication on the funeral clothing of Pope Clement II, where the whole of this group of textile material is discussed, Sigrid Müller-Christensen presents the opinion that the ornamentation used in the textile patterns is very much related to decorations in Syrian architecture, for example, that of the Palace of Sammara. To this she adds the important fact that some of these mono-chrome and consistently high-class silks are inwoven with Arabic inscrip-tions, showing quite clearly that they were made in Mohammedan territory, in these particular cases quite certainly in Syria. The reader will recall the favoured status enjoyed by the Syrian merchants in the Byzantine capital which was mentioned on p. 129.

Western Islam

Though geographically outside Asia the western parts of Islam, Spain and North Africa may reasonably be treated in succession to the main area in the east. The Arabs, or the Moors, as they were known here, are said to have introduced sericulture in Spain soon after their conquest of that country, with the result that Almeria was already a silk-weaving town in the ninth century. There is a great deal to suggest that for a considerable period Moorish silk products were chiefly *tiraz*, that is, veil-like fabrics with tapestry borders in Cufic, a particular form of Arabic script. The oldest known specimen has an inscription of this kind referring to the Caliph of Cordoba who reigned between 976–1009.

In the course of her comprehensive researches into Islamic textile art, Dorothy Shepherd has studied some draw-loom woven silks which must undoubtedly have been produced in Spain. The name of a Moorish ruler woven into one specimen dates it to the period between 1107 and 1143. As can be seen from Pl. 25, the general composition is of Sassanian origin, while the stylization and the execution of the details bear the unmistak-able hallmark of Mohammedan art but it is quite different from other contemporary textiles.

A thoroughly Islamic design, and one of the finest products of this branch of art, is to be seen in the chasuble of Saint-Sernin in Toulouse

(Pl. 26), a masterly composition of paired peacocks whose tail-feathers form the apex of a Moorish ogee arch while their podium is embellished with a Cufic inscription ('supreme blessing'). There is also a series of small animals surrounding a tree of life shaped like a candelabra. All this stands out in bright colours — but only two colours in the same horizontal row — against a blue-black background.[16] The detail reproduced in Pl. 28a is taken from another liturgical vestment, now in the Archiepiscopal Museum in Utrecht. Here too we see rows of paired peacocks together with stylized details standing out alternately in red, yellow and green against a dark blue ground. This fabric was probably woven in the early twelfth century — whether in the eastern or western region of the Islamic world may for the time being be left an open question. Its resemblance to the, probably Syrian, silk found in an Egyptian tomb, shown in the same plate, speaks in favour of the east.

Not far from the ancient capital of Burgos in northern Spain is *Las Huelgas*, 'the Pantheon of Castile', where between 1181 and 1375 no less than thirty eight persons of royal birth were buried, each enclosed in a lavish coffin and dressed according to his or her rank. Many of the textiles are in a relatively fair state of preservation. One surprising fact, bearing in mind the mortal enmity between Christian Castile and the Mohammedan Moors, is that these funerary accessories — the many textiles as well as the rich stucco decorations in the burial chapel, show influences of Moorish art, indicating that Moorish skills were indispensable, even here. A short enumeration of the main textile categories represented in the catalogue of Gomez Moreno follows. Among the woven fabrics are a number of veils with tapestry borders, mostly of silk and gold thread, a typical Islamic technique. Among the draw-loom fabrics are silks of a distinctive type which seems to be a Spanish speciality: 'double-faced weft weaves' (D3) with only one warp system of very thin thread and shiny, untwisted silk wefts forming lozenges or other composite twill effects, sometimes combined with single ornaments or emblems. Of the weft-faced compound weave there are two different types: the common all-silk quality sometimes in-woven with gold, characterized by very small pattern repeats often depicting heraldic motifs such as the arms of Castile but also geometric or abstract patterns. In contrast to these fabrics there are a few specimens with large designs of paired animals in roundels with Cufic inscriptions, which are executed in the kind of weft-faced compound twill in which the main warp is of coarse linen (cf. below). Among the many other textiles may be mentioned gold brocaded tablet-woven bands, innumerable specimens of very fine pattern knitting as well as cross-stitch embroideries, the latter two categories mostly displaying heraldic patterns. It is worth mentioning in this context that, under the heading 'Spanish Silks', the papal inventory of 1295 describes patterns with heraldic motifs which seem to resemble the nearly contemporary specimens still preserved in *Las Huelgas*.

The generally anti-pictorial attitude of Mohammedan art continued to make itself felt after 1492, when the allied kingdoms of Castile and Aragon succeeded in pushing the Moors southward, thus expelling some of them to North Africa (Morocco), where for centuries to come the Moors continued to weave multicoloured silks in the so-called Mudejar style, which is characterized by polygonal patterns of stars and interlace ornaments together with arabesque borders and Cufic lettering. Between the fourteenth and sixteenth centuries there was an extensive commerce between certain towns on the Spanish Mediterranean coast and the Italian trading cities, which favoured mutual influence. For example, we know of Spanish velvets which, except for minor details, are exact imitations of ordinary fifteenth-century Italian fabrics (cf. below, p. 151). During the sixteenth century as well, there seems to have been a great deal of silk weaving in Spain, but recent Spanish research (Nino y Mas) has revealed a definite decline during the century that followed. At the same time, however, Spain continued to be an important producer of raw silk.

Asia Minor

The Seljuks were the first of the nomad tribes of Turkestan to advance west. Eventually they subjugated Asia Minor, where in about 1100 they founded the great kingdom of Rum with its capital, Konia. In about 1300 this state was forced to capitulate to another Turkish tribe, the Ottomans. They soon expanded their empire to include the Balkan peninsula and in 1453 they made Constantinople their capital. The Ottoman dynasty remained in power until 1924. Initially the invaders adopted the predominant art styles of the countries they conquered. It was not until the fifteenth century that this area began to develop anything that can be classed as specifically Turkish art.

All the Turkish silk manufactories were situated in Asia Minor, the oldest of them in Bursa, the ancient capital of the Ottomans. Silk production was important because, here, as at other Oriental courts, clothing etc.

was distributed on a very large scale to court functionaries as well as to prominent foreigners. As a result of the close political contacts existing between the Swedish crown and the Sublime Porte, especially in the seventeenth century, many precious Turkish textiles found their way to Sweden where many of them were made up into ecclesiastical vestments and given to churches. At the Turkish court the costumes which had belonged to each Sultan were carefully preserved and deposited in the Topkapu Serai. These rich collections have recently been arranged in an exemplary manner and are now accessible for study.[17]

VII, fig. 17. Motif from a Turkish silk and gold cloth, fifteenth to sixteenth century

The Turkish style of silk weaving is pre-eminently decorative. The designers were influenced by both Persia and Italy, especially Venice and Genoa, at the same time as they evolved a style of their own. This style is distinguished by a few fresh colours, well-dyed, with a predominance of cherry red, hyacinth blue, white and gold. The Persian influence is apparent above all in the form of naturalistically drawn flowers: tulips, hyacinths and carnations, often depicted in profile. There also occur certain heraldic emblems, for example, the crescent, the so-called tiger stripes and the three crystal balls supposed to have been Timur's device, together with a characteristic abstract ornamentation that may be Seljuk in origin. The technique used in the best products may be termed a kind of 'lampas' (D6) based on a clear contrast between warp satin and weft effects. There are several superb examples of this kind (Pl. 59). Concerning some of them, opinions divide fairly evenly between the following attributions: Turkish work influenced by Venice, or Venetian work influenced by Turkey, examples which testify to mutual influence, particularly in the seventeenth century. One common Turkish technique, which might have been relatively cheap, is a weft-faced weave consisting of a thin, well-spaced warp and very thick and loose wefts in two, or occasionally three, alternating colours. Velvet, often with very large, debased pomegranate patterns, occurs frequently but is, technically speaking, of a rather low quality, and often mixed with cotton.

VIII *Silk Weaving in Europe*

The origins of the Italian silk industry go back to the centuries-old Levantine trade. As we have already seen, a number of Italian towns had had trading depots of their own in the ports of the eastern Mediterranean from which they could keep an eye on the local productions and also purchase commodities brought in by the caravans from places further afield. The luxury commodities thus obtained, spices, incense, precious stones and, above all, grège silk and silk fabrics, were sent by sea to Italian and other western Mediterranean ports, including Marseilles, from whence they were carried further north. In France these fabrics were commonly termed *étoffes d'outre mer*.[1]

As a result of the crusades, however, political conditions became progressively more unstable and, accordingly, less favourable to peaceful trading. The East Roman Empire steadily declined, and in 1203 Constantinople was sacked by the crusaders. Meantime the Italian merchants had been prudent enough to start similar industries in their own country. These native enterprises were headed by Lucca, the first town to admit skilled Saracen craftsmen, then by Venice, soon Genoa, Milan, Florence and other towns of northern Italy followed the pioneers in this respect.

The paramount role formerly ascribed to Sicily has been reduced considerably in the light of the researches of von Falke, who established that most of the surviving silk fabrics formerly attributed to Sicilian workshops must have been made in Lucca or Venice. Since then, the Italian historian Monneret de Villard has shown that developed silk weaving can only have existed in Sicily on a very limited scale and that Sicilian textile art was above all concerned with embroidery and *tiraz*, that is, thin, veil-like weaves with inscribed borders or decorative compositions mostly done in tapestry technique. A very rich example of this art is shown in Pl. 5, now forming part of the lining of the famous coronation mantle in Vienna.

Historical data

In the course of the thirteenth and fourteenth centuries, many of the Italian trading republics succeeded in establishing a native silk industry that marked the inauguration of a new and unique era. Thanks to skilful and determined co-ordination of the various stages of production and commercial organization, the Italians acquired a paramount status that was to remain unassailed for almost four hundred years, until they began to meet with serious competition from the French in the mid-seventeenth century. Nevertheless, intense rivalry existed between the different towns. At the same time as they protected their own specialities against imitation, they used all the means at their disposal to obtain skilled workers and trade secrets from elsewhere. But in spite of these methods, or rather because of them, the different Italian manufactures came to resemble one another more and more closely as time went on. With only a few exceptions it is almost impossible to decide where a given fabric might have been produced. But the all-pervading, specifically Italian character, realistically observed details, a clear, almost plastically firm line and an unfailing soundness of quality, remained practically unaltered through the centuries.

The Italian silk industry played a prominent part in the trade with northern Europe during the Middle Ages and the sixteenth century and well into the seventeenth century as well. The various Italian towns had their own permanent representatives in the major commercial cities of Europe, one of the most important of these towns being the Flemish port of Bruges, by virtue of its links with the Hanseatic League, which mainly covered the northern market. Bruges and Lübeck were the main points of departure for the export of fine Italian fabrics to Scandinavia, where a large number of medieval specimens have survived, mostly preserved in Swedish churches.

A document from this very significant environment provides a first-class illustration of the social and political role of textile art at the time. The writer is referring to the procession of foreign merchants who escorted Duke Charles the Bold on the occasion of his ceremonial entry into Bruges in 1468. The Italian contingent is described as follows:

First rode the Venetians, wearing costumes of red velvet. Then came the Florentines, with an advance guard of sixty torch-bearers clad in blue and and pages clad in cloth of silver and with short cloaks of red velvet. The horses wore covers of white silk with borders of blue velvet and the merchants themselves were dressed in black silk damask with red cloaks. Their leader, the powerful Tommaso Portinari, was as finely arrayed as the Duke himself!

After reading this account and others like it, one can well understand the proclivity shown by the Netherlands painters, led by the van Eyck brothers and Hans Memling, for depicting both sacred and secular persons dressed in the most sumptuous Italian fabrics mainly showing so-called pomegranate patterns: it was this practice that first gave rise to the quite erroneous supposition that these fabrics had been manufactured in the Netherlands (J. Kalf).

The Development of Design

The development of Italian silk weaving is multifarious, due probably to internal competition. The technical advances and the new types of weave have already been dealt with (in Chap. vi) and we shall therefore be able to dispense with detailed descriptions. Our knowledge of the leading textile art of this period is founded on an invaluable source material in the form of ecclesiastical inventories. The most detailed of these concern the papal treasury, one dating from 1295 and a later one from 1361 and there are similar documents from other large churches in various countries.[2] The descriptions found in the papal inventories are distinguished by their precision and by an impressive degree of expert knowledge concerning origins and other matters, and also by a concise terminology. All this enables us to match many surviving fabrics with the descriptions given.

The 1295 inventory employs straigthforward headings which indicate either the nature of the articles described, or the origin of the materials. The latter group includes the following headings: *panni tartarici* (Tartar silk), which, judging by the descriptions, would seem to have been both Chinese and Persian (viii, figs 2–3), *panni de Romania* (the contemporary name for the Byzantine Empire), possibly resembling viii, fig. 1, and *panni hispanici* (Spanish). But the heading *panni lucani*, fabrics from Lucca, also includes a Venetian fabric (one only!) which may reflect the relative status of the two foremost Italian industries of that time. Both of them frequently occur in the detailed descriptions of the articles. The patterns of the Italian silks are for the most part described as consisting of griffins, lions, birds or other ferocious animals in roundels (viii, fig. 1), *in rotis* being the term often employed. These are the same kind of patterns as were found in the Byzantine fabrics, which were there called either *panni* or *hexamiti* (samitum, D2). On the other hand the technique used for the Italian silk fabrics was often called 'diasper', a kind of 'lampas' (D5), which appears as a new Italian speciality, though it may originally have been a Saracen (Syrian-Islamic) invention. The 'diasper' (Lat. *pannus diasperatus*) was an all-silk fabric described either as monochrome or two-coloured, in either case with certain details, such as heads and feet, brocaded with gold.

We can recognize the same execution in a type of pattern without any kind of framework. This type of design is best described with direct reference to existing specimens (Pl. 35). The strikingly large pattern repeats invariably comprise two different kinds of animals — for example, a peacock, a gazelle or a long-tailed dragon or 'basilisk', — arranged in pairs and often as if they were standing on the edge of an onion-shaped plaque consisting of several concentric borders of Arabic ornaments thus showing the origin of the design. In Latin this motiv is called *pina* (pine-cone).

VIII, fig. 1.   Monochrome silk, Byzantine-Syrian area, eleventh century

It was Otto von Falke who first identified the term *diasprum* with the combination of pattern and weave reproduced in Pl. 35a. Exactly the same type of pattern, however, also occurs in a variant which contains less silk: one of the weft systems is replaced with a *filé* consisting of gilded or silvered membrane strips wound around a core of linen or hemp. Oddly enough, three different specimens of this kind of fabric have survived in Uppsala Cathedral, all reliably dated to before 1293 and 1295. Two of them (Pls 35b, 36) form part of a magnificent cope, which Archbishop Nicolas Alloni brought home in 1295 from Anagni where he had been consecrated by Pope Boniface VIII. The other piece, with silver membrane on a red ground, forms the main part of a rectangular cover still preserved in the reliquary of St Erik. Concerning this item the *Miraculae Sancti Erici* records that in 1293 *unum pretiosum baldechinum* was donated to the shrine of the martyr King in thanksgiving for a miraculous cure. Thanks to this document, the *baudekin* fabric in the shrine of St Erik seems to provide full evidence of the exact significance of the term, or at least its significance at that date. The same word (*baldakin* etc.) is quite often recorded in Scandinavian documents from the Middle Ages, for Sweden about fifty times between 1270–1346. Originally it must have denoted a fabric from Baghdad (It. *Baldacco*), but later on a special kind of fabric made in Italy — which also might have been termed 'half-silk'.

VIII, figs 2–3. Chinese silks with lotus designs, symmetrical and asymmetrical.
From about 1300

The above leads into a complex of problems which have been dealt with by Donald King. The first result of his investigations is the convincing evidence of a Venetian origin for the famous retable belonging to Regensburg Cathedral, donated by Bishop Heinrich von Rotteneck (1277–96). It is a large figural representation centred around the Crucifix group which is displayed on a surface of 125 by 265 centimetres, a free design executed in weft-faced compound twill, an all-silk weave brocaded with metallic gold, most of which has now worn off. It is a masterpiece in all respects (note the details in Pl. 31).[3] O. von Falke's arguments concerning this piece had run round in a circle. He considered that the retable had been made in Regensburg, and supposed also (erroneously) that the weave was a half-silk comparable to certain fabrics (of which a great number are known from northern and central Europe) which are indeed half-silks (weft-faced twills with a main warp of flax or hemp). Through this conclusion, the latter type came to be termed 'Regensburg cloths' (*Regensburger Stoffe*) which is certainly wrong. Later on a Spanish attribution was put forward (Shepherd 1951), but this has also been questioned. By a thorough study of the rich contemporary inventories and by comparing them to the Regensburg masterpiece, Donald King reached the conclusion that woven figure subjects were a Venetian speciality. This seems very probable indeed. On the other hand, it is doubtful whether every figured half-silk in weft-faced compound weave which is still extant was necessarily made in Venice. It also seems wise to hesitate before making general rules about the term *baudekin*, used in connexion with some of the descriptions. With regard to Donald King's quotation from the French royal account of 1318, *draps à or sur chanvre, de Venise*, it seems preferable to identify this kind of half-silk with the *baudekins à or sur chanvre* (*i.e.* with gilt membrane on hemp thread) preserved in Sweden (Pl. 34a) and mentioned in Swedish records, see above.

Referring to the above facts, the technical types of silk fabrics current in the Italian silk manufacture of the period can be summarized as follows: (1) the old weft-faced compound twill, either all-silks in two or more colours and possibly also including gold brocading, or else what King terms 'half-silks' (employing a main warp of coarse linen threads and a binding warp of silk, usually together with wefts of alternating silk and membrane threads) — the latter type of weave appearing in very different qualities, and probably to a certain extent also made somewhere outside Italy. (2) the 'diasper' type described above, that is, all-silk, employing two warps and two wefts, either two-coloured or monochrome; (3) the same kind of weave, perhaps termed 'half-silk', in which one half of the weft consists of gilded or silvered membrane (Fr. *or sur baudruche*) wound round a hemp or linen core. For the technical interpretation of the term 'half silk' both alternatives can be considered, and perhaps both are correct.

The next phase of development of Italian textile art was an explosive one, bringing in the 'free' or 'wild' style. At the beginning of the fourteenth century, the regularly symmetrical and static schemes of composition previously paramount in the silk weaving of the western world are partly supplanted by asymmetry and movement; birds on the wing and running quadrupeds, both real species and fantastic ones such as the phoenix and Chinese dragons appear. Another novelty is the abundant use of plant motifs, including luxuriant floral scrolls that sometimes make up the whole of a pattern (VIII, fig. 3). Inscribed bands with illegible Arabic lettering are often used for purely decorative purposes to underline the exotic nature of these imaginatively and ingeniously composed patterns, sometimes incorporating such heterogeneous elements as people, ships, fragments of landscape and so on. Undoubtedly the individual motifs were borrowed from a number of quarters, not least from the Moslem world. But the crucial impulse behind this revolutionary change of style can only be attributed to more remote influences — those of Chinese silk weaving, in which asymmetry has been an essential feature from the earliest times.

In 1240 Genghis Khan and his hordes had battered their way through Asia. But the route thus established was also conducive to peaceful traffic, and Marco Polo, who made his famous visit to the country of the Great Khan between 1269 and 1294, was only one of a number of travellers to China. We know from the papal inventory that there were many 'Tartar', that is, Chinese, fabrics in Rome before 1295. As far as is known, nothing remains of these fabrics that could serve as historical evidence, except the gold and white silk of Pope Benedictus XI in Perugia — the famous garments of Can Grande delle Scala in Verona being later. One of the very few silks in Europe surviving from this early period is the red damask (VII, fig. 5) employed sometime before 1300 for the head-shaped reliquary belonging to Turku Cathedral.[4]

Thus the foundations of the 'wild' style would appear to have been laid by the beginning of the new century, the *trecento*. Although no reliable evidence has been found of any Italian silks in this style at so early a date, there can be no doubt that such specimens once existed. Reviewing the hundred or so specimens chosen by von Falke to illustrate this group, a selection which could well be supplemented, by for example, specimens in Sweden, one can distinguish, stylistically and typologically, between earlier and later stages. Some specimens probably do not go back further than the beginning of the fifteenth century, when this type of pattern was still quite in fashion, as can be seen with a fair degree of certainty from contemporary paintings. On the other hand there is some documentary evidence dating certain specimens to the beginning of the fourteenth century.

The surviving specimens of these Italian silks, which are only a minute fraction of all that originally existed, give a unanimous impression of restless versatility, an abundance of themes and varying types of composition, ingenuity and imagination, perhaps sometimed coupled with a straining after new effects. Not all of them are designed in the same good taste, but a very large proportion of them bear witness to a degree of artistry suggestive of the participation of many of the great artists of the period. The sketch book of Jacopo Bellini, now in the Louvre, and the drawings of Pisanello constitute direct evidence of such participation as do later decorative fabrics woven after sketches commissioned from Antonio Pollajuolo. The general artistic standard was effectively maintained. As a rule the guild organizations of the various towns and cities seem to have engaged pattern designers of their own. For instance, in a contract drawn up in Genoa in 1424, Master Baldo Franchesi of Lucca undertakes to deliver no less than sixty new patterns a year. The demand for new patterns must have been enormous. On the other hand there seems to have been relatively little technical variation as far as patterned fabrics were concerned. True, the velvet technique (*velluto*) began to appear in the thirteenth century, but the so-called diasprum or 'lampas', (D5) still remained the predominant technique during the first part of the fifteenth century, though its quality declined towards the end of the period.

The Quattrocentro

The consummate art of silk weaving that was to be the worthy partner of the architecture of the fifteenth century was not fully developed until towards the middle of the century. On the other hand the pattern schemes that were to be used were fully evolved before then, as were the individual motifs. The crucial stage of stylistic evolution came with the application of new techniques, above all those of velvet and damask.

Unlike the *trecento* style with its superabundance of heterogeneous patterns, nearly all executed in the same technique, the *quattrocento* is above all distinguished by a variety of technical execution. The excellent new techniques of damask and velvet now attained their peak, velvet in the form of several technical variants. On the other hand the pattern types are surprisingly few and uniform, being dominated for the most part by a single theme, the so-called pomegranate, about which more later. The animals and all the other disparate motifs have vanished, apart from heraldic emblems and coats-of-arms made to order, which still play a significant part. In its fully developed state, the new style is characterized by an emphasis on the surface and the structure of the weave; the texture. Use is made of the property of a binding to obtain a certain structure of the weave, thus varying the sheen or depth of the colour in such a way that the patterns appear quite distinctly without colour contrasts. True silk damask is a contrast of dull and shiny surfaces. The velvet technique affords an even greater contrast of shades than damask: the cut pile gives a deep and intense colour effect in clear contrast to a voided, plain-ground weave that appears light in comparison. Additional effects are obtained with uncut velvet, which gives an intermediate shade, and with such refined techniques as variations in the height of the pile (pile on pile) — a very exacting

VIII, fig. 4. Pomegranate design, gold and silk cloth. From the burial of Sigismundo Malatesta, d.1468

method which the Italians call *alto-e-basso*. In order for a pattern of this kind to 'come out', in either velvet or damask, it must contain fairly large areas of surface and the drawing must not be excessively detailed. In other words: the aesthetic effect of this technique requires comparatively large shapes and simplified drawing. To this are added in certain cases, on top of the patterning effects of the ground weave, supplementary colour effects such as brocading in gold and colours or, in the case of velvet, a weft of gold or silver thread in the ground weave.

Turning now to patterns and themes, the so-called pomegranate can resemble a pineapple, or rather a pine-cone — this was how the compilers of the papal inventories saw it — but it can also be compared to a thistle flower. But this flower or fruit is associated with a large, almost round, leaf with shallow lobes which forms the background to the motif in question. In purely formal terms, this composite motif is related to the ancient palmette, which in turn is descended from a lotus flower in profile, as seen for example in Chinese silks, where the lotus flower with its stalks and leaves forms a symmetrical pattern subdivided into ogival fields (VIII, fig. 2). Other patterns originally of Chinese inspiration comprise diagonal tendrils undulating in a single direction which, however, are larger than the Chinese originals. The term pomegranate first began to be used in German works on the history of art during the nineteenth century and is thus devoid of any traditional standing. The fruit of the pomegranate when it has ripened and split, a common theme in Chinese art (cf. Pl. 55a) is different in appearance. Although the term 'pomegranate pattern' is a misnomer, it has proved impossible to eradicate since it covers such a special concept.

This greatly abbreviated description has unduly emphasized the element of uniformity. It would be a great error to suppose that Italian silk weaving during this period of its apogee, from the second third of the fifteenth century and about a hundred years onwards, was in any way stereotyped. It included several different types which it has not been possible to describe here, among them the unique masterpieces drawn by Antonio Pollajuolo at the behest of the King of Hungary, Matthias Corvinus, and Pope Sixtus IV. These fabrics have a 'living' decorative ornamentation closely related to the superb silver work and wood carving of which the Florentine Renaissance was then capable. In other sumptuous fabrics too, the same sense of style in the execution of details is found even where the main composition adheres to the traditional pomegranate pattern. The relative conservatism of style apparent in the surviving fabrics, intended mainly, it should be noted, for export to northern Europe, was probably due to the standardization dictated by the exigencies of a large-scale export trade.

Outside the confines of large scale silk manufacture come the figured borders, fabrics with a stout weft of coarse material, specis of 'lampas' (D5) with repetitive figure scenes of a Biblical character, intended to be cut up and used for adorning ecclesiastical vestments, in other words a relatively inexpensive substitute for embroidered orphreys. Their execution organized on a routine basis as in most Italian silk weaving, is presumably derived from graphic prototypes. They are not really to be regarded as textile art in the true sense.

Italy was probably also the country of origin of a group of sumptuous fabrics from the sixteenth century in rich velvet technique with patterns of greatly enlarged arabesques. One such velvet brocade is shown in Agnolo Bronzino's well-known portrait of Eleanor of Toledo (the consort of the Medici prince Cosimo I), and in view of the antecedents of the lady in question, this has been taken to imply that the fabric was Spanish. For many reasons, the design seems more likely to have been made in Italy, perhaps specially commissioned in Florence by Cosimo himself. At all events, fabrics of this particular kind are far from uncommon in Italy, while in Sweden (St Olai Church, Norrköping) there is, among other things, a cope of this very material, decorated with embroideries which are either Italian or Polish, a combination indicating Italian and not Spanish origin.

The pomegranate patterns developed in the fifteenth century retained their popularity far into the sixteenth century. Their distinctive character is very much bound up with their perfect execution. It is above all the large leaf that catches the eye. In the type of monochrome velvet where the pattern appears as lighter lines voided in the pile, the leaf gradually supplants the tendril, which almost disappears. In another type it may be the tendril which gets the upper hand or it may be transformed into a garland or a branch forming a distinct framework round a central ornament, for example a vase with flowers as in VIII, fig. 5. This brings us back to a pattern scheme which is admirably suited for renaissance forms, and this type of composition is very common throughout the succeeding century.

VIII, fig. 5. Two-coloured, voided velvet, Italy, sixteenth century

1550–1650

Until the beginning of the sixteenth century, large-patterned silks were used for every conceivable purpose, including clothes. During the sixteenth century, however, there patterns became differentiated according to purpose. The so-called Spanish costume, black for men, gave the ladies, too, a preference for small and relatively discreet patterns. On the other hand increasingly luxurious interior design had generated a rising demand for still more decorative, that is, larger, designs and more vividly-coloured fabrics for wall decoration and upholstery.[5]

VIII, fig. 6.   Italian silk damask, 1550–1650

This period also produced scattered patterns, usually in asymmetrical arrangements: ornamentally stylized flowers on a short twig, scattered more or less densely and often in very small pattern repeats (Pls 51a, 53a). These patterns were executed in various brocading techniques in damask and, the costliest of all, in fine quality velvet, cut and uncut, on a shiny atlas ground. The period excelled in bold and refined combinations of colour, for example, wine red and turquoise, salmon pink and grass green with silver, mauve and straw yellow, besides the long-established combinations of red or green against a yellow ground shot through with gold. Scattered patterns were known in Italy in the fifteenth century, though they were not common: the inspiration probably came from Persia, where this method of decorating a surface had long been highly developed (cf. Pls 46a and 56–57).

On the other hand the typical wall-covering fabrics were given stout symmetrical designs composed in such a way that the pattern filled the entire loom width which was then often used in alternation with a plain length in some contrasting colour. These fabrics were frequently woven with a coarse ground weft (waste silk, flax or hemp) which was invisible on the face, with the result that they were somewhat rigid; quite often such fabrics were used for ecclesiastical textiles. The most sumptuous wall coverings had large flower designs in polychrome velvet, for which Genoa acquired great fame, and which retained their reputation as late as the eighteenth century in France, where they were known as *velours de Gênes* or *velours jardinières* (Pl. 50).

Italian silk weaving has invariably displayed a high standard of craftsmanship, providing the foundation for the successive technical innovations that occurred, particularly during the fifteenth century, and resulted in products of superb quality.[6] The silk industry was able to maintain this standard for a long period, but this very excellence also carried with it the seeds of the conservatism which caused Italy to begin to lose its market during the seventeenth century. The Italian specialities, damask and velvet, had been created for monochrome surface ornaments and were not suitable for the lively fashion patterns which the French designers began to introduce towards the end of the seventeenth century. Consequently the Italian workshops were eventually forced to specialize in heavier fabrics while the French developed the fashionable products. Savary's famous *Dictionnaire de Commerce* offers the following description of the situation at the beginning of the eighteenth century: 'Although Italy still exported large quantities of gold and silk fabrics to France, Italian persons or rank preferred to buy the elegant silk for their clothing from France.'

FRANCE

Historical data

The constantly rising imports of costly silk from Italy prompted Louis XI to take steps to establish native production. First of all, approaches were made to the great commercial city of Lyons, but they met with resistance there from the merchants engaged in the silk import trade. Instead it was Tours that, by virtue of its closer proximity to Paris, obtained a royal privilege for silk manufacture in 1470. The new venture was so successful that the authorities in Lyons had second thoughts, and in 1536 they were granted a similar privilege at their own request. Both these ventures were supported by the state. Among other things they were protected by repeated import prohibitions and by detailed ordinances favouring domestically produced fashions. Skilled Italian craftsmen were encouraged to come and teach various technical methods to the French weavers. One of them was the famous Claude Dangon of Milan, who between 1605–1607 seems to have produced some particularly fine luxury fabrics which earned him tokens of royal favour as well as the jealousy of his colleagues in Lyons. During the decades that followed, French craftsmanship, under the leadership of Tours, advanced by leaps and bounds. Thus a distinctively French style of fairly high quality seems to have been evolved in the 1640s, in time for the drastic reforms of the 1660s, when the great Colbert, Louis XIV's ingenious Minister of Finance, carried out his reorganization of the whole structure of French industry.

It is well known that French silk production concentrated on fashionable products, on the constant creation of new costume materials for ladies and gentlemen in high society and for the court of the French monarch, the fountain head of all changes of taste and fashion. This tendency became apparent at an early stage and was observed by, for example, the Venetian ambassador in Paris, who as early as 1546 remarked for the benefit of manufacturers in his own city that the French always preferred lighter and less durable fabrics than the Venetians and that they soon tired of wearing costumes of the same material.

Modern research has shown for the first time exactly how fashions were created: Colbert's purposeful programme of 1667 stipulated that manufacturers were to produce new patterns every year. This decree was adhered to, and in fact by the end of the seventeenth-century manufacturers were producing new patterns twice yearly. The intention was to generate a growing demand and thus stimulate the French silk industry in order to make it more and more profitable. Colbert expected it to cater for all the other courts and capitals of Europe as well as Paris. It has been generally supposed that the exodus of skilled craftsmen which followed the revocation of the Edict of Nantes (1685) was a disastrous reverse to the French silk industry. It would now appear as though these events have been somewhat over-dramatized. Although the revocation may have been something of a reverse to such a young industry, there were obviously positive forces capable of surmounting the difficulties.

The vital prerequisite for the essential implementation of Colbert's ambitious programme was provided by the extraordinary efforts of a large number of talented designers. Contemporary spokesmen have recorded the demands that had to be met in order to become a skilled pattern designer. The training involved was inevitably long and expensive: apart from being a skilled draughtsman one needed a bold imagination and a fundamental knowledge of weaving. The designer also had to be able to make an independent assessment of the direction of the wind of fashion and of the preferences of his clientèle. As a rule designers in France enjoyed an acknowledged social status and were well-paid, assuming they were not factory owners themselves, which was often the case. This was very different from Spitalfields in England, where the standing of a draughtsman was far more modest by comparison.

The publications of Thornton and Rothstein have made it possible for extant silk fabrics from about 1700 to be assigned to exact dates. With very few exceptions, silk fabrics are never actually dated but pattern drawings often are, and a large number of them have come down to us, most of which were used in Spitalfields in the silk weaving workshops established by Huguenot refugees from France. Some of the designs were drawn by James Leman, who worked for the family enterprise, while others were the work of Anna Maria Garthwaite, who was a freelance. Both designers had access to pattern drawings smuggled out of France. Designs of this kind are often inscribed with a date and in many cases silk fabrics can be dated by comparison with the designs.

The seventeenth century

Whatever their themes and other stylistic traits, the patterns of the Middle Ages and the Renaissance were consistently two-dimensional, showing a clear distinction between background and pattern forms. In spite of the relative relief effect which can be obtained using the rich velvet techniques, the older patterns retained the character of a flat surface. The general striving of the baroque style for three-dimensional effect is also apparent in this field. But developments moved slowly; it took time for viable methods to evolve. The first advances were made by the use of weaving techniques: a secondary pattern was introduced, a ground pattern serving as an accompaniment to the principal motif. Ground patterning was executed in damask but also with an extra floating weft or with varying bindings. Softening effects of this kind began to appear towards the middle of the seventeenth century. The tendency to avoid rigid surface contrasts also resulted in large shapes being filled with small patterns executed in damask or various bindings. Applied to large symmetrical compositions this became the type which, owing to general resemblance to some forms of needle-point or bobbin lace, has inappropriately been termed 'lace pattern'. Fully developed 'lace patterns' existed before 1690 and were still popular towards the middle of the eighteenth century (Pl. 65).

The second half of the seventeenth century witnessed the emergence of numerous asymmetrical compositions made up of many kinds of floral motif. Often they consist of fanciful flowers depicted in a realistic manner, contorted as if they were growing out of each other. Sometimes the shapes employed are strictly stylized, for example, in the form of leaves or inorganic twisted shapes suggesting metal objects or other artefacts. It is characteristic of these extremely heterogeneous and complex patterns that they are produced by means of what might be termed unorthodox techniques: different variations of lampas combined with brocading and extra wefts in which various metallic effects often play a prominent part. Thus one and the same fabric could involve the use, not only of silver and gold but also of several different kinds of metal thread or frisé giving a more or less shiny or glittering surface.

It is not until the very last years of the seventeenth century that the special tricks whereby the pattern designer created the illusion of a third dimension appear: intersections and contortions of the objects depicted in perspective — all kinds of inorganic shapes combined with surrealistically portrayed fanciful plants. On closer inspection many detailed motifs can be recognized which had previously occurred separately and which have now been drawn into a vortex of fantastic or exotic shapes forming what have been called 'bizarre designs'. This peculiar genre is distinguished by a virtuosity of draughtsmanship and by a complex and extremely refined textile technique. As a rule the pattern repeats, which, without having any particular 'up' or 'down', are usually very long, are dominated by a principal motif executed with various metallic effects, accompanied by a ground pattern in damask forming an accompaniment. Although 'bizarre' silks were eventually manufactured in many different places, there can be little doubt that this genre originated in France.[7]

The eighteenth century

The 'bizarre' period, one of the most interesting in the history of textile art, was brief and hectic. The style can be said to have been fully evolved by about 1695, but artistically speaking its greatest successes occur between

IV. *From the cover of the Russian-Swedish peace treaty of 1721. Cf. Pl. 69.* *(Swedish State Archives).*

1700 and 1710 (Pls 68, 69 and colour plate IV). After 1720 there came a process of artistic disintegration, entailing among other things the exaggeratedly illusory rendering of an abundant but unreal flora and a sometimes irritating tendency always to be searching for new motifs.

The 1730s marked the coming of the rococo and the introduction in the design of silk fabrics of the special naturalism expressed by the contemporary painting. This trend was pioneered by Jean Revel, a leading silk designer in Lyons who was originally trained as a painter. The paramount themes of this important artist were garden flowers and the greenery of parks, depicted with shadows and highlights sometimes interspersed with portions of landscape à la chinoise or with so-called rocailles, resembling fluttering clouds. Colour became a principal means of expression more than ever before. The use of brocading made it possible to dispense with practically all technical restrictions. Revel devised a new technique, the point rentré, permitting colour transitions to be shaded into each other. There were many skilful designers active in Lyons at that time, but Revel was their incontestable leader, acclaimed by his contemporaries as a great artist. It was he who paved the way for Philippe de Lasalle, who was active some decades afterwards.

However artistic it was, people soon tired of this colourful impressionism, which in the long run seemed too obtrusive when applied to clothing. By the 1740s the scale diminishes and the floral motifs are succeeded by casually scattered twigs or gracefully curved tendrils standing out against a light ground. The ground weave could be plain taffeta: squared or striped, or else accentuated by a more or less neutral ground pattern, very often self-patterned. The flower tendril could also be juxtaposed with motifs resembling lace frills, or even fur trimmings. As time went on the colouring became more subdued and the flowers were collected in wreaths and garlands in the somewhat classical manner typical of the Louis XVI style.

These 'great silks' (les grandes soies) with their brocaded patterns took a great deal of time to weave and were therefore bound to be very expensive. This in turn created a need for simpler techniques and smaller patterns which could be made in a simpler loom such as the métier à la petite tire (cf. Chapt. VI). Many fabrics of this kind were known as droguet. Others were of the kind known in Sweden as ras de Sicile, a weft patterned weave, usually in two colours, which could have fairly large designs. There were many variations and many different names: the manufacture of almost two hundred different designations was registered in Lyons during the

1740s and this provides sufficient indication of the impossibility of identifying all of them. Mention will be made here of only a few classes.

Chiné was the name of a light and apparently simple clothing fabric which was nevertheless far from cheap. The term *chiné* indicates the oriental origin of the techniques, in which the yarn is patterned before it is woven. Originally this was done by resist-dyeing (as in Indonesian *ikat*), but in Europe a similar effect was later achieved by printing on the warp. *Moiré* is a fabric deriving its distinctive characteristics from an after-treatment: a plain silk rep, in some cases also woollen or linen, is folded double and pressed in a calendre which gives a 'watered' effect. Another technique was termed 'lustring', which involved the impregnation of the fabric in question (taffetas or similar thin qualities of silk), with some substance increasing its lustre but also, unfortunately, making it brittle.

Men's fashions were also supplied with suitable fabrics, which were often woven with all the parts of the costume marked out and complete with their edging borders, thus ready to be cut out and sewn up. Velvets with very small patterns were particularly popular for this purpose. Here, it should also be mentioned that clothing accessories and decorative articles of all kinds, from lace-making to ribbons, purses and other small items going by the more or less adequate collective term *à la petite navette* had been a Parisian speciality ever since the Middle Ages. Naturally this tradition lived on (see Clouzot).

Silk which was to be used for wall coverings and upholstery required quite different properties from the ever-changing fashion fabrics. For various reasons, patterns developed more slowly in this sector. Thus the *velours jardinières* or *de Gênes* mentioned above, either imported from Italy or less highly-prized French imitations, were still quite in vogue in the early eighteenth century. The French breakthrough in this sector did not occur until the 1730s, with the new inventions of Revel. Unfairly enough, his successor, Philippe de Lasalle, is more widely known, above all because his compositions survived long after the Revolution, manufactured as they were by long-standing enterprise by Pernon, who was Lasalle's partner. The silk industry in Lyons attained its apogee in the early 1780s. Almost eighteen thousand looms are said to have been in operation in 1783, two-thirds of them producing patterned silks, as against twelve thousand in other parts of the country. Soon afterwards, however, came the decline, due among other things to a change in fashion which called for lighter and predominantly monochrome fabrics.

The consequences of the Revolution

In 1789 came the Revolution, which immediately paralysed the whole of the French silk industry. To the oppressed workers of Lyons it provided the signal for bloody fighting and even for the destruction of implements and stocks as an act of vengeance against the wealthy *marchands-fabricants* (merchants and manufacturers were often the same people) who had established the fame of the city, with the workers' assistance but to their detriment.

After Napoleon seized power, the taste for luxury, so essential to the silk industry, was restored and Lyons revived. The costly furnishing textiles known as *le grand genre* were generously encouraged by the First Consul and Emperor, who even promulgated decrees to the effect that all persons of high rank should wear silk from Lyons, and renew their clothes as often as possible. The Emperor himself placed gigantic orders for new furnishings for all his palaces — and not only those in France: the foreign residences (in Turin, Rome, Strasbourg, Amsterdam) were decorated with Lyons silk, the upholstery, etc., invariably matching the wall coverings.

The great painter David exerted a powerful influence. Pattern designers of the *Ancien Régime* were commissioned to provide patterns for a new style which was given its most consistent formulation and application during the Empire by the architects Percier and Fontaine. This pre-eminently architectural ornamentation totally discarded the plant motifs and the painterly colouring used previously, substituting all kinds of classical ornamentation, warlike emblems and scattered stars together with the crowned monogram of the Emperor Napoleon, all rendered with three-dimensional effects in a uniform colour against a monochrome plain ground in a radically contrasting colour, each ornament being depicted as if superimposed on this ground. The range of colours was very limited, seldom including more than two. During the first Napoleonic era interior design was dominated by a basic shade of cool blue with white and silver ornamentation, but the increasing use of mahogany furniture with gilded mounts gave rise to a predilection for golden yellow ornamentation against a cherry red or myrtle green ground. Commonest of all was a damask-like technique with extra binding warps for the wefts that were needed to model detail effects in the ornamentation. The background was generally executed in glossy warp satin.

As time went on, the severe, grandoise style of the Empire was gradually softened, one might even say dissolved, by the addition of illusionistic details. These, usually naturalistic, additions provide the first evidence of the abolition, by the Jacquard loom, of the technical restrictions associated with the manually-operated looms, restrictions which in a manner of speaking had disciplined line and composition. In fact the grouping of the warp threads necessitated by the figure harness system (which was operated by hand) had given rise to a more or less distinct, stepped contour and a more stringent stylization, unlike the relaxed, curving lines that automatically characterize the Jacquard woven patterns. The introduction of Jacquard's invention was a great technical advance that reduced the cost of human labour input to a revolutionary degree. This ease of patterning, of illusionistic reproduction of practically any painted prototype, offered unprecedented possibilities. These possibilities were utilized without restraint, and the results were encouraged by a public that uncritically yielded to technical perfection. But the beneficial artistic tension of the struggle with technical limitations was lost in the process.

All the flood gates were now open to the romantic luxuriance and virtuoso naturalism that are typical of all textiles of the nineteenth-century rococo, the style which marks the beginning of the whirligig of nineteenth-century historical styles: nineteenth-century renaissance, nineteenth-century gothic, nineteenth-century baroque and even a third rococo period. This amalgamation of historical styles went hand in hand with a mixture of materials and techniques. The limitations which had been so beneficial from an aesthetic point of view were increasingly eradicated as one technique quite unashamedly imitated the other. Essentially unique works of art such as tapestry woven wall-hangings now came to be mass-produced by means of the Jacquard machine, and, to make matters worse, they were made from bad and cheap material and in false, drab colours. Similarly, solid cross-stitch embroideries were reproduced by machine printing on thin, flimsy cotton fabrics.

Such was the general tendency of nineteenth-century textile production. The dissolution of styles inevitably affected the silk manufacturers of Lyons, in spite of their sound traditions of craftsmanship and the honourable efforts made by many manufacturers to safeguard the standards of silk weaving. The powerful status of the artist designers in their companies was an important French tradition, and in the long run it was probably their efforts that saved the silk industry of Lyons from destruction.

Towards the end of the nineteenth century artists and intellectuals in many countries began to react against the falseness of these imitations of styles and materials and against the general deterioration in taste. Eventually a completely new style was developed. In France it was termed *l'art nouveau*, while in Germany and other countries it was called *Jugend* after a journal of the same name published in Munich. The trend was an international one with many national ramifications, especially in England, with artists such as William Morris and Walter Crane, who were both particularly concerned with designing textile patterns, above all for printed fabrics, which were traditionally of great importance in England. The *Jugend* movement embraced all types of handicraft, the aim being to establish a process of interaction between them. As a characteristic expression of the emergent twentieth century, *art nouveau* can be taken to mark the conclusion of this short survey.

OTHER EUROPEAN COUNTRIES

Silk weaving in the countries of central and northern Europe was more or less directly dependent, first on Italy and later on France. The countries concerned long continued to work with native materials. Silk weaving did occur in some parts as early as the Middle Ages, but it was of a very simple quality. Silk was far too expensive an import commodity for ventures of this kind to be profitable. Moreover there is evidence from London to show that the Italian merchants, who still dominated the market in the seventeenth century, tried to prevent the establishment of enterprises that might compete with the Italian silk industry. France had succeeded in breaking the Italian hegemony during the seventeenth century. But France herself incurred competition through the revocation of the Edict of Nantes. The thousands of Huguenot craftsmen thus expelled from their country became the founding fathers of silk manufacture elsewhere in Europe. Safeguarded by the artifices of mercantilism, these new industries enjoyed a period of vigorous, though artificial prosperity during the eighteenth century.

The following is a brief outline of the major enterprises in central Europe. A relatively exhaustive account of corresponding activities in Scandinavia, that is, in Denmark and Sweden, will be given in Chap. IX.

The Netherlands

Ever since the Middle Ages the one-time Spanish Netherlands and the ultimately independent Dutch Republic had maintained their highly developed woollen and linen industries which for centuries to come remained export industries on the grand scale. Silk weaving was a late starter and does not seem to have played an important part at any time. It is true that the practical preconditions were satisfied to a certain extent after the Portuguese discovery of the sea route to India (1498) had made raw silk directly available. The import of raw silk to the southern part of the Low Countries is said to have given rise to the manufacture of the kind of half-silks called *satin de Bruges*. Moreover, after the establishment of the Dutch East India Company in 1602, Holland was also in a position to embark on silk weaving, parallel to the rest of its textile production. Here the same workshops would often work with both linen and silk, and both branches of manufacturing were affected by this combination. But silk weaving in the Netherlands aimed at mixing or replacing silk with some other, indigenous material, linen or wool, to provide a cheaper commodity than was supplied by the great silk manufacturing countries, Italy and France.

Central Europe

In Germany silk weaving seems to have been a sporadic phenomenon during the sixteenth century. A few silk weavers existed in Hamburg, probably subsidiaries of the Dutch enterprises, and Italian silk dyers are said to have taken up residence in Nuremberg in 1573. During the mid-seventeenth century, many small German states experimented with the cultivation of silk, but most of these ventures foundered due to adverse climatic conditions. It was only in southern Austria, around the two cities of Görz and Gradiska, that these ventures proved successful and developed into the silk production that provided the foundation for a flourishing silk industry.

The Hamburg workshops enjoyed a period of considerable prosperity during the seventeenth and eighteenth centuries. But the most important silk centre in Germany lies in the Rhineland, in the area surrounding the town of Krefeld, where as early as the seventeenth century the van der Leyen family from Holland had started to trade in silk and linen products, ribbons and suchlike. In 1724 they founded the first dyeing shop. Forced as they were to economize on precious material, the Germans could never rival the French products. Apart from silk and half-silk fabrics they manufactured scarves and handkerchiefs in 'Indian' patterns. The Krefeld industry gained ground especially after the decline of the Dutch silk industry.

The manufacturing industries which, carefully fostered by Frederick the Great, developed in Berlin and surrounding areas of Brandenburg, are a typical instance of the artificial policy of industrial mercantilism. After Frederick's death, the industries declined, but the Berlin factory survived until about 1870.

Silk weaving in Austria began more or less with the Board of Trade established in 1666 by Count Zinzendorff and the Electoral physician Becher, by Imperial command, and with the recruitment through this office of French and Italian instructors. Results were a long time coming and contemporaries therefore regarded the venture as a failure, but when the silk weavers of Vienna formed a guild in 1710 there proved to be between twenty-five and thirty masters. Many new initiatives were taken during the reign of Maria Theresia. A quality ordinance issued in 1751 regulated widths, qualities, etc. Technical skills were improved by instruction and better machinery. That same year, for the promotion of velvet weaving, three Frenchmen, Fleuriet, Telier and Gautier, were commissioned to teach Austrian apprentices. A host of Italians and Lyonnais took up residence in Austria on their own initiative. A school for draughtsmen, organized on French principles and staffed by French teachers, was founded in 1758. The silk manufacturing enterprises active in Vienna and its surroundings had a wide repertoire, and their qualities are praised by Savary. The leading manufacturers were Beywinkler and Hebenstreiter, later succeeded by André and Bräunlich. Except for certain years of crisis, output covered demand fairly well and there was quite a considerable export trade, above all with Poland and Russia. But the fact that the importation of brocaded fabrics was still permitted in 1774 suggests that skills were limited in this respect. One example of Austrian silk is a damask from the 1790s, designed by the architect Henrici, the vigorous post-Rococo rocailles of which are typically Viennese.

The Austrian silk industry derived considerable impetus from the paralysis imposed by the French Revolution on the leading silk manufacture in Europe. Austrian production increased and so did exports. Here as elsewhere, the extensive silk industry that developed during the mid-nineteenth century is less impressive artistically than technically and economically.[8]

Switzerland and the Tyrol specialized among other things in ribbon making. Thus a new type of loom, commonly known as the Zürich loom, was invented in the eighteenth century for weaving several ribbons parallel to one another.

According to the latest research, Poland has never possessed a silk industry of any importance.[9] Ever since the Middle Ages, contacts with

Italy had been so active that the demand for costly fabrics could be catered for more efficiently by importation. The trade was mainly organized by Italian merchant houses, established in Cracow, especially during the early seventeenth century; their very extensive imports are known from account-books, custom lists and other documents which are still preserved in Polish archives. On the other hand there was a native production of the typical 'Polish sashes' which formed an essential part of the costume of the Polish nobility. The decorative ends of these long sashes, which hung down in front, bear witness to their origin in the Mogul courts of India. The long, narrow fabrics, stiff with metal thread, were initially imported from Persia and Turkey, but were later produced in Polish workshops specializing in free imitations of the oriental girdles, as recently described by Dr Maria Taszycka.

Sericulture is said to have been attempted in Russia, though without any great success. Silk weaving shops are also said to have existed in Yaroslav and some other towns, but they would seem by all accounts to have been of little importance. The luxury articles of this kind consumed in the country, no doubt in very large quantities, were mainly imported by Persian merchants, who were strongly represented in Moscow.

England

The large number of silk workers, most of them women, who were registered in London as early as the fifteenth century were probably engaged in *passementerie* or similar work and, above all, in embroidery Silk weaving did not exist as yet. The first silk weaving manufactories were established during the reign of James I and they received valuable reinforcements after the revocation of the Edict of Nantes, in the form of exiled French Huguenots. The Huguenots settled in East London, in Bethnal Green and Spitalfields, which eventually became England's modest counterpart to Lyons. As in the metroplis of the French silk industry, work here took the form of domestic industry. Eventually there are said to have been seventeen thousand looms. The main products were damask and soft brocaded silk. As mentioned above a large number of pattern drawings have come down to us providing a fair indication of the nature of this manufacture which is being studied by English scholars, especially Natalie Rothstein.

IX

Silk Weaving in Scandinavia

In Scandinavia as in other northern parts of Europe, climatic conditions affecting silk cultivation were quite different from those in southern Europe, where sericulture had developed since the Middle Ages. Great efforts were made in several centres to establish sericulture, in Sweden they extended as far as the 64/65 degree of latitude, but they were all doomed to failure in the long run. Consequently silk manufacturers were for the most part dependent on imported raw material, and this was too expensive for manufacturing to be profitable.[1]

DENMARK[2]

No other country has devoted more care and expense to its silk weaving, in proportion to the results obtained, than Denmark. The beginnings were highly auspicious. In 1619 Christian IV purchased a property in Copenhagen, from Købmagergade to Pilestræde, where he had a street laid out and lined with fourteen workshops on either side. A large contingent of silk and damask weavers, dyers, etc. was summoned from the Netherlands. This contingent also included the famous damask weaver Pasquier Lamertijn, from Courtrai. The number of workers was impressive: there were fifty-two master weavers and eleven dyers in the city. Products began to be delivered as early as May 1620. The new enterprise was protected by various import prohibitions. The Silk-works apparently specialized in patterned fabrics. Apart from pure silk fabrics, half-silks and linen damasks were also produced, apparently being woven in the same workshops as seems to have been the rule in the Netherlands.

As results worthy of the ambitious enterprise three tablecloths still survive: one, of white linen damask, is in Rosenborg Castle, Copenhagen, while two others, of blue-white and yellow-red silk respectively, are in the Kremlin in Moscow. The interesting and lavish design, similar in all these cases, includes a bird's-eye view of a ready laid table, while the long side borders are filled with a sequence depicting a naval battle and large hunting scenes. Finally, the ends bear the crest and monogram of Christian IV together with his ancestral device. The execution has been attributed, no doubt correctly, to Lamertijn. The designer was probably the Dutch painter Karel van Mander. The two tablecloths in the Kremlin were gifts presented by the Danish king to the Tsar in connexion with an embassy in 1627. Far less impressive examples of the production of the Silk-works are provided by the cushion covers bearing the royal coat of arms, a few specimens of which have been preserved at Rosenborg Castle. The decorative design, rather unusual for a silk fabric, is executed in a primitive technique that is very prodigal of silk. Looking at this example one can readily understand why the silk manufacture ran at a loss. Unfortunately things did not turn out as King Christian had intended. The merchants refused to have anything to do with the new products, which could not rival the foreign fabrics in terms of price or quality. Stocks accumulated remorselessly and in 1623 the venture was taken over by a private company consisting of wealthy foreign merchants. Not even they could keep the business going, and early in 1627 it was wound up completely.

The next attempt was made by Christian V, who began in 1680 by issuing strict import prohibitions. The silk manufacture which was then established is represented in the Rosenborg collections by a piece which speaks well for the technical capacity of the enterprise: a red and silver silk with a specially designed pattern of laurel garlands and the insignia of the Order of the Elephant. These enterprises were dependent on complete import prohibitions, which were rigorously enforced. Confiscated goods were burned in public and heavy fines were imposed for wearing costumes of foreign fabrics. The Danish production on the other hand was encouraged by an ordinance providing that anybody investing more than 500 dalers in a silk manufacturing enterprise should be entitled to dress 'above his station', or more exactly to wear 'velvets, taffetas and other plain silks made in this country', which incidentally indicates that patterned silks were somewhat uncommon. The native manufacture could never have been made to pay without auxiliary measures of this kind, and when the Dutch compelled Denmark to abolish her import prohibitions, it sank into a rapid decline. By 1690 all silk weaving in Denmark had come to an end.

A third attempt was made in 1735. This also fell short of commercial success, but activities were kept going after amalgamation, until the close of the century. After long negotiations the business was taken over by a consortium of merchants, and it seems to have made progress for a time. Something of a peak was attained in 1763, when up to 938 workers were employed at the silk factories in Denmark. The furnishing material shown in Pl. 64, with the crowned monogram of Christian VI, belongs to this period.

SWEDEN[3]

The beginnings of silk weaving in Sweden were a great deal humbler than those in Denmark. Here too the pioneer was a Dutchman, namely Jakob van Utenhofen, who in 1649 was granted privileges for the manufacture of plush, damask, 'padesoy' (*peau de soie*) and brocade and also for dyeing of silk and other fabrics. But his products were not as good as might have been expected. This man had been encouraged by Queen Christina with large orders, but the merchants complained that his silk products were more expensive than foreign ones and inferior to them in quality, so that nobody would buy them. Many other foreigners sought and obtained privileges in Sweden towards the end of the seventeenth century. Although their products were protected by import prohibitions and high tariffs their workshops never became going concerns.

Swedish silk weaving in the eighteenth century

The Swedish silk manufacturers enjoyed a period of amazing prosperity thanks to the special circumstances applying during the Age of Liberty. During the 1738/39 *Riksdag* the Caps had been ousted by the Hats. One of the salient points of the Hat party's programme was the increase of national wealth by the promotion of native manufactures. The *Manufaktur-fond* set up for the distribution of the subsidies was placed under the immediate jurisdiction of the *Riksdag* and soon developed into a Ministry in its own right, known as the *Manufakturkontor*. The management of this office came to have a profound influence on the arts and crafts in the country as a whole.

In the first instance encouragement was given to manufacturers of various handicraft products, such as the Rörstrand faïence factory, the silk-weaving enterprises and the Flor factory of linen damask (about which more in the following chapter). Those responsible also realized the importance of recruiting artistically and technically talented people, efforts in this direction being justified by the hope that native products would become good enough to compete with foreign ones. This idea was fully in line with the chimerical principles of the mercantile system, but the way in which it was implemented bears witness to a more pragmatical view and a realistic policy that was capable of bearing fruit independently of political circumstances.

An urgent need was now felt for a Swede who would be capable of taking charge of both technical and artistic developments. The man appointed was a 23-year-old fortification officer by the name of Jean Erik Rehn, who was allowed to travel to Paris in 1740 to study there. Rehn's first instruction in the French capital was given by the talented engraver Le Bas, under whose guidance he made such progress that he was offered an appointment in Paris. If he had accepted he would have been lost to Sweden, and of course the matter was reported to the appropriate authorities in Stockholm. To save the situation it was decided to offer Rehn a permanent appointment as *dessinateur* to the Swedish manufacturies. This appointment was confirmed in 1745 by a contract for life under which Rehn's obligations were focused entirely on the textile industries. He was to invent models and draw coloured designs and to make patterns for silk, woollen, linen and other fabrics produced by factories in Stockholm and elsewhere and he was also to inspect the factories to ensure that his patterns were adhered to, and to provide the technical advice and instruction which these required. With a view to his own technical education he was to study machinery, cloth dressing, etc. in the factories of Paris and Lyons to which he had gained admittance. These studies, or, to put it more bluntly, industrial espionage, were certainly not at all appreciated by the French silk manufacturers. At the same time as Rehn was dispatched to Paris a skilled silk manufacturer, Bartholomé Peyron, was summoned from Lyons. Peyron, who opened a workshop in Stockholm in 1741, was evidently allotted the most exacting tasks and seems in all respects to have occupied a leading position in his trade.

By January 1746 Rehn was hard at work. One of his first measures was to set up a machine for printing squared paper for the 'point paper plan' (*mise en carte*) serving as a guide for setting up the loom. The silk manufacturers were now informed that they could order such point paper plans or drafts. To attend to the purely technical tasks, Rehn engaged a cousin of his (Olof Rehn) and, later on, additional assistants.

In 1755 Rehn went on a second study trip by way of Vienna to Venice and from there to Rome, Naples and other places, returning home via Lyons and Paris. All along his route he purchased large quantities of samples, materials and machinery, though this time he was concerned with the porcelain and faïence industries as well as textiles. The reason was that Rehn had become more and more interested in tasks involving a wider artistic frame of reference, particularly on behalf of the court, with the result that, following his return home (1757), he was appointed Surveyor to the Royal Household, his former responsibility for the textile manufacturing industries was now transferred to Olof Rehn.

Although silk factories had existed in Sweden before the Hats came to power, a rapid expansion now ensued and during the 1750s production assumed impressive dimensions. In 1765, by which time the decline had already set in, there were thirty-four silk factories in Stockholm with a total of 458 looms in operation employing 1,157 workers. There were also several silk factories in the provinces, for example, in Gothenburg, Mariestad and Norrköping.

In 1765 and 1766 the situation was completely transformed by another reversal of political fortunes: the Caps gained power and support was withdrawn from the manufacturing enterprises. Measured by the number of looms, production fell by half, and two years later there were only 221 looms working. But silk weaving was far from extinguished, and the number of factories remained generally unaltered for several years to come. But in 1850 there remained only sixteen factories, of which one, Almgren's, stayed in business until well into the present century.

The nature of Swedish silk manufactures is illustrated by an unusually abundant source material and excellent research. The reports and accompanying fabric samples submitted every year to the Board of Trade by the different factories throughout the country have survived from 1751 onwards, though unfortunately a great many of the samples have vanished. Equally important are the series included in *Theatrum oeconomico-mechanicum*, a collection of samples of all kinds, made by Anders Berch, Professor of Economic Laws at the University of Uppsala. The remaining parts of this collection are now in the custody of the Nordiska Museet. The 'Berch Collection', which is interesting in more ways than one, contains both Swedish and foreign textile samples with inscriptions stating their origins and names. Another important source is the stock of silks acquired by the Royal Household for furnishing the royal castles and palaces. Important particulars concerning these fabrics are often to be found in the accounts of the various residences. Mention should also be made of the royal gala costumes preserved in the Royal Armoury, some of the materials in which are documented as being of Swedish manufacture.

The oldest extant specimens of precious silk from this period are probably the material for the costumes worn by King Adolf Fredrik and his consort Lovisa Ulrika at the coronation in 1751. These fabrics were woven at Peyron's factory. As can be seen from these and many other specimens, Swedish manufacturers were for the most part content to make fairly straightforward copies of French prototypes of which Rehn had contrived to obtain samples.

Upholstery and wall-coverings for the royal residences were made for the main part by Peyron after drawings by Rehn. One of the most splendid of these (Pl. 72b), in gold and red, was made in 1753. In a style which lacks any counterpart in the French production, Rehn created a number of symmetrical damask designs (Pl. 74) which, with their intertwined frames, their plain or squared surfaces and their taut line, are somewhat reminiscent of Italian silks of the sixteenth century but also give something of a classical impression. For this reason the former supposition that they were made before Rehn went on his journey to Italy seems questionable.

The Berch collection includes two separate samples with very similar genuine French rococo patterns brocaded in gold, silk and chenille in bright colours but with different coloured grounds, of yellow, and of azure blue. Labels attached to the samples (Pl. 73b) state that the silk material was produced at Drottningholm 'under the gracious patronage of H.M. Queen Lovisa Ulrika'. Records concerning the blue silk, made by 'Fabriqueur Abraham Ekstedt', also indicate that in 1766 forty ells were presented by the Estates to Princess Sofia Albertina, who was then thirteen years old. The major part of this blue silk is still extant in the form of ecclesiastical yarns of Slaka church. But the greater part of the output of the Swedish factories probably consisted of entirely plain or small-patterned silk and velvet fabrics. *Droguet* was usually the main item mentioned in the production catalogues. Warp patterned silks of this kind, with small pattern repeats in one or, less frequently, two colours, were produced by many Swedish factories. A similar fabric, though with a larger pattern repeat, was known as *droguet lustrin* and fetched a higher price. *Ras de sicile* and *cammage* came in the same price range as *droguet*, and all three can be seen in the sample book illustrated here (Pl. 73). *Ras de sicile* was a relatively large-patterned silk. *Cammage* was the name given to a small-patterned silk with two floating coloured wefts against a ribbed ground. *Peruvienne* was a striped warp and weft patterned silk which probably antedates the 1770s. Even such technically demanding articles as small-patterned fabrics for men's costumes in cut and uncut velvet were made at the Swedish factories, but they were very expensive to buy.

The most important article to be produced by the Swedish factories from the mid-nineteenth century until the First World War was silk kerchiefs or headcloths, which were then commonly worn by country-women. Such kerchiefs were also exported in large quantities to Norway, Åland, Finland and even to Russia.

X

Linen Damask and other Table Linen

A white linen cloth on the table, be it at the Lord's table or the household table, was already standard practice in the Middle Ages. Paintings from the fifteenth century sometimes show tablecloths which appear to be decorated with ornamental borders in openwork or needlework of multicoloured silk, or coloured woven borders. The blue and white so-called 'Perugia towels', a folk-art production which survived until recently in Italy, no doubt can trace its origin from similar medieval textiles.[1] Sometimes the medieval painter has shown a diagonal pattern, what we would now call lozenge twill, white on white, covering the entire area of the cloth. Linen fabrics of this kind have been preserved from the Middle Ages (Pl. 82b) and are in fact not dissimilar to the self-patterned silks woven much earlier in China and also in Spain. A Dutch scholar has identified weaves of this kind with such names as *kruiswerk*, *lavendel*, *pavy*, *pellen*, and *kraaneoog* occurring in a weaver's will. Such fabrics were commonly used on the tables of wealthy middle-class homes in Holland and Scandinavia throughout the seventeenth century.

THE NETHERLANDS AND GERMANY

Linen damasks with specially designed patterns, large tablecloths complete with oblong napkins, were a refined artistic product that came into fashion at the princely courts of the sixteenth century and were a luxury article that remained an expensive status symbol of the upper reaches of society during the seventeenth century.[2] The establishment of this distinctive production was due in the first place to two quite separate phenomena: Flemish linen thread and the Italian technique of silk damask. The high quality of the linen thread was the achievement of a centuries-old, well-organized linen industry comprising everything from the cultivation and preparation of flax to the spinning and weaving of the finest linen tabby or 'batiste' and subsequent bleaching processes. Damask, densely woven to bring out the two contrasting surface effects, had been evolved experimentally by the Italian silk weavers. The two phenomena were brought together because Flanders included the powerful port of Bruges, the most important Italian trading centre in northern Europe, where large quantities of Italian silks were always on sale or being exported. Linen damask, was brought to perfection by means of technical and artistic inventions by the local craftsmen.

A natural beginning was to imitate the patterns of silk damask, as shown in Pl. 60 including regular pomegranate patterns. Soon, however, certainly not later than about 1500, another type was introduced which seems, with its contrast between dark and light surfaces, to have been modelled to a great extent on woodcuts. Later, other kinds of graphic pictures provided models for table damask. With large princely orders, coats of arms and monograms, were a natural kind of motif particularly suitable for decorating the surface of a large napkin. Figurative scenes were predominantly employed for the large tablecloths, for example, battle scenes, allegories, mythological or Biblical themes, often provided with explanatory inscriptions (cf. Pl. 63). Figure subjects of this kind were invariably executed with point repeat, that is, with the entire pattern unit repeated in reverse several turns across the width, while vertically there could be a succession of many different scenes, sometimes giving a vertical pattern unit of several metres. The long sides were generally decorated with an almost uniform tendril border.

Although his surviving works differ from those of his successors, the master weaver Pasquier Lamertijn must be seen as a pioneer of the style described above. He was born in Courtrai (Kortrijk), one of the leading linen-weaving towns of Flanders, which as early as 1496 had obtained an *octroi* of manufacturing linen damask. Together with many other skilled damask weavers, Lamertijn was obliged to leave his native town on account of the religious persecutions beginning about 1580. The fugitives settled in Haarlem and Alkmaar, with the result that these towns became the principal centres of damask weaving in Holland. Lamertijn settled in Haarlem, where he was active for many decades and won great renown by supplying table-linen to the royal houses of Europe. He is credited with the invention of a method of weaving very large and complex patterns with 'all manner of pictures, histories and battles' (Pl. 61). Thus, unlike the commoner type described above, these patterns were not invariably executed in point repeat. But Lamertijn's 'free' damask technique was very laborious, with the result that his products were extremely expensive and sometimes had to be sold at a loss. Consequently his professional work earned him more glory than profit, and this may have been the reason why he accepted the invitation of the King of Denmark to move to Copenhagen (cf. p. 165). At all events, it was here that he executed the masterpieces which today testify to his unique skill: the great linen cloth at Rosenborg Castle and the two silk cloths in the Kremlin.

Another famous Haarlem weaver was Quirin Jansz Damast, active until 1650, the year of his death. The exhaustive and detailed inventory of his estate compiled by his daughter provides an interesting insight into his wide-ranging activities.

By this time the art of weaving linen damask in the Flemish-Dutch style had spread to several other countries. These new manufacturing ventures were reinforced by the many French Huguenots who were forced to leave their country after the revocation of the Edict of Nantes (1685). The Irish damask factories were especially successful because they acquired a very gifted instructor in Louis Crommelin from Picardy, who raised the Irish linen industry to a high pitch of excellence.

Next to the countries along the Channel and North Sea coasts, the most important continental flax-growing areas were Silesia and Saxony, where linen tabby had long been manufactured on a considerable scale. It therefore seemed a natural step for damask weavers to be established on the same lines as in Flanders and Holland. Efforts were made in this direction during the sixteenth century, but nothing came of them, owing to local resistance against the professional workshop organization that was necessary for high-class damask weaving. The Silesian linen tabby weaving, on the contrary, could be carried out as cottage industry, organized on an outwork basis. It was not until 1666 that a real damask manufacture materialized in Saxony, in Gross-Schönau near the little town of Zittau, which soon underwent a considerable expansion. During the eighteenth century it began to overtake the Dutch industry, which by that time had entered on a decline.

The eighteenth century brought with it new types of patterns characterized by a striving after all-over compositions fitted to certain sizes. The borders, now on all four sides, became more prominent and were adapted to the format, preferably with symmetrical corners. The napkins, which were always square, were often given a concentric design, while the central part of the tablecloths had a large centre ornament or were given repetitive patterns, which were quite often imitated from silk patterns (cf. Pls 51b and 80a).

SWEDEN AND THE OTHER NORTHERN COUNTRIES[3]

It is hard to say when linen damask or other kinds of patterned linen were first produced in Scandinavia. There were guilds of linen weavers in several Swedish towns, including Malmö, Gothenburg and Piteå as well as Stockholm, and also in Borgå (Porvoo) in Finland, which in about 1700 was the foremost linen weaving town in the Swedish Empire. Most, if not all, of this production was plain tabby (Sw. *lärft*), but Countess Sophie Brahe, a Danish noblewoman, in her interesting account books for the years 1627–40. mentions one professional weaver making *damnasch dreyel* (probably damask with geometrical patterns like Pl. 82c–d) beside several women weaving linen tabby on a domestic basis.

However, there were damask weavers working in Stockholm before 1696, when detailed records mention a very large order placed by the court. It was Hedvig Eleonora, the energetic Queen Dowager and Regent, who took the initiative on behalf of the royal court in starting damask production, which began in 1698. Jürgen Hoffmann, evidently a very capable and respected master from the linen weaver's guild, who was repeatedly summoned to the Palace, is referred to as 'damask weaver' indicating that he was the owner of a damask loom. This loom, however, was not of the very great size required for the cloths ordered by the Queen which were to be 4½ ells wide (270 centimetres). Nothing has survived of this material commissioned by the royal court, but we do have three napkins ordered personally by the Queen Dowager. The centre contains the crowned monogram HERS (*Hedvig Eleonora Regina Sveciae*) surrounded by scattered triple crowns; along the four edges is a narrow tendril border. Finally there is a woven inscription, 'Stockholm 1700', '1701' and '1703' respectively.

Flor's linen manufactory

The efforts made during the Age of Liberty to repair the war-torn national economy by starting industries in various parts of the country were praiseworthy in themselves; unfortunately, they were not always well planned. The idea of exploiting the linen industry that had been developed in Hälsingland during the early Middle Ages was a good one, but the gentlemen who were awarded special privileges for the purpose in 1728 were hardly equal to the task. By the merest coincidence, one of them, a Stockholm merchant, finally settled in the village of Östra Flor, which eventually became the home of the remarkable textile enterprise 'Flor's Linen

Manufactory'. The sponsors were fortunate enough to find the right man for the job. The Englishman Stephen Bennet, who was unusually well endowed with technical knowledge, experience and a capacity for organization, took over the management of the enterprise in 1736 and managed to get it well and truly on its feet within a few years. It is particularly interesting to note the diversity of the activities that were maintained. The instructional activities concerning flax processing and spinning, which Bennet inaugurated and which extended into the neighbouring province of Ångermanland and along the coast of the Gulf of Bothnia, were of fundamental importance. As a result of this practical teaching, there were almost two thousand women spinners in the surrounding parishes working for Flor when the business was at its height. In this connexion it is worth noting a statement by Bennet to the effect that the flax grown in Hälsingland and Ångermanland was better than the imported product, but also that the flax fibres could be destroyed during processing. For example he points to the necessity of keeping cattle, 'for without milk whey for the perfecting of the bleaching, all labour is in vain'.

The main task, of course, was the manufacture of linen damask, and accordingly there were always a number of looms working for the royal store rooms. The Flor factory also received a great many other orders, on one occasion for six royal courts simultaneously. To keep these activities going and at the same time to make rational use of material resources and technical installations, Flor carried on a great deal of supplementary production which seems to have been extremely comprehensive. Above all, this production was concerned with linen tabbies and similar fabrics, but it also included quantities of cotton fabrics, some of them of very fine quality, a kind of openwork fabric called *skirduk*, and sometimes even silk. Cotton stockings, plain and openwork, for men and women, were another important article. Printed fabrics were also produced, mostly 'blue-print', or coloured blue by resist dyeing on linen. Productions of this article in 1765 totalled 3,055 ells. For forty years, between 1753 and 1793, Flor had its own hallmark, which was a unique occurrence, this privilege normally being reserved for towns. In 1845 declining profits forced the owners to close this high quality enterprise.

The Vadstena manufacture

When in 1752 the *Manufakturkontor* began to consider plans for the establishment of a linen factory and flax plantation in Vadstena, it was only natural that they should consult Stephen Bennet of Flor and ask him to send them somebody who was an authority on water retting, flax dressing and spinning. A skilled linen weaver and suitable tools for flax dressing were also requested. It is said that a spinning wheel and a reel were sent down from Flor to serve as models, but we do not know whether the persons requested ever put in an appearance. Meanwhile, those in charge of the Vadstena factory had also engaged foreign craftsmen. The first to arrive were one German and two Frenchmen together with their families. They were specialists in manufacturing fine linen batiste, which at that time was a novelty in Sweden. The factory thus started existed from 1753 until 1778, though not without difficulties. It was not until 1778 that the Vadstena factory changed over to damask weaving, which became its main item of production. All the foreign workers except one had left the country by 1778, so that the entire workforce were now Swedish.

Towards the end of the eighteenth century the Vadstena damask manufacture underwent a great deal of improvement regarding both patterns and technical execution. The products were now carefully signed and dated, and this shows quite clearly that older patterns were used: for instance a square napkin with Rococo pattern which was signed as late as 1797 (Pl. 80b). The first decades of the nineteenth century were a period of continued prosperity during which Vadstena actually surpassed Flor. But in 1843 the Vadstena factory too had to close down, two years before the demise of its rival.

Apart from the two large enterprises, Flor and Vadstena, a number of smaller damask workshops with fairly good capacity developed in various towns, though only a few of them stayed in business for any length of time. Of particular note, the Stenberg factory in Jönköping was founded in 1820 by the industrious and competent 'councillor dowager' Ulrika Stenberg, a descendant of the famous Ulrika Oxelgren, the wife of a rural dean and the ancestor of many other clergymen's wives in the province of Småland, who were all remarkably active in textile work. The damask factory was eventually expanded and was managed with the assistance of Ulrika Stenberg's two daughters and a master weaver. After Mrs Stenberg died, in 1858, they carried on the business until 1883. During the 1840s Ulrika Stenberg visited Stockholm, where she purchased a Jacquard loom from Almgren's silk factory. As a result her damask weaving came to differ from that of other Swedish factories, which still employed the draw-loom with 'simple cords' (cf. Chap. VI). There was also a great difference in terms of patterns and quality. Generally speaking, the patterns can be characterized as 'floral nineteenth-century rococo' using detailed and predominantly naturalistic designs. The quality was dense and very fine, due among other things to the later use of English machine-spun linen thread or, occasionally, of cotton thread as well. Stenberg damask fetched high prices and enjoyed a high reputation, as witness the orders received from the royal court and the prizes won at exhibitions in both London and Paris.

All the damask weaving described so far seems to have differed in character from the enterprises which arose in the province of Skåne during the nineteenth century and which have become well known through the book on the Malmö guild of linen weavers. The members of this guild were termed 'linen weavers' pure and simple, and most of them seem only to have woven coarse tabby. On the other hand there were weavers outside the guild residing in the country and usually moving from one customer to another, generally owners of manorial estates or other wealthy people. This was the case with two skilled weavers who had emigrated from Finland in the 1730s and 1740s. Both of them handed on their trade to several succeeding generations.

The kind of native table-linen, striped, chequered or patterned with stars and other geometrical ornaments, generally woven as true damask, which was frequently used in the nineteenth century, is something quite different from the workshop-woven damasks which during the eighteenth century were still being produced by the trained craftsmen mentioned above. The native Scandinavian production of the nineteenth century woven on a domestic basis was greatly influenced by the standardized weaving equipment gradually developed in England and Scotland, sources of many industrial inventions in the eighteenth century. During the nineteenth century these methods rapidly spread within the united kingdom of Sweden and Norway. The introduction of the new methods was very much the work of the Swedish Ekenmark family. This talented and industrious family numbered seven persons, men and women, all of whom were active as teachers, both by means of travelling courses through Sweden and Norway and through the medium of no less than eight publications which appeared between 1820 and 1848. These books, which have long, elaborate titles, contain practical notes about the new methods, drawings of loom constructions, advice on the treatment of materials, patterns and drafts, etc., all adapted to conditions in the Norwegian and Swedish countryside and the general knowledge of weaving that already existed in both countries. Not all this information was originally devised by the Ekenmarks. Essential parts have been taken from a book by John Duncan, printed in Glasgow in 1807–08. But Duncan's book was explicitly addressed to 'Manufacturers of Cloth and Operative Weavers', while the Ekenmarks's publications were intended for non-professional women working in their own homes. John Ekenmark is to be regarded as pioneer for making an unknown variety of weaving equipment known and used in Sweden and Norway. The achievements of the Ekenmarks has been excellently described by A. Bugge and S. Haugstoga.

XI

Knotted Pile Fabrics and other Fleecy Textiles

The rya-rug of the Nordic countries and the Oriental carpet

Although geographically and functionally they are two very different phenomena, technically the Nordic rug and the Oriental carpet have so much in common that one is bound to ask whether there is some historical connexion between the two. Did the technique become widespread at an early stage, or did it occur spontaneously in different places?

Both techniques are knotted pile, meaning that an additional yarn, which does not belong to the ground weave, forms some kind of 'knot' around the warp threads and is thus kept from slipping out of the finished weave. This is the general criterion of knotted pile. The tufts or knots thus formed may be tied in different ways, they may be long or short, densely or sparsely placed, of one or more colours, executed with pre-cut short ends (inserted one at a time) or with a continuous yarn which is either pulled up by hand between each pair of knots or else laid over a stick or rod so that the tufts will be of equal length after they are cut (see XI, figs 1, 2).

The basic functional difference between the Nordic rya-rug and the Oriental carpet is important to bear in mind. In the Nordic countries, from ancient times, the woollen pile rug has served as a warm bed-cover which is used with the pile inside or downwards. The Oriental carpet on the other hand was placed on the floor with the pile uppermost, to be sat on. As time went on, the wool for the knotted pile came to be dyed in different colours, and the knots were arranged in patterns, so that the carpet also became an adornment for the tent or the palace.

THE NORDIC RYA-RUG

We will start with the rya-rug because, apart from the abundance of rya still remaining in the Nordic countries, the development of this type can be traced from other sources, especially inventories, accounts, wills, and other written documents. In this way, especially where Sweden and Finland are concerned, we can survey half a millennium during which the rya-rug has been woven and used in various forms. The history of the rya-rug is a

XI, fig. 1.   Various pile loops executed with a continuous thread.
a–b from Swedish rya-rugs, nineteenth century. *c–e* looped weaves,
late-Roman or Coptic, Egypt third to ninth century

topic that has attracted many scholars in the Nordic countries. Recent research into the currency of the rya-rug in Finland during the sixteenth and seventeenth centuries has also given us a wider perspective of the development in Sweden which, as has not been understood previously, was the Nordic country from which this innovation first spread. But where it actually originated is another question. The first rya-rug in Sweden may have been luxury articles reserved for the privileged few, which would point to foreign influence.

Rya-rugs are first mentioned in the rules of the Bridgettine order for Vadstena Convent, whose members were recruited from the leading families of medieval Sweden. The relevant rule concerns the sisters' bed-clothes: 'Over them they are to have a piece of white *wadmal* (plain woollen cloth). And also a rya-rug (*ryio*; the Latin version says *pannus villosus*, that is fleecy cloth). And a sheepskin during the winter.' The oldest written version of these rules dates from about 1420, but there is no doubt that they were in force in the fourteenth century, when the convent was already established. The rule must mean that the rya was a lighter alternative to an animal skin. The latter was necessary during winter, but in the convent could be nothing more luxurious than sheep-skin. Persons of rank would have costly furs, such as otter and beaver, of which, for instance, the Norwegian bishop Aslak Bolt had two bed-covers among the rich furnishings he brought with him to his diocese of Nidaros (Trondheim) in 1429. The rya-rugs and the plain woollens that the sisters needed were made within the monastery, just as castles, manors and large farms would provide for their own needs. We know that work of this kind was already being done in the fourteenth century, because the Vadstena diary for 1424, recording the death of the lay sister Helena, recalls that for forty years she had been in charge of the *lanificium*, the preparation of wool

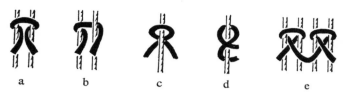

XI, fig. 2. Pile knots of various types: *a* Ghiordes, *b* Sehna, *c–d* one-warp 'Spanish' knots, *e* continuously worked knot

and woollens. No doubt a similar arrangement was practised at Nådendal, the daughter foundation of Vadstena in Finland. Among other things, rya-rugs from this convent are known to have been given in part payment for buildings on two occasions during the fifteenth century, which suggests that they were being produced on a considerable scale.

Scattered references to rya-rugs have come down to us from fifteenth-century Scandinavia. The following two notices from the early sixteenth century show that, locally at least, the rya-rug was very common indeed. Following the annexation of Öland by Sweden, Gustav Vasa issued letters patent confirming the 'ancient right' of the Öland farmers 'to sail to Germany and sell rya-rugs and woollens in order to buy salt and broadcloth'. Then again, the much travelled monk of Vadstena, Peder Månsson, who originally hailed from Småland and eventually became Bishop of Västerås, in his *Art of War* advised people defending a house to sew their old rya-rugs into sacks and fill them with sand. Evidently, then, it was quite common for people to have large numbers of ryas at home.

Throughout the Vasa period there are abundant references to ryas in the accounts of the royal castles, bailiffs' reports and so on, which show quite clearly that rya-rugs of various qualities were an important item in the large-scale subsistence economy of Gustav Vasa, as practised at the various castles between which the court moved at fairly regular intervals. Rya-rugs were woven at all the royal castles, and on a very large scale at some of them, such as Turku (Åbo) in Finland. There the making of rya-rugs was organized at royal manors in the countryside and the products delivered to the Crown. Large quantities were needed for the military establishments that had to be maintained during the wars against Russia, for example at Viborg Castle and at Olovsborg.

There is a great deal of documentary evidence on this subject for the period when Duke Johan resided in his Duchy of Finland and kept his court at Turku Castle. Everybody, from the members of the ducal family to the courtiers and servants, had rya-rugs on their beds, as well as blankets (*vepor*) and, in some cases, furs or fleeces.

The rya-rug was soft and warm and its great advantage over the fur was that it could stand up to the wet without becoming stiff and un-manageable, and it was also easy to dry again. For this reason it was very popular among seafarers of all ranks. Five rya-rugs were withdrawn from the stores of Turku Castle when Duke Johan was preparing to sail to England and plead his brother Erik's suit to Queen Elizabeth, and he was similarly equipped for a subsequent journey to Poland. We also read of persons on royal service being presented with a rya-rug for their journey.

Sometimes the Turku inventories give an idea of what these rya-rugs looked like. For instance, the ground weave, which was turned upwards when the rug was used, could be patterned with many-coloured wefts, such as red, yellow, green, and black and white. This weave was termed *lessen* weave (or *wippelessen*) and may well have resembled 'bound' rose-path. In some cases the inventory description has led to a surmise that the many-coloured ground weave was imitating a *vepa* or a double-cloth blanket which was superimposed as decoration on the plain rya. The knotted side of the very best rya-rugs could be decorated with stripes or squares (perhaps checkered black and white) or else given a coloured border. Needless to say, these ryas were of a superior quality, of specially selected fine wool and executed with greater care than the ordinary rugs. On the whole, all ryas seem to have been fairly similar, the pile being mostly of grey, white or black wool, resembling a fleece — a *pellis artificialis* (artificial pelt) as Linnæus put it some centuries later. This generalized description refers to the common bed rya, a purely utility object not to be confused with the 'decoration rya', which represents a later stage of development.

In Finland, at least, the rya-rug as an everyday article was still confined to the upper reaches of society even in the sixteenth century. The garrison-ing of the East Finnish castles does not seem to have caused the practice to spread to the surrounding permanent population. It was only in the seventeenth century that the rya became popular among the urban bourgeoisie and the lesser nobility and clergy in the countryside. It is worth noting that this new fashion grew up in the south-western part of Finland which once formed part of Johan's duchy, where the technique had been propagated as a result of the manufacture originally based on the royal manors. Much the same applies during the seventeenth century to

Sweden south-east of a line between the northern border of the province of Uppland and the Göta River in the west.

The 'ornamental rya' first appears in the form of the double-piled rya, which is simply the old utility rya woven in one piece together with a decorative bedcover. This tendency is already perceptible in the descriptions from Turku Castle. As was pointed out by Vivi Sylwan, the idea of executing the decorative side also in the pile technique evolved in Sweden, where it was probably inspired by imported items in so-called 'Turkey work'. The decorative side of the rya-rug was done using finer wool and short knots, which made the pattern more distinct, while the utility side retained its original shaggy character.

The next stage in this development was that the many-coloured upper side became independent, developing into an exclusively ornamental rya used as a ceremonial coverlet, especially for the bridal bed. This change took place in Sweden during the eighteenth century, with the result that the one-sided ornamental rya soon came to predominate. The double-pile rya is comparatively rare in Sweden, while in Finalnd there are still about two hundred in existence. This type of rya-rug was still being made in Finland in the nineteenth century, especially in the old rya districts, side by side with the purely decorative variety.

The utility bed rya also lived on, though in various guises. A type that can be termed medieval was particularly common in the ancient rya-making provinces of Uppland and Öland during the eighteenth and nineteenth centuries. These are woollen rugs with fairly long knots made close together, the smooth side often consisting of a many-coloured, striped or checked twill, while the pile side is undyed and devoid of decoration apart from a coloured marking to distinguish the top end from the foot (Pl. 91c). A different type of patterning, occurring in southern Sweden, is formed by the back of the knots being allowed to pass through the ground weave thus forming a geometrical decoration on the plain side. The third variant is the unpretentious utility article known as the 'fisherman's rya' or 'sailor's rug', which was still being made and used in the early years of this century, particularly by seagoing people along the coasts of Finland, Sweden and Norway. These unsophisticated textiles, which can be made out of every kind of material, including strips of cloth, etc., are in fact closely akin to what may have been the original of the rya-rug, the 'artificial fleece'. The geographical and social distribution of the rya-rug and the models which may have inspired the individual ryas have been described by different scholars. Various fabrics and embroideries, both native and foreign, have been suggested. Embroidered samplers are known to have played an important role because in these, mainly executed in cross-stitch, the design was broken up into small squares which could easily be translated into knots.

Seen in an international perspective, the documentary history of the Scandinavian rya-rug is relatively short, lasting for about six or seven centuries. This is one reason why the development of the type is fairly easy to trace. The study of this topic has yielded knowledge that can be profitably applied to certain problems concerning the development of the Oriental carpet.[1]

THE KNOTTED CARPET OF THE ORIENT

The Oriental carpet, a fascinating phenomenon both artistically and historically, first began to arouse general attention during the nineteenth century, when it also became a subject of scientific study. Museums and private collectors vied with each other in acquiring early Oriental carpets. The first major exhibition, held in Vienna in 1891, marked the beginning of a new epoch.[2]

Kurt Erdmann supposed that the knotted pile carpet or rug had originated among primitive nomad peoples in Central Asia as an imitation of an animal fleece, which would make it something of a counterpart to the earliest Scandinavian utility rya-rugs, and that the transition to a decorative textile took place in these surroundings. According to this view, the technique would have been taken westwards by the Seljuks or other Turkish peoples, who might have been the first to introduce this craft to Anatolia from whence carpets are known to have been exported to Europe. This thesis was based on the following facts: after some ten to twelve fragmentary carpets of a previously unknown type were found in a mosque in Konia and later on in Beyshehir (both towns in Asia Minor) they were related to a statement by Marco Polo, who visited the country about 1271, that 'the most beautiful carpets in the world are made in the kingdom of the Seljuks of Rum', of which Konia was the capital. For this reason the 'Konia carpets' were supposed to date from the thirteenth century and thus to be the oldest Oriental carpets still extant.

But this thesis is very questionable for several reasons. The main argument against it is constituted by the well-preserved carpet from Pazyryk, which was discovered in 1949 in the grave of a Siberian chieftain and dated archaeologically as far back as the fifth or fourth century B.C.

The high technical quality and the perfect design of the carpet (a square of roughly two metres with concentric borders depicting horsemen, deer and ornaments directly related to Assyrian and Iranian-Achaemenian art) bear incontrovertible witness to a level of civilization which can only be attributed to Iran under the Achaemenian dynasty (550–330 B.C.). From this point a line of development may be postulated leading on to later Persian court art, at its height about 1500. Between these two poles, then, are at least 1800 years of rising achievement. Looking backwards in time for a primitive stage corresponding to the utility rya-rug of the Nordic countries, we are reduced to guesswork: 3000 B.C. or perhaps a thousand years earlier.

But the main thing, now that we have an actual carpet from Achaemenian times, is that we know Iran to have been proficient in the art of carpet-making long before the Seljuks appeared. This sophisticated artistic production may for various reasons be assumed to have reached its height under the Sasanian rulers (224–651). Just as the court of the Great King was served by its own silk- and tapestry-weaving workshops (cf. pp. 84 and 117 f.), it must also have had workshops for carpet-making. There are, in fact, Greek references to 'soft carpets' which were said to be used by Babylonians and Persians. Certainly it is difficult to envisage the very famous carpet known as *The Spring of Chosroes*, which in 637 was seized by the Roman army at the sack of the Sasanian royal palace at Ctesiphon. It may have been what is termed a 'garden carpet', but the description 'worked of gold and silver and set with innumerable precious stones' appears rather puzzling. A more intelligible description is given of the carpet on which an Abbasid caliph was murdered one October night in 861: it indicates that the border consisted of portrait medallions with Persian inscriptions.

There are still enough specimens of Sasanian silk fabrics in existence to give a rough idea of what a floor carpet could have looked like at that time. In attempting a hypothetical reconstruction of the Sasanian Carpet, should be considered the so-called animal carpets, showing animals in octagonal frames (like the Marby rug Pl. 6a). These are more or less folk-art renderings of earlier prototypes belonging to a higher class of carpet manufacture.

Two types of design: which is the older?

If we reconsider the dating of the 'Konia carpets', it is clear that they cannot possibly date from as far back as the thirteenth century as was supposed. In two of them, at least, the design of the main field consists of repeated pattern units obviously derived from silk fabrics which cannot possibly be dated further back than the fourteenth and fifteenth centuries respectively. In one of these two cases the immediate prototype can actually be identified as a Chinese silk damask, a specimen of which has been discovered in an Egyptian burial (cf. xi, figs 3, 4). The entire 'Konia group' therefore must be post-dated by at least two hundred years.[3] This in turn implies that the above mentioned animal carpets often depicted by Italian painters of the fourteenth and fifteenth centuries must represent an older type than the carpets of the Konia group. Two such animal carpets

xi, fig. 3.   Chinese silk damask with asymmetrical palmetto design. From an Egyptian fourteenth century burial

xi, fig. 4.   Centre pattern of a pile carpet from Konya (Asia Minor), inspired from a silk similar to fig. 3. (Thus not older than the fifteenth century.)

have come down fairly intact. One is the famous 'Marby Carpet' (Pl. 6a) in Stockholm, for many years serving as an altar frontal in a little church in northern Sweden. The other is the 'Dragon Carpet', which was acquired by Berlin from an Italian church but perished in World War Two. The principal motif of the 'Marby Carpet' is a simplified Tree of Life flanked by a pair of birds, while the Berlin fragment depicts a dragon which appears to be of Chinese descent. Both animal motifs are enclosed in an octagonal frame, which is an angular rendering of the more or less circular frame seen in silk designs — the natural result of a coarser technique (cf. xi, fig. 5 and Pl. 6a).

Parallels to the device of birds or other animals flanking a Tree of Life are easily found in silk fabrics belonging to the Sasanian artistic tradition, and they are particularly common in the group which is known to have been made in Sogdiana, a peripheral region of Iranian artistic influence, and an obvious area for a folk-art production (Pl. 18c). These coarse silks with Sasanian design (schematized by the weaving technique) may have been the direct prototypes of the type of rugs we are concerned with.

It should be borne in mind here that folk-art, or popular art — particularly textiles and above all Oriental textiles — is an extremely conservative form of production whose working methods and repertoire of motifs are passed on from generation to generation, subject only to a cautious and gradual process of transformation. In a tradition of this kind, a few centuries make very little difference. The Sogdian silks date from the seventh to ninth centuries, which means that at least 500 years, involving various stages of imitation, separate the silk-woven prototype from the 'Marby Carpet' and similar products. But such rugs might not necessarily have been made in the same area as the silk fabrics: one is inclined to believe that they were woven a long way away. Some five centuries seems

XI, fig. 5. Iranian silk with paired ducks of Sassanian type. Eighth to ninth century. To be compared with the Marby rug, plate 6

sufficient for a textile motif to travel around, especially when one considers that similar themes of identical origin have lived on in the Nordic countries, as, for instance, in the beautiful *rölakan* tapestries from Skåne with animal motifs called *bäckahäst* (Pl. 95b) (something of a Scandinavian Pegasus) and *varulalejon* (a leonine beast whose name defies translation).

The above instances of design prototypes for pile carpets, all of them silk fabrics, made far away and long before, are symptomatic in more ways than one. Owing to the expensive material employed, the new themes portrayed and the craftsmanship involved, silk weaving occupied a leading position in the textile arts which gave added impact to its patterns. New trends in textile design made their first appearance in silk weaving. Moreover, silk fabrics were easily transported, with the result that they were distributed far and wide. All these factors helped to make patterned silks the most effective means whereby textile ornament and pattern motifs were communicated from one place to another. In the case of the carpets from Konia and the relatively simple craftsmanship that no doubt predominated after the city lost its political status and its court, and, consequently, its court workshops, it is perfectly understandable that a

xi, fig. 6.   Fragment of a pile rug of Caucasian type, fourteenth to fifteenth century, found at Fostat

Chinese silk, which happened to turn up, should have provided the model for a carpet design (cf. XI, figs 3, 4).

Specially designed carpet patterns are hardly likely to have occurred anywhere except in the Persian court workshops between the fifteenth and seventeenth centuries, and even then the same group of artists, the miniature-painters, provided the designs for practically all branches of artistic activity. The main difference between a pattern for a silk or velvet fabric and the design for a carpet was that the former had to be limited to a pattern repeat which could be repeated automatically again and again. But relatively similar repetitions sometimes occur in carpets, even though they are not technically necessary. It was probably not uncommon for the same design to be used for carpets as well as for loom-woven fabrics.

When considering early remains of knotted carpets the following observation may be appropriate. One of the most conspicuous of the Egyptian finds is a fairly large fragment in the custody of the Metropolitan Museum in New York, whose pattern can be interpreted as a replica of a marble mosaic floor from late antiquity. This textile, then, provides further evidence for the above contention concerning the use of similar designs for quite different media.

European painting often bears witness to the importation of Oriental carpets, and it also shows what use was made of these colourful and exotic decorative fabrics. In Italy during the fourteenth and fifteenth centuries they would often be hung from windows and balconies on festive occasions. In northern Europe during the sixteenth and seventeenth centuries they were above all used as table covers in secular surroundings, while on the other hand Memling's depiction of an Oriental carpet on the floor in front of the enthroned Madonna indicates a treasure that could only be placed on the floor on the most auspicious occasions.

The heyday of the Oriental carpet

The Oriental carpet is essentially a unique, one-off product. This applies equally to the simple popular type, rustic in both design and colouring, and to the masterpieces of artistry and technical skill that could only be produced under the aegis of powerful patrons. Carpets are a supreme example of teamwork, highly artistic teamwork in which the effort and individual ability of every weaver is hardly less important than the pattern designed by a leading artist.

There are in general three basic types of production: folk art, craftsmen in small workshops, and court workshops. The purest form of folk art is the domestic handicraft practised by farmers and cattle-herding nomads. The nomads were restricted to a small, easily portable loom, while farmers permanently settled in one place could use larger and more stable implements, both kinds being so-called tapestry looms, in which the weaver starts from the bottom and works upwards, beating with a heavy iron comb. There would be no specially composed patterns in communities of this kind. The weavers employed well-known traditional themes that could be learnt by heart. Alien themes were sometimes adopted, but only in isolated communities. Outside influences were assimilated in a conservative spirit.

Town craftsmen in their permanent workshops generally worked to orders from merchants or private clients. Of course, they had better resources than the domestic craftsmen, in terms both of looms and of pattern motifs, including designs which had originally been conceived in palace workshops and successively gained wider currency. However, these patterns had to be schematized in order to suit the techniques of a rather primitive town workshop. Here again there were no complete models to be followed. For the sake of simplicity, certain pattern elements, borders and repeating patterns for the main field, were standardized and repeated on a routine basis, sometimes to chanted instructions. This working method is recognizable from the way in which pattern units are broken off to suit the size of the carpet, without regard for the composition as a whole.

The Persian palace workshops used small cursory sketches: there were no full-scale cartoons of the kind employed in the corresponding type of European work. Many of these compositions resemble those of book-covers, displaying a lobed central medallion which is repeated in quartered sections in the corners inside the border. But, as already mentioned, consistently repetitive patterns also occur. The use of the small sketch demanded a great deal from the weaver, who had to translate it into full size on the right scale. As an example of this mastery may be mentioned the splendid 'hunting carpet' belonging to the King of Sweden, which measures no less than 285 by 555 centimetres.

All 'genuine' Oriental carpets, older than about 1850, are made entirely of wool from the long-haired breeds of sheep living in the highland areas where these rugs were originally manufactured. As a rule the palace workshops also used wool for the pile, whose deep, saturated colours could only be produced with this material. On the other hand, during the period of highest achievement, it was almost the rule for the most precious carpets (which had to be very closely knotted for the sake of the details) that the ground weave, or at least the warp, was of silk. Among the fine old Persian carpets only some rare sixteenth-century ones were made with a silk pile, as in the case of the 'hunting carpet' mentioned above. A special kind of silk carpet was made in Persia but not for use there. It has a thin, almost flat pile of silk and was made solely for presentation to foreigners. Because a large number of such carpets found their way to Poland they were formerly believed to have been made there and are thus generally but misleadingly termed 'Polish carpets', Persian miniatures of the fifteenth century bear abundant witness to the high standard of Persian carpet-making at that time. Only a small number of such specimens have come down to us. But there are sufficient examples of sixteenth-century Safavid court production to testify to its superb quality. At its best, the Persian carpet is a complex work of art which does not yield all its secrets at first glance. Professor Richard Ettinghausen has written well on this point in *Oriens* (Leiden, 1958):

The Safavid carpet had functions of a psychological nature beyond its basic service as a warm, soft and handsome floor covering. The key to a proper understanding of it lies in so much of the Persian landscape, those immense, barren, monotonously brown or grey vistas, glaringly hot or windswept; and in the compact but equally monotonous earth-coloured towns or villages haphazardly built up without planning or loving care. Like the gardens the carpets provide the mental antidote for these ubiquitous sights. . . . Better than a garden, these carpets are *in* the house and exist in all seasons. Similarly, as in certain Safavid palace pavilions where the architect tried to bring the house into the garden by having a large open portico jutting out into it, so the designer of the Safavid carpet, conversely, brings the beauty of the garden into the house. The studied order in the carpets, with all their intricacy, was undoubtedly just as deeply satisfying as was the formalism of the Persian garden.

In a wider sense, too, the underlying idea of the Persian carpet can be described as that of a blossoming garden, the synthesis of ideal existence for the Oriental. The whole of Oriental carpet-weaving can be compared to an enormous flower garden including the widest variety of species, great and small, colourful decorative plants requiring good soil and a mild climate and less pretentious herbs that can do well on poorer ground, all children of the same earth and subject to its peculiar characteristics, and only to be transplanted at the expense of their character and vigour. The land of the Oriental carpet is like a gigantic meadow which has long yielded splendid harvests, not least in the form of wild plants, products of folk art, with all its strengths and weaknesses.

The later development of the Oriental carpet

As the seventeenth century drew on and during the eighteenth century Persian carpet-making developed a certain artistic debasement, at the same time as its technical standards degenerated. Later this comparative recession became still more noticeable, as lines gradually became more relaxed and angularized while at the same time ornaments were dissolved and began to revert to their folk art antecedents. 'The garden plants run wild and their seeds spread far and wide in a process of hybridization. New species develop which are sometimes difficult if not impossible to define.' During the twentieth century it has become increasingly common practice for Oriental carpets to be sold under geographical designations which are supposed to indicate where they were manufactured, or rather, where the dealers have bought them. A name of this kind implies a certain type of carpet with a special combination of themes, colours and technical characteristics. However, the progressive commercialization of the carpet trade has given rise to so many names (some of them impossible to verify) that one is more inclined to speak in terms of trademarks. The main essential, therefore, is to know the respective native areas of the four main groups: Persia, Central Asia, the Caucasus, and Anatolia.

The carpets least affected by outside influences are those which until recently were made in Central Asia by various Turcoman tribes leading a nomadic existence on the far-flung steppes of the Asian interior. Bokhara, the ancient capital of the Sogdians, was the common trading centre of these tribes, hence the somewhat misleading commercial designation 'Bokhara carpets'. All these carpets are distinguished by their dense and usually low pile, their lustrous wool and their deep colour range in various shades of red. The somewhat monotonous patterns are composed of highly geometrical repeat ornaments. They often look very ancient, but none of them is likely to date back further than the eighteenth century.

The Caucasus, together with the neighbouring country of Armenia and the north-eastern parts of Anatolia, is the home of a genuine and distinctive folk art with an independent, conservative sense of style which has been very sparing in its assimilation of foreign themes. Compositions vary, and the repertoire of patterns displays an abundant diversity. Certain alien motifs or types of composition evidently date from a very long time ago, which accounts for the completeness of their assimilation. Interesting proof of folkart conservatism is given by some Caucasian carpets which, although probably made no earlier than the nineteenth century, have patterns of the same kind as those depicted by such fifteenth-century

European artists as Memling. The Caucasian carpets are distinguished by their fresh colouring and clear, well-balanced colour contrasts. The pile is often deep.

Anatolia, the old name for Asia Minor, which roughly corresponds to present day Turkey, has long been regarded by Europeans as the heartland of Oriental carpet-making. It was from there that the first Oriental carpets came to the west. But although the history of the knotted carpet goes back a very long way in this country, in the absence of any documents concerning the age of Anatolian carpets and because, as has already been made clear, no very ancient carpets can be identified with complete certainty as Anatolian, it is hard to say exactly how long the art of carpet-making has been established in Anatolia. However, some of the towns in the western parts of the Anatolian highlands, particularly Ushak, Ghiordes, Bergamo, Kula, Ladik, Konia, etc., had long been practising a craft of folk art character. The carpets thus made were for the most part exported by way of Smyrna (present day Izmir) to Europe, where they were known as 'Smyrna carpets'. Some of them were made to order and incorporated crests, etc. The workshops had no separate artistic management but tended to reproduce local patterns, the pattern units being repeated regardless of the size of the carpet. A certain amount of influence must have been derived from earlier princely workshops, though these never attained the artistic capacity of the Persian court manufactories. Passing influences left various marks, some more noticeable than others, on the shaping of the various local types.

Off-shoots from the original carpet-making areas

Apart from the areas whose own production of wool occasioned the production of carpets for sale, special workshops were organized to produce carpets for the courts of the Moslem rulers, who demanded a high artistic standard. One particular type of very high quality, with abstract, finely worked patterns mainly in two-colours, was formerly supposed to have been woven in Damascus but is now generally considered to have been made in Cairo for the Mameluke court, probably in the sixteenth and seventeenth centuries.[4]

The Moorish occupation of Spain brought carpet-weaving to that country, and there is written evidence to this effect from the twelfth century. The oldest extant carpets date from the fifteenth century: this is known from the coats of arms that are woven into them. These carpets differ from all those known from the Orient, by reason of the knot, which includes only one warp thread, and also through the typical small geometrical patterns, which in fact are reminiscent of contemporary or earlier Spanish silks with their small pattern units.

FLEECY TEXTILES OF VARIOUS SHAPES AND ORIGINS

The Latin word *villosa* may have signified various kinds of weave with additional pile, either knotted or otherwise inserted, but it could also have referred to woven materials which have been made hairy by some secondary treatment. There are a number of late medieval occurrences of the word which refer unambiguously to knotted pile rugs of the kind dealt with in the preceding sections of this chapter, but in the great majority of cases it is impossible to deduce the appearance of the fabric or the textile techniques they involved. One is therefore thrown back on hypothetical identifications with recent material and with a limited number of archaeological finds.

The solid execution of the two categories, the bed-cover and floor carpet, already dealt with, had an important bearing on their practical function. A bed rya of the old type contained a large quantity of wool, for instance, a sixteenth-century Finnish rya-rug could require no less than 17 kilograms. The knotting technique was more or less essential in order to prevent the pile yarn from sliding out of the ground weave as a result of heavy use. Similar considerations must have applied to the unknown precursors of the Oriental carpet. A textile destined to lie on the ground of a tent or on the floor of a palace, where people would either sit on it or walk on it barefoot, had to be thick and firm and the tightly set knots gave added stability to the weave. In view of the large numbers in which these articles were produced, it is only natural that the technique eventually became standardized in the form known to us from both rya-rugs and Oriental carpets; the differences between the common varieties of knot are of little significance, although rya-rugs include several deviations from the normal technique. Whether the different kinds of knotted pile are to be regarded as mutually independent inventions is another problem, and it is this problem that the following account sets out to investigate.

Early references and illustrations

First of all it should be observed that there were, and still are, several other types of piled and napped ('hairy') fabrics. It is hard to give exact translations of their names, because these derive from early texts in Latin and other languages and words referring, not to the technique but to the visible effect. Many of these pile fabrics served mainly as articles of clothing, a function demanding very different properties from those of a bed rya or a carpet, above all, lightness and flexibility.

There are two French sculptures of John the Baptist providing an excellent illustration of what these pile fabrics may have looked like in thirteenth-century Europe.[5] In both of them the mantle is draped and worn with the pile outwards. When John the Baptist retreated into the wilderness, the hairy garb of the shepherd, 'raiment of camel's hair', was the obvious thing for him to wear. In Christian art, this became the Baptist's attribute and as such can be seen in countless representations both earlier and later than the two examples referred to here. One of the very earliest, dating from about 550, adorns the famous archiepiscopal throne in Ravenna. An apparently similar garment, with distinct and regular tufts, is depicted on sculptures from a far earlier period, namely from Sumerian Mesopotamia (*c*.3000 B.C.). This *guenna*, mainly worn as a skirt (hanging below the waist), has been compared or identified by some scholars with the *kaunaké* of classical Greece. There is a fairly exhaustive reference to the *kaunaké* in Aristophanes's Wasps, first performed in 422 B.C. In verses 1131–1156 the young snob Bdelycleon is made to foist on his old father an expensive cloak said to be of a kind never before seen in Athens. It was probably dyed purple. Aristophanes mentions that these luxurious cloaks, also known as 'Persian' cloaks, were made in the town of Ecbatana (later called Hamadan) and that they were (in *c*.422 B.C.) the height of fashion in Sardes (the capital of ancient Lydia). Later on, similar fabrics also became fashionable in Rome. In his *Historia Naturalis VIII*, Pliny the Younger remarks: 'In my father's day, people began wearing the *gausapa* (a coverlet or cloak with the pile or nap on one side), while *amphimallia* (cloaks with pile on both sides) and *ventralia villosa* (hairy or pile-woven girdles or skirts?) have only come to be worn in my own lifetime. Now people have also started weaving tunics with wide borders of the same kind as in a *gausapa*, that is, with the pile or nap on one side.'[6] Pliny the Elder died in A.D. 79 and his son died before 114.

In Latin documents from eighth-century Europe, above all on the subject of Frisian trade, there occurs a term which seems as far as we can judge to refer to something similar, namely *villosa*, as a description of cloaks and coverlets. Unfortunately how they were made is unknown. Perhaps more precise information — information that can be checked against the archaeological finds — could be gained from a fresh perusal of the original texts.

These texts were studied by an Austrian archivist (P. Kletler) who in 1924 published a work that has frequently been quoted by Scandinavian archaeologists. Kletler showed clearly that *villosa* fabrics could be of various qualities, ranging from coarse 'goat-hair' to the very fine. He believes that they were made in the north-western parts of the continent of Europe and exported from there to England and Italy, and he says that they were used as bed-covers and rainwear. Here as in other similar cases, it is regrettable that the original wording is not quoted together with the German interpretations, for example, *Regenschirme* (umbrella), which is probably an erroneous translation. Scepticism is also aroused by the various evaluations of quality, as in the assumption that a goat-hair fabric is bound to be coarse and inferior. Evidently it has escaped the author's notice that natural fleeces, especially those from primitive breeds of sheep, contain both soft wool and hairs, both of varying quality; that there are breeds of goat having hair of extreme fineness and high quality; that the hairs serve to keep out the rain, and, a matter of no little importance in this connexion, that the same function can be imparted to a fabric made of similar material if, by one method or the other, it is made hairy or shaggy.

Inventories from the chateaux of medieval France include frequent references to hairy or shaggy fabrics under the name *tapis veluz*, which is again an unsatisfactory term, because *tapis* means a cover, which could be hung on the wall, placed on a bed or laid on the floor, and of course *veluz* is the same word as *villosa*. A very detailed inventory of the valuable estate of Charles V of France (d. 1380) refers to large quantities of *tapis veluz*, but nothing is mentioned concerning their colours or decoration.[7] Evidently they had been woven in small, narrow looms: when the width is specified, it is about an ell.[8] The format of each piece is stated in terms of the number of widths and their length. These pieces, which were relatively small, seem to have been used as a means of insulation from cold floors, beside the beds, upon or underneath chairs and benches fixed to the wall. In cases of this kind, the fabrics used were undoubtedly simple utility products woven by native craftsmen. Perhaps they resembled the *tapis nostrez* which were being made in Paris in the thirteenth century. But they may also have resembled the *rya* which the nuns of Vadstena were permitted to use. On the other hand an inventory of somewhat later date, compiled in 1409, mentions a *tapis veluz* with large patterns and coats of arms. This must have been a knotted carpet of Oriental or Spanish type.

Similar references are quite common in later periods. All that can be said with any certainty is that *villosa, veluz* and similar terms refer not to the actual technique, but to its effect.

Surviving specimens of napped or piled fabrics

This section deals with the napped fabrics and pile weaves that exist today in the form of archaeological finds and recent materials, together with the manner of their execution.

Egyptian burial finds from between A.D. 200 and 800 include several variants. Even in a single fabric both voided pile weave of multi-coloured wool, forming patterns, and deep, dense pile of linen thread forming a hairy rim can be found. The latter variety, which is always linen of a single colour and uncut, is executed by means of a continuous thread drawn up into loops without forming knots — 'looped weave' in other words.

The oldest known European examples of piled textiles come from a Bronze Age find made in Denmark, though it is not really relevant here because, according to Hald and Broholm (1940) the pile threads were inserted afterwards, presumably with a needle. A very rich chamber burial, dated to the fourth century A.D. and including fragments of knotted pile, was excavated in Pilgramsdorf in East Prussia in 1937. According to the German scholar who analysed the textiles, the knots were of the Ghiordes type and were done in woollen yarn on a ground weave of hemp, the density 13–14 knots per 10 centimetres width. Referring to the other burial furniture, part of which (e.g. silks) was Oriental, the writers assumed that the knotted pile fabric was Oriental too. However, the hemp of the ground weave casts some doubt on this conclusion.

During her excavation of grave 6 at Valsgärde (Uppland, Sweden), dating from the mid-eighth century, Professor Greta Arwidsson recovered tiny remains of a rya-like coverlet which had been laid over the dead man and the abundant treasures that were interred with him. Two shields had been placed on top of the coverlet, thus emphasizing its value as decoration. A still perceptible difference of shading suggests that the pile was of more than one colour. The analysis pointed to a peculiar and otherwise unknown technique with plied pieces of yarn being twisted around each other and at the same time at intervals bound down into the ground weave.[9]

The so-called *Terpen* or bog finds from Holland contain a special kind of shaggy or coarse pile weaves, which unfortunately can only be dated approximately between A.D. 500 and 1200. There is, for instance, a corner piece of a thick coverlet which has long thick ends of yarn sparsely hanging on one side of the weave, probably inserted during the weaving process. Because of the very strong felting, however, the weave is difficult to analyse. At least five more finds of this kind are known from the Viking period. Two of them come from the west of the British Isles, one from Kildonan on the island of Eigg of Scotland (A.D. 850–900) and one from Jurby on the Isle of Man (*c.* A.D. 900). The finds made at Birka included a scanty fragment of two-coloured unspun wool but of an unidentifiable technique. A few years ago a well-preserved Icelandic textile find was published by Elsa Guðjonsson, who subjected it to an interesting investigation which also included the finds from the British Isles. A find from Volynia, dated to the ninth century, has a technical resemblance to the Kildonan fragment.[10] Lastly a similar textile found during the investigations of medieval town remains in Lund in southern Sweden, may be mentioned.

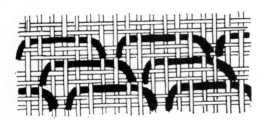

xi, fig. 7.   Technique of pile weave from Volynia, nineth century

The Icelandic fragment was discovered near the old homestead of Heynes in the south-west of Iceland, and its position, at a depth of about 2 metres, indicated that it dates from between 900 and 1000. It comprises two somewhat different pieces, joined by a secondary seam, which probably come from two separate cloaks. The ground weave is a four-end twill. Interestingly enough, the pile consists, not of spun yarn but of continuous locks or tufts of long hair, between 15 and 19 centimetres long, taken straight from the fleece. Each lock has been inserted in the shed under two or more warp threads and secured with a loop round one of the warp threads — a knot which has not been observed previously. The Kildonan specimen is similarly executed, but without the loop. The most interesting thing about this find is that it can be related to ancient Icelandic law writings, *Grágás*, containing descriptions of different commodities. Wool and woollens were of course staple Icelandic exports, and certain carefully described standard types were legal tender. Woven pile cloaks — corresponding to the rectangular plaid which until recently formed part of the traditional costume of the Scottish highlander — were known by the following names: *vararfeldir* had to be rectangular, measuring 204 by 102 centimetres and with thirteen 'locks' across the weave; *hafnarfeldir* was of a finer quality, and then there were *roggvarfeldir* and *feldir*, which could also be semicircular. Since the locks on the Heynes fragment are much closer together than is required for a *vararfeldir*, it must have come from a *hafnarfeldur* or some other superior *feldur*. These regulations are thought to have remained in force until about 1200, when the production of *feldir* is said to have ceased. During the same period, mention is made of another name for a similar thing: *loði* and *loðkapa*, which latter could also have sleeves. The Icelandic author thinks that these terms denote a napped weave resembling the Slovakian specimens and other products which will be discussed shortly. Yet another term, *kögur*, is sometimes used during the Middle Ages and even later in connexion with *feldur*. The Icelandic writer surmises that *kögur* denotes an imported product used as a coverlet. Previously that word was related to *kavring*, a term which in southern Sweden was used to denote a rya-rug.

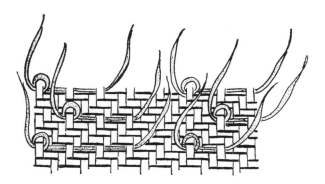

XI, fig. 8. Technique of pile weave from Heynes, Iceland. tenth to eleventh century

On the subject of these different products, the question arises as to why, as a general rule at least, they were worn with the pile outwards. No doubt the reason was that already alluded to: the long hairs from the natural fleece of the animal were the best possible means of keeping out the rain. First and foremost, then, the hairy cloak was a practical outer garment, whether, like John the Baptist or the wandering shepherd, the owner lived in the wilderness, or whether he was merely going on a journey. Clearly, however, the 'hairy cloak' could also be a luxury garment. According to *Gragas*, an Icelandic *feldur* from the twelfth century could be shaggy on one or both sides, and the locks could be either fine and close together or coarse and sparse. The cloak could be grey, white, black, red or blue, and it could be striped or decorated with bands, in short, a status symbol which may have resembled the Heynes fragment. Perhaps the *villosa* of the Frisian merchants were of this kind?

At this stage of my writing a new publication came to my notice which serves to amplify the above observations in several respects. A Slovakian scholar, Dr Ema Markovà, presented the results of her studies of a long-haired clothing material which until very recently had been made in Slovakia and Hungary, as well as in the Balkans and the Ukraine.[11] This production, which takes the form of both domestic and professional handicraft, is based on a breed of sheep whose hairy fleece is ideal for the purpose, forming as it does long and virtually straight hanging locks. These sheep, which are known as 'Wallachians' in Slovakia, are distinguished by their long, spiral horns. They are above all associated with the Carpathians and the nearby highland areas, but the breed is now almost extinct. These shaggy materials were invariably used, it seems, for making outer clothing, above all sleeved coats which were used by shepherds among others, but they were also used for trousers and even full military uniforms, according to a drawing of 1570.

It is a fundamental characteristic of this product — a characteristic that has never been explained before and for which the Slovakian writer has found evidence in ancient Greece — that the weft is not spun. The vase-painting (I, fig. 1) shows the wool being shaped to rolls ready for entering the shed as weft. A special implement, known throughout the Carpathians as the *druga*, is used to produce this sliver and to wind it up. As a result of

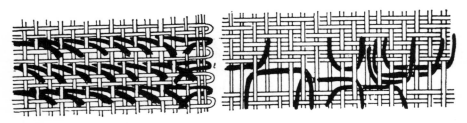

XI, fig. 9. Techniques of 'shaggy mantles' recently manufactured in the Carpathians, generally used in Slovakia and Ukraine, respectively

this procedure, the wool retains its porosity. The treatment which follows weaving releases the long hairs, thus forming a long nap. There are three different weaving methods, the most important of which will be considered shortly. The other two methods appear to be time-saving substitutes for an earlier and more painstaking procedure. In one of them the thick *druga* yarn passes directly as weft in a shed consisting of sparse warp ends of hemp, and is very well beaten in. Afterwards the fabric is teazled and fulled in water by means of a wheel construction. Another method, from Eastern Slovakia, involves plucking up the *druga* weft to loops here and there (xi, fig. 1c), after which the fabric undergoes more or less the same treatment as in the previous instance. The most widespread and apparently, the original procedure in this connexion was for relatively short pieces of *druga* yarn to be inserted in the main weave with long ends left hanging and torn off by hand. After it has been duly processed, the surface of the weave bears a striking resemblance to the natural fleece, with its long locks of hair, and it also serves the same practical purpose of excluding damp and rain. The garments made from this material were extremely useful in all kinds of weather.

As can be seen from the diagrams in xi, fig. 9 the ground weave is usually tabby, and the thick yarn ends in alternate sheds are inserted straight, behind two or three warp threads. It is only at the edges that the weave is looped round a warp thread so as to resemble a species of knot. A specimen from the Ukraine incorporates partially longer, irregular insertions, and the ground weave there is four-end twill.

Knotted pile weaves from medieval Europe

Opinions differ as to when and how the technique of knotted pile was first introduced into Europe, or whether it was in fact invented independently in the West. However, there are records from Moslem Spain which bear witness to carpet-making as early as the twelfth century. Mention should also be made here of the fragments of knotted pile rugs — single-warp knots tightly set, all wool — which belonged to the funeral cloths of the Emperors Conrad II (d. 1039) and Henry IV (d. 1106), buried in Speyer. S. Müller, in her publication rightly considers these carpets, originally very fine, to be of Oriental or possibly Spanish origin. One important source, namely the Paris guild regulations has proved to be highly controversial. The earliest of these, the *Livre d'Etienne Boileau* of 1258, which is based on conditions during the twelfth century, mentions two separate corporations: the *tapissiers* producing *tapis nostrez*, coarse woollen coverlets of native type, and the very highly qualified *tapissiers sarazinois*. In a later version of the statute published in 1302, the latter category is distinguished from another group of *tapissiers*, namely those working *en haute lice*. Certain French scholars now believe these last two categories to refer to the technique which has been known for centuries in France as *tapisserie* but also as *hautelisse* (in both cases meaning tapestry technique). Other authorities, such as Betty Kurth and Kurt Erdmann, maintain that 'Saracen' must have meant *tapis veluz* — 'hairy' knotted pile carpets — a not improbably but, unfortunately, unproven explanation. Whatever type of craftsman the term *tapissier sarazinois* may have referred to in thirteenth-century Paris, there are other very good reasons for supposing that knotted pile with a many-coloured, dense nap did not occupy a very prominent position in the textile art of the West during the Middle Ages. Perhaps the most telling argument of all is the well-documented and extraordinarily rich production of tapestry wall-coverings which, starting in Paris, developed in the towns and cities of northern France and Flanders during the fourteenth and fifteenth centuries.

From medieval Central Europe there is one great work in knotted pile: the originally very large figured wall-hanging in Quedlinburg. This work, remarkable in more ways than one, was made between 1186 and 1203 and was originally intended as a gift to Pope Innocent III from the Abbess of Quedlinburg, Agnes, who seems to have been an outstanding personality. In her authoritative work on figured tapestries, Betty Kurth, the late Austrian scholar, ranks this gigantic composition — thoroughly classical in style and conception — as the high-water mark of the period of artistic development that occurred in twelfth-century Saxony. This wall-hanging is also unusual from the point of view of textile technique. The knot is made over a single warp thread (XI, figs 2c, d), as in the funeral rugs in Speyer mentioned above and in later Spanish carpets, while the ground weave consists of a stout hempen thread as used in the contemporaneous Halberstadt tapestries. Thus the Quedlinburg wall-hanging is based on an independent procedure specially devised for the task in hand, which testifies to a very high degree of technical skill and also to an artistic leadership that was by no means common in the workshops of medieval convents. It is impossible to tell how those in charge of the Quedlinburg workshop had acquired their knowledge of this technique, which they adapted (probably for the first time ever) for a figure composition, in a way which represented a technical refinement of the best contemporary painting. Apparently, this new departure was never emulated, and four hundred years were to pass before anything comparable was produced in Europe in this particular textile technique.

European pile carpets since the Middle Ages

The first European-made pile carpets were all imitations of the carpets imported from the east, the aim being to replace these imports with less expensive native products. For example great efforts were made in sixteenth-century England to establish carpet manufacture according to the 'Levantine' method. A few specimens have come down to us, including a fragment with a coat-of-arms which probably belonged to Queen Elizabeth. In 1597 a dyer named Hubblethorne was sent to Persia to collect as much technical knowledge as he was able, but little came out of it all.

It was in France that the first genuinely European pile carpets saw the light of day. Some time before 1604, a man by the name of Fortier approached Henri IV with a project for manufacturing *tapiz de Turquie en façon de Levant*. In fact the enterprise took shape under the leadership of another man, Pierre Dupont, who was allowed to set up his workshop in no less a place than the Louvre. His pupil Lourdet acquired premises in the Chaillot Palace in 1626, and from there the factory moved to the old soap factory called *La Savonnerie* in 1672. It was under this name that the firm became famous for its *tapis veloutés* in the current French ornamental style. The *Savonnerie* carpets were invariably woven after pattern drawings adapted to the rooms where the carpets were to be installed. In 1825 *La Savonnerie* amalgamated with *La Manufacture des Gobelins*.

In England the success of the *Savonnerie* led to French instructors being summoned to London in the mid-eighteenth century, which in turn gave rise to English court production on similar lines. Long before that, however, there were a number of minor workshops producing what was known as 'Turkey work', rather a cheap commodity (often with an inlaid instead of a knotted pile). It was used mostly for upholstery or for other purposes requiring small sizes. These products were also exported.

Carpets aspiring to the name of *Savonnerie* were also made in Sweden. This happened during the eighteenth century, when work was resumed on the new royal palace in Stockholm, and weaving operations were directed by French 'tapisiers' (Pignan, Duru and Serre) who were engaged in 1744 to weave tapestries and train Swedish pupils. They found a really promising pupil in Per Hilleström, who was given further encouragement by means of a visit to France, where in 1757 and 1758 he was enabled to study work at *La Savonnerie* and *Les Gobelins*.

On his return to Sweden, Hilleström produced several excellent pieces of work in both techniques. He also had a number of pupils, including his own son Karl Peter Hilleström, who was later to acquire greater renown as a painter.[12]

SUMMARY

To recapitulate the last few pages and the data, in both words and pictures, that serves to indicate the early occurrence of some form of pile textiles: the material from the Carpathians, partly of recent date, shows how difficult it is to tell what technique can have been meant by the Latin *villosa* and similar terms. The first question to be answered is whether hairiness — the pile or nap effect — has been produced by the insertion of extra yarn in the ground weave during the weaving process, or whether it is merely the result of napping, teazling and other forms of after-treatment.

Concerning the addition of extra yarn, investigations have revealed a host of technical variants ranging from the straightforward and evidently random insertion of locks or yarn ends, sometimes tied around a warp thread, to systematically regular knots of the kind known from the Oriental carpets. On closer investigation the Nordic rya-rugs are found to have been quite variable. In fact there is no evidence to prove that the oldest rya-rugs, those of which only documentary evidence remains, were executed in exactly the same way as most of the ryas that are extant today. The trend has naturally been towards standardization and similarity, which of course was further encouraged by the organization of large-scale productions, as in the case of the royal manors of Finland and Sweden during the sixteenth and seventeenth centuries and by the existence of workshops and, particularly during the past 100 years, by the existence of weaving schools, courses, and books. Perhaps the 'inlay technique' of the oldest Nordic ryas resembled the Icelandic cloak fragment (xi, fig. 8), where the inlay material was shown to consist of a lock from the untreated fleece. At least this is not impossible. In this connexion the etymological interpretation of Hj Falk the ancient Norse term *ryja* (to pick up the wool naturally shed by the sheep) may be relevant. Sheep shearing is considered a relatively novel practice which did not occur in the Scandinavian countries until the twelfth century. Both the Slovakian study and the Heynes find enhance the probability of this interpretation: the porous tufts of wool no doubt made excellent *druga* yarn, to borrow the

Slovakian term for it. Comparing the technique exemplified by diagrams of textiles from the area of diffusion thus identified — the Near East, Egypt, the Carpathians, Spain, the British Isles, Iceland and Scandinavia during a period of about 2,000 years — it is hard to draw a line of demarcation between the incidence of simple inlays and, on the other hand, what may be classified as 'knots'. Inlays with a fastening loop occur in the Carpathians in the same garments as straight inlays, and archaeological finds from north-western Europe have yielded specimens incorporating both techniques. On the other hand it is probable that the use of paired loops combined to form a 'knot' (for example, the Sehna and Ghiordes knot) was evolved in the Orient three thousand years ago; the technique is fully developed, for instance, in the Pazyryk carpet (500–300 B.C.). In the Scandinavian rya-rugs that have come down, very few of which antedate the mid-eighteenth century, the pile usually consists of tufts bearing quite a close resemblance to the Oriental knots. But, as was already mentioned, there are also irregular types of ryas, and there is no evidence to show how the pile was executed in earlier times, that is, during the fourteenth, fifteenth, sixteenth, and seventeenth centuries. Possibly there was a gradual and natural standardization of an originally more primitive technique which may have arisen and evolved quite independently.

There is no need to be constantly on the look-out for influences as an explanation for technical similarities. At least, this applies to the following case, which came to my knowledge as a result of some photographs which I received from New Zealand a long time ago. The photographs show a number of Maori men wearing cloaks which obviously have a kind of pile on both sides (Pl. 91a). Bengt Danielsson of Stockholm states that these cloaks are plaited by hand from a kind of raffia. When the Maoris came to New Zealand from the Friendly Islands, in about A.D. 1000, they did not have looms. It must have been the considerably cooler New Zealand climate that induced them to insert dog hair or feathers to form something resembling a fleece. The outside of this garment was often decorated with hanging threads, as shown in the pictures. This type of pile must have been invented by the Maoris without any outside cultural influence, a fact which is certainly relevant to the problem considered above.

XII *Dyeing, Textile Printing and Pattern Dyeing*

Colour is something very essential to textiles, especially when the woven material, besides its utilitarian purpose, is intended for the adornment of dress or decoration in general. The colour effect can be attained in different ways: by the varying shades of the natural fibres, by painting (applying pigmental colours with a brush or a stamp), or by regular dyeing.

DYEING

Dyeing is a chemical process executed by immersion in a dyebath in combination with various treatments especially adapted to the different colouring agents as well as to the kind of fibre material which is to be dyed. The preparation of the textile fibre with a mordant of some kind is of decisive importance in getting the fibres in question to absorb a certain dyestuff. In several instances, however, further treatment may also be necessary to attain the required shade of colour and to make that colour fast, that is, resistant to the influence of light and washing. As a general rule the animal fibres (wool and silk) will absorb a dyeing agent fairly easily, while vegetable fibres are not very amenable to any dyeing process. These observations, of course, refer to natural, not synthetic, dyestuffs.

These dyeing procedures can be applied 'in piece' or 'in yarn', the latter being the method required for most kinds of patterned weaves. Wool may also be dyed 'in wool', especially when it is to be used for blending and multicoloured fabrics. But there are also other kinds of methods for the additional application of a design on a woven material; these methods are described below, under the heading 'Pattern Dyeing'.

Surviving silk fabrics from the last centuries B.C. show that the Chinese had developed methods of dyeing silk yarn in several colours for use in their most exquisite weaving. Still older woollen textiles, preserved in the famous Siberian burial sites, bear witness to a corresponding proficiency within the Iranian civilization. Moreover the Old Testament contains similar references. Thus Exodus XXVI includes a description of the

Temple veil adorned with cherubim 'in artistic weave' (no doubt tapestry) 'of white linen thread and blue, purple and scarlet woollen yarn'. The latter colours may probably have been dyed with indigo, true purple and some kind of kermes, perhaps the kind of cochineal for which Persia became famous during Roman times. Here may also be mentioned the intricate methods of dyeing cotton developed in India long before, the technology of which did not become known to Europe until the eighteenth century.

Some important dyestuffs

The art of using the *purpura mollusc* to make red, violet and even black dyes is considered to have been developed by the Phoenicians during the first millenium B.C. It was in the nature of things for this work to be done on the coast where the molluscs were caught, the eastern shore of the Mediterranean. Very large quantities were needed to dye even a small amount of wool, and collecting the molluscs was a laborious business. The expense of this method as well as the aesthetically pleasing result gave purple its special status as the colour of the ruler. Thus the officers of state of the Roman Empire were entitled to wear the *toga praetexta*, a cloak with one or more purple stripes, emblems of rank or status symbols that soon prompted imitations and developed into a fashion.

Generally speaking, textiles in bright red colours have always been much sought after, but it has always been very difficult to dye a red that will be fast to light and washing. The commonest red dye was obtained since ancient times from the root of some species of the *Rubiaceae* family (madder), which grew practically everywhere, either cultivated by man or in its natural state. Thus the dye itself, which has remained in use until recent times, was not expensive, but the quality of the colour (a medium red generally with a touch of yellow), and its durability, very much depended on the method used and the skill with which it was practised. Very often this kind of red gradually changes to a more or less brownish tint resembling tanned leather and therefore known in English as 'tan' or 'buff'.

Durable and very bright shades of red, with a tinge of blue, were derived from certain species of scale insects, which prey on various plants. One of the dyeing substances most highly rated during the Middle Ages was called kermes, a name deriving from an Arabic word meaning 'insect'. Since these small insects or lice were sold dried, they resembled berries or grains and were therefore called *grana* in Italy.

The genuine kermes, or rather a related species used in Iran during Sasanian times and called 'Persian cochineal', was used to dye the brilliant woollen material of the so-called riding-coats from Antinoë.[1] This very precious kind of material, a napped woollen fabric of the highest quality, was dyed in various colours. Originally it was the material itself that was called *scarlatum* in Latin. It was only gradually that this word came to denote a red colour and in that sense entered many European languages: scarlet from *écarlat* (Fr.), *scharlachrot* (Ger.), *skarlagen* (Old Norse). Another term for the bright tints of red is 'crimson' — in French *carmin* or *carmoisi*, in German *karmosin* — all names deriving from the above mentioned Arabic *kermes* (insect).[2]

The red animal dyes of the Old World, however, were ousted by another insect, the Mexican cochineal. Following the conquest of Mexico, where these insects lived on a species of cactus, the Spaniards soon began introducing this dyestuff to Europe. Eventually the cultivation of Mexican cochineal spread to other countries with suitable climates and it came to play a very important part in various kinds of dyeing. It was not really supplanted until the introduction of synthetic dyes, towards the end of the nineteenth century.

A cheaper dyeing material for everyday use was orchil, derived from a species of lichen of the *Rocella* family. Orchil gives a short-lived blue-red colour which in time changes to an unpleasant shade of mauve and bluish-pink.

In China, yellow was reserved for the Emperor. The colour generally remains unchanged in Chinese silks, whereas Chinese red has often changed to tan. As far as woollens and European material are concerned, yellows, possibly obtained from weld (*Reseda luteola*) or some other herb, seem generally to have faded or disappeared. According to Père Coeurdoux (see below) the same also applied to yellow dyes on Indian cotton.

Indigo blue, one of the most durable dyes, is obtained from plants, namely various species of the *Indigofera* family, which to a great extent were cultivated in India and exported from there. Blue could also be obtained from woad, also termed pastel (*Isatis tinctoria*), which was widespread in Europe but had also been used in the Near East since the beginning of the Christian era. Pastel contains the same colour ingredient as true indigo but in a weaker concentration. Both dyes can be used for different kinds of fibres.

Sometimes two dyeing procedures were combined. For instance, to obtain brilliant shades of green, especially for the foliage of tapestry wall-hangings, known as *verdures*, yellow and blue dyes would be applied in succession, one on top of the other. After it has been exposed to daylight for some time, however, the yellow will fade, so that the darker portions take on an increasing shade of blue, thus contrasting with the lighter and originally more yellowish areas. Today the resultant colouration is much appreciated. It is often seen together with a tan (see above), which has gradually replaced an original bright red, from a non-fast dye. Aesthetically indeed, this colour scheme may be extremely attractive, but historically speaking it is misleading to extol the 'quiet, restrained colour sense of past ages', as sometimes happens in cases of this kind.

The dyeing substances mentioned above are those which have been most important, but many others have also been used. Some dyeing ingredients were imported from far away and became very expensive, but it should also be emphasized that the result, particularly where durability was concerned, was no less dependent on the method and personal skill of the dyer. A really good dyer, one with hereditary trade secrets that were never divulged to strangers, was a highly individual specialist, indeed something of a magician. A comparison between the materials surviving from different periods shows, however, that the professional skill of the dyer has varied, or that the methods used must have been less conscientious at some times than at others.

A literary illustration of the state of the dyer's craft during ancient times and during the Middle Ages is provided by the statutes issued as late as the seventeenth century, when the French manufacturing industries were reorganized by Colbert. These statutes, no doubt founded on medieval traditions, show that there was a world of difference between the skilled master dyer, *le teinturier de grand et bon teint*, and all those who were only capable of *petit teint*. This example was quoted by Pfister, in his penetrating study of dyeing in classical times (1935). He also came to an interesting conclusion regarding the two papyrus manuscripts of technical recipes, the most comprehensive of which, the *Papyrus Holmiensis*, belongs to the Royal Library in Stockholm.[3] All these recipes (which refer to different crafts) bear witness to technical ignorance and most of them refer to methods which have never been of any major practical importance. Pfister points out that the professional dyer was always illiterate: he had his recipes in his head and would certainly never have revealed them to an ignorant clerk. Pfister concludes that the manuscripts in question, dated to about the first century A.D., originated in an Egyptian temple whose priests often had a liking for technical problems with a touch of alchemy. The learned philologists who wrote about these documents were pure theoreticians with no inkling of technical matters.

One final observation: those who are concerned with more recent textiles frequently encounter the results of *petit teint* in more or less home-made, vegetable dyeing especially in folk textiles.[4]

PRINTED FABRICS

Technically speaking, the method of textile printing practised in Europe during the Middle Ages was rather primitive, closely related to book printing and above all to the art of woodcut. Printing on fabrics, as well as on paper, leather, etc., was done by means of wooden blocks in which the design was cut in relief, the raised parts being smeared with paint. This paint consisted of some kind of pigment plus a binding agent, generally linseed oil, which could adhere to the ground fabric and then be dried. The fabric to be printed could be of practically any material, but linen tabby was commonest. Most of the paint stayed on the surface of this fabric, which only barely absorbed the paint. Black paint was the easiest colour to produce and was therefore the most commonly used. Dull black patterns were often supplemented by water colour painting, usually in red or green, which, however, soon disappeared. Needless to say, a printed fabric of this kind was not water-fast.

Technically speaking, the printing operation was easily performed and did not require any professional ability. The cutting of the block, on the other hand, was, or should have been, a very skilled job. Particularly during the Middle Ages, European printed fabrics could be characterized as cheap substitutes for expensive loom woven textiles of silk or other materials.

There are a number of such printed fabrics which may have been manufactured in Germany during the late Middle Ages, but there are also single pieces of different origin, some of them earlier. A detailed description in Cennino Cennini's *Trattato della pittura*, considered to have been written in Florence in about 1400, testifies to the practice of this craft in Italy. It is possible that this Italian document was known to a certain Swedish monk who spent several years in Rome (1508–24) observing many technical processes which he then wrote about for Swedish readers. Among his writings was a letter called *Säterverks konst med stockar* ('the art of making stamp work with blocks') giving instructions on how to apply the block-printing method to leather and to woven material. It is interesting to note the same term in Norwegian and Swedish texts from the fifteenth and sixteenth centuries: *säterverk* often occurs in a context obviously indicating identity with the block-printing materials which still exist.[5]

Block-printing survived into post-medieval times, but it was gradually very much transformed, both technically and artistically. Under the influence of the Indian calicoes which appeared in the late seventeenth century, European printed fabrics also became multicoloured, the leading countries in this respect being France, Britain and Holland. As early as the seventeenth century, engraved copper plates began to be used for printing fabrics, just as they were employed for printing engravings on paper. This technique came to be more widely used in the middle of the eighteenth century, especially for figure designs. The method of printing with metal rollers developed comparatively late in the day. Although the first patent was taken out in 1783, this method was not applied on any considerable scale until about 1815.[6]

In about 1730 cotton printing factories were also set up in Sweden, some of them were in the Stockholm area. The so-called 'blue printing' on linen, using the resist dyeing method (see below), was practised in several parts of the country, for example, at the Flor Linen Factory (cf. Chap. x). Compared with other countries, the products of the Swedish printing factories have survived in fairly large quantities.

METHODS OF PATTERN DYEING

Unlike block-printing and similar techniques, the methods of decorating woven fabrics alluded to under this heading are all based on true dyeing, which means a chemical process produced when the textile is immersed in a dye bath. In this respect, however, two quite different procedures can be applied, depending on the capacity of the special dyes to be absorbed by certain kinds of fibre. As far as cotton is concerned, either a resist or a mordant must be used; in practice, resist dyeing is mainly used for indigo, and mordanting for madder. The resist substance (Fr. *réserve*) may consist of hot fluid wax, rice paste or the like, applied to the areas which are intended to stand out in white and thus remain undyed. This substance is removed by washing after the dyeing process has been completed. The resist can be applied with stamps (a kind of printing), with large blocks (sometimes double) or by using stencil and brush. Rich designs are worked free-hand with brush and pencil, the latter being similar to the Javanese *tjanting*, which may be described as a kind of fountain pen with an onion-shaped receptacle for the hot wax. A rather primitive type of resist method, termed tie-and-dye or *plangi* (Indonesian), is applicable to woven fabrics as well as to yarn intended to function as warp or weft. When occurring in Europe, partially dyed yarn of this kind is usually named *chiné* or *Flammengarn* (Ger.), but it may equally be termed *ikat*; this is an Indonesian word also used for woven fabrics ('double-ikat', 'warp' or 'weft ikat').[7] Madder dyeing on cotton cannot become colour-fast without a mordant. In practice this can be applied in roughly the same way as the resist, but when the results of the two are compared, the final appearance of one is more or less the reverse of the other. Indigo resist dyeing presents the pattern in negative, white on a blue ground, while the mordanted madder design will stand out red against a white ground.

INDIAN PAINTED AND PRINTED COTTONS

It is known that in India, the homeland of cotton, methods of colouring this fibre with non-fugitive dyes were evolved long before the Christian era. Indian craftsmen succeeded at quite an early stage in executing decorations by partially dyeing cotton fibres, by the methods here called pattern dyeing. Examples of this invention are illustrated in the famous Ajanta frescoes, dating from the fifth century A.D.

The earliest extant specimens of patterned cottons seem to have been found at Fustat, the harbour site of Old Cairo, where textile fragments of several kinds were retrieved from ancient rubbish heaps. The quality of these fabrics is consistently coarser and they are much less carefully worked than the high-class products which entered Europe via the East India Companies. Red and blue are the only colours occurring. The majority of the fabrics are resist dyed, the design standing out negatively in white against a blue ground. Most of the patterns may have been executed with small blocks or stamps, but beautifully worked specimens of free-hand painting were also found among these 'rags'. In comparison to other textile categories found in Egypt, these discoveries occurred rather late. The circumstances of the finds — in so far as they were known — were of no help in dating them. Attributions concerning age and origin must therefore be founded entirely on other criteria, primarily on the analysis of each item. Evaluation of these problems was started independently by two different scholars, who published their investigations almost simultaneously: the Swedish orientalist and art historian C. J. Lamm (at that time resident in Cairo as professor at the university) and the late R. Pfister, the eminent textile specialist. It should be pointed out that the two publications deal with the same kind of textiles though not with the same specimens. Pfister believed that the Fustat material had been made in Gujarat, on the western coast of India, and as late as in the fourteenth and fifteenth centuries. Referring to Arabian authors mentioning textiles especially of cotton, Lamm considered that some of the dye-patterned cotton fabrics dated from as early as the Abbasid dynasty (eighth to ninth centuries).

In any case, the main shipping route passed through the Red Sea to Egypt, and in fact to Fustat. This export trade, which also extended eastwards, was organized by the Arabs. Large quantities of dyed and undyed cotton fabrics were already being exported in the eleventh century to south China, where this material was considered a luxury in comparison with silk. The Arab writer Ibn Battuta relates that a single coat of cotton fetched the same price there as several coats of silk. Marco Polo has also left an admiring description of dyed calicoes and gossamer-like veils of cotton.

The products revealed by the Fustat finds resemble the simple Indian utility articles that are known from more recent times — a timeless product that often looks older than it is. But these fragments are particularly interesting because they exemplify the cotton fabrics which, according to written evidence, must have been known in medieval Europe and even in the Scandinavian countries, but which have now vanished. But traces of their presence have been preserved in several languages. From the Middle Ages onwards many textile designations were derived from the names of manufacturing places or trade centres: for example, *baudekin* or 'baldachin' a precious silk fabric, originally presumed to come from Baldacco, the Italian name for Baghdad; damask from Damascus and muslin from Mosul. Fustian was a cotton fabric probably named after the important transit harbour of Fustat, where Arab goods changed hands and were carried further afield by merchants from Italy and other western countries. Red fustian is mentioned in the Norse Sagas, for instance *Egil hafdi fustans kyrtill raudan* (a shirt of red fustian) but also several times in later Norwegian and Swedish texts. A foreign term could also continue to be used. The word *qutn, qoton* was latinized to *cottonum* which was assimilated by most western European languages: *cotton* (Fr., Eng.), *Kattun* (Ger.) as well as the Spanish *algodon*, being derived from the Arab form with the definite article, *al-qoton*. The same Arab word is considered the origin of a name occurring in old Icelandic texts: *guðvefr* which has been compared among other things with Anglo-Saxon and Old High German *godweb, gotaweppi*. Such fabrics are described in old Icelandic as *tvilitadr*, literally 'two dyed', which reminds us of the two-coloured cottons from Fustat.[8] Another word for cotton sometimes occurs in medieval Scandinavian texts: *seather/seter*. It was I. Henschen who first pointed out that this word must have had a different meaning from *säterverk*, which is identical to block printing. Linings of *red seter* are mentioned in the will of Queen Blanka (dated 1365) and in a document of 1489. Using relevant dictionaries she traced the origin back to the old Hindu word *chit* (from which later the English *chintz*) via intermediate forms in the Middle High German (Schiller-Lübben) as well as Rumanian and Turkish (*zeter — czetar — citcitary*, etc.). It may be asked whether these linguistic traces have any connexion with more easterly trade links with Scandinavia than those passing the Mediterranean and Western Europe.

The East India cotton trade

The foundation in 1600 of the English East India Company was followed in a few years by a Dutch, a French and a Danish organization of the same kind. The principle purpose of these enterprises was to compete with the Portuguese for the profitable spice trade, which centred on the Malay Archipelago. However the primitive economic system of the Indonesian islands, which did not use coinage, necessitated a suitable barter material. Such was the multicoloured Indian cotton fabrics which were coveted by Malayans as well as by other inhabitants of the tropic areas. The highly developed Indian cotton industry varied considerably between the different districts as regards the quality of the fabrics, the dyes and the methods of patterning, the types of design, etc. The piece-goods in demand for the spice trade were mostly the coarser and cheaper grades of cotton cloth, both plain and printed or painted. The harbours which were used by the European shipping were situated within three main areas: the western coast around Gujarat, the Coromandel coast along the south western side of the Indian peninsula and finally the Bengal area including the states of Bihar and Orissa. The European nations in question had acquired territorial settlements, so-called factories, with their own resident agents. From here production could be organized and the goods collected until the ships arrived to load cargoes which would be bartered in Indonesia for pepper and other spices. As time went on, however, the Company directors in London ordered the ships to retain some of the cotton goods until they reached an English port, though not for consumption in England. For economic reasons the cottons were to be re-exported and sold at profit, mainly the slave markets in northern or north-western Africa. It was a long time before the London directors dared to present Indian cottons on the home market. But from 1660 onwards the demand for Indian calicoes increased enormously in England, a circumstance which may be due to a better supply of real *chintz* or *chit*, the latter word being the Hindu name for cottons with painted design on white ground, that is, the category called *pintados* in Portuguese. The years 1670–1700 were the boom period, suddenly terminated by the Act of 1707, which imposed serious limitations on the import of Indian fabrics. But the prohibitions intended for the protection of the native textile industry were hardly effective. The flow of calico-chinz, etc. with their 'exotic' floral designs and, especially, their bright, durable colouring was not to be stemmed. Even as contraband, these fabrics continued to be all the rage in fashionable European circles during most of the eighteenth century.

Imports of Indian textiles — 'Indian' being used in the widest geographical sense — are an important episode in the history of textile art. An overwhelmingly important part was played in this connexion by the East India companies; although they were not the only actors on the scene. Goods of roughly the same kind reached Europe by other routes across the Levant to the Mediterranean and also by the lesser known route across Russia, about which the *Mercatura Ruthenica* has a certain amount to say; see Chap. xiv.

Most of the very brief particulars given above refer to the British East India Company, mainly because this is the Company which has attracted the greatest amount of historical research. Without in any way belittling the achievements of earlier British scholars, mention should here be made of John Irwin of the Indian Section of the Victoria and Albert Museum. Apart from his own writings, Irwin was one of the founders of the valuable *Journal of Indian Textile History*, which has published articles by himself and by many other scholars. These publications have included three papers by the late P. R. Schwartz of Mulhouse, a prominent textile chemist who provided an expert commentary on three unique accounts concerning Indian chintz design. The most exhaustive of these, the Beaulieu MS of 1734, was not previously known. The letter sent from Pondicherry in 1742 by the Jesuit Father Coeurdoux was already famous thanks to Baker's great publication, but it was not known *in extenso*. Schwartz's third contribution concerned a well-informed report written in 1795 by W. R.

Roxburgh, a famous English botanist. All three documents testify to the great problems connected with the production of Indian chintz.

So far only a few salient features of the basic technical and commercial development of this trade have been considered. But this is also an important chapter in the history of art — a whole chain of thematic developments, aesthetic preferences, artistic creativity, and in the designs provided for the craftsmen, all of which show that developments followed a completely different course from the one previously supposed. In a paper in the *Burlington Magazine*, entitled 'The Origin of "Oriental Art" ', John Irwin shows that this well-worn phrase is a myth. The fanciful 'Indian' flowers were in fact based on European models — hand drawings or engravings which the Indian textile painter enlarged and reproduced in the manner dictated by traditional techniques, following instructions from the factories or their agents. The exhaustive correspondence between the British factories and the directors in London provide ample evidence of this relationship, and it also indicates that use was often made of Dutch patterns. At the same time, however, many of the models drawn in England were not really English but 'chinoiseries', directly inspired by Chinese works of art imported to Europe; this is particularly true of the popular *palampores* (Port.) decorated with the 'flowering tree' motif, an Indian version of which, moreover, was exported to China, where it provided a model for embroideries in silk, and even for painting with pigments on silk satin, for shipment to European ports. This more or less completes the circle.[9]

Miscellaneous Textile Techniques

BANDS AND BRAIDS

Bands of all kinds form an interesting and very important chapter of textile art and one which has not been given the attention it deserves. Bands were always put to widespread and multifarious use, both for practical purposes and in all manner of decorative contexts. Different practical functions called for very different properties, ranging from various degress of flexibility and elasticity to rigid firmness and the greatest possible resilience — requirements which were excellently catered for by the ancient band-making methods.

Anyone who wishes to study band-making should particularly look for specimens in the following categories of textiles: (1) folk-art, particularly in Scandinavia, which presents a wealth of patterns and techniques (2) ecclesiastical textiles of the Middle Ages, including pictorial subjects, where a very important part is played by bands or orphreys (3) archaeological finds, from nothern Europe, Egypt and Asia. The student will find that certain techniques recur in all three categories though in very different materials. Whereas the popular bands are of linen and woollen yarns, the ornamental bands from the Middle Ages are usually made from multicoloured silk together with gold or silver thread. Needless to say, the difference in materials greatly affects the appearance of the product.

Technically speaking, bands can be divided into two main groups. Firstly there are 'woven bands', which to all intents resemble 'true' woven fabrics, in that they comprise a warp and a weft and, presumably, were executed on a weaving implement with a shedding device, that is, some kind of heddle. Secondly there are many 'primitive' methods of braiding which can be executed with very simple tools or by the human hand alone.

Woven bands

As regards some bands woven until recent times in the rural areas of Scandinavia and eastern Europe, it is impossible to determine solely from the finished product whether they were made on a bandloom of some kind or by means of a rigid heddle combined with body tension weaving (see Chap. II). Both implements have been used for plain and patterned bands alike. Ornamentation, if any, is executed by manipulating the warp, which always dominates the binding. The weft is beaten into the shed with a knife beater. In bands with a two-coloured warp, simple pattern effects can be produced by alternations of colour. A common technique capable of producing very rich patterns entails picking up by hand an additional warp in a contrasting colour and making it float on the surface of the ground weave, which is always in tabby weave.[1]

It is hard to generalize concerning the making of the broad bands or borders of costly material which were used during the Middle Ages, especially on ecclesiastical textiles. The Latin term *aurifrisia* (gold band) which occurs so frequently in the inventories can mean a variety of techniques, including woven gold braids and embroidered borders. It is clear, however, from the specimens which have survived that the woven braids were of many different types, several of them produced locally and on a small scale. Among the local productions from the Middle Ages there is a type which has been found in tombs of German princes and bishops buried some time between 1150 and 1250 (Pl. 94a). These borders generally include animal motifs and bear a certain resemblance to true silk fabrics, but their technical execution is relatively primitive. In this respect they are very different from the perfectly executed gold bands with which several contemporary French embroideries were trimmed, or with the magnificent 'Sicilian' borders, often including Latin inscriptions (Pl. 93d), whose true origin still awaits thorough investigation.[2] Mention should also be made of the well-known 'Cologne borders', the oldest extant specimens of which may hardly be earlier than about A.D. 1300 (Pl. 94b, c). They were manufactured on a large scale in the late Middle Ages, and exported to several countries beside Sweden. The technique was invariably the same, a coarse version of 'samitum' (type D2) in which the weft consists mainly of thick gilt membrane thread forming the background to ornaments in multicoloured silk. As shown earlier, Cologne was a major producer of this kind of gold thread, which was spun in the convents of the city to provide a cheaper substitute for metallic gold thread.

However, mass production of a similar kind seems to have been more the exception than the rule during the Middle Ages.[3] Instead, the leading workshops, especially the convents, often produced their own trimmed bands, which could be of a very high standard. This was the case in the convent of Vadstena (Sweden), whose embroidered vestments are notable for their exquisite trimmings. From the sixteenth century onwards trimming bands, etc., so-called *passementerie*, were generally produced by specialist workers or by lace workshops. The type of braid here named 'kilim band' (because of its similarity with the true Oriental *kilim*) is known from medieval specimens which were manufactured in convents at Vadstena and Danzig (Pl. 95a). But it is also known from modern Norway where such bands were made until recently for the traditional women's costumes. The geometrical pattern is formed by multicoloured wefts, which are inserted in the warp by means of a flat, pointed kind of shuttle. The weaving implement mainly takes the form of a box supporting two rollers, for the warp and the finished band, but it has no shedding mechanism (II, fig. 23). It may be mentioned that similar 'weaving boxes' are reproduced in pictorial representation from the Middle Ages.

Tablet weaving

The implements for tablet weaving consist of a number of square plates with a hole in each corner, in which four threads are threaded. As a rule tablet weaving is based on continuous twisting as follows. If a tablet fitted with its threads is turned around several times the result will be a twisted cord. If several tablets are positioned parallel in the direction of the warp, they can all be turned simultaneously (II, figs 20–21). For every quarter of a revolution thus performed, a shed will be formed in which wefts can be inserted, as shown in the drawing XIII, fig. 1. The result is a dense, firm weave, with a corded appearance on both sides, the weft being invisible on the reverse and face alike.[4]

This description applies to the basic technique. For patterning there are many variations, the simplest of them being to alternate the direction of the twist, with every second cord turned in the opposite direction. Very rich patterns can be produced by turning individual tablets separately and by threading yarn of different colours into the holes (Pl. 92a, b). Additional wefts can also be inserted, sometimes of gold or silver threads covering the face of the weave, with shorter brocading stitches superimposed on top of the gold woven surface (Pl. 92c–g). Another quite different application of this method is two-coloured 'double cloth'. The tablets are for the most part turned alternately backwards and forwards, two of the four sheds being used for each colour, which is thus woven in tabby. This variant of tablet weaving is known from Iceland and the Near East. Tablet weave (Sw. *brickväv*, Ger. *Brettchenweberei*, Fr. *tissage aux cartons*) is in current use throughout the ancient world. Its exact age has yet to be ascertained, but there is every reason to suppose that it is very ancient indeed. Because of its unsurpassed ability to provide a firm and resilient band, tablet weaving was often used for reins and belts. As shown in Chapter II this technique was employed in arranging the warp for the warp-weighed loom.

Over and above these practical functions, however, tablet weaving has undergone an artistic development which qualifies it as a luxury manufacture (see Pls 92–93). Norwegian and northern Swedish burial finds from the fifth and sixth centuries (Snartemo, Evebö, Högom, Norrala) have yielded bands up to about 4 centimetres wide, individually patterned and bearing witness to a highly sophisticated technique. Later specimens, also of wool, are known from Denmark and Finland, all of which were undoubtedly made within the Scandinavian area.

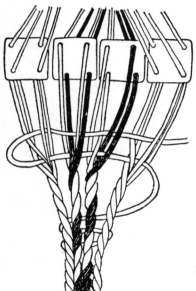

XIII, fig. 1.   Plain tablet weave with four tablets

A different category is encountered in the tablet-woven bands of silk with extra wefts of drawn gold and silver wire, many of which were among the Viking finds from Birka. No less than sixty graves contained such bands (see Pl. 92d–g). During the 1930s, when I was engaged on the analysis of the Birka finds, I thought that all these bands had been made in Sweden. Since then, however, their consistent and high quality has increasingly convinced me that the tablet bands in Birka were imported from the

Orient, probably via the Russian trade routes, like so much of the other material in these finds. It follows that this kind of band must have originated in large-scale manufacturing centres of the Byzantine area. Presumably this luxury manufacture gradually spread westwards to Europe, which during the Middle Ages appears to have been swamped by precious gold bands, very often tablet woven. Such bands can be recognized in the *aurifrisia* of the early church inventories and in the 'red gold band' of the Nordic folk song.

There is a great deal of evidence to show that tablet weaving was a smart hobby practised in distinguished circles. The Oseberg Queen was buried with a set of tablet weaving that she seems just to have started. Another queen, Hemma, the consort of Louis the German (d. 876), gave Bishop Witgarius of Augsburg a belt with a woven inscription done in tablet weave, using red silk with gold brocading. This exquisite piece of work is still to be seen in the Augsburg Cathedral Museum (Pl. 93a).[5]

Diagonal braiding

This technique is completely independent of any implement, being executed with the fingers only, starting from the middle with a few threads, and gradually drawing in more and more parts (threads or groups of threads). If several colours are used, diagonal lines are formed. The plaited band is very elastic. The technique is often practised using coarse woollen yarn. In Scandinavia it occurred during the Viking era (the Birka finds) and, centuries earlier still, in Central Asia (for finds made by the Hedin expedition in Lou-Lan, see XIII, fig. 2). Plaited braids of multi-coloured silk and gold thread, of this type, have been made in many parts of the world, from China to medieval Europe.[6]

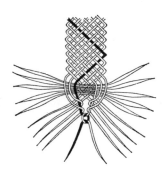

XIII, fig. 2.   Diagonally plaited band with decorative finish. Central Asia

Sprang

The technique called *sprang* can be defined as 'plaiting parallel threads with fixed ends'. Work starts by stretching a continuous thread to and fro between two firmly anchored pegs or sticks, for instance, attached to the backs of two chairs at a distance of about 2 metres. Plaiting begins from the middle by intertwining threads two by two in alternate rows. The worker uses his fingers and a few small sticks, always moving the sticks towards the ends in order to concentrate the plaiting, and during the work successively removing the sticks (see XIII, fig. 3 and Pl. 94d and e). Since the threads are not free the same sequence of twists is formed towards both ends, resulting in two identical parts of fabric. When all the stretched threads are plaited together, forming a continuous band, this may be cut into two identical parts. Especially when worked in woollen yarn the result is a supple and elastic band, which in Scandinavia often was used

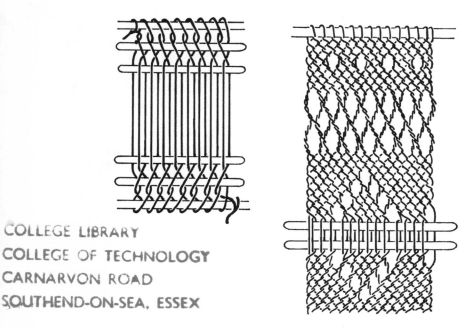

XIII, fig. 3. 'Sprang' plaiting, diagram showing the basic work and a patterned open-work. Sweden

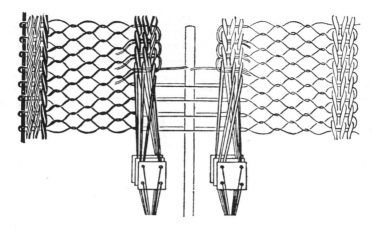

XIII, fig. 4.   Diagram showing the combined procedures
of Sprang plaiting and tablet weaving, as exemplified
by the legging from Tegle, Norway, fifth century A.D.
    1 : the sprang threads are stretched by being used as
weft in the two outer-most tablet bands. 2 : Then
working from the centre, all the threads are plaited in
sprang, resulting in two similar parts. This work finished,
the threads are successively cut off and inserted into the
next two tablet-woven bands, and are fixed by being
turned backwards

for garters. In Sweden this technique was generally called *pinn-band* (*pinne*
in Swedish being synonymous with the English 'stick').
    Patterned sprang plaiting is a further application of the plain sprang
just described — the twists varying to form a pattern in openwork. The
great number of threads required makes it necessary to stretch the yarn on
some kind of frame in order to organize the inter-twining. This work might
result either in an openwork net or a dense fabric. The openwork type
was used for the hoods and hair nets, some of which have been found in
Danish burials from the Bronze Age and subsequent periods, exhaustively
described by Margrethe Hald. In these cases the sprang piece was retained
undivided which, however, required a kind of 'locking' by a transversal
'chain' of stitches in order to prevent the twining becoming undone.
Another method is illustrated by a unique piece of textile — probably
one of a pair of leggings — belonging to the bog find from Tegle (Norway,

fifth century); the reconstructing diagram, fig. XIII, 4, shows how the sprang work was started and finished with tablet woven bands.

This kind of plaiting technique, internationally known by the ancient Scandinavian term *sprang*, has been widespread both in terms of date and location. It is known from antiquity until recent times and in all parts of the world. There are archaeological finds of this type from Egypt and ancient Peru, and the technique has an ethnographical distribution among North American Indians, south European peasants and Scandinavians. The word 'sprang', in Norwegian and Swedish medieval texts, *spranging/språngning*, *sprangadher*, *stockesprangning* clearly refers from the contexts to an openwork textile of decorative character executed in linen or sometimes in silk threads. This kind of textile work was particularly noted by Olaus Magnus (1490–1557).[7] In his important work *Historia de gentibus septentrionalibus* (History of the nordic peoples, printed in Rome, 1555) he praises the textile skill of the Nordic woman, laying stress on that whitest of net work *candidissimo illo opere retiario quod spraangning vocant* (splendidly shining white-work which they called 'spraangning'). The identification with the technique described above is no doubt correct, but it seems possible that the term sprang was sometimes given a wider sense. What sprang was called during the Bronze Age is hard to tell.[8]

FELT AND TAPA

Both kinds of fabrics are made by the compression of fibres.

Felt was originally a very primitive technique involving the kneading and pressing of loose wool under the influence of moisture and warmth so as to produce a coherent thick fabric or rather, a 'mat'. The felting method is generally supposed to have originated in Central Asia, where there was an abundance of animal hair and where man needed protection from the severe cold. It was an ideal technique for the nomad tribes of these areas, because it did not require bulky implements such as looms. As a matter of fact, loom weaving was unknown to the Mongols.

The felting technique must have been applied to decorative purposes at an early stage. In primary method differently dyed wools may have been kneaded together by placing suitably shaped tufts on a prepared ground of the same material. Naturally this procedure gives inarticulate patterns with poorly defined colour boundaries. The earliest known specimens are of a high quality, small mats with elegant floral patterns set against a white background, forming part of the Shosoin treasure (eighth century). The technique has survived in Syria and Iran, among other countries, where it is applied to the making of large carpets.

Another, more effective, method is the following, which entails several operations. First of all, figures and ornaments are cut out from ready-made felt in a kind of inlay technique in contrasting colours. The figures are then put together, either edge to edge in the technique called *intarsia* or else as applied work on a monochrome background. In both cases the figures are secured by stitching, which can sometimes add further effects by the application of gilded leather, cut out in narrow strips or in ornamental shapes. In this technique the patterns, mostly consisting of animal forms, are distinguished by their sharply defined silhouettes. Impressive examples of the technique were found in 2000-year-old Siberian graves (Noin Ula, Pazirik, etc.). In this art-genre, motif and technique are harmonized in a strong, very decorative style. This vigorous art should also be viewed as the historical background of much pattern-weaving, in silk and other materials, which flourished in the Sasanian-Iranian sphere of civilization, spreading from there to the western world.

Tapa is the Polynesian name for a paper-like product commonly used in Polynesia and Melanesia, but also in Indonesia and Mexico. The inner bark from certain bushes, principally species of mulberry and rubber tree, is soaked in water and cut in strips. The strips are pounded or beaten until the overlapping parts adhere to each other, forming large sheets. The sheets are left to dry and afterwards often decorated with painted ornaments. The finished pieces are used to make cloaks, skirts, ponchos or coverlets.

XIV *The Textile Trade with the Orient*[1]

TRADE ROUTES FROM THE MEDITERRANEAN AND
SOUTHERN EUROPE

The countries of the eastern half of the Mediterranean, known collectively as the Levant, have long been the first to receive luxury articles from the Orient. From India and East Africa came gold and precious stones, spices and incense. The 'Silk Road' described in Chapter VII was opened up a century or so before the Christian era. Textiles had the advantage of being easy to transport — they weighed little and they were comparatively strong, which partially explains why they came to be so prominent in long-distance trade, especially by overland routes. The detailed account from 1674 of the Russian trade with the Orient (see below) is undoubtedly applicable to earlier centuries as well and shows that textiles of various kinds far outweighed other commodities.

The leading nations which have peopled the Levant and succeeded one another as the paramount traders — the Phoenicians, the Greeks, the Arabs, the Italians — have all contrived to occupy strategic positions, harbours and colonies from which they have been able to control the various access routes from the East, in so far as political or climatic conditions rendered these routes passable. Their geographical position gave the Levantines the power partly or entirely to exclude other nations from the trade routes in question.

Thirteenth-century Europe was confronted with the disastrous menace of Genghis Khan and his Mongolian hordes. The situation remained critical for a number of years, but as far as southern Europe was concerned the danger was ultimately averted. The Levantine trade, now dominated by the Italians, was soon reorganized after the period of disruption. A number of Europeans who managed to travel the long road through Asia to China, and even back again, during the latter part of the century are known by name. Most of them were monks or missionaries dispatched by the Pope (Carpini, Ruysbroeck, Montecorvino, Pordenone, Pegolotti, etc.), but there were also merchants such as the Polo brothers of Venice, Marco's uncles. In fact the onslaught of the Mongols had the effect of stimulating the influx of goods and art forms from the East. This is reflected by the many silk fabrics of East Asian origin mentioned in the written sources (church inventories) though less frequently preserved, and above all by the new style, inspired by Chinese motifs, which came to revolutionize the Italian silk industry during the fourteenth century.

The Levantine trade spurred the Iberian peoples to many daring enterprises in the hope of finding a route of their own to India. Columbus himself sailed west in the hope of reaching India and believed himself to have done so when he came to America in 1492. During the fifteenth century the Portuguese had made several vigorous attempts to circumnavigate Africa and then sail on to the promised land. In 1498 Vasco da Gama managed to reach the western shore of the East Indies by this route. The first European colonies were founded there, giving the Portuguese control over the trade with the Indies for a century to come. The successes of the Spaniards and the Portuguese increased the demand for Oriental goods in other western countries. English, Dutch and French East India Companies were therefore set up in 1600, 1602 and 1604 respectively to import goods from India and China by the sea route round the coast of Africa. In 1616 Denmark also founded an East India Company and established a colony of her own at Tranchebar on the Coromandel coast. Sweden on the other hand concentrated all her energies on reviving the trade with the Orient by way of Russia. Thus the Swedish East India Company did not materialize until 1732, well after the final collapse of the south-eastern policy.

The above facts are all common knowledge. On the other hand it is less widely known that there were other routes to the Orient, by way of Russia, sometimes even by way of the Arctic Ocean. Nor are there many who know how important a part was played in this trading area by Sweden, both during the Viking period and subsequently.

THE VIKING TRADE THROUGH RUSSIA

The voyages of the Norsemen in and through Russia to the Byzantine Empire and other countries to the eastward are amply recorded by written sources and archaeological remains. 'The Chronicle of Nestor', written during the twelfth century at a monastery in Kiev, tells the story of a Swede named Rurik and his brothers who in 852 (or 862) founded a domain of their own which came to include the cites of Novgorod and Kiev. The Russian sources call both the Swedes and their kingdom *Rus* (cf. map. p. 230). The Rus were experienced navigators. The earliest route they took went across the Baltic and the Gulf of Finland to Lake Ladoga and on via the Volkhov River to Novgorod, which became their first main centre. After a short overland passage, rolling their ships on logs, they reached the Dnieper, along which they sailed past Kiev and into the Black Sea, where the route lay open to Constantinople. Here the Vikings often served in the Imperial guard, where they were known as *Varangians*. The Rus could also take a route further to the east, down the Volga, which led them to the kingdom of the Khazars on the Caspian Sea. At the Volga Bend was the trading town of Bulgar, offering goods from the rich land of Perm. Here too they could meet caravans from Merv and other parts of Eastern Persia, a link with the Silk Road from China. They could also follow the Volga and its tributaries in the opposite direction and, assuming they did not travel home westwards by way of the Gulf of Finland, continue northwards, through the country of 'Bjarmaland' with its Lappish population and on up to the Arctic Ocean. Here the Swedish Vikings could meet Norwegians who had sailed round the north of Scandinavia and the Kola Peninsula. A third route started from the Baltic ports and followed the Vistula or the Oder through Poland. This route was not opened up until the tenth century, when the eastern routes had begun to grow too hazardous.

The trading activities of the Swedes in Russia and the Orient were organized business enterprises on the grand scale, a form of colonization, in fact. If necessary garrisons would be established near the river routes from which the native Finnish or Slavonic population could be kept in check and goods obtained through them. The main commodities were furs, but there were also amber and slaves, which could be exchanged for precious metals, silks and other textiles and spices. The earliest written record of this commercial traffic is to be found in French annals from the year 839, when Louis the Pious was visited by Swedish envoys on their way home from Constantinople. They had probably been sent by the King of the Swedes on some kind of commercial mission to the Byzantine Emperor. It is assumed that they travelled there by way of Russia but, finding the route unsafe, decided to return by way of western Europe.

During the tenth century the Swedish Rus seem to have begun to be assimilated by the Slavonic population, though in 1018 the majority of the inhabitants of Kiev, which had become the capital of the kingdom of Rus, could still be said to be Swedes, or Danes, as they were also called. Dynastic alliances bear witness to friendly relations with Byzantium and the mother country. Prince Vladimir, whose mother was Swedish, was married in 989 to Anna, daughter of the Byzantine Emperor, while Prince Yaroslav of Kiev married Olof Skötkonung's daughter, Ingegerd.

There are many rune stones commemorating men who were killed while travelling in the Orient. Often they name the place or the country where the dead man met his fate, for example, Gardarike (Russia), Holmgård (Novgorod), Miklagård (Byzantium), Jursalia (Jerusalem), Greece and 'Särkland', which presumably stands for Persia, the country south of the Caspian Sea from which silk (*sericum*) was obtained.

The archaeological evidence of the eastern ramifications of Viking civilization comprises graves found in Russia containing objects of Swedish or Scandinavian design and, above all, the finds of objects of Russian or Oriental origin which have been made in Sweden. A very instructive part of the Swedish finds are the oriental silver coins the distribution of which plainly indicates the homelands of those taking part in these trading ventures, above all Gotland, the area surrounding Lake Mälar and the east cost of Sweden. So far roughly 60,000 Arab coins have been registered, while the number of Byzantine coins is far smaller. Does this mean that the northerners acquired larger quantities of goods, that is, silk, from Byzantium?

The unique discoveries that were made on the island of Björkö (Birka) provide a more detailed and in some respects more enigmatic picture of Scandinavian links with the Orient.[2] The trading town of Birka was not only the terminus of Swedish trade with the Orient, it was also linked with a trade route going south-west towards the Rhine valley and the North Sea coast, via Hedeby in the frontier tract between Denmark and Germany. As some of the finds from Birka are dealt with at length in other connexions (Chap. IV), attention here will be confined to some textile categories which certainly came from the Orient. Among the silk fabrics there is a single example of a fine self-patterned silk of Chinese origin (type C2, III, fig. 19) which was in all probability imported by the Volga route. Apart from some specimens of plain taffeta, the other silk fabrics, from some fifty graves, are all weft-faced compound twills (type D2) which may originally have had multicoloured patterns. They generally occur in narrow strips which seem to have been applied as trimming on plain woollen garments similar to the Iranian 'riding caftans' from Antinoë.

At least seventy variants of tablet woven braids of silk with gold or silver wire were found, all of them of very high technical quality (Pl. 92). Another, quite unique category consists of costume ornaments of gold or

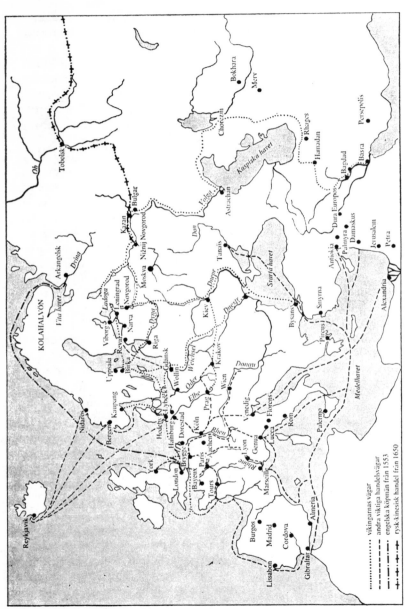

Map 1.   General map of Europe and Western Asia. Principal trading centres and towns with a significant output of textiles together with the commonest trade routes: the Vikings, ninth to tenth centuries; the English Merchant Adventurers about 1553, the Sino-Russian trade from c. 1650 and other main routes

Map No. 1 is compiled with the aid of a sketch for which I am indebted to Prof. B. Almgren

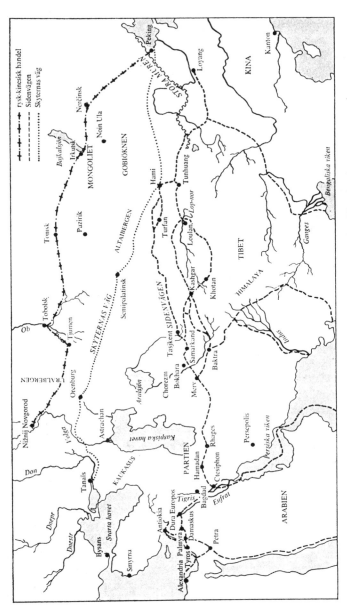

Map 2. Trade routes through Asia: furthest to the North the seventeenth century Sino-Russian caravan route, then the Scythian route sixth century B.C. and the various courses followed by the Silk Road under the Han dynasty and subsequently.

Map No. 2, apart from a few modifications, is due to J. I. Miller, who for his part has followed W. Willett's map of the Silk Road. Note the route indications silver wire embodying several distinct techniques. There can be no doubt that most of this work, which is of a remarkably high standard, was done somewhere in the Orient, while isolated and far cruder imitations may have been produced in Scandinavia. The Birka material includes ninety-two species of this kind, but similar objects have also been found in isolated graves of the same period, at Valsgärde, north of Uppsala, and at Mammen in Denmark.

The prosperity of Birka came to an end about 975, and during the eleventh century most of the Northmen seem to have abandoned the long trading voyages in the East. Not so the Gotlanders, who, with progressively greater infiltration by the Hanseatics, took charge of the Russian trade and still had a factory of their own at Novgorod in the thirteenth century. Kiev, however, was captured in 1240 by the Mongols, who had previously conquered the whole of south Russia. The trading town of Novgorod, which had managed to retain its independence under a Christian prince, concluded a commercial treaty with the Hanse in 1270. But to the south of Novgorod was the Golden Horde, the powerful empire of the Mongols, which for a long time to come was to isolate the whole of the area to the northward. For the time being Scandinavian trade was forced to look for other routes. More than 300 years were to pass before Russia once again became a factor to reckon with as a link between Scandinavia and the Orient.

EUROPE DISCOVERS RUSSIA

The Muscovite Empire long remained completely unknown to the majority of Europeans, but the dawn of a new era produced a general inquisitiveness linked with mercantile interests. Behind this inquisitiveness lay a vague awareness of the possibility of obtaining via this country Oriental products of the same kind as the Portuguese and the Italians were collecting from their ports in India and the Levant. Even before Ivan III, Tsar of Muscovy, had conquered Kiev (1480), thereby destroying the 'Mongolian Yoke', he received his first visit from a prominent westerner, the Venetian diplomat Contarini, who was on his way home from an embassy to Persia, where he had conducted negotiations directed against Turkey, the mutual adversary of both Persia and Venice. The Italian diplomat's observations make amusing reading. Some decades later (1517) the Austrian Baron von Herberstein came to Moscow as the emissary of the Emperor Maximilian. He paid two protracted visits which provided the material for a famous book, *Rerum Moscovitarum Commentarii*, which was published in several languages. A wealth of literature now began to appear concerning Russia. Other writers on the subject included Adam Olearius from Holstein, who travelled extensively in Russia, Persia and various other countries.

The great trading nations, England and Holland, contrived to realize their hopes concerning the transit possibilities offered by Russia. Bold plans were based on the circumnavigation of Norway and penetration via the Arctic Ocean and its tributaries into the Russian interior — in other words, the route taken by the Norwegian Vikings through Bjarmaland. The first of these 'Merchant Adventurers' was Richard Chancellor, who reached Moscow in 1553 and was received by the Tsar, Ivan the Terrible. As a result, in 1555, England was awarded extensive privileges for her Muscovy Company. The Dutch followed the same route and they were principally responsible, in 1583, for the foundation of the important town of Archangel where the River Dvina flows into the White Sea. During the following century Archangel was a centre of great activity by the two commercial rivals.

Swedish trade via Russia during the sixteenth and seventeenth centuries

Unlike the western Europeans, the Swedes had long been familiar with the Russian trade routes. Their trade in this quarter had presumably never completely died out but had been mainly confined to home produced articles such as furs, sole leather, flax, wax and soforth. The import of Persian silk products appears to have been mooted once again during the reign of Gustav Vasa, for an exchange of letters between the King and the Swedish Governor of Finland indicates that Persian textiles had been offered for sale in Viborg. The King agrees with the Governor's recommendation that the Russian merchants be treated well and says that he would like to buy their fabrics. Similar conclusions can be drawn from a Russo-Swedish treaty of 1557, which provides that Swedish merchants may travel freely to Novgorod, Moscow, Khazan and Astrakhan for trading purposes.

No doubt the Swedish assault on Ingria and the conquest of the important commercial town of Narva in 1581 — two years before the foundation of Archangel — were prompted by plans to gain control of Russian trade with the Orient. One of the principal aims of Swedish foreign policy down to the beginning of the eighteenth century was to attract to the Baltic ports all Oriental merchandise arriving in Russia. But transit traffic was now far more complicated than it had been during the Viking period and the Swedish plans came up against obstacles in many different quarters. The ultimate trading partner, the Shah of Persia, was usually amenable, while the greatest opposition came from the Russians, for the trade in silk, both raw and processed, was a monopoly of the Tsar. The matter was handled by the *gosts* (merchants ranking as state officials), who could be very obstructive. This trade was only sanctioned in a small number of places (principally Moscow, Astrakhan and Khazan) and in return for the payment of tolls. Moreover foreign merchants were not allowed to trade with each other on a 'guest to guest' basis, even though this principle was sanctioned by treaty. On top of all this came the rivalry with merchants from other countries, the Dutch and the English. This meant competition between the two export routes — the route via Archangel and the route via the Baltic ports. True, the northern route was much longer and was icebound for a great deal of the year, but it was unaffected by wars and did not entail any extra dues over and above the Russian transit duty. By contrast the far shorter Baltic route, which had the advantage of being passable for the greater part of the year, was more liable to be disrupted by outbreaks of war. Moreover, the expectations of profit entertained by the free Baltic trading cities of Reval and Riga, as well as the extra dues that would have to be paid in the Sound had to be taken into account.

Due to the geographical proximity of the two countries, the Swedish Crown had long kept itself well informed concerning the internal affairs of Russia — so well informed, in fact, that a modern Russian historian has maintained that the Swedes of the period knew more about Russia than the Russians themselves. Time and time again observers or delegations were dispatched, and on returning they had to submit exhaustive reports, most of which are still in the custody of the Swedish National Record Office, which is considered the most important source for anyone wishing to study the domestic history of seventeenth-century Russia. The small number of these authors whose works have been published includes Petrus Petrejus (Per Persson), who visited Russia for a total of four years before 1611 and after his return home composed a weighty description which was published in six volumes. Another such author is Johann de Rodes, Swedish trade delegate in Russia between 1649 and 1655. To an ambitious great power like Sweden, the Baltic ports were of vital significance. Commercially speaking, the Swedish empire, which during the seventeenth century comprised Finland and large areas of the Baltic and North German coastal areas made the Baltic a Swedish *mare clausum*. But other countries in northern Europe also hoped to benefit by co-operation with the Swedes. Accordingly a large number of 'legations' or 'embassies' visited Russia and Persia in the hope of getting the trade in Persian exports re-routed via the Baltic ports. The first of these expeditions was a joint Swedish and north German venture. In 1633 and 1635 Duke Frederik of Holstein-Gottorp dispatched two embassies led by a lawyer of international repute, Philip Crusius, with Olearius, already mentioned, serving as secretary on both occasions. The many prominent members of these embassies included a young Mecklenburger, J. A. von Mandelsloh, who went on to India and subsequently publised descriptions of his journeys containing some interesting observations on the subject of textiles. Crusius later entered Swedish service (and was raised to the nobility under the name of Krusenstierna). As Director of Commerce in Esthonia and Ingria, an office established in 1653, he came to play an important part in Swedish trade policy. Krusenstierna also led a Swedish embassy to Moscow in 1655, but it was not very successful, for the Russians invaded the Baltic provinces and incarcerated the delegates. Some years later a prolonged rebellion broke out in the Volga valley under the leadership of Stenka Razin. Astrakhan was ravaged, the stocks of silk were destroyed and the entire textile trade was paralysed for many years to come. The rebellion was not put down until 1671.

Two years later a new Swedish delegation was dispatched under Lillienhof, a naturalized German merchant who had succeeded Krusenstierna as commercial expert. This venture was extremely bold, for it was aimed at nothing less than the establishment of a supranational trade route between western Europe and the Orient — an international route which would be immune to wars and tariff barriers, a peaceful trade route cutting clean through all the national boundaries. France and Holland were prepared to guarantee the enterprise. The legation was extremely well prepared, but for all its skill the gigantic task it had been set proved impossible. On his return to Sweden, Lillienhoff was deeply pessimistic regarding the prospects of the Baltic route. But the Swedes did not give up.

When a person appeared who could be said to be uniquely qualified for the task, it was decided to change tactics and to attempt first and foremost to influence Persia. The new man appearing on the scene was Ludwig Fabritius. He was born in Brazil, the son of a Dutch physician. He accompanied his stepfather to Russia, where as a young man he obtained a commission in the Imperial army. During the campaign against Stenka Razin he was captured by the rebels and sold as a slave to a mountain Tartar but redeemed by an Indian merchant, who took him to Persia. From there he returned to Astrakhan and re-entered the Imperial army, where he obtained promotion. He then moved to Sweden. After he had come into a large inheritance from Holland, he offered to lead a Swedish expedition to Persia, where in his opinion there was every prospect of participating in the profitable trade in silk. Fabritius even went so far as to offer to finance the expedition. A delegation left Sweden for Persia in 1679. In Isfahan Fabritius tried to persuade the Persians of the advantages to themselves of exporting their silk products via Narva and the Baltic ports instead of the long route via Archangel. He returned to Sweden in 1682 but later went on two further expeditions, in 1683–88 and 1697–1700. On his final return journey he even managed to obtain an audience with Peter the Great, two months before Russia declared war on Sweden. After his second visit to Persia, Fabritius was accompanied all the way to Stockholm by some Persian-Armenian merchants who are said to have been received with great interest and cordiality. Apart from two 'free years', they were offered one year's exemption from customs duty. Perhaps the fairly numerous Persian silks from this period (Pls 56–57) still extant in Sweden were brought into the country by these Persian merchants or by the members of the legation? Or were they sold by Russian merchants in the so-called 'Russian shops' at Slussen in Stockholm?

The Swedish legation of 1673 included two young men who had compiled extremely useful reports of their observations (almost trade espionage) in Russia, Erik Palmqvist and Johan Philip Kilburger. Kilburger in particular was closely acquainted with various parts of this enormous country. On his return to Sweden he started work on a description entitled *Mercatura Ruthenica*, which he intended to have printed. Presumably the work was banned from publication because the authorities found it far too up to date and politically inflammable. Among other things it included the very latest tariff schedules for trade via Archangel and Livonia.[3]

The 'Mercatura' description provides a detailed account of textile products and includes some unique particulars in this respect. Concerning Russian output it reports that the native linen tabby is invariably coarse and never more than 3/4 *archin* (about 46 centimetres) wide. All fine linen fabric comes from Holland, except for that woven in Sloboda Radaschowa, an exclusive manufacture conducted solely on behalf of the Tsar. Russian wool is said to be coarse and of inferior quality, though it improves as one goes further south (presumably Kilburger is referring here to the Caucasus) Persian wool is very fine. In Russia all fine woollens, known as camelots, were invariably imported. The highly informative chapter dealing with the Persian trade indicates that most silk is produced in the province of Gilan, south of the Caspian Sea. Many different varieties of raw silk and woven silk fabrics are named, and prices and customs duties are also quoted. It relates how, immediately on its arrival by boat in Astrakhan, some of the raw silk is purchased by Englishmen and Dutchmen, who then 'comfortably' forward it by boat up the Volga to Archangel and then overseas. Kilburger also reports that the Persians send some of their raw silk by caravan to Aleppo, but are reluctant to do so owing to their enmity with the Turks.

Most of the trade in silk takes place in Moscow. The Persian and Indian merchants have trading areas of their own in the centre of the city where they display their goods in vaulted shops. Many of the Persians and Indians have lived there for years, but after the Stenka Razin disturbances they became involved in several disputes with the Russians, who in Kilburger's opinion do not appreciate the advantages they derive from this trade. The Persians' goods are described under seven headings, which, apart from raw silk, 'saffian' leather and a miscellaneous category including precious stones, incense, indigo, rice, naphtha, etc., mentions the following four groups of textiles:

Damask, velvet and 'all kinds of Indian and Persian stuffs', many of them skilfully worked with gold and silver. — To this may be added an interesting statement by Johann de Rodes to the effect that, particularly where flowered patterns were concerned, these fabrics were as good as the Italian silks, their only defect being that they were sold in short lengths measured for a coat of the kind worn by Persians, Turks, Russians, and others.

The next heading is devoted to printed cotton (Ger. *Kattun*) or chintz. The writer distinguishes between *gefärbte Kattun* (dyed cotton) also termed *kindiak*, a mysterious word which may possibly have meant resist-dyed, and 'flowered' Indian cotton. It seems that not very much of the latter variety comes out of Persia but that, remarkably enough, a great deal of it comes from Holland by way of Archangel. Mention is also made of tablecloths and bedspreads with printed(!) patterns adjusted to their format. Kilburger does not say where these goods were manufactured, but presumably most of the chintzes were of Indian manufacture and the kind imported from the Dutch may have come from a different part of India from that of those imported directly.

The next heading refers to *Nasstucher* (kerchiefs or neck cloths), *Schärpen* (probably wide sashes of the kind worn round the waist by the Polish gentlemen of rank in Pl. 58b, c) and *Flohr* (veils). All these products are evidently made of silk and are said to be either Indian or Persian.

The final item is confined to two words, *gewirkte Tischteppiche*, which in the context must refer to what would today be called pile rugs. Persian or Turkish carpets of this kind generally served as table-cloths in seventeenth-century Europe. In a short section on the trade in Greek products which then follows, mention is made of *turkische Tapeten*, which may refer to much the same thing. The Greek merchants also had a trading area of their own in Moscow where they lived all the year round.

One subject which earlier travellers to Russia had not known about is the trade with Cathay, as China is called in Russian. Kilburger records that in 1654 the Russians sent a commercial embassy to the Great Khan in Peking, which resulted in the opening of a new trade route, with the important Siberian town of Tobolsk serving as an entrepot. Coloured Chinese and Tartar silk fabrics were brought here and reference is also made to a coarse Kattun cloth (possibly of hemp?) always measuring $8\frac{1}{4}$ *archin* (5.85 metres) and known to the Russians as *kithaika*. In addition, porcelain, tea and many other Chinese goods were bartered to the Russians in Tobolsk and, finally, also raw silk, which is said to be far superior to the Persian variety. Thus in 1673 the Tsarist monopoly purchased Chinese silk at 25 roubles per *pood* (16.38 kilogrammes) and then sold it to a Hamburg merchant for 120 roubles.

Interest in the Orient is a consistent theme in the history of Swedish foreign policy. Approaches had been made to Turkey even before the plans for transit trade through Russia had conclusively foundered. And during his involuntary stay there (1709–14), Charles XII made considerable efforts to recover this sphere of interest, both culturally and economically. To the latter end he founded the Levantine Company and in the former connexion he dispatched a succession of young scientists to explore different parts of the Orient. An important cultural contribution was also made by many of the three-thousand soldiers from the Swedish army who were taken prisoner by the Russians after the battle of Poltava and, at best, were obliged to spend several years in Siberia or still further afield. The same tendency is reflected by the lively interest taken later in the Orient by Linnaeus and by the voyages of exploration undertaken there by many of his disciples.

There is a tendency for all unusual luxuries from the seventeenth century extant in Sweden, textiles above all, to be classed as spoils of war. Admittedly a great many things were simply appropriated, especially during the Polish wars of Charles X, although regular trade still occurred even then. In the case of Persian commodities, however, there can hardly be any doubt that large quantities entered Sweden through trade during both the sixteenth and seventeenth centuries. After all, it is known that Russian, Persian and Armenian merchants were regular visitors to Stockholm and Narva, near to the Russian Estonian frontier, where they maintained the stone buildings that were needed for the storage of their valuable merchandise.

Another completely different way in which Oriental textiles reached Sweden arose from the typically Oriental custom of presenting coats of varying degrees of sumptousness as a token of respect. A notable instance of this practice is to be found in the coat of gorgeous Persian velvet presented by the Tsar of Russia to Queen Christina (Colour Pl. III). The parish churches of Sweden also possess numerous chasubles, etc. which have been made out of Turkish coats brought back by travellers from the Orient.

XV *Textiles and Textile Crafts in the Scandinavian Countries*[1]

In relation to European culture the Scandinavian countries have served in many respects as a conservation area, where inherited crafts and working traditions — to a great extent connected with the production of textiles — have continued to exist until quite recent times. This situation is primarily due to the fact that the industrial production of textiles which for centuries had been established in western Europe — abolishing most domestic crafts and folk-arts in those regions — came very late to the northern countries. The historical picture formed by this trend of conservationalism is advantageously completed by a very large number of extant textiles of various types and ages, domestic products as well as foreign commodities. The reason that all these have been preserved lies in the fact that these countries, especially Norway and Sweden, have been spared devastating wars on their own territories, but the preservation could also be due to the generally poor conditions and the relative rareness of materials which were too precious not to be taken care of — a positive side of the average poverty through the ages predominant in the northern lands.

In the previous chapters, many of the textile phenomena, in the form of materials and inherited working methods still preserved in Scandinavia, have provided illustrations of worldwide developments. In some cases this has resulted in an imperfect picture of things specifically Scandinavian. I have therefore chosen to give a separate, continuous survey of our knowledge of textile work and textile art in the Scandinavian countries, from the very earliest times until the coming of the Industrial Revolution. This will also provide an opportunity of considering varieties which have not yet been dealt with. To avoid unnecessary repetition, the account is confined in places to brief mentions containing references to earlier sections. The main emphasis, of course, is on native products, but because foreign textiles have naturally played a part in developments, they must be taken into account as well, in so far as they can be distinguished from the rest.

Archaeological finds are practically the sole source of knowledge concerning prehistoric times. Finds occur very irregularly, owing to the variable physical conditions affecting the preservation of textile fibres: Thus there are large areas and long periods in which no traces whatsoever are to be found of any textile products, though this must not of course be taken to imply that no textiles in fact existed. It should be noted here that the relative value of a textile find from a particular period — the extent to which it represents an average or supreme achievement within its own epoch or area of civilization — is connected with the direct reason for its appearance (or disappearance) in the soil, for example, as part of a lavish funerary rite, as a votive offering or as the simple clothing of a convicted criminal. Or again it may be included in stratified refuse from a work place or a settlement, it may be a single item mislaid by its owner or, the commonest occurrence of all, it may have been saved from destruction by pure chance and nothing else.

The Stone Age and Bronze Age

The only Stone Age textiles to have survived in Europe are probably the brittle fragments found in the Swiss pile-dwellings: tabby weaves, some of them with in-woven ornamentations and with starting borders indicating that they were woven on a warp-weighted loom.

The Bronze Age, on the other hand, is represented by unusually well-preserved material, thanks to the practice then occurring in Denmark of burying the dead in the hollowed-out trunks of oak trees, in which entire costumes and articles of clothing have been preserved. The best-preserved finds are those from Egtved and Skrydstrup, which were excavated as recently as 1921 and 1935. All the Danish finds bear witness to an exalted social status: they are superb individual achievements, some of them embodying highly intricate techniques and sometimes made from specially selected wool. Particularly noteworthy are two women's hoods in the kind of open-work braiding known as sprang, some large pieces of cloth woven on a warp-weighted loom, and some remarkable men's caps, worked with the needle in imitation of a curly fleece. Less well-preserved fragments of similar finds have been discovered in Schleswig-Holstein. Mention should also be made of fragments of coarse tabby weave from about ten different finds in southern Sweden which, like the major Danish finds, have been dated to the Early Bronze Age. Two similar Bronze Age finds have also been made in Norway, both of them in the Rogaland area.

The Gerum mantle, woven in a four-end twill enriched by alternating dark and light shades of woollen yarn, differs from all other known Bronze Age fabrics (cf. Post, Walterstorff, etc.). Both the Danish cloaks and that from Gerum are oval in shape.

The Iron Age

The first centuries of the Iron Age were formerly supposed to be devoid of textile finds, but this has changed following the emergence of a series of southern Danish and north German bog finds from Celtic and Roman times. One of the most important objects is the large twill piece from Huldre bog, which Dr Hald showed to be tubular-woven, a method which she believes occurred simultaneously with the warp-weighted loom.

Scandinavian textile finds from the Roman and Migration periods (*c*.300–550) are dominated by two different techniques: four-end twill made on the warp-weighted loom and tablet-woven braids. The latter occur both separately and interwoven with the cloth, in the warping of which they were a constructional necessity, but sometimes also a decoration. The majority of these high quality finds have been made in Norway. Particularly noteworthy among them are those from Gjeite in north Trondelag, Blindheim in Möre and Setrang in Buskerud, all from the Roman period (fourth century); also from Veien in Buskerud and Vestrum in Vestfold, from the transition to the following period, as well as some very splendid finds from the Migration period, above all in the graves at Snartemo in Vest-Agder, the finds from Evebö in Gloppen, Nordfjord, and Övre Berge in Lyngdal. Finally there is the unique bog find from Tegle, so important in various respects and thus frequently discussed in this book.

In Sweden all that was formerly known from the whole of this period (*c*.300–550) were two diminutive textile finds; the Öremölla burial find and the probably somewhat older find from Nykvista in the parish of Varnhem, both in the province of Västergötland. Then in 1949 and 1961 two very important Migration period graves were discovered at Högom and at Norrala, in north-eastern Sweden. The first of these graves contained an unusually well-preserved man's costume; the other furnishings of both burials closely resembled the Norwegian finds from the Migration period.

On reviewing the finds which antedate the Viking period in Sweden and Norway, it is striking that regular plain twill occurs during the latter period, while the technically more advanced type in lozenge twill, often of a finer quality, occurs in Norwegian and Swedish finds from the Roman period. This, coupled with the fact that some of these fabrics have been found together with imported Roman objects of glass or bronze, has led to the supposition that the textiles too were imported, which in turn implies that the plain twill of the Migration period is the oldest native Scandinavian product, as far as twills are concerned. As things stand, this must be left an open question. One notable phenomenon is the very great loom width, about 2 metres, characterizing all these cloaks or mantles, from the north German Torsberg mantle to the majority of the Norwegian ones mentioned above, as well as the weave-starting 'fringe' in the Tegle find.

During this period, tablet weaving occurs in a multitude of variations. The basic type, with a straight twist, is used when the braid is woven together with a fabric. But many different techniques bearing witness to an impressive degree of individual skill were developed for freely-executed trimming borders. By varying the twist of individual tablets, the holes of which had been threaded with different coloured yarns, it was possible to produce very effective patterns, either with geometrical motifs (Snartemo V and Övre Berge finds) or with animal figures. Weft effects could also be obtained by brocading. This exacting technique, which was also used for animal motifs, was evidently quite common in Scandinavia; it occurs in both the Snartemo and the Evebö finds and in Norrala and Högom, invariably in combination with the clasps with round buttons that are typical of the same period. A further type is represented by a Norwegian bog find, from Helgeland in Rogaland. A geometrical interlace pattern has been brocaded on the plain ground weave, in a way which reminds one of Swedish *krabbasnår* (Chap. III, B2), a technique which was quite common during the Middle Ages as well as later. Such fine examples of these types must have been preceded by a long process of development in Scandinavian tablet weaving.

No doubt the same also applies to sprang, examples of which have survived from as early as the Bronze Age, particularly in Denmark. All that has been found in Sweden are a few diminutive fragments among the Birka finds, while Norway possesses a specimen which is as unique as it is well-preserved from the Tegle find. The cylindrical garment — it is uncertain whether it was intended as a legging or a separate half-sleeve — also presents a unique combination of sprang and tablet weave (see XIII, fig. 4).

Another technique which is executed with a large wooden sewing-needle, is sometimes called one-needle knitting (Sw. *nålbindning*). It is a very old technique, often used, up to the present day, for mittens and socks. The oldest example, dated by means of pollen analysis to the fourth or fifth century, was found in a bog of Åsle.

THE VIKING PERIOD

Our knowledge of textiles from the Viking period is mainly founded on two unusually large groups of finds; namely the complex collections from Oseberg and Birka, supplemented by smaller and less important finds. The lavishly furnished funeral ship of Oseberg, dated to c.860, is unique. But more varied light has been shed on this period by the multifarious finds from Birka which in its time, c.800–950, was a commercial centre of international importance. Denmark's most essential textile contributions from the Viking period come from burials in Mammen and Hvilehöj which were discovered by chance during the nineteenth century and were, unfortunately, not subjected to archaeological research on the site. Here may also be mentioned the famous burial site at Valsgärde, north of Uppsala, carefully excavated from 1928 onwards. Here members of the same chieftain family are thought to have been interred for many generations (c.400–1050). Among the fifteen ship burials Nos 6–8 were excavated by G. Arwidsson who managed to recover some textile remains. Finally in this connexion some interesting textiles should be mentioned which emerged during the 1950s and 1960s in Skåne, at Norrvidinge, on the island of Gotland, at Väte-Mölner (not published), as well as numerous finds of less impressive categories, from burial grounds in western Norway (a few specimens have been preliminarily published).

The great burial mound of Oseberg, the grave of Queen Åsa, was discovered in 1903 and excavated during the following year. The excavation of the well preserved ship, now to be seen in the Viking Ship Hall outside Oslo, and the salvaging of the various artefacts found in the ship, was an achievement of the utmost scientific value. The textiles are of different kinds including imported silks and fine woollens, but there are also domestic products of a high standard, among them series of figure scenes executed in a kind of tapestry weave. The last mentioned type, naturally, attracted the main attention and interest of the two scholars, Hans Dedekam and subsequently the late Björn Hougen, who were entrusted with the exacting investigation of the textiles. Apart from special papers by both these scholars, the remaining textiles still await final publication.

The site of Birka, situated on the island of Björkö, on Lake Mälar, was discovered in 1871 by Hjalmar Stople, who then proceeded to excavate the burial grounds. In the course of a few years approximately 1,100 graves were excavated — in an exemplary manner by contemporary standards, but far too superficially by those of the present day — with the result that important textile materials must have been irretrievably lost. Textile remains were found in nearly two hundred graves. This percentage seems low, but nevertheless it comprises a unique quantity of varied and important material, most of which can be accurately dated. It should also be noted that this was the first time that textiles were systematically retrieved in any European excavation.

Imported textiles

The Viking period was essentially international. Foreign goods began to be common, and this is particularly evident from the Birka finds, which to a great extent reflect the living conditions of a community of wealthy merchants. Birka had regular links with Byzantium and the Orient via the Russian trade routes (see Chap. xiv) but it was also in direct touch with Haithabu in Schleswig, in the south-western corner of the Baltic Sea and thus with the trading towns of the Rhine.

Among imported commodities pride of place must go to the fine worsted fabrics dealt with at length in Chapter iv. The largest selection comes from Birka, but specimens of this manufacture, especially the standard type of twill, named 'W 10', have also been found in several other Scandinavian and northern European finds from the period between A.D. 600 and 1000. However, the same commodity is found in the Palmyra and Aintinoë finds, which must imply Oriental production on a large scale, probably in Syria. It seems probable that these fine woollens, in common with other Oriental luxury articles, were transported to Marseilles or other ports along the French Mediterranean coast, and from there were taken north by the Frisian merchants trading with the Scandinavian countries (cf. map on p. 230). That would be an explanation of the term *pallium fresonicum* (Frisian cloth) much discussed by the historians.

Silk fabrics have been found in both Oseberg and Birka; in Birka silk occurred in about fifty graves. With the exception of a few fabrics, including one of Chinese origin, the majority represent the multicoloured, weft-faced compound twill type (also called samitum) which was manufactured in Byzantium and the eastern Mediterranean. Strips of this material were used as trimmings on garments of some plain material, probably woollen. Clearly of Oriental origin are the artistically executed costume ornaments of gold and silver wire, the techniques employed being related to both braiding and needlework.

My present opinion — contrary to that expressed in 1938 in *Birka III* — is that the fine tablet-woven bands made of silk with extra wefts of gold and silver wire, must also be of Oriental origin. This is probable on account of the consistently high quality and the uniformity of pattern (with only insignificant variations) among the large number of specimens that have survived in Birka alone — some ninety variants in sixty graves — and hardly anywhere else in the Scandinavian countries. There are two exceptions to this: the Mammen find, which, however, also includes other Oriental costume ornaments, probably Persian, and the relics in Durham Cathedral associated with St Cuthbert. But, as has already been seen, tablet-weaving for utilitarian and luxury purposes was widely current in Scandinavia from a much earlier date.

The native textiles of the Viking period

The partly finished tablet-weave, containing fifty-two tablets, placed near the Oseberg queen herself is the most eloquent testimony remaining that tablet-weaving was a native Scandinavian craft.

The most important specimen of early Scandinavian textile art is a kind of tapestry with varying stitches and binding effects executed in multicoloured wools on a linen warp (the latter material often decayed). The earliest known specimen of this kind was found in Valsgärde 8 (seventh century). More recent fragments were found in Valsgärde 6, in two Birka graves and in Norway: beside all the Oseberg *refils* three finds from Ostfold and Rogaland. Adding to these the later specimens of north Swedish 'soumak tapestries', the *refils* from Överhogdal and Skog, which are to be seen as folk-art successors to the refined textile art that was practised at the court of Queen Åsa, there is justification for speaking of a native Scandinavian art form. The trail may be followed still further back in time if the tablet-weaves portraying fantastic animal figures are to be considered as precursors of the pictorial weaving of the Oseberg find.

In the Queen's burial chamber were found some thirty fragments, evidently remains from several oblong hangings depicting a host of figures. The height, or width of the weave, was remarkably small, between 16 and 25 centimetres. The pictorial style might be compared to the style of a miniaturist, with very small elaborate figures: persons of both sexes, warriors, and perhaps even Amazons, carrying shields and spears, with

xv, fig. 1.   Figured weave, 'Soumak tapestry' representing a battle scene.
Oseberg ship burial, about 850 A.D.

horses, either carrying riders or pulling great carts (see XVI, fig. 1). There is also a stylized Tree of Life, which Hans Dedekam interpreted as the Tree of Odin, thus reflecting the view that the entire cycle would represent religious rites and mythological scenes. In his masterly study of the Oseberg pictorial textiles, Björn Hougen endorses this view but emphasizes that the scenes must in the first instance have been epic portrayals of historic events of the kind mentioned in Old Norse sagas. Hougen remarks on the similarity of pictorial weaving and wood carving in the Oseberg find: carts, the sleigh, etc. It is tempting to continue this comparison to the extent of characterizing both categories as 'polychrome relief', a plastic rendering closely bound to the surface, the effect of which was originally heightened by a multiplicity of colours. To heighten the effect still further, the sculptured animal figures were sometimes incised with geometrical surface patterns bearing a striking resemblance to the woven patterns seen on the figures of the hanging. It should be noted that these too formed a kind of relief, accentuated by means of colour against the white ground weave. Moreover, from a close study of the animal-shaped bed-posts, the incised surface patterns seem to be imitations of woven patterns.

THE MIDDLE AGES

In view of its international character and the important part played by imports, the Viking period is generally characterized as a transitional period leading up to the Middle Ages. If on the other hand the textile remains of these two periods are considered in terms of the use to which they were put, two very different pictures emerge. All that has come down from prehistoric times is archaeological evidence, most of it from burials and accordingly in the form of fragments of costume. Starting from the early Middle Ages, on the other hand, very few articles of clothing have been preserved and textiles in general are rarely found as a result of excavation. Subject to a few exceptions, everything that survives today in the way of medieval textiles has been preserved in churches, owing to the paramount role of ecclesiastical art during the Middle Ages. The sources of knowledge are now supplemented by written documents: dated records or 'diplomas', wills, legal documents, inventories, stories from the Norse sagas, folk songs, etc. The Icelandic and Norwegian sagas, written down in the thirteenth century, also describe events that occurred several generations earlier. These stories provide abundant evidence of the role played by luxury fabrics. It was above all on these writings that the Norwegian philologist Hjalmar Falk based his important study of Old Norse textile terminology, in which he attempted to interpret and explain textile terms of native and foreign origin.

The written sources contain several names for the textile furnishings in the home that were intended to serve both as decoration and as protection from the cold. The walls were hung with two kinds of hangings, mainly called *tjald* and *refil*, which were frequently used together, in which case the latter, being the more elaborate, would be hung above the former. If there were benches fixed to the walls of the house, the hangings, often termed *ryglaken* (dorsal), would be put up to adorn the inside walls, behind the backs.

Surviving textiles of foreign origin

The large silk textile donated in memory of St Knut on the occasion of his translation in 1101 is still in the possession of Odense Cathedral. This somewhat debased design of eagles in dark blue and purple is a direct copy of one of the Imperial *pallia* woven on the Byzantine court looms.

The cathedrals of Turku (Åbo) and Uppsala still possess some remarkable textile treasures connected with the cult of the martyr king St Erik and with the religious ceremonies that took place in Uppsala during the latter decades of the thirteenth century. The most famous of these is the red cope of Archbishop Folke, embroidered in France with a number of scenes of martyrs and brought from there to Sweden in 1274. No less remarkable is the Roman vestment of Archbishop Nicolas Alloni, which he himself brought home from Italy in 1295 after receiving his insignia with the papal blessing on his nomination. The textiles still kept in the shrine of St Erik date from the same period. They include a splendid Italian fabric, of the same kind as the cope of Bishop Nicolas, both of which were discussed in Chapter VII. The unique reliquary in Turku, made from a Chinese silk (VII, fig. 5), dates from the same period. Apart from the episcopal vestments already mentioned, Uppsala Cathedral possesses a number of silk fabrics, some Italian and some of Chinese or other Asian origin, which were probably bequeathed to the Cathedral in about 1320. Two silk fabrics, once the property of Århus Cathedral in Denmark, are of Italian manufacture but clearly influenced by Islamic textiles. Here may also be mentioned some interesting silk fragments in Bergen Museum, from the convent of Selje (Pl. 33b, c). These are varying types of self-patterned weaves with only one warp system; they are undoubtedly of Spanish origin.

The above survey includes most of the early medieval silks preserved in the Scandinavian countries. Those dating from the later Middle Ages — the fifteenth century and the opening decades of the sixteenth — are far more numerous, especially in Sweden, where one is entitled to speak about large quantities. This is particularly true of Italian silk fabrics from the period, which are now far more numerous in Sweden than in Italy itself. This remarkable situation, paralleled on a lesser scale in the other Scandinavian countries, is due above all to the relatively lenient implementation of the Reformation: the Catholic practice of wearing ecclesiastical vestments remained current in Sweden until the eighteenth century. The costly medieval vestments were appreciated and taken good care of by the Swedish churches, which as a result of Gustav Vasa's confiscations were too poor to be able to afford replacements. Another reason for the survival of such a large number of medieval ecclesiastical textiles until the present day is that practically no wars have been waged on Swedish soil, that is, within the boundaries of sixteenth-century Sweden.

The textiles primarily referred to here are those which were particularly costly: products of the Italian silk looms, which were at the peak of their achievement at that time. But various kinds of costly orphreys with figural representations in needlework were also imported for adorning ecclesiastical vestments. The Middle Ages also saw the importation of patterned textiles of wool and linen, coarser and cheaper commodities that probably played quite an important part as models for native textile production. Uncommon as they now are, due to normal wear and tear, these products are interesting in the context of textile history because they constitute examples of the application of ancient silk techniques to coarser materials and of copying and adaptation of older silk-weaving patterns.

A total of some ten woollen coverlets, one of the most interesting groups of articles in this category, have survived in various parts of Norway, Sweden and Finland (Pl. 83b). The material is coarse woollen yarn for the weft and a spaced warp of flax or hemp. The technique is a weft twill in two colours, similarly patterned on both sides though in reversed colouring. In fact this is a coarsened translation of a type of silk principally known from Spain. It is uncertain where these woollen coverlets were made. On the other hand it is obvious that their patterns were in turn imitated in Norwegian and north Swedish double cloth.

Although it is believed that plain woollens for 'superior clothing' were imported from other countries, there was for a long time no specific evidence of what they looked like — with the sole exception of the complete dress of a fourteenth-century man which was found in the Bocksten bog. It is only in recent years that more materials of this kind have been brought to light through excavation of medieval areas of some Swedish and Norwegian towns. This material invariably consists of refuse, to both worn out rags of clothing and unworn pieces with cut edges that probably came from a tailor's workshop. Some isolated finer pieces (silk strips and gold braid) may have been lost by their owners. Preliminary analysis suggests that most of the cloth was of foreign manufacture.

Native textile production

It is the commonest plain fabrics, the everyday commodity, about which least is known, because as a rule they have all been destroyed. Practically all that remains in the way of domestically woven woollens from the Middle Ages are the clothes of the Scandinavians living in isolation in Greenland whose graves have been excavated by Danish archaeologists, and a man's costume from c.1500 found in a bog in northern Norway. Most of these articles of clothing are coarse four-end twill, obviously woven on a warp-weighted loom, in contrast to the rather fashionable costume worn by the 'Bocksten man' mentioned above, a three-end twill which by definition must have been woven in a treadle loom and, accordingly, was probably imported.

In the Scandinavian countries practically all plain woollens were produced in the countryside for the requirements of the individual family and as a source of extra income, particularly through barter. This state of affairs persisted throughout the Middle Ages and, doubtless, for a considerable period afterwards. Thus there were no professional weavers in medieval Stockholm and it was a long time before Swedish towns, like the towns of Germany and the Netherlands, acquired professional craftsmen of this kind. Textiles were generally produced on a domestic handicraft basis at various levels, but the larger households, manors, royal estates and palaces doubtless provided scope for differentiation and professional specialization, and were probably in a position to get hold of prototypes and patterns that could be used for local production on a minor scale.

There is much information concerning one of these manors, which was excellently organized by an experienced and ingenious *mater familias*; this was the convent founded in Vadstena during the fourteenth century by St Bridget. The exhaustively detailed rules of the convent stipulate hard work as well as spiritual exercises. The various tasks were meticulously apportioned. After their midday meal the sisters were to go about their various tasks. Those who could write were to do so, and those who could sew were to do needle-work or sprang-work, while others again were to cut out clothing for the brethren and sisters. Each was to do the work that she was best suited for. The records give us the name of a widow, Helena, who for a period of forty years was in charge of the *lanificium*, where wool and woollens were prepared and stored. Other tasks, as well as surviving articles, testify to various kinds of weaving: coarse woollen cloth, pile rugs, plain linen tabby and tabby brocaded on the counted thread of the Dukagång type. It is almost certain that the textile activities of the convent provided a school for various kinds of textile work and that the training given here profoundly influenced the surrounding area.

A brief account will now be given of existing medieval textiles of Scandinavian origin, most of which are well known and frequently discussed in the literature of the subject. The specimens have survived because, sooner or later, they became the property of a church, but it should be noted that many of them, nonetheless, are of a secular character.

Reference has already been made to the wall-hangings from Överhogdal and Skog, which were described as folk-art versions of the aristocratic textile art of Oseberg (see above). The simplification affected both technique and stylization, but the design and the narrative style are so closely related that there can be no questioning their ancestry over a period of three or four centuries — through intermediate stages which have since vanished. In 1910 a large cover, joined together at a later date by five long and narrow textiles of which four were worked in a kind of soumak technique and one in double cloth, was found in the parish church of Överhogdal in the north Swedish province of Härjedalen. Two years later another piece of 'soumak weave' was discovered in the parish church of Skog, in the neighbouring province of Hälsingland. The first of these finds was later taken apart, and the pieces, *refils* (cf. above), are now on show in the Östersund Museum, while the Skog *refil* was acquired by the Historical Museum in Stockholm.

The hanging from Skog and the related pieces from Överhogdal are of the same format (33–37 centimetres high), and thus somewhat larger than the Oseberg *refils*. The coarser hangings are on a larger scale and are executed in a technique which is less rich and varied than that of the earlier ones. The pictorial conception is much the same: a crowd of different figures one after the other, the upper and lower edges being marked by a geometrical border. The colours, warm red, dark blue, and greenish blue against a white background, still retain their freshness and provide a fair indication of the original spectrum of the Viking Age counterparts which are now devoid of all their colouring.

These Swedish pictorial textiles have interested many scholars. Time and time again, new interpretations have been proposed for details of the scenes and the original pictorial content. As regards the Överhogdal hanging, the narrative scene is generally taken to have been based on the Völsunga saga and the story of Sigurd Fafnesbane. The Skog hanging obviously depicts a stave church, but beside it there stand three crowned men concerning whom opinion is very divided. They have been said to represent either of the three Magi; the three Holy Kings of the Scandinavian countries, St Erik, St Olav and St Knut; or the three pagan idols, Odin, Thor and Frey, as they once stood in the temple of Old Uppsala. The latter suggestion rests as the evidence of the chronicler Adam of Bremen who visited the place during the eleventh century. The last of these interpretations is principally based on the observation that the man on the left has only one eye and would thus appear to represent Odin, who, the saga relates acquired wisdom by pledging one of his eyes in the well of Mimer. This interpretation was then taken to imply that the scene in its entirety depicted a historical event, namely the overthrow of the pagan temple at Uppsala and the erection of the first Christian church. However, this exciting theory will have to be abandoned since a careful investigation by A. M. Franzén has shown that the one-eyed figure originally had two eyes. The riddle remains unsolved. Opinions have also varied concerning the dating. Broadly speaking this has been successively brought forward in time from the original suggestion of the eleventh century to the more likely proposal of the thirteenth. The nature of folk-art in which the motifs are reptitious of remote prototypes makes exact dating particularly hazardous.

The custom of decorating a festive interior with long narrow hangings showing narrative figure scenes also existed on the continent. The most famous example of this practice is the so-called Bayeux tapestry, a 70-metre long pictorial narrative of the conquest of England by William the Conqueror in 1066. This dramatic representation, however, is not a tapestry weave, but needle-work executed in laid and couched work with coloured woollen yarns on a linen ground. Remarkably enough several early specimens of this very embroidery technique have been found in

Iceland, Norway, and Sweden where it is generally called '*refil* stitch', indicating its use for similar purposes.

Norway, however, possesses two very remarkable wall hangings from the early Middle Ages which are also oblong *refils* but executed in different techniques. The hanging from the demolished parish church of Höylandet, now in the Museum of Antiquities in Trondheim, is obviously a native product, even though the scene it depicts, the three Magi, reveals that the skilled artist who designed it had access to a foreign model, probably an English manuscript of the thirteenth century. The silhouette-like figures are embroidered in richly varied geometrical patterns, which are executed in white linen yarn and multicoloured woollen yarn on a red woollen fabric. This unique work was presumably done in one of the many convents in the archiepiscopal city of Nidaros (Trondheim), which at that time was a very wealthy community.

The Baldishol hanging is the sole representative from medieval Scandinavia of the homogenous all-over tapestry technique frequently met with on the continent. The composition as well as the subject, the Twelve Months of the Year, also belongs to the international repertoire of the twelfth century. Of the original twelve subjects only two, April and May, have survived. Some anachronistic details coupled with a close resemblance to medieval Norwegian wood sculpture and the dovetail technique of the colour changes show beyond any shadow of doubt that this colourful work of art was made in Norway, probably during the early thirteenth century.

As regards other techniques suviving in Scandinavia, the following are represented in woven items which are reliably dated to the Middle Ages: double cloth (D4), *Dukagång* and *Krabbasnår* (B2). No doubt other techniques were also in use, but unfortunately no definitely medieval specimens have survived, neither of any rya-rug or of sprang. But anyhow the folk-art textiles can for the most part be regarded as a continuation of the average production of the Middle Ages. Naturally this kind of production was successively influenced by the general artistic trends of the following periods or by individual prototypes, but on the whole it has preserved its medieval character amazingly well. This conservative tendency is already apparent in textiles from the end of the medieval period, which in design and type often seem to be at least a century older than they actually are.

There are two varieties of medieval doublecloth, the main difference between which concerns the technical execution of the colour-change. The oldest type is composed of a layer of white linen forming an irregular design against the other layer which is of wool, often chequered in red and blue. The repertoire of patterns includes knots and interlace motifs together with swastikas and geometricized animals. Both the narrow *refil* from Överhogdal (Pl. 86) and the cover from Kyrkås present surface arrangements reminiscent of certain rare silks of hitherto unknown origin.

The blue and white hanging from Grödinge (Pl. 87b) introduces a newer type of doublecloth, which was to be long-lived. The decorative pattern of fabulous beasts on chequerboard squares is a stylistically skilful simplification of the well-known Persian-Byzantine kind of silk designs consisting of various animal motifs, generally in frames, circular or angular. Some remains of this kind, among others the above-mentioned *pallium* of St Knut of Denmark showing eagles, represent the kind of prototypes that it may have been possible to study in our latitudes.

It is, however, hard to say with any certainty whether this excellent composition, so artistically adapted to the coarse woollen material, really was made here in the North. But the following facts seem to make this probable. There is a closely related parallel to the Grödinge wall-hanging which has belonged to the church of St Martin in Finland. And the type corresponds quite closely to descriptions in the court inventories for the Vasa period, which in detail account for many two-coloured weaves, mostly identifiable with our double cloth and termed 'Russian' or 'Finnish' weaves. The designation 'Finnish' is also known from Bohuslän in western Sweden where the technique survived until quite recently.

Dukagång (B2) is known above all from south-eastern Skåne where horizontal wall-hangings with predominantly Romanesque motifs were used to embellish interiors on festive occasions (Pl. 88a). However, none of these textiles date further back than the eighteenth century. On the other hand there are other dukagång hangings with related patterns, with a ground weave of either white linen or red wool, which were undoubtedly made before the end of the Middle Ages (Pl. 85a). They were preserved in the Bridgettine convent of Nådendal in Finland, where they were probably woven. This raises the question as to whether similar fabrics were made at Vadstena. An altar-cloth in a Swedish church with borders in dukagång may constitute evidence for this conjecture. This assumption is corroborated by the existence of other techniques which were probably practised in both places. This is the case, at all events, with a number of silk embroideries from the Finnish daughter-convent which, in spite of a certain awkwardness in the design, bear a close resemblance to works from the Vadstena workshop, which was pre-eminently skilful in this particular art. But the same applies to other, coarser techniques, specimens of which have been preserved in both Swedish and Finnish churches, which lead to the assumption that the skilled sisters of Vadstena did weave doublecloth of the Grödinge type.

The art of needlework in Sweden

Sewing with costly materials — silk, gold, silver, and pearls of various kinds, sometimes with the addition of metal spangles — was a demanding occupation whose male practitioners were known as 'pearl-stitchers'. This art was employed above all in ecclesiastical textiles, as a supplement to the Italian silk fabrics.

A great deal of this kind of work was done in Vadstena, the mother convent of the Order of St Bridget, where the art of needlework reached a very high standard. About thirty specimens from the Vadstena workshop have come down to us, among them the splendid altar-frontal of Linköping Cathedral, which can be dated to about 1400 by means of the coats-of-arms belonging to prominent donors. Many of these textiles are beautifully trimmed with braids and bands of characteristic types. A large number of existing ecclesiastical vestments together with written documents make it possible to reconstruct the activity of an important embroidery workshop in Stockholm associated with a burgess of the city named Albert, who was known both as a 'pearl-embroiderer' and as a painter of church murals, in the latter capacity sometimes signing himself as *Albertus Pictor*. He is mentioned in the Stockholm city records between 1465 and 1508. The greatest period of this embroidery workshop came during the 1480s. Some of the most important works belong to Uppsala cathedral and were probably commissioned by the powerful Archbishop Jakob Ulfsson. Among other works may be mentioned two remarkable tomb covers of which one was commissioned by some of the country's leading families. Certain features of the embroidery which are attributed to Albert and which, even from an international standpoint, are distinguished works, betray the influence of Danzig or the nearby cultural area which in turn may reflect something of Albert's antecedents. Swedish medieval documents also mention other embroiderers, but apparently none of these can challenge Albert's authorship of the works now known.

Here may be described another category of needlework, mostly large coverlets or other furnishing textiles made of thick woollen cloth in bright colours, often red and blue. The technique is a type of inlay work (here called *intarsia*) meaning that the same motif is cut out in two rectangular pieces of cloth in contrasting colours. The two motifs are then interchanged and the edges are sewn together, after which narrow strips of gilded leather are applied over the seams and as extra decoration. Behind the monumentally stylized designs can be discerned the ultimate influence of Persian-Byzantine silks depicting fantastic animals, while the technique itself is reminiscent of the decorative textiles, known from the rich Siberian burials from the fourth and fifth centuries B.C. The oldest specimen (preserved only in a coloured drawing) bears a coat-of-arms, probably of north German origin, dating the cover to the early fourteenth century and suggesting that this cover was a foreign prototype on which the other woollen intarsia pieces were modelled. The remaining textiles as well as the records, especially from the royal castles and manors, indicate that this type of work continued to be in fashion as late as the sixteenth century. They were in secular use notably as coverlets for the state bed, as wall hangings and as cushion covers, but not as canopies, as was earlier erroneously supposed. For that purpose these coverlets would certainly have been too heavy.

Both geographically and historically, the commonest embroidery technique was cross-stitch of multicoloured woollen thread covering most of the ground material of linen tabby and often employing designs derived from silk fabrics.

TEXTILES FROM THE SEVENTEENTH CENTURY ONWARDS

In his *Svenskt arbete och liv* (Life and Labour in Sweden) Eli Heckscher states that 'During the Middle Ages the overwhelming proportion of the Swedish people must have been farmers'. But he continues, 'on the other hand they did not live by farming alone'. They also had to build houses and practise various crafts. The subsistence economy required and stimulated versatility on the part of the individual, within the family, household and estate and in the surrounding community. Within this more or less confined group there developed a division of labour conditioned by the changes of the seasons and by other practical considerations. Customs were established by which some tasks became by definition men's tasks while others were allotted to the women. It was the prerogative and duty of the housewife to assume responsibility for all the work connected with the preparation and management of food, the care of livestock and all the seasonal chores entailed by the production of textiles.

In the Scandinavian countries particularly, these tasks came to comprise the specific occupation of women, a state of affairs which remained practically unaltered until the turn of this century.

It is above all external, political events, not domestic conditions, that justify the nomination of Gustav Vasa as the harbinger of a new epoch. The social structure, working life and the economic system did not change. On the contrary, if Heckscher is to be believed, the period down to about 1600 witnessed the organization and consolidation of the medieval economic system, some facets of which survived for a great deal longer still. Indeed, according to the same authority, since the medieval techniques of iron-founding survived in the province of Dalarna until 1870, this date could be argued as the true end of the medieval period. Where textile production is concerned, at all events, there are a striking number of similarities between the late Middle Ages and the century that followed.

Foreign textiles

After the coming of the Reformation, imports of textiles were still very considerable, but they were now of quite a different kind. The nature of the fabrics purchased testifies to a degree of sobriety and parsimoniousness that stands in strong contrast to the very costly luxury articles, above all Italian silks, that were acquired while the Catholic Church was still a wealthy patron of the arts. The problem now was that the King's personal servants and the officers of the Crown (from ministers downwards, and particularly the army and navy) should receive at least part of their pay in the form of clothing. But nothing like the amount of material required for this purpose could be produced within the country, and in any case the native *wadmal*, a rough cloth without the complete after-treatment or finish, was only good enough for the rank and file and the meanest servants. The surviving accounts record purchases of innumerable kinds of broadcloth (*kläde*) a fulled and shorn article, sometimes of very high quality, which was imported and which may also have been dyed. Such fabrics entered under a variety of names showing that they came from various towns in Germany, the Low Countries and England. To check the outflow of money caused by these imports, Gustav Vasa eventually saw fit to sponsor native production. Craftsmen and suitable sheep were brought in from Germany. Sheep farms and fulling mills were established in various towns and developed into considerable wool-producing enterprises during the seventeenth century.

The Vasa period, however, was by no means hostile to sumptuous textiles. It has already been seen how interested Gustav Vasa was, for all his penny-pinching, in establishing contact with Persian silk merchants. The fabrics he wished to buy were of the luxury kind which were later sold in Stockholm in the 'Russian shops' near Slussen. Some of the ways have already been mentioned in which oriental textiles could find their way to Sweden (see Chap. XIV).

Of course, luxury textiles were also imported from countries nearer at hand, but most of these imports appear to have been connected with special orders, especially from the Court and for particular occasions, such as weddings and coronations, requiring a great deal of ostentation. Festivities of this kind were meticulously prepared: detailed particulars have come down concerning the purchases made in London and Antwerp for the coronation of Erik XIV and also concerning the orders placed by Gustav II Adolfus in Hamburg. In both cases the orders concerned lavish costumes with embroidered decorations. During the eighteenth century corresponding orders were placed in Paris. But even then it is scarcely possible to speak in terms of any continuous importation of luxury textiles — those which were brought into the country were generally contraband or war booty. Native production was protected by high tariffs.

Native Swedish textile production

The woollen factories founded by Gustav Vasa prospered during the seventeenth century in keeping with the mercantile system, which became more and more influential after 1720. Mercantilism prescribed the reduction of imports by encouraging native production, above all through manufacturing industries. Among the most cherished of these industries were those concerned with silk weaving and linen damask, which were protected by subsidies, import duties on corresponding foreign products, and special ordinances designed to prevent competition from home crafts, which were directly opposed by the state, all hopes being pinned on the towns and their craftsmen instead (cf. Chaps IX and X).

As has already been observed a number of times, home craft was a form of production which, apart from catering for the direct needs of the practitioner in many respects could also provide an important supplement to a family's occupation, which was usually agriculture. Textile work in particular has occupied this dual role for centuries. This in turn fostered a considerable degree of manual skill and technical knowledge, which also benefited the manufacturing enterprises and provided the foundation for a certain amount of collaboration with them. Despite the disfavour shown by the authorities, home crafts did very well on the eighteenth-century market, but as business trends rose and fell it was the handicraft practised in individual homes, generation after generation, that created the living tradition which in turn enabled ancient implements, working methods, techniques, patterns, and terminology, etc. to survive as the centuries passed.

Turning now to consider the products of genuine home craft, a category is distinguishable which can justifiably be termed textile folk-art: more or less decoratively designed fabrics, embroideries, etc. which were originally intended for the personal environment of the maker. These patterns and motifs are impregnated with the traditions and beliefs of that environment but sometimes also by influences from outside. The fusion of inherited techniques and patterns with chronologically heterogeneous motifs, and the practical consequences of such local circumstances as the availability of certain dyes and spinning materials — all these things together are ingredients in the chains of development resulting in the various provincial types of textile work.

The surviving corpus of old folk textiles reflects a course of development with a retarding tendency, a characteristic which is typical of all folk-art, perhaps supremely typical of the extraordinarily conservative textile art of the Orient. Swedish textile art and the textile art of the other Scandinavian countries are unusually variegated and technically versatile. But what is more, an historically valuable situation occurs here in which many textiles produced during the past three or four centuries and still extant are supplemented both by written documents and by a number of even older textiles which were undoubtedly made during the Middle Ages, if not earlier still. Together they reveal a course of development extending over millennia and covering the entire world, evidence which can contribute towards an understanding of phenomena in textile art everywhere. It is considerations of this kind that make a knowledge of Scandinavian textile folk-art a matter of international relevance.

Detailed accounts of the various weaves are to be found in Chapter III, in which Scandinavian material constitutes an important ingredient in the classification of textile techniques. But various aspects of specifically Scandinavian textile art have also been discussed in other sections.

WHAT WEAVING IMPLEMENTS WAS USED?

This is an intricate question, but it has to be asked. I shall endeavour here to answer it as far as is possible, approaching it in the same order as that used to describe the different types in Chapter II. Marta Hoffmann is probably correct in regarding the small vertical frame from the Oseberg find (II, fig. 9) as a loom for weaving a tubular warp, used especially for weaving the figured *refils* in the same find. On the other hand it has been proved that at least one of the horizontal hangings from northern Sweden (shown on Pl. 87a), generally considered to be descendants of the Oseberg hangings, was woven on a warp-weighted loom.

The part played by the tubular loom (type 4) in Scandinavian textile art was not realized until Margrethe Hald indicated several examples from Celtic and Roman times. This type of weave may be even older than the warp-weighted loom (type 5), although it would be hard to prove this.

As has already been said, the occurrence and worldwide use of the warp-weighted loom are relatively well documented, not least as regards the Scandinavian countries, where it survived longest.

The distribution of the warp-weighted loom in Scandinavia

In 1921 a find of the utmost importance to textile research was made at Tegle in western Norway. This find consisted entirely of textiles which had evidently been carefully deposited in a lake which was eventually transformed into a bog, thus preserving the material. Archaeologists classify it as a votive offering of about the fifth century A.D. Two items are of particular interest for present purposes, namely a piece of four-end twill including the starting border in tablet weave, and a similar starting border with the warp ends assembled in balls, the whole ready to be fastened to the beam (cf. II, figs 10, 11).

Hans Dedekam's publication of the Tegle find came at a fortunate moment in that it led his Swedish colleague Emelie von Walterstorff to the discovery which she presented in 1928 in her important article 'En vävstol och en varpa' (A Loom and a Warping Implement). A Lappish *rana* cover produced on a warp-weighted loom and the warping tool on which the warp was arranged, served to present the explanation as to how the Tegle warp had been made and used. From this initial discovery, Marta Hoffmann proceeded first and foremost to save what could be saved of warp-weighted weaving in Scandinavia and the knowledge connected with it.

Geographically the Scandinavian material divides into three main areas: the west Norwegian, the Lappish, and the Icelandic, to which must be added the Faroes. Structurally speaking, these groups differ from one another, but are mutually complementary. Each of them has in its own way preserved different stages of the weaving method once current throughout Europe, a technique which, moreover, has followed an independent course of development in Iceland. Taking the groups one by one — the surviving artefacts together with theoretical and practically inherited knowledge — produces the summary which follows.

Of the west Norwegian group twenty-three looms are now left, some of them incomplete, plus two or three women who have directly communicated an inherited knowledge of the use of the warp-weighted loom, which has remained in use there during the present century for making a special kind of cover in geometrical tapestry (rutevev). There are also a number of other fabrics which might have been woven on the warp-weighted loom.

The extensive *Lappish* group still survives today in a tradition which has never quite been broken. This production is now located around Lyngenfjord within the western portion of the vast area of the Scandinavian Arctic where only a few generations ago *rana* (the Swedish and Finnish term for the Norwegian *grene*) was woven on a considerable scale, both for domestic use and for sale. Written records from the sixteenth and seventeenth centuries show that *rana* covers were of great economic importance to the Lapps. Here was a universal article of exchange, used until quite recently for the payment of taxes. There are linguistic reasons for supposing that this type of weaving was adopted in northern Norway at an early stage, since a number of old Norse loan-words show that the Lapps acquired the implement from their Scandinavian neighbours not later than the seventh century. But the simple striped *rana* of today — a heavy fabric in weft-faced tabby with a spaced warp — so well-suited to the climate, is a greatly coarsened descendant of the refined twill weaves represented by, for example, the Tegle fabrics, which are some 1,500 years older.

The human tradition in the *Icelandic* group was broken in the early nineteenth century and all that remains of the loom itself is a single specimen (unfortunately radically altered about fifty years ago) and a small model dating from about 1870, by which time the warp-weighted loom had already been ousted by the treadle loom. But the lack of direct practical evidence and a living tradition is counterbalanced by sources of other kinds which, even by international standards, are of the utmost importance. The engraved picture of an Icelandic loom published in 1780 by Olaus Olavius in *Oeconomisk Reise igiennem . . . Island*, has often been reproduced, but the original on which the engraving was based, drawn in 1777 by Saemundur Holm and completed with detailed instructions, is a more valuable document which has only recently become known, after a long period of oblivion in the Royal Library in Copenhagen. Marta Hoffmann has been able to supplement Holm's instructions with a number of exhaustive descriptions in the National Museum of Iceland concerning the warping and weaving procedures for the ancient loom. Apart from these sources, Iceland has a considerable collection of written documents — lawbooks from the Middle Ages (*Grágás, Jónsbók*) and, from more recent times, written codifications of customary law, *Bualøg* — containing information about the wool production that played such an important part in the economy of the country through the centuries. Practical experiments based on the descriptions provided a successful substitute for a living tradition, and these experiments showed quite conclusively that the warp-weighted loom was a highly efficient weaving implement.

The experiments yielded a great deal of information of universal relevance, but they also helped to explain certain technical peculiarities previously noticed in archaeological finds. Whereas warping as it is known in the Lappish *rana* gives a division into two sheds only, the Icelandic method which has now been revealed produces four sheds, resulting in a four-end twill. It has already been observed that this type of warping only calls for three heddle rods, hence the Icelandic term for it 'three shaft'. It was also found that, when the twill binding turns to form either a chevron or a lozenge twill, this will invariably result in an assymetrical turnover, forming a sharp score, as indicated by Pl. 90b. This study revealed a circumstance of great importance, namely that the warping method automatically gives even numbers in the binding repeat, that is, either two or four, but never three. Thus a three-end twill cannot be woven in a warp-weighted loom.

Icelandic legal texts contain several rules concerning the measurements, weight, etc. required for a piece of cloth to be approved, and they also tell a great deal more about this form of production, which was of such vital importance. The standard regulations were necessary because a piece of woollen cloth could be used as legal tender. At a certain point during the thirteenth century, the length of a piece of cloth could not be less than 22 ells, which, indeed, is a remarkable achievement for this weaving implement, used for thousands of years to produce comparatively short pieces. The loom type illustrated by Holm can only be explained as the result of a native Icelandic invention, occasioned by competition with continental weaving. The professional woollen industry, developed in the countries bordering the English Channel, was based on the south-eastern type of loom, which was fitted with treadles and beams and thus constructed for weaving long loom pieces.

The reason why the Icelanders retained their ancient loom until during the eighteenth century (when Danish merchants forced them to adopt the treadle loom) was no doubt that it required so little space. In this unforested country, houses were generally built of stone and turf and had very small and narrow rooms.

The above summary suggests that the warp-weighted loom was the weaving implement commonly used in the countryside all over Scandinavia during the Middle Ages, and even later — particularly for weaving woollen cloth, which was the most important textile material. Apart from considerations of space, there is another and more positive answer to the question as to why this ancient implement persisted for such a long time: it made it possible to decide in each case the exact width of the fabric desirable for the purpose in hand. All that was needed in order to obtain a broader weave was to find a long enough beam. The treadle loom, on the other hand, was usually built for a narrow width and could not be altered. This meant, for example, that a coverlet had to be woven in two lengths, which afterwards had to be joined together. This was aesthetically displeasing, especially as it was difficult to get the patterns to fit perfectly. By means of a warp-weighted loom, on the contrary, the entire textile could be woven in one piece, thus avoiding a disfiguring join, as exemplified by the two related coverlets from Skåne and from Norway which are illustrated in Pl. 95b and c.

XVI *When and How Textiles have been Preserved — and should be Preserved*

ARCHAEOLOGICAL FINDS

The textiles occurring in archaeological finds are a minute fraction compared to objects of metal, stone, pottery, glass, etc. — categories on which archaeological research has particularly concentrated. It may be speculated whether this specialization, due above all to practical circumstances, has not sometimes had a disastrous effect on the recovery of still extant but half-decayed fragments of textiles. In earlier excavations many such fragments doubtless passed unnoticed and were thrown aside as being 'only dirt'. More recently, however, it has been found that fragments which are almost destroyed can in fact be salvaged, at least sufficiently to benefit research. It is to be hoped that this will encourage all practising archaeologists to keep a careful watch during their excavations.

Elsewhere it has been shown how the physiological properties of different spinning materials played a fundamental part in the development of the various branches of textile art. This chapter will consider instead how the various properties of textile materials, combined with extraneous circumstances of one kind or another, can determine the survival of a textile product left in the soil for hundreds or thousands of years, and also the extent to which it survives. First, a few examples which on the whole can be taken as establishing general rules, though it should, however, be emphasized that there are exceptions to these rules and that many instances of the preservation of textiles are still awaiting a satisfactory scientific explanation.

The general verdict that animal fibres have better prospects of survival than vegetable ones is founded on extensive experience, particularly in northern Europe. Vegetable fibres are seldom actually preserved, since they are more susceptible to disintegrating bacteria, which in damp soil will annihilate every single thread of linen, for example. On the other hand certain traces may survive. For instance, by observing holes pierced in a woollen or silk fabric one might be able to tell that there was once a linen or other vegetable thread. The appearance of a linen fabric can moreover be preserved if the fabric has lain next to iron which has deposited rust, in which case the rust will have been absorbed by the linen threads and then hardened. When this happens, the surface structure of the fabric is preserved although the actual fibre material is destroyed. Under similar circumstances silk and wool (the hair of sheep and other animal species) have proved to be relatively immune to decay, but in all cases the character of the immediate surrounding earth must have played a decisive part. Copper salts from oxidized objects of bronze or silver have quite often acted as disinfectants, thus preserving, for example, a piece of the fabric with which the ornament in question was originally associated. Thus the Birka graves yielded innumerable specimens of tablet-woven braids consisting of a silk warp interwoven with wire of silver or pure gold. The corroded silver has generally preserved the silk material, which, however, is destroyed when interwoven with pure gold, since the latter is not chemically affected and, consequently, does not emit any preservative salts. On the other hand a rare specimen alternately interwoven with gold and silver has survived fairly intact (Pl. 92d–g).

Hermetic sealing from air, permanently and from an early stage, gives various kinds of fibres a fair chance of resisting decay. This, probably, is the reason why textiles of bast fibres (flax) have been preserved in the Swiss pile dwellings of the Neolithic period. Presumably they fell directly into the water, were saturated and then sank to the bed of the lake, where they were soon encapsulated in the fine clay sludge deposited by the lake and were thus hermetically sealed by natural means. The absence of woollen fabrics from these finds has been discussed by archaeologists, some of whom assume that any woollens must have disappeared because wool cannot survive in water. As has been seen, this cannot be accepted as a general rule. On the other hand it must be remembered that special circumstances are required — even in the case of animal fibres — to prevent decay occurring in damp soil. The lack of finds should therefore not be taken to exclude the possibility that woollen textiles were used parallel to the consistent vegetable finds yielded by the pile dwelling sites. But why did not both kinds of fibre material survive, given the same circumstances? As everybody knows from experience, a woollen object takes time to become wet through: the air which collects in cavities keeps it afloat. Thus it follows that any woollen textile which was dropped in the water must have kept afloat and been carried further on by the flow before sinking, while the vegetable material sank straight to the bottom and was covered by the mud. Another case of preserved textiles is exemplified by the famous Oseberg ship burial. There intentionally applied protective layers of turf — coupled with an underlying foundation of blue clay pressed upwards by the weight of the stone cairn — are considered to have saved the textiles, for the main part woollens and silks, but also tiny remains of bast fibres.

Why, however, did the textiles of two very similar sixth-century graves fare so differently? An almost complete costume of fine woollen fabric trimmed with tablet-woven bands fastened to bronze clasps survived in the burial mound of Högom, in the province of Hälsingland, while in the Norrala grave not far away, hardly anything remained of a similar item, except the clasps surrounded by half-decayed though unmistakeable fragments of tablet weave and cloth. As yet the riddle remains unsolved.

Seclusion from the air, combined with constant humidity, and, possibly, with the presence of methane, is taken into account for a series of bog finds in Scandinavia and in the regions to the west and south of the Baltic, for example, the Bronze Age mantle from the bog at Gerum in Västergötland, and the medieval man from Bocksten in Halland. The crucial factor in the survival of the usually very well preserved Danish Bronze Age costumes is a matter of dispute. A decisive role was formerly attributed to the tannic acid in the oak coffins, but this explanation has been questioned.

In this age of refrigeration technology, it is not difficult to appreciate that constant freezing can be an excellent means of conservation. In fact, however, the archaeological potential of this mode of preservation is strictly limited. One notable series of examples came from the medieval cemeteries of Greenland, where relics of a 'Norse colonization at the ends of the earth' were recovered from the perpetual ice.[1] The most remarkable examples of archaeological refrigeration have been recovered by Russian archaeologists in Noin Ula in northern Mongolia and in the Altai region (Pazyryk and other sites).[2] These discoveries are the graves of powerful nomadic princes belonging to the equestrian peoples that for centuries dominated large tracts of Central Asia. The finds, which date from the centuries about the beginning of our era and roughly 400 years earlier exemplify such different categories as native works of felt and leather, Chinese silks, woollen embroideries in the Greek style as well as the famous pile carpet (cf. Chap. XI) and some small tapestry pieces. The textiles are particularly impressive because of their relatively well-preserved colouring which is unusual for archaeological textile finds. In other cases where colours could be observed soon after the textiles were unearthed, they generally faded soon afterwards.

Colours can be preserved, however, in certain circumstances, when textiles have been kept constantly dry and in darkness, for example, in fine sand. In conditions of this kind even vegetable fibres can survive fairly intact. Thus the dry desert climate provided the best possible conditions for the survival of textile remains, as witness the finds made by expeditions following the ancient caravan routes through the deserts of Central Asia, mentioned earlier. But the most abundant source of textile finds is Egypt, where the arid climate has preserved vast quantities of the most varied textiles: linen fabrics from Pharaonic times, finely patterned silk fabrics of Sassanian Persian manufacture, printed or pattern-dyed Indian cottons but above all native textiles and complete articles of clothing, usually of linen woven with coloured decorations of woollen yarn.

TEXTILES ABOVE GROUND

What has been said above concerning the resistibility of textiles is also basically applicable to textiles preserved above ground: disintegration due to oxidization or for other reasons is still a menace, though a less immediate one. It must be realized, however, that climate means a great deal. A humid and, above all, a tropical climate will have disastrous effects within a short space of time, owing among other things to predatory insects. Silk and animal fibres differ somewhat in this respect. Silk turns brittle more rapidly in dry heat, while the greatest danger to woollen textiles, as long as the temperature does not fall below about 10°C, is from moths and other harmful insects and calls for very special preservative action. Linen material is particularly treacherous because atmospheric humidity in itself enhances the strength, that is, the elasticity, of a sound thread, at the same time as its propensity for absorbing moisture can easily give rise to infection, mould and decay. On the other hand temperatures in excess of about 80° are harmful to linen fibres.

Light is the enemy of all kinds of textiles. This is particularly true of sunlight but also applies to ordinary daylight and moderate artificial light, all of which omit harmful ultraviolet rays. The harmful effects of these various sources of light differ considerably. The light can change or destroy colours, though the extent to which it is capable of doing so will vary according to the dyes and the dyeing methods used. Light can also cause the disintegration of the fibres.

The avoidance of all these dangers is a complex problem which is not made any simpler by the conflict between the rational solution and the justified interest of museums in displaying the objects concerned. However, the following should be borne in mind. If future generations are to inherit any of the textile art that exists today, greater account must be taken of this danger than is commonly the case. Museum displays aimed at aesthetic effect are often a direct menace to the survival of the textiles themselves.

There is perhaps only one collection in the entire world that has been ideally managed in this respect, and this is the Japanese Shosoin temple treasure, whose textiles have been so carefully stored that after 1,200 years they still look almost new — when it is possible to see them! In recent years they are said to be exhibited for a few weeks in the year and even then only a selection is shown. The custom of the old manors and country houses whereby inherited precious textiles were packed away most of the time and only got out on special occasions, was based on the same practical experience as the strict Japanese regulations concerning the care of the priceless temple treasures.

Another aspect of the survival prospects of textiles may be termed 'the human factor', which in the long run is responsible for the careful or less careful handling of brittle fabrics and also for direct action of various kinds. Basically the action taken can be divided into three categories: (1) heavy-handed repairs and re-sewings (2) restorations aimed at recreating a more or less hypothetical original state (3) conservation aiming to save the textile document as such and to safeguard its continuing survival with an eye to future research requirements.

Method one is completely unacceptable. So too is the second method if its practical implementation encroaches on the character of the ancient material and jeopardizes its survival by unduly radical measures (gluing with injurious substances, unduly dense sewing, etc.). Obviously the conservation principle is the proper one, but its implementation requires above all experience, special knowledge and skills combined with a capacity for antiquarian and artistic appraisal. Irreparable damage has resulted from deficiencies of human capacity in one or other of these respects.[3]

FADING AND CHANGES OF COLOUR

In referring above to the harmful effects of light on textile colours, the term 'fading' was deliberately avoided, because this word is often given too narrow a definition, being taken to imply that the colour shade is weakened or disappears altogether. Naturally, it does happen that textiles fade in the restricted sense of the term, with dark blue changing to light blue, bright red to pale pink and so on. But it is no less common where old textiles are concerned for certain colours to be totally transformed. This phenomenon, however, is due not only to the effect of light but also to chemical processes gradually brought about by the dyes used in the different cases and also by the usually very complex dyeing process connected with each colour — or rather by some defect in the process.

The above is intended as food for thought and an aid to seeing and understanding what an extant textile may originally have looked like. This is no easy problem: much examination and comparison is necessary before things really begin to be observed. Only then does it become clear how mistaken an assessment of the aesthetic intention, or the artistic achievement, must be if it is based solely on the present state of the material. A pictorial scene with burning flames or red roses — which tone has turned buff — is an example as obvious as it is common of the transformation brought by time. A similar change of colour in a non-figurative composition based on a balance between different colours of equal strength is far more difficult to discover and reconstruct.[4]

XVII   *Concluding Remarks*

'It was textile art that first enabled man to overcome the exigencies of climate . . . Textile art is so closely bound up with the whole of human development that, archaeologically speaking, it is perhaps more than anything else a measure of the civilized status of mankind. In its developed form as woven fabric it is such a striking product of sophisticated thinking that it must be assigned to a stage in the history of human civilization which is very superior to the early days of man, when the hides of slain animals were sufficient for his simple needs.'

The quotation comes from an epoch-making article on 'Prehistoric textile art in Scandinavia' by G. J. Karlin, the famous founder of *Kulturen* (the museum of cultural history in Lund). It is worth noting that, when his paper was written, in 1903, most of the more important and now well-known archaeological textile finds had yet to be made, while those which had been made had not been properly published. There was, in fact, hardly any textile research worthy of the name at that time. In current accounts attention was concentrated on the motifs of the design, normally to the exclusion of technical aspects. Karlin's study, although mainly confined to the archaeological collections in Lund and Copenhagen, is therefore to be regarded as a pioneering effort, valid not only for Scandinavia; and his eloquent statement, with which this chapter opened, still holds good today — to an even greater degree than Karlin himself could have imagined. It provides the historical perspective for the technical intricacies of silk weaving, as well as for primitive production intended solely for everyday necessities.

Elsewhere in Europe, as in Sweden, people had long been content with merely collecting. The closing decades of the nineteenth century were the halcyon period of the collectors and saw the founding of most of the European museums of arts and crafts. During this period, with its delight in ornamentation and its preoccupation with the 'historical styles', a great deal of interest was taken in old textiles because they were regarded as suitable models for contemporary applied art at that time so much in favour.

The first scientifically based contributions to our knowledge of the distribution and importance of textile art in earlier times were, in fact, made by philologists and linguistically trained historians. One of the first was Francisque Michel, whose erudite and imaginative work was published in Paris in 1852, with the descriptive title *Recherches sur le commerce, la fabrication et l'usage des étoffes de soie, d'or et d'argent*. A documentary researcher of wider significance was W. Heyd, whose *magnum opus* of 1878 is still considered a fundamental work for the history of the Levant trade during the Middle Ages.

Naturally the gradual discovery of surviving textiles, chiefly in medieval church treasuries, and the first attempts to identify these textiles by means of data in early written documents often resulted in attributions which are no longer acceptable. The correct assessment of the age and origin of surviving textiles — which nearly always lack explicitly dated inscriptions — was found to involve more than merely deciphering the written documents.

Towards the end of the nineteenth century and the years about the turn of the century, a few publications concerning the textile art appeared, most of them written by museum directors and other leading art historians of the period. Three names can be singled out: Moriz Dreger in Vienna, Julius Lessing and Otto von Falke in Berlin. Dreger's lavishly illustrated *Künstlerische Entwicklung der Weberei und Stickerei* (1904) was devoted to various manifestations of European textile art. The two German scholars limited their project to silk weaving — a large enough subject in its own right. Lessing started systematically with a set of illustrations on the grand scale (in giant folio) published between 1900 and 1908. The plan was for this series to be gradually supplemented by an 'explanatory text'. The latter task devolved on Otto von Falke, who on Lessing's death succeeded him as director of the Kunstgewerbemuseum in Berlin. Von Falke developed his task into a quite independent publication, the great *Kunstgeschichte der Seidenweberei*, published in 1913. The character of this work is best summed up by his statement that to present history of the art of silk weaving means describing the development of surface decoration in Europe and the Near East — a limitation of the problem which we are hardly prepared to accept nowadays. As an art historian of the old school, von Falke was mainly interested in the motif as such and in its typological development. On the other hand, he showed little concern for the weaving techniques, which have had a decisive effect on the stylistic execution of the designs.

Otto von Falke was a synthesist. His comprehensive training in the history of art was combined with a rare capacity for general perspectives, a quality which becomes all the more impressive when it is remembered that, to help him get his bearings in this very complex field, he had very little help in the way of the abundant photographs that any present-day art historian regards as indispensable tools of his trade. Von Falke's *magnum opus* remains unsurpassed as a general account, and its value is not impaired by the fact that some of his conclusions later proved to be historically untenable. Nor is he to be blamed for the fact that important finds have since emerged that have transformed the total picture, or for the increasing refinement and the consequent change of course undergone by scientific method during the half century following the publication of his work. Von Falke's historical edifice has long remained notably unassailed, presumably because his universally acknowledged authority and the sheer magnitude of his book have deterred any serious assault. Instead his work has encouraged imitators who (apart from more or less meritorious contributions of their own) have schematized him, sometimes with disastrous results.

The period after von Falke, after the First World War, is characterized by the publication or the discovery of many individual finds or groups of finds. Thanks to the discoveries made by Aurel Stein, Sven Hedin and others, the role of Asia in the history of textile art began to emerge with increasing clarity, as witness the following place names: Noin Ula, Lou-lan, Tun Huang, Palmyra, Dura-Europos, Shosoin in Nara, Pazyryk, etc. and, during the last few years, innumerable finds made by Russian and Chinese archaeologists.

The same period was also notable for a growing understanding of the importance of techniques and of the need for accurate analyses of materials. The new attitude was expressed in specialist publications based on careful studies of textile techniques and also, eventually, on the application of scientific methods to the identification of fibres and chemical substances. The pioneer of the use of scientific methods of analysis on textile material was the French scholar Rudolf Pfister (d. 1966), who in other respects too was a paragon of scholarship in this field. A trained textile chemist, formerly practising in this field, as early as the 1920s Pfister developed an interest in the ancient textiles that had been discovered in Egypt. He carried out a number of systematic analyses of this abundant material and succeeded, with instructive results, in collating his findings with written and historical documents and with other available forms of specialized knowledge. The primary investigations generated many ideas which Pfister developed and successively published in articles in various periodicals and separate publications, including his fundamental paper on dyeing and alchemy in the Hellenic East (1935) and the weighty contribution to the debate on Iranian textile art (1948). The widest attention — together, unfortunately, with incompetent and grossly unfair criticism — was aroused by Pfister's exemplary study of the textile finds from Palmyra, published in three volumes between 1934 and 1940.

From the next generation of leading scholars in textile research Harold B. Burnham should be mentioned. His premature death in May 1973 is deeply regretted by colleagues all over the world, not least for his important contributions towards the achievement of an internationally practicable textile nomenclature.

QUESTION OF METHODS

The general outline given here has been aimed (among other things) at bringing out something of the universality which is typical of textile products as a whole and also, to a very great extent, of historical research into textile art and related problems. One cannot make any headway in this sector without continually crossing over boundaries — world wide relationships are constantly in evidence, as are relationships to many other disciplines: especially the study of languages, history and natural science. Textile research is therefore bound to be very much of an international concern. It is equally apparent that the study of textile phenomena has a part to play in many interdisciplinary problems, both as donor and as recipient. The textile historian is bound in the nature of things to consult technical literature in other languages and to enlist personal contacts with colleagues in other countries in the course of his own tasks. But not even the student of the general history and problems of textile art can dispense with international literature on the subject.

In either case one is liable to have difficulty in really assimilating this kind of literature, even if in other respects one has mastered the language concerned. This is because literature about textiles inevitably contains a great many technical terms which are not intelligible to the uninitiated. Nor as a rule are they to be found in ordinary dictionaries, and, even if they are, one cannot always rely on the explanations given. Since the same kind of uncertainty occurs in many languages, a great confusion of tongues is liable to result. Worse still, there are sometimes cases of different authors writing in the same language but not employing the same nomenclature. This does not matter very much in so far as different words are applied to the same phenomenon, but it may be disastrous when the same word is used in completely different senses. Circumstances of this kind can give rise to serious misunderstandings and can be a stumbling block to co-operation by students and scholars in different countries.

To remedy this state of affairs, an attempt has been launched to establish internationally identical norms. This very ambitious undertaking is being sponsored by the *Centre International d'Etude des Textiles Anciens* (CIETA), a liaison body for international textile research established in 1954 in the French silk manufacturing city of Lyons. The plan is for vocabularies of practically useful terms to be compiled within homogeneous language areas. Each reference word is to be accompanied by definitions in the language concerned and by corresponding terms in several other languages. To begin with, attention has been concentrated entirely on terms connected with woven fabrics and their production. First in print was a Scandinavian collaborative work compiled by E. Strömberg, A. Geijer, M. Hald and M. Hoffman: *Nordisk Textilteknisk Terminologi* (Oslo, 1974, 1979 — 'NTT-74-79' — Tanum Publ.) which included entries with definitions in Swedish and Danish, Icelandic, Finnish as well as English, French and German synonyms. The English edition of a textile terminology was fulfilled by Dorothy K. Burnham, continuing her husband's work. Her book, *Warp and Weft, A Textile Terminology*, splendidly illustrated with photographs and instructive drawings by the author, has been published by the Royal Ontario Museum of Toronto, 1980.

NOTES

1. The Swedish version here translated into English was a free interpretation from *Snorri's Sagas of the Norwegian Kings*, translated into modern Norse by G. Storm.

I. Materials (pp. 1–18)

1. Concerning recent and general textile matters the reader is referred to current manuals and encyclopedias. Basic works about Antiquity are H. Blümner's *Technologie und Terminologie . . . bei Griechen und Römern*, 1912., cf. also, *Studies in Ancient Technology* by the Dutch scholar R. J. Forbes. Concerning early Nordic culture, entries are to be found in *K.L.N.M.* (Dictionary of Nordic Medieval Culture).

2. On sheep breeds in early Britain *see* Ryder. On collecting and spinning wool in early Norway, *see* Falk; in Asia *see* Montell, 1941.

3. Further information regarding different silk species will be found in Willett, 1958.

4. The early occurrence in the Nordic countries of the different bast fibres has been studied by many authors, *see K.L.N.M.* The three species (flax, hemp and nettle), being difficult to analyse before refined microscopic methods came into use, have often been confused in the archaeological literature.

5. For different methods of pleating linen fabrics *see* Geijer, 1938, and Täckholm.

6. Lopez.

7. Godwin.

8. The global occurrence and manifold use of the nettle plant was extensively treated by M. Hald, 1942.

9. The result of this new investigation confirmed the opinion of G. Hatt that flax did not appear in Denmark before the fifth century A.D. In this connexion may be mentioned information kindly given by A. M. Rosenquist, Oslo University Museum: from among her analyses of textile fibres from the Oseberg finds there are several instances of nettle but, remarkably enough, none of flax fibre. From these two examples the conclusion can be drawn that old determinations of bast fibres are not to be taken for granted. This might perhaps also be the case with certain finds from the Swiss lake dwellings earlier identified as *Linum angustifolium*.

10. The early history of cotton was extensively treated by Lamm, 1937, and by Pfister, 1938.

11. An early attempt by O. von Falke, 1913, to compile facts concerning gold thread was only partly correct. More detailed research on this matter was presented by the present writer, 1938.

12. Membrane gold was formerly identified with the term 'Cyprian gold', which appears in old texts, but this was undoubtedly a mistake.

13. In his work, *Sino-Iranica*, the American linguist B. Laufer quotes texts from the Chinese annals describing flameproof fabrics. Among them, one piece measuring 20 feet was used as the mantle of a Buddha statue given to the Chinese emperor by the king of Kashgar in the fifth century. Laufer tells that this extraordinary material, at this time well known to Persians and Arabs, came from Bajistan in the central Asian highlands.

14. The opinions concerning the word *byssos* have long been controversial. Dr Wipszykas's elucidation of the industrial conditions clearly proves that the *byssourgi* were weavers of very fine linen, and not of cotton, the latter is all the more absurd an hypothesis as this raw material may not have been imported into Egypt before the Arab conquest in A.D. 642.

15. Primitive and old spinning methods have been studied by many Scandinavian scholars: Frödin and Nordenskiöld on South America, Montell on Asia, 1941, Jirlow, 1931, Hoffmann, 1942, 1964, and Vallinheimo, treating Scandinavian conditions, 1956.

16. This matter was considered by E. Markovà in her article extensively discussed in Chapter x. She pointed out that the ancient Greeks made a clear difference between the strongly spun thread needed for the warp and the special type of loose yarn which in many cases was used as weft.

17. Different shapes of spinning implements are illustrated in the pamphlet *Spinning Wheels* from the Ulster Museum. Details on Scandinavian conditions are given by Hoffmann, 1942 and 1945.

II. *Looms and Practice of Weaving Implements (pp. 19–41)*

1. The construction and function of various looms have been studied by many scholars. The evolution of weaving techniques outside Europe was investigated by the German ethnographer H. Ephraim (1905) while his compatriot C. H. Johl described ancient looms among Egyptians, Greeks and Romans (1917, 1924). The English specialist Grace M. Crowfoot made many important observations concerning the Near East as well as the Antiquity which she presented in several short papers, one in collaboration with L. Roth. Among Scandinavians in this field may be mentioned E. Nordenskiöld and G. Montell on South American and Asiatic matters, E. von Waltertorff, M. Hald, M. Hoffmann and G. Grenander-Nyberg on Scandinavian looms. Two important papers by the Danish philologist Poul Andersen are also to be considered.

2. Thus, for instance, some two-thousand-year-old Chinese silks were copied in Japan by Jacquard mechanics. The fragment of a unique linen fabric with pick-up pattern (happily preserved in the coat of a twelfth-century sculpture) was recently reconstructed in a modern Swedish loom with multiple harness.

3. The Royal Library of Copenhagen owns an illustrated manuscript 'Nueva coronica y buen gobierno' by Don Felipe Guaman Poma di Ayala. Translated into French, published 1936 in Paris, Institut d'Ethnologie. Recent looms of this type occurring in Latin America investigated by M. Hald, 1961, cf. Montell, 1929.

4. Montell, 1934, Hald, 1961.

5. This is more a method than a loom, the tools for stretching a tubular warp being of very different shapes. This type of weaving in the Scandinavian languages is called *rundväv*, the words *väv* (n.) and *väva* (v.) related to the English 'weave', having maintained the basic signification connected with the activity. The varying methods of tubular weaving were observed quite early by several ethnographers: Nordenskiöld, Montell (Sweden), as well as W. B. Grubb, Lila O'Neale, W. E. Roth, Grace M. Crowfoot. But the first to carry through a wide technical investigation has been the Danish expert Margrethe Hald.

6. Some scholars, from Dedekam to Hald, assumed this tool to be a frame for plaiting *sprang*, while others considered it a loom for weaving, cf. Hoffmann, 1964, p. 330. I feel that both opinions are justifiable and that the same kind of implement may have been used for different purposes.

7. The diagram is borrowed from Dr Hoffmann's extensive publication on the warp-weighted loom.

8. This loom picture is correct as to details while most of the other vase paintings are roughly sketched — after all, this was a very ordinary implement! But the well-known loom of Penelope from the Chiusi vase — so very often illustrated in the literature and much discussed — can never have been meant to reproduce a real

loom. The artist, no doubt, desired to draw a supernatural, divine loom, capable of producing a luxury tapestry and a plain fabric as well. He created a hybrid. cf. Geijer, 1977.

9. Figure 14 goes back to a drawn reproduction, the original of which, the so-called 'Kuer Book' from 1363 containing the regulations of the wool-weavers in Ypres, was destroyed in World War I. The German MS, the *Mendelsche Hausbuch*, contains a loom picture from *c*.1425.

10. The Polish scholars Kaminska and Nahlik dated these finds according to the stratigraphic order to the period 1000–1300. All the textile remains belong to a local production of low quality.

11. M. Hald (1961, 1963) observed several recent specimens of this loom in use in the Near East. The Hungarian example described by W. Endrei (1961) derives from an old settlement which was destroyed in A.D. 1240.

12. According to information kindly given by E. Guðjonson, Reykjavik, National Museum.

13. Compare Hoffmann, 1964, pp. 106 f.

14. According to recent investigations such triangular leaves instead of a pulley were in use in Norway and western Sweden for weaving three-end twill.

15. See Lehmann-Filhés, Hald, 1930, 1950, etc.

16. This kind of bandloom as well as the following tools, were described by A. Noss.

III.   *Weaves and Woven Fabrics (pp. 42–62)*

1. As a rule the textile terms used in this book are in accordance with the vocabularies compiled under the auspices of the Centre International des Etudes des Textiles Anciens (CIETA). In the first place it is relevant to mention the English version of 1964 (stencilled) compiled by delegates from Britain, Canada and the U.S.A., and the (printed) edition of the Scandinavian textile terminology, *Nordisk Textilteknisk Terminologi*, edited by Geijer and Hoffmann, Oslo, 1974. This contains an extended selection of terms compared with the earlier vocabularies which were all mainly concerned with words for silk products.

2. Besides the general textile terms, there are some Swedish words referring to old folk-art textiles which to a certain degree have come into international use. Through the influence of the national romantic movement for the revival of old crafts, many such words, being of local origin, were adapted as technical terms with a precise meaning.

3. The wide dispersal of 'overshot weaves' (Sw. *daldräll*) all over Europe and North America was studied by H. Burnham, who besides the numerous wool-linen coverlets found specimens of spun silk from the seventeenth century.

4. These two German terms were introduced into the CIETA terminology in 1971. Long before this the misleading word *Doppelköper* (used by von Falke and others) had been replaced by another term which also occurs in the literature: *Köper mit zwei Ketten* or *zweikettige Köper*, which is directly translated from the Swedish equivalent.

5. According to the great *Dictionnaire de l'Académie Francaise*, 1835 edition, and later French dictionaries, the word 'lampas' meant only a kind of silk fabric with large pattern of Chinese origin and used for furnishing purposes. See also M. Heiden, *Handwörterbuch der Textilkunde*, 1904.

6. Natalie Rothstein, 'Tissue', *CIETA Bulletin*, no. 11, 1960.

7. Following von Falke's example of using the word 'Diasprum' as a technical term. This should not be understood as claiming the full historical significance — *see* D. King, *CIETA Bulletin*, no. 11 'Sur la signification de "Diasprum" '.

IV. *Development of Plain Weaving (pp. 63–81)*

1. However, one specimen of the warp-weighted loom set up with a linen warp does exist. It is from the Faroe Isles, and was brought to Copenhagen and published by Worsaae in 1849 (Hoffmann, 1964, p. 141). But this must have been an isolated case. Even though it was difficult, the wool weavers of that island, not knowing any other loom, must have been able to succeed in weaving with linen.

2. The Sigtuna pulley was published in 1939 by Anderbjörk and Geijer. Two other medieval pulleys were later excavated in Lund and Lödöse: they are of similar shape but made of wood and much coarser.

3. Textile remains were found in the giant Neolithic site of Chatal Huyuk and in the old layers of Jericho, published respectively by H. B. Burnham (1965) and E. Crowfoot (1960).

4. The frequency of loom-weights accounted for by G. M. A. Richter, *Handbook of Greek Art.*

5. The main part of the burial finds from Birka was published by H. Arbman in 1943, the textiles having already been given a detailed investigation by this writer in 1938.

6. Engaged as the university 'opponent' for M. Hoffmann's doctoral thesis, I returned to the problem of the worsted twills. The result was an article 'The Pallium Fresonicum of the Viking Age, was it Manufactured in Syria?'. Agreeing with Hoffmann's arguments against my own early hypothesis of a Frisian origin for several reasons, I was able to quote a verbal comment from the Dutch archaeologist A. Halbertsma, that excavations in Holland obviously had shown that during this period sheep-breeding played no significant role there.

7. Among the Antinoé finds preserved in the Musée des Tissus, Lyons, remains of the described fabric were observed by Pfister, who analysed the red dye and the extremely fine wool. Both analyses indicated an Iranian origin, see Pfister, 1948. Some years later large quantities of the same woollen material came to light in the reserves of the Museum. They were sent to Stockholm, to the *Riksantikvarieämbetet*, for laboratory investigation and subsequent treatment. The fragments were found to be parts of at least four caftans or 'riding-coats' of which one was entirely reconstructed, first mentioned by me in *Orientalica Suecana*, vol. XII (1963).

8. This interesting note comes from Hoffmann (1964) who has the information from a paper by G. Crowfoot (1961).

9. The first part of the argument seemed to point towards Iran (see Hoffmann). But linguistic experts claimed that the word was not of Iranian origin. The final solution was found in an article by Professor F. Rundgren, *Orientalica Suecana*, III (1954): the word *sillagdun*, etc., is derived from Latin *sigillatum*, which probably meant originally some hallmarked commodity imported to the Roman empire.

V. *Individually Patterned Weaves (pp. 82–95)*

1. Articles by Grabar, 1956, and Müller-Christensen, 1966, of which there was a detailed review by Geijer in Fornvännen, 1975.

2. The amount of literature on tapestry in various languages is considerable. Of fundamental value is the *Histoire de la tapisserie* by Guiffrey (1886), the vast survey *Wandteppiche* by Göbel (1923–28), the scholarly masterpiece on medieval German *Bildteppiche* by B. Kurth (1926), and Weigert's books on French tapestries (1956, 1964). The extensive Swedish work by Böttiger (1895–98) is still of basic importance. Entirely devoted to Scandinavian folk-art tapestries are Thor Kielland's *Norsk Billedvev, 1550–1800* (1953–55) and Ernst Fischer's *Flamskvävnader i Skåne* (1962).

3.   This very numerous category, generally inappropriately termed 'Coptic', was often published in groups belonging to special collections: Wulff and Volbach treated the Berlin collection, Pfister and later Père du Bourguet the Paris collections, Kendrick the Victoria and Albert Museum textiles, and Egger equivalent items of the Kunstgewerbemuseum in Vienna — to mention but a few. See also a short survey by Beckwith in *CIBA Rundschau*, 1959, and a well illustrated Russian publication *Koptische Stoffe* by L. Kybalova (1967).

4.   The diagram Fig. 5 derives from an extensive laboratory study by A. M. Franzén treating an unusually well preserved Coptic tunic. (*Rig*, 1961, English summary.)

5.   The following description follows E. v. Waltertorff, 1925.

6.   Unfortunately the term 'draw-loom' has become controversial, and is sometimes used in a very specialized sense. There are, however, quite a number of types of construction varying in detail but all fitted with arrangements for drawing the heddles in order to produce the pattern; these are all covered by the general term 'draw-loom' (*métier à la tire, Zugwebstuhl, dragvävstol*, etc.).

7.   After Burnham's article in the *CIETA Bulletin*, 1965 (discussed here) several other contributions on this type of weaving appeared (by Vial, Endrei, King, Riboud, Lubo-Lesnichenko, etc.). Here should also be mentioned the publications on the textile finds of the Pelliot expedition to Touen-Houang, published by K. Riboud and G. Vial in *Arts Asiatique* and in a separate volume. None of these contributions seem to me seriously to affect my suggestions.

VI.   *Mechanical Patterning (pp. 96–106)*

1.   The description of the draw-loom functions is based on the well-known manuals by Cyrus-Zetterström (Swedish, also issued in English and French) and by Ingers and Becker. For special viewpoints cf. note v, 6.

2.   The unexpected discovery of a Sassanian silk in Swedish possession prompted me to give an account in favour of Pfister's argumentation of 1948, against that of Falke (1913) in connexion with the Antinoë finds (*see* Geijer, 1963).

3.   Concerning silk weaving in France I am quoting my own account of 1931 (Sylwan & Geijer) which is mainly based on Clouzot, *Le métier de la soie en France*, n.d.

4.   Our fig. 3 (*métier à grand tire*) is drawn after a photograph illustrating the *Arts et Metiers* catalogue. The drawing was reproduced by Glazier, 1923.

VII.   *Silk Weaving in Asia (pp. 107–140)*

1.   The basic importance of China in the world's silk production was by no means unknown to Europe, see Pariset. But it was not until the 1920s that the early silks became a reality. Only a very small number of T'ang silks were known by Falke, from literary sources. The first silks from the Han period were revealed through the great discoveries in Turkestan by Kozlov, Aurel Stein and Hedin. It took a considerable time before all this remarkable material was treated in a scholarly fashion. It should be mentioned that the American scholar P. Simmons has written an excellent review of relevant publications, see *Bulletin of the Museum of Far Eastern Antiquities* (*B.M.F.E.A.*), 1956.

2.   These important excavations were led by P. K. Kozlov and the material was taken to Leningrad. A short catalogue in English by C. Trever appeared in 1932, and in 1961 the extensive studies devoted to the Han silks by E. Lubo-Lesnichenko, sinologist of the Hermitage Museum, were published. Here I must acknowledge the kindness of the late Harold Burnham, who allowed me access to the translation of the Russian text, which had been made in Toronto at his instigation.

3. Sir Aurel Stein described his great finds, representing the Han and the T'ang periods, in two great publications *Serindia* (1921) and *Innermost Asia* (1928). A condensed study of the Han silks by F. H. Andrews appeared in the *Burlington Magazine*, 1920. Pfister's basic publication on the *Textiles de Palmyre* came out in 1934, 1937 and 1940. It led to important special studies by O. Maenchen-Helfen in *The Art Bulletin*, xxv (1943) and by R. J. Charleston, in *Oriental Art*, I, 1948. See also Sylwan's volume on the Hedin-Bergman finds, *Investigation of Silk from Edsen-gol and Lop-nor*, issued in 1949. Finally, there is W. Willett's *Chinese Art*, which gives an excellent introduction to the silk weaving of the Han dynasty. The book first appeared in a pocket edition in 1958, and later in a magnificently illustrated volume in 1965.

4. The calligraphic signs have been interpreted by Lubo-Lesnichenko.

5. An instructive volume on the Shosoin has been published by M. Ishida and G. Wada.

6. A great number of similar fabrics with fantastic foreign designs belong to the large collection of ecclesiastical vestments formerly belonging to St Mary's church in Danzig; magnificently published by W. Mannowsky, *Der Danziger Paramentenschatz*, Berlin, 1931–38. Cf. note VIII: 4.

7. One of the first scholars to show serious interest in Iranian textile art was Ernst Herzfeld: *Am Tor von Asien* (1920), *Die Malereien von Samarra* (1928), *Iran in the Ancient East* (1941). In contrast Phyllis Ackermann, co-author of the *Survey of Persian Art*, mainly followed Falke's suppositions, while at the same time consistently disregarding all Pfister's conclusions, including those concerning the Palmyra silks which she supposed to be Parthian products. Ackermann's latter hypothesis, however, was sharply refuted by, among others, O. Maenchen-Helfen, R. J. Charleston and P. Simmons, who were all convinced that the silks were Chinese.

8. Abundant examples of such decorations, small ornaments of gold plate, were found long ago in southern Russia and are now on show in the Hermitage treasure rooms. Similar ornaments in the form of gold bees were found in the grave of Childeric.

9. Concerning the whereabouts of early Persian silks, the following should be mentioned: the silk fragments from Antinoë are dispersed in several museums, beside the French collections, those in London, Berlin, Leningrad, Vienna, Boston. Many similar items have been preserved in European church treasuries and have been published as collections: the *Sancta Sanctorum* of the Vatican by Volbach, the Sens cathedral treasury by Abbé Chartraire while a number of interesting fragments used as reliquary covers and owned by Swiss cathedrals have been investigated by E. Vogt, 1958, 1963, 1964.

10. A thorough description of the *linceuil de Saint-Remi* was published in the *CIETA Bulletin*, no. 15, 1962.

11. I would like to thank Dr Anna Ieroussalimskaja, Hermitage Museum in Leningrad, for showing me this extraordinary garment and many other interesting textiles from Mochtchevaja Balka which have come to light during a number of expeditions in Caucasia under her leadership. Cf. article in the *CIETA Bulletin*, no. 24, 1966, and recent papers in Russian.

12. D. Shepherd has called her article 'Zandaniji Identified?'. It should be added that many examples of silks belonging to this 'Sogdian group' are among the recent finds mentioned in the preceding note.

13. The Saint-Josse silk, now in the Louvre, was first published by Migeon (*Syria*, 1922) and later by Ebersolt (*Orient et Occident*, 1928).

14. The so-called Buyid textiles should be mentioned here. It was claimed that they had come from a royal mausoleum near Ray in Persia and had been found by

commercial diggers. The textiles were attributed to the Buyid dynasty (932–1055) or possibly to the Seljuk period (eleventh to twelfth century) but the details of their discovery were somewhat obscure. As time went on rumours of the outstanding 'discovery' reached London. The Victoria and Albert Museum acquired a large specimen which later, judged from the artistic point of view, proved to be one of the best. Other specimens from the group passed into the hands of art dealers. After World War II they appeared on the international art market and were acquired for high prices by many collections in the U.S.A. In 1948 G. Wiet, the renowned expert in Arabic epigraphy, published his *Soieries persannes*, commenting directly on the Buyid silks, the designs of which contain many Arabic inscriptions. Wiet's work was reviewed by Florence Day (*Ars Islamica*, 1951) who questioned the authenticity of the textiles mainly because of iconographical and technical anomalies.

Spending six months in winter 1953–54 in the U.S.A. the present writer was confronted with the 'Buyid problem' and was able to study most of the specimens then in the States as well as to discuss the whole question of their authenticity. This resulted, finally, in a strong personal doubt about the origin of these textiles, which I could not accept even as medieval, this opinion being based on a life-long acquaintance with medieval textiles. Amongst other things, the over-intricate composition and many of the iconographical details do not seem to me to be in keeping with what is known of the historic development of textile design. This opinion appeared in the original Swedish edition of this book, published New Year 1972.

In Autumn 1973 the ordinary Congress (*Assemblée générale*) of the CIETA was invited to Riggisberg near Bern in order to discuss the Buyid silks belonging to the Abegg-Stiftung in Riggisberg. Since the authenticity of these textiles had been doubted by several experts, Mechthild Flury Lemberg, Curator of the Abegg-Stiftung, decided to carry out a thorough investigation. An account of this was published in no. 37 of the *CIETA Bulletin*, containing a detailed introduction by Mechthild Lemberg, a technical account of thirty-nine Buyid fabrics belonging to the Abegg-Stiftung by Gabriel Vial of Lyons, and a dyestuff analysis by Judith Hofenk de Graaff of Amsterdam. As a result of their investigations there seemed now to be many reasons to doubt the authenticity of thirty-one of the thirty-nine fabrics. The ensuing discussion by the meeting is reported in no. 38. Nos. 39/40 contain Dorothy Shepherd's categoric 'refutation of the Riggisberg Report'. Prompted by D. Shepherd's refutation of their previous investigations the authors of the Riggisberg Report presented renewed examinations confirming their original suspicions as to the authenticity of the Buyid silks in question (*Bulletin*, no. 43).

I personally took no part in the discussions of recent years but I feel it my duty to acknowledge Mr Werner Abegg, primordial collector of this important textile material, for having so generously allowed, and actively supported, the investigations which will no doubt be of great value to future research.

15. Notes giving details on the history of this very precious and important textile, a gift from the Emperor Constantine to King Pepin the Short, as well as technical *dossier de recensement* by F. Guicherd were published in the *CIETA Bulletin*, no. 17, 1963. Cf. A. Grabar, *L'Empereur dans l'art byzantin*, 1936; J. Beckwith, *The Art of Constantinople*, 1961.

16. This beautiful silk was earlier considered to originate from a palace workshop in Palermo (von Falke, Kendrick), but since the Italian scholar Ugo Monneret de Villard (1946) has found evidence which reduces the importance of the Sicilian looms, a Spanish-Moorish origin seems more probable.

17. The richest collection of Turkish woven textiles outside Turkey belongs to the Victoria and Albert Museum in London. See *Brief Guide*.

VIII.   *Silk Weaving in Europe (pp. 141–164)*

1.   The content of this chapter is based on the same historical facts as are the corresponding parts of *Siden och brokader*, Sylwan and Geijer, 1931. As far as Italy is concerned this was based on von Falke and the Italian authors Brenni and Podreider. With the publication by Branting and Lindblom, *Medieval Textiles in Sweden*, more Italian material has come to light. Also relevant are the investigations by U. Monneret de Villard and other Italian scholars, chiefly concerned with historical circumstances, questions of organization, etc.

2.   The Papal Inventories were published by Molinier, Paris, 1882–88.

3.   S. Müller-Christensen in *Das Münster III*, 1950, and in *Sacrale Gewänder des Mittelalters, Ausstellung*, Munich, 1955.

4.   The burial garments of Can Grande della Scala in Verona were published (together with some other textile studies written in the 1920s) by G. Sangiorgi in *Contributi allo studio dell'arte tessile*, Milan, undated. Cf. A. Santangelo, *Tessuti d'arte*, Rome, 1958.

5.   See Geijer, in *Erik den Helige, Historia, Kult, Reliker* (1954).

6.   In Polish archives Dr Maria Taszycka has found rich material (order books, samples and detailed correspondence) originating from Venetian merchants residing in Cracow and testifying to a very large import of Venetian silks. A great deal of the recorded material can be identified with extant silk fabrics.

7.   The expression 'bizarre design' was coined by the Danish art historian V. Slomann. In his lavishly illustrated book *Bizarre Designs in Silk* he maintained that a certain group of fantastic designs were of Indian origin. This hypothesis was sharply refuted by John Irwin, a renowned connoisseur of Indian art, who based his criticism on a number of working drafts on paper, with related designs, which had recently been found in English possession but originating from France. Thornton took up the hunt for bizarre designs, studying French records and as well as referring to published material, about *inter alia* the Danish royal costumes by S. Müller-Christensen, 1940, and some single dated specimens in Swedish possession by A. Geijer, 1959 and 1966.

8.   On the Austrian silk industry see M. Dreger, 1915, and H. Deutsch, 1909.

9.   Compare note 5 above.

IX.   *Silk Weaving in Scandinavia (pp. 165–170)*

1.   This chapter is a condensed version of the corresponding section in Sylwan and Geijer, 1931.

2.   Research on Danish silk manufacture began in 1902 with an article on the 'Silk House' of King Christian IV by Bernhard Olsen, followed by Elna Mygdal's studies on Paschier Lamertijn and the history of the tablecloth. Sigrid Müller-Christensen's great work on the royal costumes in Rosenborg appeared in 1940. Some notes for this book were kindly given to me by Gudmund Boesen, director of the Rosenborg collection.

3.   The Swedish silk manufacture, less ambitiously launched, but more consistent, attracted the attention of many scholars of about the same generation: Sigurd Wallin (1920, 1924), Ingegerd Henschen (1921), Gösta Malmborg (1927), Torsten Lenk and Martin Olsson (both 1932) and Carl Hernmarck writing about J. E. Rehn (1944). A basic publication in this field is *Alingsås manufacturverk* by Stråle, 1884.

X.   *Linen Damask and Other Table Linen* (*pp. 171–178*)

1. According to Elisa Ricci, in *The Studio* of 1913, there are historical records proving the existence of this type in the fifteenth century.
2. The small volume *Alte Tafeldamaste* by M. Braun-Ronsdorf gives a good survey of the European manufacture of table linen. A more pretentious volume by G. T. Ysselstein (1962) has excellent illustrations but the text has been severely criticized.
3. The remarkably extensive information on linen damask in Sweden (either imported or made in the country) is due mainly to the devoted activity of one person, Miss Elizabeth Thorman. She started to compile a series of regional inventories of linen tablecloths which were documented in a number of catalogues, articles and books, covering individuals and enterprises in this genre. An important contribution was also made by Dr Ernst Fischer through his investigation of the linen weavers' guild in Malmö (1959). The work *Damast* by G. Ingers and J. Becker (1955) was written mainly to serve as a manual of practical damask-weaving, but also contains historical details on Swedish and Danish damask-weavers. In Denmark, too, investigations have started and a publication may soon be expected. In spite of its title (Damask Weaving in the Peasant House), the Norwegian work by Bugge and Haugstoga (1968, English summary) may be of international significance. The register of master weavers and workshops active in Sweden from the late eighteenth century until about 1900 (p. 325 in the Swedish edition of this book) has been omitted here, as not being of general interest.

XI.   *Knotted Pile Fabrics and other Fleecy Textiles* (*pp. 179–205*)

1. The basic work on the history of the Nordic rya started with an inventory covering the whole of Sweden which in 1914 resulted in an exhibition at the *Nordiska Museet* in Stockholm. The organizer of this enterprise was Axel Nilsson (later the creator of the Röhss Museum in Gothenburg). After the premature death of Dr Nilsson his scholarly principles were carried through by V. Sylwan; her *Svenska ryor* appeared in 1934. In the meantime the Finnish ethnologist Professor U. T. Sirelius presented his work on the rya-rugs of Finland (1924, in both Finnish and Swedish). Sirelius's younger compatriot Riitta Pylkkänen, successfully broadened the view of the development of the Nordic rya by extensively studying historical records and extant comparative material. Her publication in Finnish in 1967 (English summary) was followed in 1974 by *The Use and Traditions of Medieval Rugs and Coverlets in Finland*. Beside the above-mentioned leading scholars, other writers have devoted themselves to the study of the Nordic rya: Hjördis Dahl (1934), Kristian Kielland (1934), Helen Engelstad (1942), Astrid Bugge (1966), M. Hoffmann (1973), E. von Walterstorff (1925), Inger Estham (1963), and, finally Konrad Hahm, *Ostpreussische Bauernteppiche* (1937).
2. The study of Oriental carpets can be said to have started in Vienna with the outstanding exhibition of 1891 and the earlier pioneer writings of Karabacek and Riegl. This was followed by the magnificent publication, *A History of Oriental Carpets*, by F. R. Martin, internationally known expert on Oriental art. The first edition of the famous manual *Vorderasiatishe Knüpfteppiche* by Wilhelm von Bode was issued in 1902. The important exhibition of Mohammedan art organized by Sarre and Martin was held in Munich in 1910. Collaboration between Bode and Ernst Kühnel produced new revised editions of the *Vorderasiatische Knüpfteppiche*, the last one in 1955 being written by Kühnel alone. Kühnel's disciple and successor as Professor of Oriental art in Berlin, Kurt Erdmann, more than anybody else, has devoted himself to carpet studies. Among other writers in this field the following

prominent scholars should be mentioned: Kendrick, Tattersall, Trenkwald, Meyer-Riefstahl, Dimand, Ettinghausen, Lamm and the two Russian archaeologists who have published the Pazyryk material, Rudenko and Griaznov.

3. This altered dating of the two types of carpets was first presented in an extensive review of Kühnel's and Erdmann's books of 1955 (the 4th edition of *Vorderasiatische Teppiche* and *Der Orientalische Knüpfteppich*). I was happy when both of them agreed with my hypothesis. Cf. Geijer, 1959b, 1963a.

4. On the question of the 'Cairene carpet', see Erdmann, 1951. On Spanish carpets see Kühnel (and Bellinger), 1953. Nowadays the literature on Oriental carpets, manuals and specialized shorter studies has grown enormously so that an impartial assessment would be impossible in this limited space.

5. One of them, illustrated by Sylwan in *Svenska ryor*, Pl. I, is a full-size sculpture from Mussy-sur-Seine, Aube.

6. The very early references, from Sumerian and Classical times, were dealt with by Sylwan in a special article, in *Rig*, 1934. Feeling doubtful about the correct meaning of some of the terms, especially those from Pliny the Younger, I asked a specialist in classical languages, Dr H. Thylander, Stockholm, who kindly offered a new interpretation for which I am much obliged and which I think has more veracity.

7. *Inventaire du mobilier du roi Charles V*, published by J. Labarte, Paris, 1879.

8. Note that a French *aune* (Eng. ell) measures about 119 centimetres 'trois pieds huit pouces' according to the great *Dictionnaire del' Académie francaise*, 1838.

9. Arwidsson, 1946, Fig. 68. However, I doubt whether the diagram is correct, since I think it more probable that the denser thread system formed the weft instead of the warp. I presume that it was woven on a warp-weighted loom which may have allowed the additional yarn tufts to hang behind the warp during the work.

10. The *Terpen* finds were mentioned in connexion with a tiny fragment from Birka, cf. Geijer, 1938. The two British finds were published by G. Crowfoot, 1948/49.

11. I am much obliged to Dr Markovà for translating into German some parts of her Slovakian text and for answering so many of my questions.

12. The above account is based on works by the following authors: Kendrick and Tattersall concerning England, Verlet concerning France, and Böttiger concerning Sweden.

XII. *Dyeing, Textile Printing and Pattern Dyeing (pp. 206–216)*

1. Analyses and comparative investigations by Pfister, 1948. Cf. Geijer, 1963.

2. Compare notes to Chapter iv, 7–9 and adherent sections of the main text.

3. In Pfister's comprehensive article, 'Teinture et alchimie dans l'Orient hellénistique' in *Seminarium Kondakovianum*, some Greek papyri, published by Berthelot and others, were subjected to scientific examination, in particular two related papyri in Stockholm and Leyden which had been published by eminent linguistic scholars, a Swede and a Dutchman, who obviously, however, did not have the capacity to judge technical recipes and relevant chemical matters.

4. In this modest attempt to delineate some of the essential features of dyeing methods my intention is to draw the reader's attention to the too much neglected problems which are fundamental for development in this vast field — problems of historical, geographical, economic and political, as well as chemical and general scientific importance. There are quite a number of manuals of technical information on dyeing but hardly any can compare with the instructive and erudite volume by the Italian chemist, Franco Brunello, *L'Arte della Tintura*, 1971, recently issued in English.

5. The monk was named Peder Månsson, and, commissioned to Rome by the Convent of Vadstena, he was finally appointed bishop in Västerås. His famous 'writings in Swedish' treating various subjects of historical value, have been utilized by many Scandinavian scholars, among them I. Henschen who wrote her dissertation on 'Printed Textiles in Sweden during the Middle Ages' (1942). In Sweden Henschen, however, is the great expert on printed textiles, especially on the productions from the eighteenth and nineteenth centuries on which subject she has published a number of articles.

6. Compare, H. Clouzot, P. Floud.

7. The distinguished Swiss scholar Professor Alfred Bühler has devoted life-long research to Indonesian and other Oriental methods of 'pattern dyeing', the high-water mark of his scholarly production being the magnificent publication *Ikat, Batik, Plangi*, 1972. His pupil, Marie Louise Nabholtz-Kartaschoff, has written a weighty work on European Ikat.

8. Further about this in an article by A. Geijer on early importation to Europe of Indian cottons (*Arkeologiska forskningar och fynd*), 1952, and 'Some Evidence of Indo-European Cotton Trade in Pre-Mughal Times', in *JITH*, I, 1955.

9. The beautiful and instructive volume *Indian Painted and Printed Fabrics* can be taken as a complete and worthy summing-up of the many previous works by John Irwin in this fascinating field.

XIII.   *Miscellaneous Textile Techniques (pp. 217–225)*

1. Domestic bands of various kinds have been studied by several Scandinavian scholars, given here in alphabetic order: Collin, 1915; Dedekam, 1924, 1925; Hald, 1930, 1946, 1950; Hougen, 1927, 1935; Kaukonen, 1965, 1968; Noss, 1966; Sylwan, 1941; van Walterstorff, 1925.

2. Apart from tablet-weaving (see note 5) and a few other exceptions, the many rich braids from the Middle Ages appear in the literature only in connexion with other textile categories. As an introduction the interested student is referred to works by the following authors: Branting and Lindblom, G. Crowfoot, 1956; Gomez-Moreno, Mannowsky, Müller-Christensen, 1955, 1961, 1972; Petrascheck-Heim.

3. The only monographic study I can recall is by E. Scheyer. See Branting and Lindblom, Mannowsky, Noss.

4. Four-hole weaving-tablets constitute the absolutely predominant type; tablets with six holes no doubt have occurred, though rarely. But a triangular equivalent probably never existed; in fact it has been proved that triangular plates of the type shown in II, fig. 21 (together with two indisputable band-weaving tablets) in western Sweden and in Norway have been employed as a kind of pulley when weaving three-end twills.

5. Tablet-weaving first attracted attention through Margrethe Lehmann-Filhés's book *Über Brettchenweberei*, 1901. This was followed by many original works on the same kind of material. The following may be mentioned: Grace Crowfoot, 1952, 1956; Dedekam, 1924, 1925; Geijer, 1938; Hald, 1930, 1946, 1950; Hougen, 1929, 1935; Schuette, 1959; Stettiner, 1911.

6. On diagonal plaiting see Collin, 1915; Geijer, 1938; Sylwan, 1941. In this connexion should also be mentioned a recent book by M. Hald, 1975, showing various kinds of plaited bands and strings.

7. Olaus Magnus (1490–1557) is renowned for his unique documentation of manners and customs in medieval Scandinavia. As a clergyman with a prominent position in the Catholic church of Sweden he had opportunities to visit many parts of the country. Forced to leave the country by the Reformation (1524) he settled mainly

in Rome where he set down his observations of his homeland, written in Latin and printed in Rome, 1555; the first Swedish edition in four volumes, 1909–25.

8. The literature on *sprang* is considerable, beginning in the 1890s with Louise Schinnerer, who analysed some plaited textiles from Coptic finds which had recently been brought to Vienna from Egypt. The plaited hair-net from Borum Eshøj had already been reconstructed in Denmark and, subsequently, via Schinnerer's publication, the technique was identified with its Egyptian counterpart. The identification with the Nordic word is probably due to Dedekam who, in a Norwegian peasant's house, had discovered a kind of frame fitted with a linen net-work which was called *sprang*.

Further basic contributions to the subject were made by Hald, 1939, 1946, 1950; d'Harcourt, 1934; Henshall, 1951; Hoffmann and Traetteberg, 1959; Markova, 1957. The latest contribution, a lavishly produced book by P. Collingwood, unfortunately should be approached with caution because of its misleading title. For a long time the old Nordic word *sprang* has been in international use as the term for a very special technique with an extensive international distribution but Mr Collingwood uses the term in too wide a sense. Several of his diagrams do not show the *sprang* technique, but types of free plaiting (with freely hanging ends), and other drawings depict a kind of mixed plaiting or interlacing, including a transversally threaded 'weft' which is quite unfamiliar to true *sprang*. Of course, this kind of interlacing is feasible — almost anything can be made by interlacing threads. But what these diagrams depict is not a genuine, traditional technique, and, above all, it is not what every textile expert means by *sprang* and its synonymous terms. I am sure that many of the drawings will appear confusing to the students and museum experts to whom the book is addressed, and who really need help in classifying enigmatic textiles, among which are the still extant specimens of this very important textile phenomenon. This is a pity in a book with other excellent qualities, *inter alia* a thorough bibliography.

XIV. *The Textile Trade with the Orient (pp. 226–239)*

1. The following may be taken as a kind of summary of the writer's publication *Oriental Textiles in Sweden*, 1951, which is mainly an account of various kinds of Oriental textiles preserved in Sweden since the seventeenth and early eighteenth centuries when they were brought to that country.

2. Geijer, *Birka III, Die Textilfunde aus den Gräbern*, 1938. Since then, however, the author has altered her opinion on some attributions. Cf. her forthcoming study in the *Festschrift* for E. Carus-Wilson.

3. J. P. Kilburger's 'Mercatura Ruthenica' or 'Kurzer Unterricht von dem russischen Handel wie selbiger mit aus- und eingehenden Waaren 1674 durch ganz Russland getrieben worden ist' was published in *Magazin für die neue Historie und Geographie angelegt von D. Anton Friedrich Büsching*, III, Hamburg, 1765, pp. 247–386. The first part gives an account of wares produced in Russia, the second part, describing imported goods, begins with custom lists from 1671 and 1674. Parts III and IV deal with coins and measures, communications, production and trading places and other internal conditions. Büsching added some reports from about 1760 and changed the word 'Commercien' to 'Handel' in the title.

XV. *Textiles and Textile Crafts in the Scandinavian Countries (pp. 240–264)*

1. This chapter is essentially a summing up of a rather extensive paper on the same subject with reference to the prehistoric and medieval period up to the ecclesiastical

Reformation in 1525. It was published in 1953 in the inter-Scandinavian series *Nordisk kultur* and included a detailed bibliography, mainly in Scandinavian languages. As it would be unnecessary to repeat all these references, with later contributions and works treating post-reformation periods, it has been decided to make a systematic grouping of the relevant authors, whose works are listed in the Bibliography which follows.

Until c. 400 B.C. (Bronze Age): Broholm and Hald, 1935, 1939, 1940; von Post, Lindqvist, von Walterstorff, 1924/25; Thomsen, 1929.

c. 400 B.C.–A.D. 800 (Iron Age to Viking period): Dedekam, 1921/24, 1924/25; Geijer, 1939; Hald, 1930, 1946, 1950, 1955, 1961, 1962; Hougen, 1930/32, 1935; Blindheim, 1946; Vahter, 1930; Hoffmann-Traetteberg, 1959.

c. 800–c. 1100 (Viking period): Appelgren-Kivalo, 1907; Arbman and Geijer, 1940: Arbman and Strömberg, 1934; Blindheim, 1945, 1946, 1947; Dedekam, 1918, 1920; Geijer, 1938, 1942, 1962, 1965; Hougen, 1940; Hald, 1950; Guðjónsson, 1962; Karlin, 1903; *KLNM*, 1956–77.

Related Iron-age Material from German Territory: Fuhrmann, 1940, 1942; Hundt, 1959–67; La Baume, 1955; Mestorf, 1900, 1907; Potratz, 1942; Sage, 1934, 1936; Schlabow, 1938, 1952, 1976; Stettiner, 1911.

c. 1100–1525 (Middle Ages): Anjou, 1935; Branting and Lindblom, 1928, 1929, 1932; Dedekam, 1918; Eldjarn, 1963; Engelstad, 1952; Geijer, 1935, 1941, 1944, 1952, 1953, 1954, 1947, 1949, 1957, 1963, 1964; Gufjonsson, 1963; Franzén, 1958, 1960, 1963, 1971; Franzén and Geijer, 1956, 1968; Karlin, 1920; Kielland, 1953/55; Lamm, 1937; Larsen, 1915; Salvén, 1923; Nordman, 1943; Thordeman, 1948; Pylkkänen, 1974.

c. 1525–1900 (Post-Reformation Periods):

Local and imported products: Böttiger, 1895–98; Boesen, 1949; Müller-Christensen, 1940; Flamand-Christensen and Mackeprang, 1950; Estham, 1964, 1974; Fischer, 1959; Garde, 1949; Geijer, 1932, 1951, 1953, 1959, 1966; Henschen, 1942, 1957, 1965, 1967; Grenander-Nyberg, 1967; Hernmarck, 1944; Hoffmann, 1942, 1945; Karlson, 1943, 1945; Lenk, 1932; Malmborg, 1927; Kjellberg, 1943; Mygdal, 1913; Nylén, 1950; B. Olsen, 1902; M. Olsson, 1932; Stråle, 1884; Thorman, 1933, 1939, 1941; Wallin, 1920, 1930.

Folk-art products: Bugge and Haugstoga, 1968; Collin, 1915, 1928; Dedekam, 1914; Ekenmark, 1827, etc.; Engelstad, 1942, 1958; Fischer, 1962; Friberg, 1931; Henschen, 1936; Ingers and Becker, 1955; Kaukonen, 1965, 1968; Laquist, 1945; Lexow, 1914; Lindblom, 1932; Keilland, 1953–55; Noss, 1966; Sirelius, 1924; Sylwan, 1932, 1934; Waltertorff, 1925, 1928, 1937, 1940, 1942; Nylén, 1969; Strömberg, 1938, 1953.

Costumes from various periods: Appelgren-Kivalo, 1907; Branting, 1911; Müller-Christensen, 1940; Falk, 1919; Gjessing, 1938, 1940; Hald, 1961, 1962, Broholm-Hald, 1935; Hägg, 1968, 1974; Franzén, 1961; Geijer, 1964; Nylén, 1947; Nörlund, 1924, 1941; Pylkkänen, 1956, 1970; Sandklef, 1937; Svenson, 1935.

XVI.   *When and How Textiles have been Preserved—and should be Preserved (pp. 265-270)*

1. Excavated by Nörlund, published 1924.
2. Trever, 1932; Griasnow, 1956.
3. This topic has been treated by the present author in several publications: 1957, 1959, 1961, 1962.
4. Geijer, 1947.

*Abbreviations and Notations used in the Bibliography and in the
List of Illustrations*
General
Engl. Fre. Germ. Dan. Norv. Finn. Sw., etc.

M., Museum in various languages
Univ., University in various languages
An., *Tb.*, Annual, Yearbook
Jb., Jahrbuch
Åb., Årsbok in Swedish and other Scandinavian languages
J., Journal
Bull., Bulletin
Mag., Magazine
Rev., Revue
Zschr., Zeitschrift
Tskr., Tidskrift

Antiquity
V. & A.M., Victoria & Albert Museum, London
B.M., British Museum, London
Met.M., the Metropolitan Museum of Art, New York
A.J., Antiquaries Journal
AJA, American Journal of Archaeology
N. & B.Cl., the Needle and Bobbin Club, New York
CIETA, Centre International d'Etudes des Textiles Anciens, Lyons
CIETA bull., ditto, bulletin de liaison
R.A.A., Revue des Arts Asiatiques
ZAK, Zeitschrift für Schweizerische Archäologie und Kunstgeschichte, Basel
KVHAA, Kungl. Vitterhets- Historie-& Antikvitets Akademien, Stockholm
RAÄ, Riksantikvarieämbetet (Council of National Antiquities, Stockholm)
ATA., Antikv.-Topografiska Arkivet (archive of Swedish antiquities connected
    with the Riksantikvarieämbetet and Historical M.)
KLNM, Kulturhistoriskt Lexikon f. Nordisk Medeltid, see Bibl.
NTT, Nordisk textilteknisk terminologi, see Bibl., Strömberg.

Some Scandinavian Periodicals mentioned below

Denmark
Aarbøger, Aarböger for Nordisk Oldkyndighed og Historie
Arbejdsmark, Fra Nationalmuseets Arbejdsmark, Copenhagen

Norway
By og Bygd (Norsk Folkemuseum), *Viking, Maal og Minne* (University, Oslo)

Sweden
Folk-Liv., *Rig* (c/o Nordiska Museet, Stockholm)
Fataburen (Nordiska Museet), *Fornvännen* (KVHAA, Stockholm)
Ymer (anthropological and geographical revue, c/o Riksmuseet, Stockholm)
Kulturen (Lund)
Tor (Uppsala, University)

Bibliography

Ackerman, Phyllis, see *Survey of Persian Art*.

Ainaud de Lasarte, J., 'La devise des rois de Grenade sur un tissu Hispano-Mauresque', *CIETA*, no. 32 (1970).

Algoud, H., *Grammaire des arts de la soie* (Paris, 1912).

Almgren, Bertil, 'Geographical Aspects of the Silk Road Especially in Persia and East Turkestan', *BMFEA*, no. 34 (1962).

—— and others, *The Viking* (Gothenburg, 1966). Sw. ed. (Vikingen) 1967. Fr. ed. (Les Vikings) 1968.

Andersen, Poul, 'Væv og Vævild', *Festskrift til P. H. Hansen* (Århus, 1949).

—— 'Forms and names of heddles', *Folk-Liv* (Stockholm, 1949).

Anjou, Sten, 'Uppsalatemplets gudabeläten avbildade på bonaden från Skog', *Fornvännen*, 1935.

Appelgren-Kivalo, H., *Finnische Trachten aus der jüngeren Eisenzeit* (Helsinki, 1907).

Arbman, Dagny, *Gobelänger och andra vävda tapeter* (Stockholm, 1950).

Arbman, H., *Birka I, Die Gräber. KVHAA* (Stockholm, 1943).

—— *Svear i Österviking* (Stockholm, 1955).

—— and Strömberg, E., 'Åslevanten', *Fataburen*, 1934.

Arne, T. J., *Europa upptäcker Ryssland* (Stockholm, 1944).

—— *Svenskarna och Österlandet* (Stockholm, 1952).

/Ayala/ Poma de Ayala F. G., *Neuva corónica y buen gobierno*, Institut d'Ethnologie de l'Université (Paris, 1936).

Beckwith, J., *The Art of Constantinople* (London, 1961).

Bellinger, Louisa, 'Textiles from Gordion', *N. & B. Cl.*, 1962.

Blindheim, Charlotte, 'Vernesfunnene og kvinnedrakten i Norden i vikingetiden', *Viking*, 1945.

—— 'En trøndersk jernaldergrav med tekstiler', *Viking*, 1946.

—— 'En detalj i eldre jernalders drakthistorie', *Stravanger Museums Årbok*, 1946.

—— 'Drakt og smykker', *Viking*, 1947.

Blümner, H., *Technologie und Terminologie der Gewerbe u. Künste bei Griechen u. Römern* (Berlin, 1912).

Boesen, Gudmund, *Christian V:s Rosenborgtapeter* (Copenhagen, 1949).

(Boileau) *Le livre d'Étienne Boileau* (1258). Ed. Depping (Paris, 1837).

Branting, Agnes, 'Knytning, knyppling och språngning', *Fataburen*, 1907.

—— *Das goldene Gewand der Königin Margareta in der Domkirche zu Uppsala* (Uppsala, 1911).

—— *Textil skrud i svenska kyrkor* (Stockholm, 1920).

—— and Lindblom, A., *Medeltida vävnader och broderier i Sverige*, Vols 1–2 (Uppsala, 1928/29) (Eng. ed. *Medieval Textiles in Sweden*, 1932).

Braun-Ronsdorf, Margarete, *Alte Tafeldamaste* (Darmstadt, 1955).

Brenni, Luigi, *La tessitura serica attraverso i secoli* (Como, 1925).

—— *I velluti di seta italiani* (Milano, 1927).

Brett, G., *European Printed Textiles*, Victoria and Albert Museum (1949).

Brett, K. B., 'The Japanese style in Indian chintz design', *Journal of Indian Textile History*, v (Ahmedabad, 1973).

Britton, N. P., *Some Early Islamic Textiles*, Museum of Fine Arts (Boston, 1938).

Broglio d'Ajano, *Die Venetianische Seidenindustri und ihre organisation* (Stuttgart, 1893).

Brunelli, Franco, *L'Arte della Tintura nella storia dell'umanita* (Vincenza, 1968).

—— *The Art of Dyeing in the History of Mankind* (Vicenza, 1973).

Bugge, Astrid and Haugstoga, Signe, *Damastvevning på bondegården* (Oslo, 1968).

Burnham, Dorothy K., *Warp and Weft, A Textile Terminology* (Toronto Ontario Canada, 1980).

——*Studies in Textile History, in Memory of Harold B. Burnham*. Edited by Veronica Gervers (Toronto, Royal Ontario Museum, 1977).

Burnham, Harold, *Chinese velvets*, The Royal Ontario Museum (Toronto, 1959).

—— 'Chatal Hüyük: Textiles and Twined Fabrics', *Anatolian Studies* (1965).

—— 'Technical Aspects of the Warp-faced Compound Tabbies of the Han Dynasty', *CIETA*, no. 22 (1965).

—— 'Han polychrome silks', *Oriental Art*, XIII: 4 (Toronto-Richmond, 1967).

—— and Burnham, Dorothy K., *'Keep me Warm One Night'*: *Early Handweaving in Eastern Canada* (Toronto University Press, 1972).

Bühler, Alfred, 'Patola Influences in Southeast Asia'. *Journal of Indian Textile History* (Ahmedabad, 1959).

—— 'Shibori und kasuri', *Folk* (Copenhagen, 1963).

—— *Plangi. Formen und Verbreitung eines Reserveverfahrens zur Musterung von Textilien* (Basel, 1969/70).

—— *Ikat, Batik, Plangi. Reservmusterung auf Garn und Stoff*, I–III (Basel, 1972).

—— and Oppenheim, Kristin, *Die Textiliensammlung Fritz Iklé-Huber*, Museum für Völkerkunde (Basel, 1948).

Böttiger, J., *Svenska statens samling af väfda tapeter*, I–3 (Stockholm, 1895–98).

Cammann, Schuyler, 'Notes on the Origin of the Chinese k'o-ssu Tapestry', *Artibus Asiae* (Ascona, 1958).

Capitano d'Arzago, A., *Antichi tessuti della basilica Ambrosiana* (Milano, 1941).

Charleston, R. J., 'Han Damasks', *Oriental Art*, 1948.

Chartraire, Eugène, *Inventaire du trésor de l'eglise principale métropolitaine de Sens* (Paris, 1897).

Christensen, Sigrid Flamand (See also Müller-Christensen), *Kongedrakterne fra 17. og 18. Aarhundrede*: De danske Kongers kronologiske Samling paa Rosenborg (English and German Summaries) (Copenhagen, 1940).

—— and Mackeprang, M., *Kronborgstapeterne* (Copenhagen, 1956).

Clouzot, Henry, *Le métier de la soie en France 1466–1815*. Paris (before 1925).

—— *Histoire de la manufacture de Jouy et de la toile imprimée en France* (Paris, 1928).

Conservatoire des Arts et Métiers. Catalogue, Industries textiles (Paris, 1942).

Collin, Maria, 'Gammalskånska band', I–II, *Fataburen* (Stockholm, 1915).

—— 'Gamla vävnader och deras mönster', ibid., 1928.

Collingwood, Peter, *The Techniques of Sprang* (London, 1974).

Cox, Raymond, *Les soieries d'art* (Paris, 1914).

Crowfoot, Elisabeth, 'Textiles, matting and basketry', Appendix to *Jericho* 1–2 by K. M. Kenyon (1960, 1965).

—— and Hawkes, Sonia Chadwick, 'Early Anglo-Saxon Braids', *Medieval Archaeology* (1967).

Crowfoot, Grace M., 'The Tablet-Woven Bands from Qau el Kabir', *Ancient Egypt*, IV (1924).

—— *Methods of Hand-spinning in Egypt and the Sudan* (Halifax, 1931).

—— 'Of the warp-weighed loom', *An. of the British School at Athens*, 37 (London, 1936/37).

—— 'The Tablet-woven Braids from the Vestments of St. Cuthbert at Durham Cathedral', *Antiquaries Journal*, V (1939).

—— 'The Vertical Loom in Palestine and Syria', *Palestine Exploration Quarterly* (London, 1941).

—— 'Textiles from a Viking Grave at Kaldonan on the Isle of Eigg', *Proceedings . . . of Scotland* (Edinburgh, 1948/49).

—— 'Textiles of the Saxon period', *Proceedings of the Cambridge antiquary society*, 44 (1951).

—— 'Linen textiles from the Cave of Ain Feschka', *Palestine Expl. Fund* (London, 1951).

—— 'Anglo-Saxon Tablet Weaving', *Antiquaries Journal* (1952).

—— 'The braids', *The relics of Saint Cuthbert, Durham Cathedral* (Durham, 1956).

—— and Davies, N. de G., 'The Tunic of Tutankhamun', *Journal of Egyptian Archaeology* (1941).

—— and E., 'Textiles and basketry', *Discoveries in the Judean Desert, Les Grottes de Murabbaat*, ed. Benoit, Milik, de Vaux (Oxford, 1961).

Cyrus, Ulla, *Handbok i vävning*, 1st edition 1950, 4th edition Stockholm, 1970.

—— *Manuel de tissage à la main* (Stockholm, 1975).

Day, Florence. *Ars Islamica*. Reviewing Wiet, A. J. (1951).

Dedekam, Hans, *Hvitsøm fra Nordmør* (Trondheim, 1914).

—— *Baldisholtæppet* (Oslo, 1918).

—— 'Et tekstilfund i myr', *Stavanger M. Åb* (1921–24).

—— 'To tekstilfund fra folkevandringstid, Evebø og Snartemo', *Bergens M. Åb* (1924/25).

Deutsch, Helene, *Entwicklung der Seidenindustrie in Österreich 1660–1840* (Wien, 1909).

Dimand, M. S., 'An Early Cut-pile Rug from Egypt', *Metropolitan Museum Studies* (New York, 1933).

—— *A Handbook of Muhammadan Art* (New York, 1947).

Documenta Textilia. Festschrift für Sigrid Müller-Christensen Forschungshefte, herausgegeben vom Bayerisches National-museum, München, 1981.

Dreger, Moritz, *Künstlerische Entwicklung der Weberei und Stickerei* (Vienna, 1904).

—— 'Beginn und Blüte der Wiener Seidenweberei', *Kunst und Kunsthantwerk*, 1915.

du Bourguet, P., *Catalogue d'étoffes coptes au Musée du Louvre*, 1 (Paris, 1964).

Dumonthier, E., *Étoffes d'ameublement*, 1–2 (Paris, 1909, 1914).

Ebersolt, J., *Orient et Occident* (Paris/Brussels, 1928).

Edler de Roover, Florence, 'The Silk Trade of Lucca', *N. & B. Cl.* (New York, 1954).
Egger, Gerhart, *Koptische Textilien, M. f. angewandte Kunst* (Vienna, 1967).
Ekenmark, J. E., *Handbok för unga Fruntimmer i Konsten att tillverka bomulls- och linneväfnader* (Cotton and Linen Fabrics). Stockholm, 1920. (The first in a series by the same family team. Further, see Bugge and Haugstoga.)
Eldjárn, Kristián, *Hundrad ár í pjodminjasafní* (Reykjavik, 1963).
Endrei, Walter, 'Le tissage à grande faconnée', *L'industrie Textile* (1957).
—— 'L'Apparition en Europe du Métier à Marches', *CIETA bulletin*, no. 8 (1958).
—— 'Der Trittwebestuhl im frühmittelalterischen Europa', *Acta Historica* (Budapest, 1961).
—— 'Une fois de plus le "métier aux baguettes" ', *CIETA bulletin*, no. 8 (1966).
—— 'Silk Fabrics from Grave I at Hana' *Acta Archaeologica scientiarium hungariae* (Budapest, 1967).
—— *L'evolution des techniques du filage et du tissage* (Paris/La Haye, 1968).
Engelstad, Helen, *Norske ryer* (Oslo, 1942).
—— *Refil, bunad, tjeld* (Oslo, 1952).
—— *Dobbeltvev i Norge* (Oslo, 1958).
Ephraim, Hugo, 'Uber die Entwicklung der Webetechnik und ihre Verbreitung ausserhalb Europas', *Mitt. M. f. Völkerkunde zu Leipzig* 1:1 (1905).
Erdmann, Kurt, *Der orientalische Knüpfteppich* (Tübingen, 1955).
—— 'Neue Untersuchungen zu Frage der Kairener Teppiche', *Ars Orientalis* (1961).
—— *Europa und der Orientteppich* (Berlin, 1962).
—— *Siebenhundert Jahre Orientteppiche* (Herford, 1966).
Espinas, G., *La draperie dans la Flandre française au Moyen Âge* (Paris, 1923).
Estham, Inger, 'En stolklädsel i knuten flossa i Upplandsmuseet. 1700-talets mitt', *Uppland* (1964).
—— *Figurbroderade mässhakar från reformationstidens och 1600-talets Sverige, KVHAA* (Stockholm, 1974).
Ettinghausen, R., 'New Light on Early Animal Carpets', *Festschrift Ernst Kühnel* 1957 (Berlin, 1959).
—— Rec. of Erdmann 1955. *Oriens* (Leiden, 1958).
Falk, Hj., *Altwestnordische Kleiderkunde* (Oslo, 1919).
Falke, Otto von, *Kunstgeschichte der Seidenweberei* (Berlin, 1913); 2nd abbr. edition, 1921. Eng. Trans. *Decorative Silks* (New York, 1922).
Feddersen, M., *Das Kunstgewerbe Ostasiens* (Berlin, 1930).
Fischer, E., *Linvävarämbetet i Malmö och det skånska linneväveriet* (Malmö, 1959).
—— *Flamskvävnader i Skåne* (Lund, 1962).
Flemming, Ernst, *Textile Künste* (Berlin, 1925).
—— *Das Textilwerk* (Tübingen, 1927). Revised ed. by Renate Jaques (1957).
Floud, Peter, *English Printed Textiles*, V. & A. M., London, 1960.
—— *English Chintz, Loan Exhibition*, V. & A. M., London, 1960.
Forbes, R. J., *Studies in Ancient Technology* (Leiden, 1957).
France-Lanord, A. and Fleury, M., 'Das Grab der Arnegundis in Saint-Denis', *Germania*, no. 40 (1962).

Franke, O., *Keng tschi t'u, Ackerbau und Seidengewinnung in China* (Hamburg, 1913).
Franzén, Anne Marie, 'Odens öga', *Fornvännen*, 1958.
—— Høyland teppet. *Norske Videnskabers Selskab Åb* (Trondheim, 1960).
—— 'En koptisk tunika' (Summary), *Rig*, 1961.
—— 'En medeltida socka i nålning', *Uppland*, 1964.
—— 'Medeltida gravtäcke' ('Another Swedish medieval tomb cover', Summary), *Fornvännen*, 1963.
—— 'Aktuella problem inom textilkonservering' (Summary), *Fornvännen*, 1964.
—— *Prydnadssömmar under medeltiden* (Medieval Embroideries in Sweden) (Stockholm, 1972).
—— and Geijer, A., 'Textila gravfynd från Trondheims domkyrka', *Nordenfjeldske K. ind. M. Åb.*, 1956.
—— —— 'Textile finds from excavations in Swedish towns 1960–1966', *Res Mediaevales* (Lund, 1968).
Frödin, O. and Nordenskiöld, E., *Über Zwirnen und Spinnen bei den Indianern Südamerikas* (Göteborg, 1918).
Fröier, Kåre, *Lin och hampa* (Stockholm, 1960).
Fuhrmann, Irmingard, 'Der Gewebefund von Pilgramsdorf. Unter berücksichtigung der Gewebe von Sacrau und Anduln'. *Prae hist. Zschr* (Berlin, 1939/40).
—— 'Zum Moorgewand von Reepsholt', *Prae hist. Zschr* (Berlin, 1941/42).
Garde, Georg, *Dansk billedvævning* (Copenhagen, 1949).
Geijer, Agnes, 'Sidenvävnaderna i Helige Knuts helgonskrin i Odense domkyrka' (Summary), *Aarbøger* (Copenhagen, 1935).
—— *Birka III. Die Textilfunde aus den Gräbern, KVHAA* (Uppsala, 1938).
—— 'Medeltida yllevävnader i samtida avbildning' (Summary), *Rig*, 1941.
—— 'En medeltida altarduk i dukagång', *Kulturen* (Lund, 1944).
—— *Orientaliska mattor*, Cat., Exhib. National Museum (Stockholm, 1946).
—— 'Medeltidens färgkonst' (Summary), *Fornvännen* (Stockholm, 1947).
—— *Oriental Textiles in Sweden* (Copenhagen, 1951).
—— 'Tidig import av mönsterfärgade indiska bomullstyger', *Arkeologiska forskningar och fynd* (in honour of H.M. King Gustaf VI Adolf) (Stockholm, 1952).
——'Chinese Silk Exported to Russia in the seventeenth century', *BMFEA*, no. 25 (1953).
—— 'Det textila arbetet i Norden under forntid och medeltid', *Nordisk kultur 15a.* (Stockholm, 1953).
—— 'Textilierna i Sankt Eriks skrin', *Erik den Helige. Historia, Kult, Reliker.* Ed. B. Thordeman (Stockholm, 1954).
—— 'Some Evidence of Indo-European Commerce in Pre-Mughal Times', *J. of Indian Text. Hist.* (Ahmedabad, 1955).
—— 'Uber die 'bizarren' Stoffe', *Festschrift Erich Meyer, 1957* (Hamburg, 1959).
—— 'The Conservation of Flags in Sweden', *Studies in conservation*, Vol. III (London, 1957).
—— 'Oriental Textiles in Scandinavian Versions', *Festschrift Ernst Kühnel, 1957* (Berlin, 1959).

—— 'Dangerous methods for the conservation of textiles', *Svenska Museer* (Stockholm, 1959).

—— 'The Conservation of Textile Objects', *Museum*, Vol. xɪv (UNESCO, 1961).

—— 'Preservation of textile objects — recent advances in conservation', *Contributions to the IIC Rome Conference* (1961).

—— 'Textilier och arkeologi' (Summary), *Svensk naturvetenskap* (Stockholm, 1962).

—— 'Some Thoughts on the Problems of Early Oriental Carpets', *Ars Orientalis*, v (Michigan, 1963).

—— 'Silk from Antinoë and the Sassanian Textile Art', *Orientalia Suecana*, xɪɪ (Uppsala, 1963).

—— *Textile Treasures of Uppsala Cathedral* (Uppsala, 1964).

—— 'Var järnålderns "frisiska kläde" tillverkat i Syrien?' (Summary), *Fornvännen* (Stockholm, 1965).

—— 'A "bizarre" silk', *Opuscula in honorem C. Hernmarck.* Ed. by the National Museum (Stockholm, 1966).

—— *Ur textilkonstens historia* (Lund, 1972).

—— *The Textile Finds from Birka. Birka III, Die Textilfunde aus den Gräbern*, revised by the author, in *Acta Araeologica* Vol. 50 (Copenhagen, 1979).

—— and Sylwan, V., *Siden och brokader* (Stockholm, 1931).

—— and Anderbjörk, J. E., 'Two Textile Implements from the Early Middle Ages', *Folk-Liv* (Stockholm, 1939).

—— and Franzén 1956 and 1968, see Franzén.

—— and Thomas, Edit B., 'The Viminacium Gold Tapestry', *Medd. fr. Lunds Univ. Hist. M.*, 1964/65.

Gervers, Veronica, 'An Early Christian Curtain in the Royal Ontario Museum', in *Studies in Textile History in Memory of Harold B. Burnham* (Toronto, 1977).

—— 'A Nomadic Mantle in Europe' in *Textile History*, published by the Pasold Research Fund Ltd, Vol. 9, 1978.

Gjessing, G., 'Sjoldehamndrakten, En senmiddelalders norsk mannsdrakt', *Viking*, 1938.

—— and Gertrud, *Lappedrakten*, Inst. f. sammenlign. kulturforskning (Oslo, 1944).

Glazier, Richard, *Historic textile fabrics* (London, 1923).

Godwin, H. 'The Ancient Cultivation of Hemp', *Antiquity* (Cambridge, 1967).

Gómez-Moreno, Manuel, *El Panteon Real de las Huelgas de Burgos* (Madrid, 1946).

Grabar, A., 'Le succés des arts orientaux', *Münchner Jb.* 1951.

—— 'La soie byzantine de l'éveque Gunther'. *Münchner Jb.* 1956.

Grenander-Nyberg, Gertrud, *Linodling och linnevävning i Själevad . . . 1750–1900.* Själevads hembygdsförening, no. 4 (Örnsköldsvik, 1967).

Griasnow, M., *L'art ancien de l'Altai* (Leningrad, 1956).

Guðjónsson, Elsa E., 'Traditional Icelandic Embroidery', *N. & B.Cl.*, no. 47 (New York, 1963).

—— 'Forn röggvarvefmaður', *Hins íslenzka fornleifafélags Åb.* (Reykjavik, 1962).

Guicherd, F., 'Le Tissu aux griffons du Monastier-sur-Gazeilles', *CIETA*, no. 7, 1958.
Guimet, E., *Les portraits d'Antinoë au Musée Guimet* (Paris, 1912).
Göbel, H., *Wandteppiche*, i–iii (Berlin, 1923–28).
Hahm, Konrad, *Ostpreussische Bauernteppiche* (Jena, 1937).
Hald, Margrethe, 'Brikvaevning i danske Oldtidsfund', *Aarbøger* (Copenhagen, 1930).
—— 'The Nettle as a Culture Plant', *Folk-Liv* (Stockholm, 1942).
—— 'Ancient Textile Techniques in Egypt and Scandinavia', *Acta Archaeologica* (Copenhagen, 1946).
——*Olddanske tekstiler* (Eng. summ.) (Copenhagen, 1950).
—— 'Olddanske tekstiler. Fund fra årene 1947–55', *Aarbøger* (Copenhagen, 1955).
—— 'Draktstudier' (Eng. summ.), *Aarbøger* (Copenhagen, 1961).
—— *An Unfinished Tubular Fabric from the Chiriguano Indians, Bolivia.* Monogr. from the Ethnogr. M. (Stockholm, 1962).
—— 'Vaevning over Gruber', *Kuml.* (Aarhus, 1963).
—— *Ancient Danish Textiles from Bogs and Burials. A Comparative Study of Costume and Iron Age Textiles* (published by The National Museum of Denmark, Copenhagen, 1980).
—— and Broholm, H. C., *Danske Bronzealders Drakter* (Copenhagen, 1935).
—— —— *Skrydstrupfundet* (Copenhagen, 1939).
—— —— *Costumes of the Bronze Age in Denmark* (Copenhagen, 1940).
d'Harcourt, R., *Les textiles anciens du Pérou et leurs techniques* (Paris, 1934).
Hatt, Gudmund, 'Jernaldersbopladsen ved Ginderup', *Arbejdsmark* (Copenhagen, 1935).
Heckscher, E. F., *Svenskt arbete och liv* (Stockholm, 1941).
Heiden, M., *Handwörterbuch der Textilkunde* (Stuttgart, 1904).
Heinz, Dora, *Der Paramentenschatz der Stadtpfarrkirche in Linz* (Vienna, 1962).
—— *Meisterwerke barocker Textilkunst* (Vienna, 1972).
Henschen, Ingegerd, 'Svenska sidenvävnader från 1700-talet', *Sv. Slöjdfören. tiskr* (Stockholm, 1921).
—— 'Dukagångsdrätten i Skåne', *Kulturen*, 1936.
—— *Tygtryck i Sverige före 1700* (Printed Textiles in Sweden before 1700) (Stockholm, 1942).
—— 'Tygtryckare i Borås under 1700-talet', *Från Borås och de sju häradena* (Borås, 1957).
—— 'Tobias Langs tygtryckeri', *Gotländskt arkiv* (Visby, 1964).
—— 'Familjen De Broen och kattuntryck från Sickla', *Nackaboken* (Stockholm, 1965).
—— 'Tygtryckerier i Stockholm 1789 — omkr. 1845', *Samf. S:t Eriks Åb.* (Stockholm, 1967).
Henshall, Audrey, S., 'Textiles and weaving applience in prehistoric Britain', *Proceedings of the Prehistorical Society* (Cambridge, 1950).
—— 'Early Textiles Found in Scotland', *Proceedings of the Society of Antiquaries* (Edinburgh, 1951–52).

Hentschel, Kurt, 'Herstellung der peruanischen und mexikanischen 2- und 3-schichtigen Hohlgewebe', *Baessler-Archiv* (Berlin, 1937.)

Hernmarck, Carl, 'Jean Erik Rehn och det svenska konsthantverket', *Fem stora gustavianer*. Studies from the National Museum (Stockholm, 1944).

Herzfeld, Ernst, *Am Tor von Asien* (Berlin, 1920).

—— *Die Malereien von Samarra* (Berlin, 1927).

—— *Iran in the Ancient East* (Oxford, 1941).

Heyd, Wilhelm, *Geschichte des Levantehandels im Mittelalter* (Stuttgart, 1879).

—— *Histoire du commerce du Levant au moyen age*. Edition considerablement augmentée par l'auteur (Leipzig, 1885/86). New ed. 1923.

Hindson, Alice, 'Canterbury seal bag No. 18', *CIETA bull.*, no. 30, 1969.

Hoffmann, Marta, 'Rokk og spinning i tukt- og manufakturhusene', *By og Bygd* (Oslo, 1942).

—— 'Om dugmagere og tøymagere og redskapene deres', *By og Bygd* (Oslo, 1945).

—— *En gruppe vevstoler på Vestlandet* (Oslo, 1958).

—— *The warp-weighted loom* (Oslo, 1964).

—— and Traetteberg, R., 'Teglefunnet', *Stavanger M. Åb.*, 1959.

—— and Burnham, Harold, 'Prehistory of Textiles in the Old World' in *Viking*, Vol. XXXVII (Oslo, 1973) Norsk Arkeologisk Selskap.

Holtsmark, Anne, 'Vefr. Darraðar', *Mål og Minne* (Oslo, 1939/40).

Hougen, Bjørn, 'Helgelandsfundet. Et myrfund fra eldre jernalder', *Stavanger M. Åb*, 1930/32.

—— *Snartemofunnene. Norske Oldfund VII* (Oslo, 1935).

—— 'Osebergsfunnets billedvev', *Viking*, 1940.

—— 'Norsk nyttevev fra oldtiden til midten av 1600-årene', *Norsk textil*, 1 (Oslo, 1948).

Hundt, H.-J., 'Vorgeschichtl. Gewebe aus dem Hallstätter Salzberg I–III', *Jb. d. Röm.-Germ. Zentral M.*, 1959–67.

Hägg, Inga, 'Some Notes on the Origin of the Peplostype Dress in Scandinavia', *Tor* (Uppsala, 1968).

—— *Kvinnodräkten i Birka* (Summary in German) (Uppsala, 1974).

Ieroussalemskaja, A., 'Trois soieries Byzantines anciennes découvertes au Caucase Septentrional', *CIETA Bull.*, no. 24, 1966.

—— 'A propos de la formation d'un centre de soierie en Sogde' (in Russian), *Srednja Asija i Iran* (Leningrad, 1972).

—— 'Western Textiles in the Far East' (in Russian) and 'A Newly Discovered Sassanian Silk with the Senmurf', *Aurora* (Leningrad, 1972).

—— 'The Great Silk Road and Northern Caucasus' (Russian text), Exhibition (Leningrad, 1972).

—— 'Le caftan aux simourghs du tombeau de Mochtchevaja Balka' (Caucase septentrional), in *Studia Iranica*, Tome 7, p. 183, 1978. Bril, Leiden. Distr.

Ingers, Gertrud and Becker, John, *Damast. Handbok i damastvävning* (Västerås, 1955).

Irwin, John, *Shawls*: Study in Indo-European influences (London, 1955).

—— 'The Origin of the "Oriental Style" in English Decorative Art', *Burlington Magazine*, 1955.

—— 'A Note on the Indian Sashes of King Gustavus Adolphus', *Livrustkammaren* (Stockholm, 1958).

—— and Hall, Margaret, *Indian Painted and Printed Fabrics*. Calico Museum of Textiles (Ahmedabad, 1971).

Ishida, M. and Wada, G., *The Shosoin*: An Eighth-Century Treasure-house (Tokyo-Osaka, 1954).

Johl, C. H., *Die Webestühle der Griechen und Römer* (Leipzig, 1917).

Kalf, Jan, *Bijdrage tot Geschiedenis der middeleuwsche Kunstweverei in Nederland* (Utrecht, 1901).

Kaminska, J. and Nahlik, A., *Włókiennietwo Gdańskie*, W. x–xii. Acta Archaeologica Univ. Lodziensis (Lodz, 1958).

—— —— 'L'industrie textile du haut moyen âge en Pologne', *Archaeologica Polona*, 3 (Warszawa, 1960).

Karlin, G. J., 'Några undersökningar om den förhistoriska textilkonsten i Norden', *Festskrift Oscar Montelius* (Stockholm, 1903).

—— *Över-Hogdalstapeten* (Östersund, 1920).

Karlson, William, *Ebba Brahes hem* (Lund, 1943).

—— *Stât och vardag i stormaktstidens herremans hem* (Lund, 1945).

Kaukonen, Toini-Inkeri, 'Soumen kansanomaiset nauhat' (Folk-Art Braids in Finland) *Suomalaisen kirjallisuuden Seura* (Helsinki, 1965).

—— 'Zum Walken von Lodentuch in Finnland', *Congressus Secundus Internationalis Fenno-Ugristarum* (Helsinki, 1965).

—— 'Om brickvävningens traditioner i Finland', *Finskt museum*, 1968.

—— 'Karjalainen pitsipoiminta' (Gauze Weave in Karelia), *Eripainos Kalevalaseuran Vuosikirjasta*, 1968.

Kendrick, A. F., *Catalogue of Textiles from Burial Grounds in Egypt*, 1–3. Victoria and Albert Museum (London, 1920–22).

—— *Catalogue of Muhammedan Textiles of the Medieval Period*. Victoria and Albert Museum (London, 1924).

—— *Catalogue of Early Medieval Woven Fabrics*. Victoria and Albert Museum (London, 1925).

Kielland, Thor, *Norsk billedvev 1550–1800*, Vols 1–3 (Oslo, 1953–55).

Kihlburger, Johann Filipp, 'Kurzer Unterricht von dem russischem Handel' (manuskript, 1674) *Büsching's Magasin* (Hamburg, 1765).

King, Donald, 'Sur la signification de "Diasprum" ', *CIETA Bull.*, no. 12, 1960.

—— 'Patterned Silks in the Carolingian Empire', *CIETA Bull.*, no. 23, 1966.

—— 'Two Medieval Textile Terms: "draps d'ache", "draps de l'arrest" ', *CIETA Bull.*, no. 27, 1968.

—— 'Some Unrecognized Venetian Woven Fabrics', *Victoria and Albert Museum Yearbook*, 1969.

—— 'Some Notes on Warp-Faced Compound Weaves, *CIETA Bull.*, 28, 1968.

Kimakowicz-Winnicki, M. von, *Spinn- und Webewerkzeuge* (Leipzig, 1910).

Kitzinger, Ernst, *The Horse and Lion Tapestries*, Dumbarton Oaks' papers, 3, Harvard University Press, 1946.

Kjellberg, Sven T., *Ull och ylle* (Lund, 1943).

Klein, E., 'Matts Holmers', *Sv. Kulturbilder*, Vol. 2 (Stockholm, 1933).

Klesse, Birgitte, *Seidenstoffe in der Italienischen Malerei des 14. Jahrhunderts*, Abegg-Stiftung (Bern, 1967).
Kletler, P., *Nordwestauropas Handel und Gewerbe im Mittelalter* (Vienna, 1924).
Koch, H., *Geschichte des Seidengewerbes in Köln 13.-18. Jht.* Staats- und sozialwissensch. Forschungen (Leipzig, 1907).
Kulturhistoriskt lexikon för nordisk medeltid från vikingatid till reformationstid (*KLNM*, Dictionary on Nordic Medieval Culture. Inter-scandinavian collaboration), Vols 1–21, 1956–77. Chief editor in Copenhagen.
Kurth, Betty, *Die deutsche Bildteppiche des Mittelalters* (Vienna, 1926).
—— 'Die Blütezeit der Bildwirkerkunst zu Tournai und der burgundischen Hof', *Jb. d. Kunsthist. Samml.* (Vienna, 1927).
Kühnel, Ernst, *Islamische Stoffe . . . des Schlossmuseums* (Berlin, 1927).
—— 'Four Remarkable Tirāz Textiles', *Archaeologica orientalica* (New York, 1952).
—— *The Textile Museum Catalogue of Spanish Rugs*, 12th Century to 19th Century (Washington, 1953).
—— and Bode, W. von, *Vorderasiatische Knüpfteppische aus alter Zeit.* 4th revised edition (Braunschweig, 1955).
Kybalová, Ludmila, *Koptische Stoffe* (Prague, 1967).
La Baume, W., *Die Entwicklung des Textilhandwerks in Alteuropa* (Bonn, 1955).
Lamm, C. J., *Cotton in Medieval Textiles of the Near East* (Paris, 1937).
—— 'The Marby Rug', *Orientsällskapets åb* (Stockholm, 1937).
—— 'Two Exhibitions in Stockholm and Some Sassanian Textile Patterns', *Ars Islamica*, VII:2, 1940.
—— 'Heliga tuppar och påfåglar', *Kulturen* (Lund, 1952).
Laquist, B., 'Iakttagelser rörande de svenska lapparnas bandvävning', *Norrbotten* (Luleå, 1945).
Larsen, Sophus, 'Kvindeligt haandarbejde i Middelalderen med saerlig hensyn til Folkeviserne', *Aarbøger* (Copenhagen, 1915).
Laufer, B., *Chinese Contributions to the History . . . of Iran. Sino-Iranica.* The Field Museum (Chicago, 1919).
—— 'The Early History of Felt', *American Anthropologist*, 32, 1930.
Laurent, H., *La draperie des Pays-Bas, en France et dans les Pays Mediterranéens* (Paris, 1935).
Lazaro Lopez, A., 'Découverte de deux riches étoffes dans l'Eglise paroissiale d'Oña', *CIETA Bull.*, no. 31, 1970.
Lehmann-Filhés, Margrethe, *Über Brettchenweberei* (Berlin, 1901).
Lexow, E., 'Gammel vestlandsk vaevkunst', *Bergens M. åb.*, 1914.
Lindblom, A., 'Från Bysans lejon till Skånes varulv', *Fataburen*, 1932.
—— see Branting and Lindblom.
Lopez, R. S., 'Silk Industry in the Byzantine Empire', *Speculum* (Cambridge Massachusetts, 1945).
Lubo-Lesnichenko, E. (in Russian, Old Chinese Silks and Embroideries, from the fifth century B.C. to the second century A.D. in the Hermitage Collection) (Leningrad, 1961).
Magnus, Olaus, *Historia de gentibus septentrionalibus* (The History of the Nordic

Peoples) (Rome, 1555). Swedish translation by I. Collijn and J. Granlund (Stockholm, 1909–1955).

Malmborg, Gösta, 'Jean Eric Rehns första verksamhetsår vid Manufakturkontoret', *Fataburen*, 1927.

Mankowski, Tadeusz, *Polskie tkaniny i kafti*, xvi–xviii (Polish Textiles and Embroideries) (Breslau, 1958).

Mannowsky, Walter, *Der Danziger Paramentenschatz*, Vols 1–5 (Berlin, 1931–38).

Markowsky, Barbara, *Europäische Seidengewebe des 13.-18. Jahrhunderts*. Kunstgewerbe Museum der Stadt Köln (Cologne, 1976).

Markowà, Emà, 'Vỳroba gúb na Slovenska' (La production des 'gouba' manteaux a long poil, en Slovaquie) *Slovensky Národopis*, xii (Bratislava, 1964).

Martin, Fr., *Figurale persische Stoffe 1550–1650* (Stockholm, 1899).

—— *Die persischen Prachtstoffe im Schlosse Rosenborg* (Stockholm, 1901).

—— *Oriental Carpets before 1800* (Vienna, 1908).

May, Florence Lewis, *Silk Textiles of Spain* (New York, 1957).

Meister, W., 'Zur Geschichte des Filzteppischs im l. Jahrtausend n. Chr', *Ostasiatische Zschr. N. F.*, xii.

(Mendelsche Hausbuch), *Das Hausbuch der Mendelschen Zwölfbrüderstiftung zu Nürnberg*. Edited by W. Treue (Munich, 1965).

Mestorf, Johanna, 'Die Kleidereste aus den Moor von Daetgen, etc', *Bericht des Schleswig-Holsteins M.* (Kiel, 1917).

Meyer-Riefstahl, R., 'Primitive Rugs of the Konya Type in the Mosque of Beyshehir', *Art Bulletin* (New York, 1931).

Michel, Francisque, *Recherches sur le commerce, la fabrication et l'usage des étoffes de soi, d'or et d'argent* (Paris, 1852).

Miller, J. Innes, *The Spice Trade of the Roman Empire 29 B.C.–641 A.D.* Oxford.

Molinier, ed., *Inventaire du trésor de Saint Siège sous Boniface VIII* (1295). Bibl. de l'Ecole des Chartes (Paris, 1882–88).

Monneret de Villard, Ugo, 'La tessitura palermitana sotto i normanni e suoi rapporti con l'arte bizantina', *Studi e testi*, no. 123, 1946.

—— 'Tessuti e ricami mesopotamici ai tempi degli abbasidi e dei selčūqidi', *Atti della accademia nazionale dei Lincei* (Roma, 1955) (French translation edited by *CIETA*).

Montell, Gösta, *Dress and Ornaments in Ancient Peru*. Oxford University Press (Gothenburg, 1929).

—— 'Studier i asiatisk textilteknik', *Ymer* (Stockholm, 1934).

—— 'Spinning Tools and Spinning Methods in Asia' (Appendix to V. Sylwan, 1941).

Mygdal, Elna, 'Af daekketøjets historie', *Tskr. f. Industri* (Copenhagen, 1913).

—— 'Paschier Lamertijn og Christian IV:s daekketøj', *Fra Arkiv og Museum*, v (Copenhagen, 1915).

Müller-Christensen, Sigrid (See also Christensen), 'Ein Frühwerk deutscher Textilkunst', *Das Münster*, 1950.

—— 'Liturgische Gewänder mit den Namen des heiligen Ulrich', *Münchner Jb.* (Munich, 1955).

—— *Das Grab des Papstes Clemens II. in Dom zu Bamberg* (Munich, 1961).

—— 'Die Tunika Königs Philipps von Schwaben', *900 Jahre Kaiserdom zu Speyer*, 1961.

—— 'Der Alexandermantel von Ottobeuren', *Ottobeuren 764–1964* (Augsburg, 1964).

—— 'Beobachtungen zum Bamberger Gunthertuch', *Münchner Jb.*, 1966.

—— *Das Bamberger Gunthertuch* (Bamberg, 1966).

—— 'Textilien in Schwaben', *Suevia sacra*. Exhibition in Augsburg 1973.

—— and others, 'Die Gräber im Königschor', *Dom zu Speyer, Kunstdenkm.* von Rheinland Pfalz, Vol. 5, 1972.

Nabholz-Kartaschoff, Marie-Louise, *Ikatgewebe aus Nord- und Südeuropa* (Basel, 1969).

Nahlik, Adam, W. *spravie rozwoju krosna tackiego* (Eng. summary). Kwartalnik Historii Kultury Materialnej (Warszawa, 1956).

—— *Tkaniny welniane importowane i miejscowe Nowogrodu Wielkiego X-XV wieku* (Woollen Fabrics, 900–1400, Imported and Local Products, Found in Old Novgorod) (Warszawa, 1964).

—— *Tkaniny wsi wschodnioeuropejskiej X-XIII W.* (East European Textiles, Eng. summary) (Łódz, 1965).

Nesheim, Asbjørn, 'Noen nordiske ord- og kulturlån hos samene', *Studia Septentrionalia* (Oslo, 1953).

—— 'Den samiske grenevevingen og dens terminologi', *Scandinavica et fenno-ugrica* (Stockholm, 1954).

Nevinson, John, *Catalogue of English Domestic Embroideries*. Victoria and Albert Museum, 1938.

Nicolescu, Corina, 'Quelques tissus orientaux dans les collections roumaines', *CIETA Bull.*, no. 29, 1969.

Nissinen, Aino, and Vahter, Tyyni, *Vanhoja kauniita käsitöitä* (Old Finnish Textiles) (Helsinki, 1955).

Nockert, Margareta, 'Tidigmedeltida textilfynd från Leksands kyrka', *Leksands kyrka under 1000 år* (Falun, 1977).

Nordman, C. A., 'Klosterarbeten från Nådendal', *Finskt M.* (Helsinki, 1943).

Noss, Aagot, 'Bandlagning' (Braid-Making) *By og Bygd*, 1966.

Nyberg, H. S., 'Ordet silke och dess historia', *Kungl. Vetenskaps-societetens åb.* (Stockholm, 1967).

Nylén, Anna-Maja, *Hemslöjd* (Lund, 1969). Engl. ed. 1976, *Swedish Hand Craft.*

Nyrop, C., *Niels Lunde Reiersen og de danske silkefabriker* (Copenhagen, 1896).

Nørlund, Poul, 'Buried Norsemen at Herjolfsnes', *Meddelelser om Grønnland* (Copenhagen, 1924).

—— Dragt. *Nordisk Kultur*, xv B (Stockholm, 1941).

Olavius, Olaus, *Oeconomische Reise durch Island* (Dresden/Leipzig, 1787).

Olsen, Bernhard, 'Kong Christian IV:s silkehus', *Tskr. f. Industri.* (Copenhagen, 1902).

Olsson, Martin, 'Jean Eric Rehns förbindelser med Manufakturkontoret under studieresan 1755–1756', *Gustavianskt* (Stockholm, 1932).

Pariset, Ernest, *Histoire de la soie* (Paris, 1862/65).

—— *Les industries de la soie* (Paris, 1890).

Petersen, Jan, *Vikingetidens redskaper* (Oslo, 1951).

Pfister, R., 'Gobelins sassanides du Musée de Lyon', *Revue des arts asiatiques* (Paris, 1929/30).

―― 'Les premières soies sassanides', *Études d'Orientalisme* (Paris, 1932).

―― *Textiles des Palmyre*, I–III (Paris, 1934, 1937, 1940).

―― 'Teinture et alchémie dans l'orient hellenistique', *Seminarium Kondakovianum* (Prague, 1935).

―― 'Coqs sassanides', *Revue des arts asiatiques*, 1938/39.

―― *Les toiles imprimées de Fostat et l'Hindoustan* (Paris, 1938).

―― 'Les textiles', *Excavations at Dura-Europos: Final Report*, IV, part II (Yale Univ., 1945).

―― 'Le rôle de l'Iran dans les textiles d'Antinoë', *Ars Islamica*, 1948.

―― 'Les tissus orientaux de la bible de Théodulf', *Coptic studies*, The Byzantine Institute (Boston, 1950).

―― *Textiles de Halabiyeh* (Zenobia) (Paris, 1951).

Pilar, Manuela de, 'Lisières et franges de toiles égyptiennes', *CIETA Bull.*, no. 28, 1968.

Pirenne, H., 'Draps de Frise ou draps de Flandre?', *Vierteljahrschrift für Sozial- und Wirtschaftsgeschichte* (Berlin, 1909).

Podreider, Fanny, *Storia del tessuti d'arte in Italia* (Bergamo, 1928).

Post, L. v., Walterstorff, E. v., and Lindqvist, S., *Bronsåldersmanteln från Gerumsberget, KVHAA* (Stockholm, 1924/25).

Postan, M., *The Trade of Medieval Europe: The North* (Cambridge, 1952).

Potratz, H., 'Das Moorgewand von Reepsholt, Ost-Friesland', *Urgeschichtliche Sammlung zu Hannover* (Hildesheim, 1942).

Pylkkänen, Riita, *Ryijyperinteitä 1500 ja 1600-luvulta* (Traditions in rya-rugs, 1500–1700) (Helsinki, 1967).

―― *The Use and Traditions of Medieval Rugs and Coverlets in Finland* (Helsinki, 1974).

Rank, E., 'Romanische Seidenstoffe aus Deutschland, sog. Regensburger Gewebe', *Die Seide* (Cologne, 1927).

Riboud, Krishna, and Vial, Gabriel, 'Les soieries Han, I. Aspects nouveaux dans l'étude des soieries de l'Asie Central, II. Analyse technique sur un specimen de Noin Oula'. *Revue des Arts Asiatiques*, Vol. XVII (Paris, 1968).

Riboud, Lubo-Lesnichenko and Vial: 'A comparative study of two similar Han documents', *CIETA Bull.*, no. 28, 1968.

Ricci, Elsa, 'Women's Crafts. Peasant art in Italy', *The Studio* (London, 1913).

Rice, Tamara Talbot, *The Scythians* (London, 1957).

―― *Ancient Arts of Central Asia* (London, 1965).

Riefstahl, Elisabeth, *Patterned Textiles in Pharaonic Egypt* (New York, 1944).

Riising, A., 'The Fate of Henri Pirenne's Theses on the Consequences of the Islamic Expansion', *Classica et Mediaevalia* (Copenhagen, 1952).

Roth, H. Ling, *Studies in Primitive Looms* (Halifax, 1934).

―― *Ancient Egyptian and Greek looms* (Halifax, 1951).

Rothstein, Natalie, 'Nine English Silks', *N.&B. Cl.* (New York, 1964).

―― 'The English Market for French Silks', *CIETA Bull.*, 35, 1972.

―― *Spitalfields Silks*. Victoria and Albert Museum, 1975.

Ryder, M. L., 'Fleece Structure in Some Native and Unimproved Breed of Sheep', *Zschr. f. Tierzücht und Züchtungsbiologie* (Hamburg, 1968).

Sabbe, E., 'L'importation des tissus orienteaux', *Revue de philologie et d'histoire* (Brussels, 1935).

Sage, Gertrud, 'Die Gewebereste aus den Fürstengräbern von Sacrau', *Alt-Schlesien*, 5 (Breslau, 1934).

—— 'Die Gewebe aus den alten Oppeln', *Alt-Schlesien*, 6 (Breslau, 1936).

Sakrale Gewänder des Mittelalters. Exhibition (Munich, 1935).

Salvén, Erik, *Bonaden från Skog* (Stockholm, 1923).

Sandklef, Albert, 'The Bocksten Find', *Acta Ethnologica*, 1 (Copenhagen, 1937).

Sangiorgi, Giorgio, *Contributi allo studio dell'arte tessile.* Milano, published before 1920 (?).

Savary de Bruslons, *Dictionaire universelle de commerce*, I–III (Amsterdam, 1726/32, 1741, 1756).

Scheyer, E., *Die Kölner Bortenweberei des Mittelalters* (Augsburg, 1932).

Schinnerer, Luise, *Antike Handarbeiten* (Vienna *c.* 1890).

Schlabow, K., *Germanische Tuchmacher der Bronzezeit* (Neumünster, 1937).

—— 'Kleidungsstücke aus der Moorfund von Damendorf', *Offa* (Neumünster, 1938).

—— *Der Thorsberger Prachtmantel* (Neumünster, 1952).

—— *Textilfunde der Eisenzeit in Norddeutschland* (Neumünster, 1976).

Schmedding, Birgitta, *Mittelalterliche Textilien in Kirchen und Klöstern der Schweiz* (Abegg-Stiftung Bern III, 1978).

Schmidt, Heinrich, *Alte Seidenstoffe* (Braunschweig, 1957).

Schuette, Marie, *Alte Spitzen*, 4th edition (Braunschweig, 1963).

—— 'The Rediscovery of Tablet Weaving', *Ciba Review*, no. 117, 1956.

Schulze, Paul, *Alte Stoffe* (Berlin, 1917).

Serjeant, R. B., 'Material for a History of Islamic Textiles up to the Mongol Conquest', published by sections in *Ars Islamica*, 1942–1951.

Shepherd, Dorothy G., 'The Textiles from Las Huelgas de Burgos', *N.&B. Cl.* (New York, 1951).

—— 'A Dated Hispano-Islamic Silk', *Ars Orientalis*, II, 1957.

—— 'Medieval Persian Silks in Fact and Fancy: A Refutation of the Riggisberg Report', *CIETA Bull.*, 39/40, 1974.

—— and Henning, W. B., 'Zandaniji identified?', *Festschrift E. Kühnel* 1957 (Berlin, 1959).

Simmons, Pauline, *Chinese Patterned Silks*, The Metropolitan Museum (New York, 1948).

—— 'Some Recent Developments in Chinese Textile Studies', *BMFEA*, no. 28 (Stockholm, 1956).

—— 'An Interim Report on Ancient Textile Collections in Japan, *CIETA Bull.*, no. 15, 1962.

—— 'About Some Chinese Weavings Observed in Japan', *CIETA*, no. 23, 1966.

Sirelius, U. T., *Finlands ryor* (Helsinki, 1924).

Six, J., 'Oud Tafellinnen', *Het Huis* (Amsterdam, 1908).

Slomann, V., *Bizarre designs in silk* (Copenhagen, 1953).

Sobolev, N. N., *Otjerki po iistri ukrashenie tkaney* (The history of textile design) (Moskow, 1934).

Stang, Nic, *Livet og kunsten i ungrenessansens Firenze*, 1. *Kunstens vilkår i borger-republikken* (Oslo, 1956).

Stein, Sir Aurel, *Serindia* (Oxford, 1921).

—— *Innermost Asia* (Oxford, 1928).

Stephani, L., *Comptes rendues* . . . (St Petersburg, 1878–81).

Strzygowski, J., 'Seidenstoffe aus Ägypten in Kaiser-Friedrich-Museum', *Jb. d. Kunsthist. Samml.* (Berlin, 1903).

Stråle, G. H., *Alingsås manufakturverk* (Stockholm, 1884).

Strömberg, Elisabeth, 'Folkliga textilier', *Nordisk kultur*, IV (Stockholm, 1953).

—— and Geijer, Hald, Hoffmann, *Nordisk textilteknisk terminologi*. Förindustriell vävnadsproduktion (Oslo, 1974). New edition 1979.

Survey of Persian art, ed. by A. Upham Pope and Ph. Ackerman, Vols I–VI (New York, 1938–39).

Sylwan, Vivi, 'Svenska dubbelvävnader', Branting and Lindblom, 1928.

—— *Svenska ryor* (Stockholm, 1934).

—— 'Svenska yror med oklippt flossa' (with Looped Pile), *Rig* (Stockholm, 1934).

—— 'Silk from the Yin-Dynasty', *BMFEA*, no. 9 (Stockholm, 1937).

—— *Woollen Textiles of the Lou-Lan People* (Stockholm, 1941).

—— *Investigation of Silk from the Edsen-Gol and Lop-Nor* (Stockholm, 1949).

Täckholm, Vivi, *Faraos blomster* (The Flowers of Pharaoh) (Stockholm, 1964).

Taszycka, Maria, *Włoskie jedwabne tkaniny odzieżowe w polsce w pierwszej połowie XVII* (Italian Silks for Costumes in Poland 1600–1640, French resumé) (Cracov, 1971).

—— 'Zagadnienie produkcji pasów kontuszowych we francji w XVIII wieku' (La fabrication, en France au XVIIIe siècle, des ceintures de la noblesse polonaise), *Biuletyn Historii sztuki*, 1976.

Thompson, Deborah, *Coptic Textiles in the Brooklyn Museum* (New York, 1971).

Thomsen, Thomas, 'Vævede stoffer fra Jernalderen', *Aarbøger*, 1900.

—— *Egekistefundet fra Egtved* (Copenhagen, 1929).

Thorman, Elisabeth, 'Det Stenbergska damastväveriet i Jönköping', *Fataburen*, 1933.

—— *Svenskt duktyg i damast* (Stockholm, 1939).

—— *Kunglig borddamast 1697–1706* (Stockholm, 1941).

Thordeman, B., 'Skogstapetens datering', *Fornvännen*, 1948.

Thornton, P., *Baroque and Rococo Silks* (London, 1965).

Townsend, Gertrude, 'Two Fragments of Late Hellenistic Tapestry', *Fine Arts Museum Bull.*, XLVI (Boston, 1948).

Trever, Camilla, *Excavations in Northern Mongolia* (Leningrad, 1932).

Trudel, Verena, *Schweizerische Leinenstickereien des Mittelalter und der Renaissance* (Bern, 1954).

Wace, A. J. B., 'Weaving or Embroidery?', Supplement to the *AJA*, Vol. LII (Wisconsin, 1948).

—— 'The Cloaks of Zeuxis and Demetrius', *Jb. d. Österr. archäol. Inst.*, XXXIX (Vienna, 1952).

Vahter, Tyyni, 'Der späteisenzeitliche Mantel im Ostbaltikum', *Congressus Secundus Archaeologorum Balticorum* (Riga, 1930).

Wallin, Sigurd, 'Siden-drouget', *Rig*, 1920.

—— 'Herrgårdens vardag', *Svenska Kulturbilder*, Vol. 2 (Stockholm, 1930).

Vallinheimo, Veera, *Das Spinnen in Finnland* (Helsinki, 1956).

Walterstorff, Emelie von, 'Vävteknik', *Bronsåldersmanteln från Gerumsberget*. See von Post, 1924–25.

—— *Textilt bildverk* (Stockholm, 1925).

—— 'Flamskvävda bänkekläden', *Från Nord. M:s saml.*, 1925.

—— 'En vävstol och en varpa', *Fataburen*, 1928.

—— 'Bondens bädd och "Stugans dragning" ', *Svenska kulturbilder*, Vol. 4, 1931.

—— 'Röllakan från Jämtland', *Rig* (Stockholm, 1937).

—— *Svenska vävnadstekniker och mönster typer* (Stockholm, 1940).

—— 'Om kypertnamn', *Rig*, 1942.

Weibel, Adèle C., *Two Thousand Years of Textiles* (New York, 1952).

Weigert, R. A., *French Tapestry* (London, 1962).

—— *La tapisserie et le tapis en France* (Paris, 1964).

Verlet, Pierre, 'Quelques considérations sur la technique des tapis de la Savonnerie aux XVII et XVIIIe siecles', *CIETA Bull.*, no. 27, 1968.

Wescher, H., 'Die Anfänge der Baumwollemanufaktur auf europäischem Boden. Die Süddeutschen Barchentmanufakturen vom 14. bis 16. Jahrh', *Ciba Rundschau*, 45 (Basel, 1940).

Wiet, Gaston, *Soieries persanes* (Le Caire, 1948).

Wild, J. P., *Textile Manufacture in the Northern Roman Provinces*. Cambridge Classical Studies, 1970.

Willetts, William, *Chinese Art* (London, 1958).

—— *Foundations of Chinese Art* (London, 1965).

Wilson, Lilian, *Ancient textiles from Egypt*, Univ. of Michigan Coll. (Ann Arbour, 1933).

Wipszycka, Ewa, *L'industrie textile dans l'Egypt Romaine*, Polskiej Akademii NAUK (Warszawa, 1965).

Vogt, Emil, 'Ein spätantiker Gewebefund aus dem Wallis', *Germania*, Vol. 18, 1934.

—— *Geflechte und Gewebe der Steinzeit* (Basel, 1937).

—— 'Geflechte und Gewebe der europäischen Stein- und Bronzezeit', *Ciba Rundschau*, 66, 1946.

—— 'Frühmittelalterliche Seidenstoffe aus dem Hochaltar des Kathedrale Chur', *Zschr. f. schweiz. Archaeol. und Kunstgeschichte*, 13, 1952.

—— 'Frühmittelalterliche Stoffe aus det Abtei St-Maurice', ibid., 18, 1958.

—— 'Die Textilreste aus den Reliquienbehälter des Altars in der Kirche St. Lorenz bei Paspels', ibid., 23, 1968.

Volavkova, Hana, *The Synagogue Treasures* (Prague, 1949).

Volbach, W. F., *I tessuti del museo Sacro Vaticano* (Rome, 1942).

—— and Wulff, O., *Spätantike und koptische Stoffe aus Ägyptischen Grabfunde* (Berlin, 1925).

Ysselsteyn, G. T., *White Figured Linen Damask* (Haag, 1962).

Sources of the Illustrations

4   *a–b* Bamberg Cathedral; *c* Stockholm, the National M. (C. J. Lamm coll.).
5   Vienna, Schatzkammer.
6   Marby Church, (ATA) Stockholm, Historiska M.
7+6   *b* the Royal Palace, Stockholm.
8   *a* Danzig, S. Mary's Church. After Mannowsky; *b* Helsinki, National M.
9   *a–b* Leningrad, Eremitage M., from Noin Ula; *c–d* from Lou Lan, now in Peking (the Sven Hedin-expedition, Stockholm).
10–11   from Noin Ula, now in Leningrad, the Eremitage M.
12–14   All these silks derive from the burial grounds in Antinoë, except Nr 13 *a* which belongs to the Aachen Cathedral Treasury; Nr 12 *a* is now in Paris, M. de Cluny; Nr 12 *b* and 14 *a* in Lyons, M. des Tissus; 13 *b* in London, V. & A. M.; 13 *c* in Krefeld, Gewebesammlung; 13 *d* in Hamburg, M. of Arts and Crafts; 14 *b–d* in Uppsala, the University M. for Egyptology.
15   Cologne, S. Ursula church.
16   The temple treasury of Shosoin, Japan. After Ishida & Wada.
17   *a* Rome, the Vatican, the collection of Sancta Sanctorum; *b* Aachen, Cathedral Treasury.
18   *a* Le Monastier, France; *b* from Astana, East Turkestan, now in New Delhi Nat. M.; *c* Rome, the Sancta Sanctorum collection.
19   *a* Brussels, M. des Cinquantenaire. From Münsterbilsen; *b* Paris, M. du Louvre. From the S. Josse church. After Ebersolt.
20   *a* Lyons, M. des Tissus from Mozac; *b* from the Oseberg ship burial. Oslo, University M. of Antiquity.
21   Milano, Church of S. Ambrogio. After Capitano d'Arzago.
22   Auxerre, France, Church of S. Eusèbe.
23   *a* Cathedral of Odense, Denmark; *b* Bamberg, Cathedral Treasury M. After S. Müller-Christensen.
24   *a* Church of Köln-Deutz; *b* Reims Cathedral.
25   From Burgo de Osma, Spain, now in Boston, Fine Arts M.
26   Cathedral of Toulouse, detail in London, V. & A. M.
27   Danzig, church of S. Mary. After Mannowsky.
28   *a* From the church in Dokkum, now archiepiscopal M. in Utrecht. (ATA photo); *b* Grave find from Egypt, now in Boston, Fine Arts M.
29   *a* Uppsala, Cathedral treasury M. (ATA); *b* Regensburg, Alte Kapelle.
30   Willigis chasuble, from Aschaffenburg, now in the National M. of Munich.
31   Regensburg, Cathedral Treasury.
32   *a* London, V. & A. M.; *b* Bamberg, Cathedral M. After Müller-Christensen 1961.
33   *a* Spanish Society, New York. From Villalcásar de Sirga; *b–c* Bergens M. Norway, from the Selje Convent.
34   *a* Skara Cathedral (ATA); *b–c* Uppsala Cathedral M. (ATA).
35   *a* Vienna, M. of Arts and Crafts; *b* Uppsala Cathedral M. (ATA).
36–37   Uppsala Cathedral M. (ATA).
38   *a* Danzig, S. Mary's church. After Mannowsky; *b* Skara Cathedral (ATA).
39   Djurö church, Sweden (ATA).
40   Strängnäs Cathedral (ATA).
41   Hamburg, Kunstgewerbemuseum. From Kloster Lüne.

42 *a* Uppsala Cathedral M. (ATA); *b* Rone church, Gotland (ATA).
43 *a–e* From various Swedish churches (ATA); *f* and *g* Norrköping, St Olai church.
44 *a–b* Cathedral of Västerås (ATA).
45 *a–c* From the Swedish churches of Vallby, Norrbärke, and Mörlunda.
46 *a* Skeppshult church, Sweden; *b* Convent church of Vadstena (ATA).
47 Bern, Historisches M. From the 'Burgunderbeute'.
48 *a* Uppsala Cathedral M. (ATA); *b* from unknown church.
49 *a–b* Roumania, Bukarest, National M. Clothes from princely burials. *c* From Ösmo church, Sweden (ATA).
50 From an altar frontal dated 1651, S. Jakobs church, Stockholm (ATA).
51 *a–b* From ecclesiastical vestments in Swedish churches; Arnäs dated 1614, Hilleshög (ATA).
52 *a–b* From ecclesiastical vestments in Swedish churches; Rimbo and unknown church (ATA).
53 From ecclesiastical vestments in Swedish churches: Skönberga, Leksberg (ATA).
54–55 The Army. M., Stockholm. Flags from the Trophy collection (ATA).
56 *a* Linköpings M. from Motala church (ATA).
57 *a* Rosenborgs castle in Copenhague; *b* Rådmansö and some other churches (ATA).
58 *a* Arboga, the town church, antependium dated 1636; *b* Indian sash, about 1724 belonging to a Prince of Hyderabad. Gotembourg, the Röhss M. *c* Polish sash signed Słuck. Private owner.
59 Örebro M., from an ecclesiastical vestment in Ödeby church.
60 *a* London, V. & A. M.
61 and 60 *b* Rosenborg castle, Copenhague.
62 From Dalarö church (ATA).
63 *a–b* Nordiska M., Stockholm.
64 Rosenborg castle, Copenhague
65 M. of Arts and Crafts, Oslo.
66 *a* Västerås Cathedral; *b* Harg church (ATA).
67 Kårsta and Stora Malm churches (ATA).
68 Tryserum church (ATA).
69 The Swedish State Archives.
70 Cathedral of Kalmar (ATA).
71 *a* Private owner; *b* Nordiska M., Stockholm.
72–73 Nordiska M., Stockholm.
74–75 Stockholm, the Royal Palace Collection.
76 *a* Altar frontal dated 1781 in Lidingö church; *b* Royal Palace, Stockholm.
77 *a* Stockholm, Royal Palace.
78–79 and 77 *b* Lyons, M. des Tissus.
80–81 Nordiska M., Stockholm.
82 *a* private owner; *b* from the Shrine of S. Heribert, Cologne; the others of various origin.
83 *a* Cathedral of Lund; *b* from Södra Råda church; *c* Heda church, *d* unknown owner, not Swedish.

84 *a* Munich, National M.; *b* Jamtli M., Östersund; *c* Norsk Folkemuseum, Oslo; *d–e* Vallbo and Ljusdal churches (ATA).
85 *a* Helsinki, National M. From the convent of Nådendal; *b* Västerås, the Castle M. (ATA).
86 Östersund Jamtli M. from the church of Överhogdal (ATA).
87 *a–b* Stockholm, Historiska M. From the Skog and Grödinge churches (ATA).
88–89 *a–b* Lund, the Kulturen M.
90 *a–d* from the Birka excavations; *e* from Sandegårda, all now in Stockholm, Historiska M. (ATA); *f* Lyons, M. des Tissus from Antinoë; *g* from Nyköping, excavations of the medieval town (ATA).
91 *a* Athens, Akropolis M.; *b* from Birka; *c* Stockholm, Nordiska M.; *d* from Australia, photo by unknown.
92 *a–b* From Övre Berge, Oslo, University M. of Antiquities; *c* from Ösmo (ATA); *d–g* from the Birka excavations (ATA).
93 *a* Augsburg, Diözesan M.; *b* Vienna, M. of Arts and Crafts, from Bamberg (?); *c* Danzig, St Mary's church; *d* London, V. & A. M. from a German church (?).
94 *a* London, V. & A. M. from a German church; *b* and *c* Uppsala Cathedral M. (ATA); *c* Haverö church (ATA); *d* from the Tegle find, Stavanger M., Norway.
95 *a* From St Mary's church, Danzig; *b* From South-Western Skåne, Nordiska M., Stockholm; *c* Western Norway, Norsk Folkemuseum, Oslo; *d* Stockholm, private owner.

COLOUR PLATES

I The authorities of the Staatliche Museen in Berlin who kindly lent me the colour diapositiv for reproduction.
II Italian silk from Simonstorp church, now in the Historiska M., Stockholm.
III From a Persian coat, gift of the Russian Tzar to Queen Christina of Sweden, about 1644. Royal Armory, Stockholm.
IV Cover for the Russian–Swedish Treaty of Peace of 1721. Swedish State Archives, Stockholm.

Index

Page references in italics are to illustrations in the text. Plate numbers are listed at the end of index entries, where relevant.

Plates

1 **a** The Lady of the Unicorn. Tapestry, France c. 1500.
  b Folk-art tapestry, southern Sweden, c. 1800.

a

→

→

b

2 a Fragment of a purple silk veil with inserted tapestry
figure of gold thread. Syria c. 200 A.D.
b Cufic inscription in tapestry weave, silk and linen. Egypt
10th C.

3 Inserted tapestry technique, Egypt 300—500. **a** Portion of a large hanging, multi-coloured wools on linen. **b** Border from a tunic, brownish purple wool on linen.

a

4 **a—b** Part of a large hanging
silk tapestry representing a mou
ed Byzantine emperor. Either
or early 11th C.
c Part of a border with Sassan
animals, wool and cotton. Sy
9th C.

5 Tapestry of gold and silk. Islan
Sicilian work c. 1100 A.D.
longing to the Coronation ma
in Vienna.

c

a

6 **a** The 'Marby rug', knotted pile. Caucasia 14th or early 15th C. **b** Detail from Pl. 7.

7 Hunting carpet of silk, Persia 1525—1550. Since 1655 in the possession of the Royal house of Sweden.

b

a

b

8 a Linen cloth, pattern in gauze weave
and brocading. East Europe c. 1500.
b Linen gauze weave from Karelia, 20th
C. Both full scale.

9 Chinese silk techniques from the Han period. **a** Warp-faced compound weave.
b Gauze weave. **c—d** Self-patterned weave. **d** ditto, type 'Han damask'.
All scale 2:1.

a b

c

d

a

b

10—11 Multi-coloured silks, warp-faced compound weaves. China, early Han
dynasty.—Note warp direction of pl. **11 b**.

a

b　→

a

b

12—13 Weft-faced compound weaves. Sassanian Iran 3rd—6th C.

12 b Of wool, 3rd C.

13 a—d The silk strips used as trimming on 'riding-coats'.

a

b

c

d

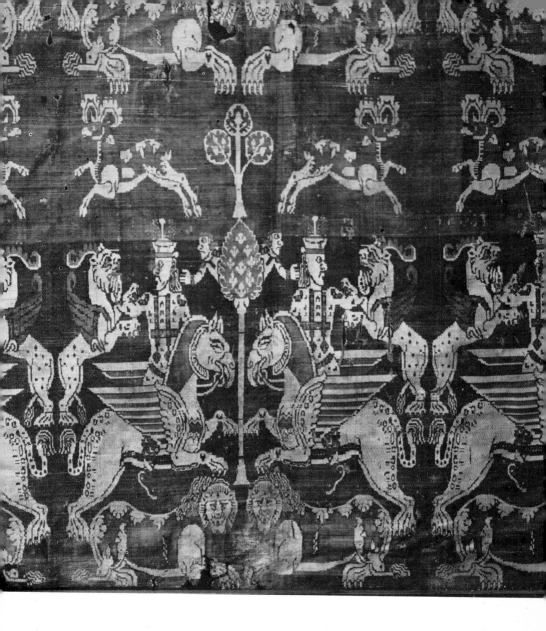

14 Weft-faced compound twills. Sassanian Iran 300—600. **b** scale 1:1, **c—d** scale 2:1, face and reverse.

15 Iranian king hunting. Sassanian silk, 7th—8th C.

16 Chinese silk in weft-faced compound twill imitating a Sassanian fabric. 7th C.

17 a—b Iranian silks, weft-faced compound twill, 8th—10th C.

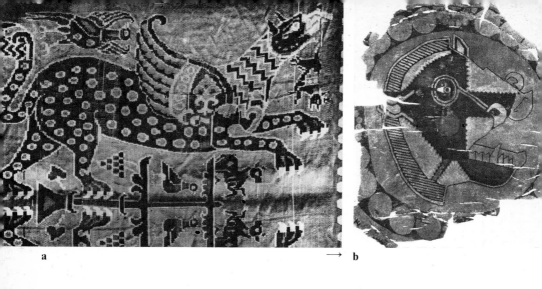

a $\longrightarrow$ b

18 Coarse silks in weft-faced compound twill. Debased Sassanian designs. Central Asia 8th—10th C.

19 a Triumphant Quadriga in weft-faced compound twill, Alexandria 7th C.
b Irregular weft-faced compound weave with a Cufic inscription, Khorasan c. 950.

c

a

b

a

b

20 a Byzantine silk with emperor hunting. Recorded as a royal gift
to the convent of Mozac, c. 750. b Strip of a similar silk, from
the ship burial of Oseberg, Norway. 9th C.

21 Large piece of white silk with hunting scenes, twill damask
weave. Syria 5th or 6th C.

22 Byzantine silk of imperial manufacture. Weft-faced compound twill ('sami-tum') in yellow-blue, c. 1000 A.D.

23 **a** 'St. Knut's cover'. Bluish-black and purple silk 'samitum', mid-11th C.
b Monochrome weft-faced weave, type 'pseudo-damask', from the burying clothes of Pope Clemens II, d. 1047.

a

b

24 a Byzantine 'pallium' with lions and inscription dated 970—1025.
b Iranian samitum with a Sassanian dragon. Given to the relics of St. Remi in 852.

25 Hispano-Moresque silk lampas, design with harpies and Cufic lettering. 11th C.

26 Samitum silk with paired peacocks, bright colours against dark blue ground. West-Islamic 12th C.

27 Black silk satin with weft pattern of flat gilt membrane. Produced in Central Asia for the western market. 13th C.

28 Two silks with related designs of various beasts surrounded by arabesque vines.
a Multi-coloured samitum, **b** lampas in two colours. Both Syrian 12th C.

29 Two silks with weft pattern of flat gilt membrane on satin ground. Turkestan or
China, late 13th — 14th C.

a

b

a

b

30 Monochrome weft-faced compound twill with 'incised' pattern. Syria c. A.D. 1000.

31 Detail of the altar frontal of Bishop Heinrich, Bishop of Regensburg 1277—93. Silk and pure gold brocaded samitum. Venice 13th C.

32 a Lampas with gold and coloured wefts on white ground: paired griffins, peacocks and Cufic lettering. Spain or Sicily, 13th C. **b** Silk veil with an Arabian inscription. Syria, early 11th C.

33 Spanish silks of various kinds, all 13th C. **a** Weft-faced compound weave. **b** Double-faced weave, **c** Lampas. **b**—**c** scale 1:1.

a

34 **a** Samitum, half silk, main warp of linen, wefts of membrane gold and silk. 14th C. **b—c** Enlarged details of pl. 37 **b** and 36. Italian diasper/lampas respectively.

35 Two Italian silks with related designs, Lucca c. 1300. **a** Two-coloured 'diasper' silk with gold brocading. **b** 'Baudekin' with weft pattern of membrane gold on a white tabby ground. Cf. pl. 36.

b

c

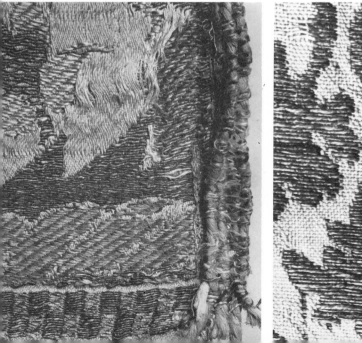

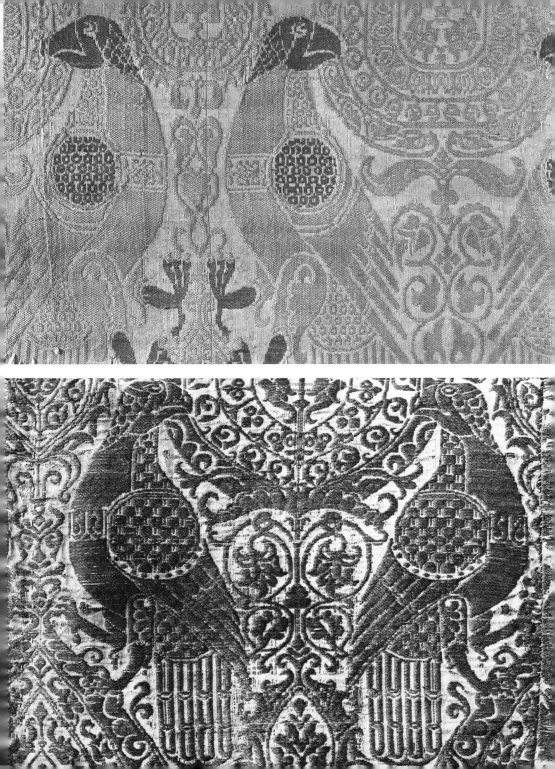

36 Part of a cope which in 1295 was brought from Rome by Nicolas Alloni, consecrated Archbishop of Uppsala.

37 Two Italian silks, probably from before 1320. **a** Design of membrane gold on tan-coloured, originally red ground. **b** Gold and multi-coloured design on white ground; cf. Pl. 35 **b**.

a

38 a Diasper/lampas with exotic motifs in gold against black ground. **b** Detail of a white silk diasper with brocaded dragons. Both Italy, late 14th C.

39 Diasper silk with pattern of various animals, originally red-green. Italy early 14th C.

b

40 Design of heterogeneous motifs. Membrane gold and some red on white ground. North Italy, 1350—1500.

41 Design with dramatic animals. Background in two shades of blue, brocaded in black, red and white. North Italy 1350—1400.

a   b

42 Designs with 'Hortus conclusus' motifs in membrane gold on tan, originally red
ground. North Italy, early 15th C.

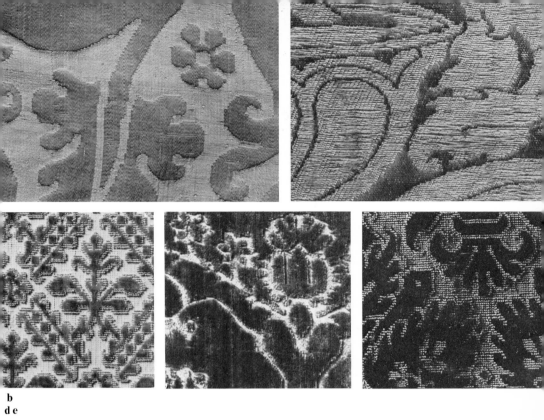

b
d e

43 Various silk techniques, Italy 1450—1550. **a** Damask. **b** Red lampas, pattern weft of thin gold wire and silk. **c** Ciselé velvet, voided. **d** Voided, cut velvet. **e** Ciselé velvet with uncut loops in two heights of pile. **f—g** Voided ciselé velvet with weft bouclé in gold. **a—f** Full scale. **g** shows a loom width executed as **f**.

f g

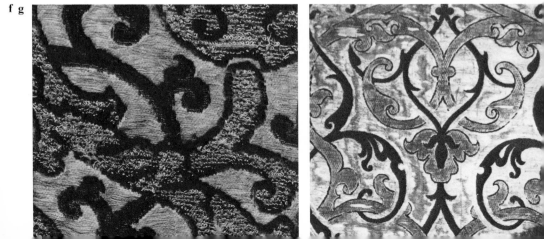

b

a

44 Pomegranate designs in velvet, Italy c. 1450—1500. **a** Standard type with voided cut pile. **b** with brocaded details in metallic gold and coloured silk.

45 a–b Damasks with pomegranates and armorial emblems of the Medicis. Florence 1450—1500. **c** Stylistically mixed design with membrane gold patterning. Italy, late 15th C., provincial production.

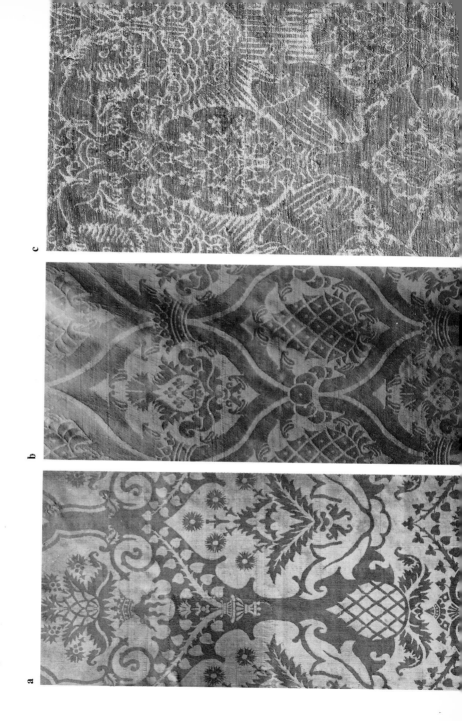

a

b

c

46 Italian velvets of unusually high quality. 1450—1500. **a** Solid pile in ruby red, green and white, details brocaded in metallic gold. **b** Ruby-red pile-on-pile velvet with brocaded palmetto motifs in gold.

47 Cloth of gold with a line pattern in red satin. Rich design of vegetative motifs in ogival lattice. Florence 1470s. From the 'Burgundian booty'.

a   b

48 **a**—**b** Cloth of gold, the design executed in velvet. North Italy, 1475—1525. Cf. colour pl. I.

49 Pomegranate designs deviating from the classical Italian types. **a**—**b** Silk velvet in deep red and gold. Probably made in Venice to a princely order from the Balkans, 16th C. **c** Red and white silk lampas, debased design. Spain c. 1500.

50 Multi-coloured ciselé velvet on a gold ground. Genoa 1600—1650.

51 a Costume material, silk satin with multi-coloured pattern wefts. **b** Mono-chrome ciselé velvet. Italy 1550—1650.

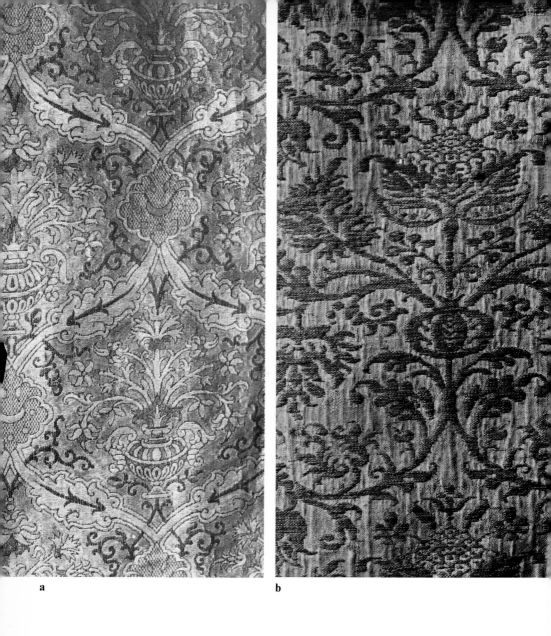

a   b

52 a Cloth of silver (thin wire), design mainly of red warp satin. **b** Half-silk lampas,
the design stands out in cotton against silk taffeta ground. Italy 1550—1650.

53 a—b Ciselé voided velvets. **a** Reddish purple pile against turquoise satin ground.
b Monochrome red. Italy c. 1550—1650.

54—55 Chinese silk damasks from Russian flags taken as war booty by Swedish forces 1700—1707.

54 a—b Early types in Ming style, the designs consisting of large vines with lotus and chrysanthemum flowers.

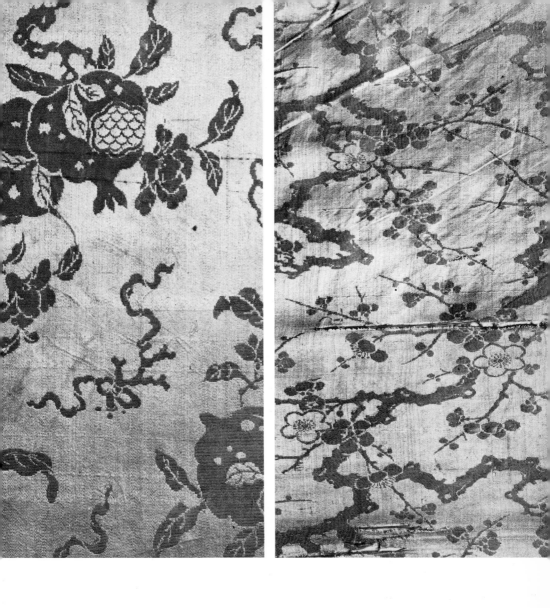

55 a—b The later types of design mainly contained scattered motifs and symbols, often of vegetative character. Here ripened pomegranates and cherry blossoms.

56 a Silk double-cloth; two layers of taffeta in red and white brocaded with gold thread. Exquisite quality. Face and reverse, full scale. Persia, about 1600.

a

57 **a** Lampas silk, multi-coloured weft pattern against black warp satin.
 b Multi-coloured silk, entirely weft-faced. — Both Persia 17th C.

b

58 a Ruby-red satin patterned in white, green and gold (gilt paper). Motif of a pineapple held by a human hand. Probably Indian, *ante quem* 1636. **b—c** Sashes, weft-faced weaves of silk and metal wire. **b** Indian, **c** Polish, signed *Stuck*.

59 Cloth of gold and silk with a magnificent flower design of Turkish type. Mid-17th C.

b

a

60 **a** Table cloth of Flemish linen damask combining framed figural scenes with the pattern of an Italian silk. Early 16th C. **b** Centre of the Danish cloth, pl. 61.

61 One of three similar table cloths from the Copenhagen silk manufacture. Signed 1621.

b

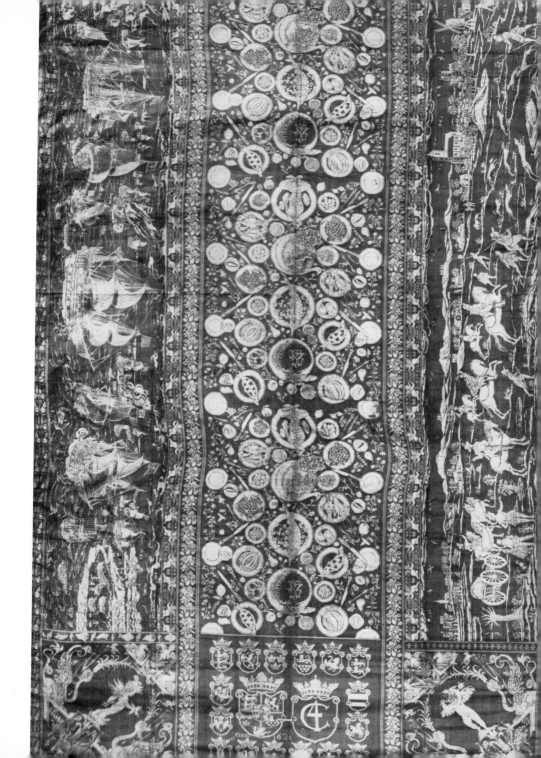

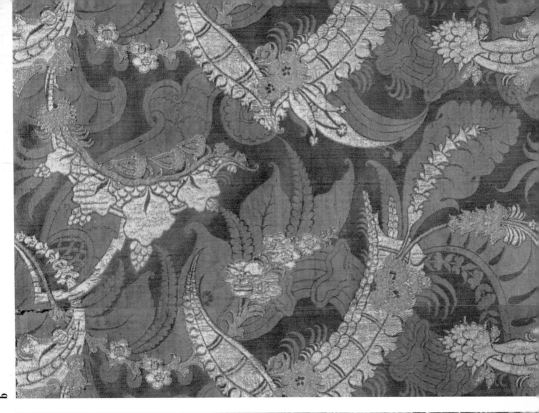

68 Azure blue silk damask brocaded with gold and some scarlet silk. Wedding
robe used 1710, later made up in vestments for a church.

69 Cover for the Russian-Swedish peace treaty of 1721. Cloth of silver with multi-
coloured design. French, early 18th C. Cf. colour p. IV.

a

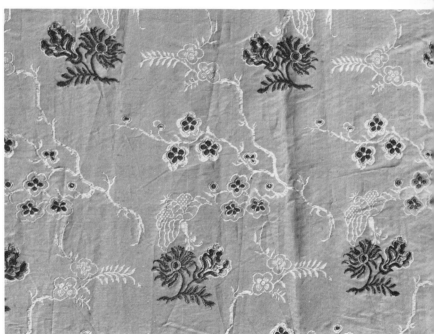

b

70 Silk and gold fabric from one of the episcopal copes ordered from Paris for the coronation of the Swedish King in 1751.

71 18th Century imitations of French rococo silks. **a** From Spitalfields.
b Chinese silk, bought in Canton by a Swedish sailor.

b

a

72—73 Silks of Swedish manufacture from the 18th century: **72a** White moiré silk for a court costume, from 1760. **b** Furnishing silk in gold and cerise, made by Peyron 1753.

73 Pattern book with samples of 'cammage', 'ras de sicile', and 'droguet', from Husberg, Mariestad. **b** Silk material from the Royal Silk Farm at Drottningholm, woven in 1766.

74 Furnishing fabric of blue damask. Design J. E. Rehn, manufacturer Peyron, Stockholm c. 1760.

75 Red silk damask bought in France in 1769 for the royal household.

a

76 **a** Striped silk in salmon pink, white, etc. France c. 1770—1780. **b** Blue and white furnishing silk copying a French 'gourgourant'. Hall marked Stockholm 1849.

b

77 a Furnishing silk in white and green. Stockholm 1846. **b** French wall silk, Napoleonic period.

a

83 Imitations of expensive fabrics. **a** Half-silk, probably German 16th C. **b** Double-faced weave with two-coloured woollen wefts, 15th C. **c** Coarse samitum weave with woollen wefts. **d** Weft-patterned tabby, wool on linen. **c—d** Germany c. 1450—1550.

b

c d

a

84 Variations on the pomegranate motif. **a** Samitum silk, Byzantium 11—12th C.
b—c Pick-up double-cloth in wool from N. Sweden and Norway, 18th C.
d Wool and linen, Italy 17th C. **e** Rich velvet, silk-gold, Italy c. 1500.

b   c

d   e

a

b

85 a Hanging in 'Dukagång' weave, brocaded of multi-coloured yarn on red woollen ground. From the Birgittine Convent of Nådendal, Finland, about 1500. **b** Woollen weft-faced weave with brocaded pattern. Swedish folk-art, mid-19th C.

86 Pick up double cloth, the one layer of linen and the other of red and blue woollen yarn. N. Sweden, 13th C.

a

87 **a** The 'hanging from Skog'. Multi-coloured figures worked in Soumak on linen tabby ground. 13th C.
b Blue and white woollen hanging in pick-up double-cloth. Middle Sweden 15th C.

b

a

b

88—89 Horizontal hangings, folk-art textiles from southern Sweden. **a** 'Duka-gång' weave with motifs of medieval character. 18th C. or about 1800, cf. pl. 85 **a**.
b 'Opphämta' weave, weft patterned tabby in blue and white, signed 1771.

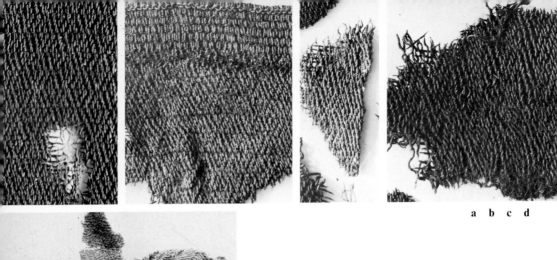

a b c d

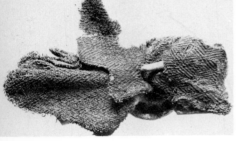

e

90 Excavated textiles. **a—e** From Viking burials in Sweden. Worsted twills, probably imported from Syria: **b** starting border, **c** sideway selvage, **e** fastened to a bronze fibula.
f From a 'riding-coat' in the Antinoë burials, 300—500 A.D. Napped fabric of extremely fine Kashmir wool, moth-eaten areas showing the ground weave.
g Hair yarn fabric from medieval stratum in Swedish town. — Scale 2:1.

f   g

91 **a** Greek marble statue rendering a woollen 'peplos'. **b** Inside of bronze buckle preserving proofs of pleated linen from the Birka finds, 9th C. **c** Swedish rya-rug, medieval type, 18th C. **d** Maori man wearing a cloak with some kind of knotted pile. New Zealand 20th C.

a

b

c

d

a b c

92 Tablet-woven bands. **a—b** Of multi-coloured woollens, shown from both sides. The tablets were individually turned for patterning purposes. Norway 6th C. **c** Silk warp, extra weft of gold wire, giving background to brocading. 15th C. **d—g** From the Birka finds, **d** is shown from the reverse, **e—f** from the face. **g** Gold wire showing impression of the pattern. All scale 2:1.

93 Medieval bands. **a** Of red silk and gold, 9th C. **b** Two-coloured silk warp and gold, 11th C. **c** Linen warp, coloured silk weft. 15th C. **a—c** tablet-woven, Germany. **d** Loom-woven band with Latin inscription, Italy 12th C.

d e f g

a

b

c

S·DIVINA·VIA·TUTA·POTENS·MEDICINA PC

d

EGE·SALVA·BENEDIC·SANCTIFIC A FAMULUM

a b

94 Loom woven bands. Germany. **a** Of two-coloured silk, 12—13th C.
b—c 'Cologne borders', 14th and 15th C.
d Sprang plaiting from Tegle. Norway 5th C. **e** Open-work sprang of linen,
N. Sweden 20th C.

d

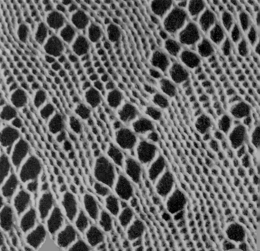

95 **a** 'Kilim' band of gold and silk, north-eastern Germany,
15th C. **b—c** Parts of folk-art tapestry coverlets from
Sweden and Norway: **b** 'Rölakan' signed 1771. **c** 'Rutevev' c. 1800. **d** Kilim from Anatolia c. 1800.